RESISTING BIG TECH

BLOOMSBURY STUDIES IN DIGITAL CULTURES

Series Editors
Anthony Mandal and Jenny Kidd

This series responds to a rapidly changing digital world, one which permeates both our everyday lives and the broader philosophical challenges that accrue in its wake. It is inter- and trans-disciplinary, situated at the meeting points of the digital humanities, digital media and cultural studies, and research into digital ethics.

While the series will tackle the "digital humanities" in its broadest sense, its ambition is to broaden focus beyond areas typically associated with the digital humanities to encompass a range of approaches to the digital, whether these be digital humanities, digital media studies or digital arts practice.

Titles in the series

Ambient Stories in Practice and Research, Edited by Amy Spencer

Digital Humanities and the Cyberspace Decade, 1990–2001, Claire Warwick

Hacking in the Humanities, Aaron Mauro

Investigating Google's Search Engine, Rosie Graham

Metamodernism and the Postdigital in the Contemporary Novel, Spencer Jordan

Reading Audio Readers, Karl Berglund

The Language of Cyber Attacks, Aaron Mauro

The Trouble With Big Data, Jennifer Edmond, Nicola Horsley, Jörg Lehmann and Mike Priddy

Queer Data, Kevin Guyan

Forthcoming titles

Herman Melville and the Digital Humanities, Christopher Ohge and Dennis Mischke

Listening In, Toby Heys, David Jackson and Marsha Courneya

People Like You, Sophie Day, Celia Lury and Helen Ward

RESISTING BIG TECH

The Personalized is Political

Niels Niessen

BLOOMSBURY ACADEMIC
LONDON • NEW YORK • OXFORD • NEW DELHI • SYDNEY

BLOOMSBURY ACADEMIC
Bloomsbury Publishing Plc, 50 Bedford Square, London, WC1B 3DP, UK
Bloomsbury Publishing Inc, 1385 Broadway, New York, NY 10018, USA
Bloomsbury Publishing Ireland, 29 Earlsfort Terrace, Dublin 2, D02 AY28, Ireland

BLOOMSBURY, BLOOMSBURY ACADEMIC and the Diana logo
are trademarks of Bloomsbury Publishing Plc

First published in Great Britain 2025

Copyright © Niels Niessen, 2025

Niels Niessen has asserted his right under the Copyright,
Designs and Patents Act, 1988, to be identified as Author of this work.

For legal purposes the Acknowledgments on pp. 257–259 constitute
an extension of this copyright page.

Cover image © viktoriya89/ Adobe Stock

This work is published open access subject to a Creative Commons Attribution-NonCommercial-NoDerivatives 4.0 International licence (CC BY-NC-ND 4.0, https://creativecommons.org/licenses/by-nc-nd/4.0/). You may re-use, distribute, and reproduce this work in any medium for non-commercial purposes, provided you give attribution to the copyright holder and the publisher and provide a link to the Creative Commons licence.

Bloomsbury Publishing Plc does not have any control over, or responsibility for, any third-party websites referred to or in this book. All internet addresses given in this book were correct at the time of going to press. The author and publisher regret any inconvenience caused if addresses have changed or sites have ceased to exist, but can accept no responsibility for any such changes.

A catalogue record for this book is available from the British Library.

A catalog record for this book is available from the Library of Congress.

ISBN: HB: 978-1-3505-0410-3
PB: 978-1-3505-0409-7
ePDF: 978-1-3505-0411-0
eBook: 978-1-3505-0412-7

Series: Bloomsbury Studies in Digital Cultures

Typeset by Integra Software Services Pvt. Ltd.
Printed and bound in India

For product safety related questions contact productsafety@bloomsbury.com.

To find out more about our authors and books visit www.bloomsbury.com
and sign up for our newsletters.

To my parents

There are no personal solutions at this time. There is only collective action for a collective solution.
   CAROL HANISCH, "THE PERSONAL IS POLITICAL" (1969)

CONTENTS

List of Illustrations xii

INTRODUCTION: THE END OF EVERYDAY LIFE 1
Everything 1
Disorganized (*Scattered and Shattered*) 8
Extraction 14
Posthuman 20

1 HOME | DREAMS AND DISHES 33
Anywhere 33
Wi-Fi 39
Metaverse 44
Presence 51
Resistance 58
Homework 64
Association (*chez soi*) 70

2 CITY | SIDEWALK COLONIALISM (*LAND ACKNOWLEDGMENT*) 85
Everybody 85
Empathy 89
Smartphone 96
Urban 102
Dividual 108
Open 117
Toronto 122

3 LEARNING | AN ABC TO DE-GOOGLE EDUCATION 131
Anyone 131
Books 133

Classroom 134
Doodle 136
Educare 137
Find 139
Grading 140
Hornbook 143
Information 144
Joy 146
Knowledge 147
Lifelong 148
Mundaneum 150
Naïve 152
Owl 153
Public 155
Query 156
Rolling 158
Soul (*Generation AI*) 160
Teacher 162
Unlearning 164
Virtual 165
Wikipedia 166
X 168
You 170
Zen 171

4 LOVE | IS EVERYTHING OK, CUPID? 183
Everyone 183
Willing 188
Dating 193
Data 199
Common 205
Conversations (*A Clouded Crowd*) 210
Consent 215

EPILOGUE: AGAINST THE STREAM FOR ECOLOGICAL JUSTICE 227
Anybot 227
Degrowth 232
Freedom 240
Cobalt (*Free Palestine, Free Congo*) 246

Acknowledgments 257
Bibliography 260
Index 278

ILLUSTRATIONS

1 WhatsApp promising more privacy than pigeon post (screen capture from video, © WhatsApp, 2022, all rights reserved) 7

2 WhatsApp promising more privacy than pigeon post (screen capture from video, © WhatsApp, 2022, all rights reserved) 7

3 Facebook's "Global Community" manifesto (screen capture from video, © PBS News Hour, 2017, all rights reserved) 12

4 "Hopefully no-one sees this poster! #Stay home" (Utrecht, March 2020, photo by the author) 34

5 "Quarantine is easier in Park Town than in Transtown" (Utrecht, March 2020, photo by the author) 34

6 Airbnb introducing "Belong Anywhere" (screen capture from video, © Airbnb, 2015, all rights reserved) 36

7 Microsoft introducing holoportation platform Mesh (screen capture from video, © Microsoft, 2023, all rights reserved) 36

8 "Hey Google, broadcast breakfast is ready" (screen capture from video, © Google, 2019, all rights reserved) 36

9 Zoom's annual Zoomtopia event (screen capture from video, © Zoom, 2022, all rights reserved) 45

10 Meta introducing the metaverse (screen capture from video, © Meta, 2021, all rights reserved) 47

11 Microsoft speaking of metaverses (screen capture from video, © Microsoft, 2022, all rights reserved) 48

12 "Home" according to Microsoft Mesh (screen capture from video, © Microsoft Mechanics, 2022, all rights reserved) 52

13 "Home" according to Meta (screen capture from video, © Meta, 2021, all rights reserved) 52

14 The "Holy Grail" of presence (screen capture from video, © Microsoft Ignite, 2022, all rights reserved) 53

15 Microsoft introducing Copilot (screen capture from video, © Microsoft, 2023, all rights reserved) 55

16 *Transcendent Man* about Ray Kurzweil (screen capture from video, © Ptolemaic Productions, 2009, all rights reserved) 56

17 "Looking for a bit of Magic? Your groceries within minutes" (Gorillas advertisement, Amsterdam 2021, photo by the author) 62

18 Esalen Institute in Northern California as seen in *Century of Self* (screen capture from video, © RDF Television, 2002, all rights reserved) 67

19 "From now on I am open" (Utrecht, June 2020, photo by the author) 71

20 "Is your journey really necessary? Have a good journey!" (Amsterdam, March 2020, photo by the author) 73

21 Home is where the heart is (photo by the author) 74

22 "Stop Spadina" (Toronto, 2015, photo by the author, made during an "official" Jane's Walk in the Annex neighborhood where Jane Jacobs lived between 1968 and 2006) 88

23 "I lived in Toronto for almost thirty years" (screen captures from video, © Sidewalk Toronto, 2017, all rights reserved) 92

24 "You can meet a new person every week" (screen capture from video, © Sidewalk Toronto, 2017, all rights reserved) 92

25 Toronto streetcar (screen capture from video, © Sidewalk Toronto, 2017, all rights reserved) 92

26 "Toronto is in an elite class of cities in North America" (screen capture from video, © Sidewalk Toronto, 2017, all rights reserved) 93

27 "Toronto has a pulse" (screen capture from video, © Sidewalk Toronto, 2017, all rights reserved) 93

28 How do *you* feel about Toronto's future? (screen capture from video, © Sidewalk Toronto, 2017, all rights reserved) 93

29 "Public" town hall meeting organized by Sidewalk Toronto (screen captures from video, © Sidewalk Toronto, 2018, all rights reserved) 97

30 "Public" town hall meeting organized by Sidewalk Toronto (screen captures from video, © Sidewalk Toronto, 2018, all rights reserved) 97

31 Artist impression in Sidewalk's *Toronto Tomorrow* development plan (screen capture from video, © Raymond Wong, 2021, all rights reserved) 100

32 City-as-platform ideology (screen capture from video, © Google TechTalks, 2016, all rights reserved) 106

33 Milky Way in downtown Toronto (2015, photo by the author and screen capture, © Google Maps, 2015, all rights reserved) 114

34 West Queen West (Toronto, 2015, photo by the author, artwork by Jesse Harris) 115

35 Downtown Los Angeles reimagined as pedestrian paradise in Spike Jonze's *Her* (screen capture from film, © Annapurna Pictures, 2013, all rights reserved) 119

36 Painting Toronto (2015, photo by the author, artwork by Women Paint Toronto) 120

37 Google's "Anywhere School" (screen capture from video, © Google for Education, 2022, all rights reserved) 132

38 Celebrating Google Books (screen capture from video, © Google for Education, 2020, all rights reserved) 134

39 Google's response to the Covid-19 pandemic (screen capture from video, © Google for Education, 2022, all rights reserved) 138

40 Google's response to the Covid-19 pandemic (screen capture from video, © Google for Education, 2022, all rights reserved) 138

41 Google's response to the Covid-19 pandemic (screen capture from video, © Google for Education, 2022, all rights reserved) 138

42 Reproduction of facsimiles part of Andrew W. Tuer's *History of the Horn-Book* (1896) (Work in public domain, image retrieved from Wikimedia Commons) 144

43 "O is for Owl" (original wood engraving and letterpress print by Rick Allen) (© copyright Rick Allen, The Kenspeckle Letterpress, kenspeckleletterpress.com) 154

44 "OK Google, how many stars are in our galaxy" (screen capture from video, © Google Home, 2017, all rights reserved) 157

45 Google's "Rolling Study Halls" (screen capture from video, © Google, 2019, all rights reserved) 159

46 Google's "Rolling Study Halls" (screen capture from video, © Google, 2019, all rights reserved) 159

47 Google's "Rolling Study Halls" (screen capture from video, © Google, 2019, all rights reserved) 159

48 Google's Class of 2030 (screen capture from video, © Google Arts & Culture, 2022, all rights reserved) 161

49 Google's Class of 2030 (screen capture from video, © Google Arts & Culture, 2022, all rights reserved) 161

50 Google's Class of 2030 (screen capture from video, © Google Arts & Culture, 2022, all rights reserved) 161

51 Moonshots! A Game of Radical Thinking by X (screen capture from video, © X, 2023, all rights reserved) 169

52 "With OkCupid you can find love, your way" (screen capture from video, © OkCupid, 2021, all rights reserved) 185

53 OkCupid's DTF billboard campaign (screen capture from video, © Overall Mural, 2019, all rights reserved) 185

54 Opening sequence *You've Got Mail* (screen capture from video, © Lauren Shuler Donner Productions, 1998, all rights reserved) 189

55 Opening sequence *You've Got Mail* (screen capture from video, © Lauren Shuler Donner Productions, 1998, all rights reserved) 189

56 Opening sequence *You've Got Mail* (screen capture from video, © Lauren Shuler Donner Productions, 1998, all rights reserved) 189

57 "Computer with a heart" (screen capture from video, © British Pathé, 2014, all rights reserved) 197

58 Love Invasion (Toronto 2016, photo by the author, artwork by Matthew Del Degan) 200

59 "Great love instead of fast sex" as promised by OkCupid sibling company Hinge (Munich 2022, photo by the author) 201

60 OkCupid's dataism according to Christian Rudder (screen capture from video, © Ted-Ed, 2013, all rights reserved) 203

61 OkCupid's dataism according to Christian Rudder (screen capture from video, © Ted-Ed, 2013, all rights reserved) 203

62 OkCupid's dataism according to Christian Rudder (screen capture from video, © Ted-Ed, 2013, all rights reserved) 203

63 Clouded love in *Her* (screen capture from video, © Annapurna Pictures, 2013, all rights reserved) 211

64 *We Need to Talk: A Film about Consent* (screen capture from video, © Tinder India, 2022, all rights reserved) 218

65 *We Need to Talk: A Film about Consent* (screen capture from video, © Tinder India, 2022, all rights reserved) 218

66 *We Need to Talk: A Film about Consent* (screen capture from video, © Tinder India, 2022, all rights reserved) 218

67 Nine great minds speculating on superintelligence (screen capture from video, © Future of Life Institute, 2017, all rights reserved) 228

68 "Don't Mess with Mother" as part of Apple's "Earth Shot on iPhone" Campaign (screen capture from video, © Apple, 2019, all rights reserved) 234

69 "Don't Mess with Mother" as part of Apple's "Earth Shot on iPhone" Campaign (screen capture from video, © Apple, 2019, all rights reserved) 234

70 Esalen Institute in Northern California as seen in *Supernature: Esalen and the Human Potential* (screen capture from video, © Jones Cinema Arts, 2018, all rights reserved) 235

71 AI for Good (screen capture from video, © Microsoft, 2020, all rights reserved) 238

72 World Economic Forum's *Great Reset* (screen capture from video, © World Economic Forum, 2021, all rights reserved) 239

73 Child labor at cobalt mine in the Democratic Republic of Congo as seen in the film *Blood Cobalt: The Congo's Dangerous and Deadly Green Energy Mines* (screen capture from video, © ABC News, 2022, all rights reserved) 249

74 Free Palestine, Free Congo (Amsterdam 2023, March for Climate and Justice, photo by the author) 250

75 Upstream along the Great River Road (Illinois, 2014) (photo by the author) 258

Experiments without Tech

1. Tracing associations 75

2. Offline map making 116

3. Automatic writing 142

4. A date with yourself 198

INTRODUCTION

The End of Everyday Life

Either the quotidian in [modern] society is taken to stand for what is organized and rational, and it is EVERYTHING—*or it is nothing.*
HENRI LEFEBVRE, *EVERYDAY LIFE IN THE MODERN WORLD* (1968)[1]

Everything

In 1968 Henri Lefebvre asked: in a society whose "basic preoccupations are rationality, organization and planning is it still possible to distinguish a level or dimension that can be called *everyday life*?" His answer: everyday life is all or nothing.[2] Or in the words of Kathleen Stewart, "everyday life is life lived on the level of surging affects … It takes EVERYTHING we have."[3]

This book analyzes how, in times of Big Tech, everyday life becomes a stream. By *everyday life*, I mean a spacetime relatively separate from state and market. Everyday life is, or was, where people made meaning, where they stayed afloat with everything they had. Everyday life was people's relative freedom to associate, alone and with others. By *Big Tech* I mean the world's most powerful technology companies, especially those promising the new American Dream of technology as second nature.

By *stream*, I mean an ever-accelerating flow in which all oppositions blur, in particular the one between public and private life that for long organized everyday life as a modern invention. The everyday stream that we're left with, and that we're living, is, in its turn, a fluctuating composition of parallel, interlocking, and interrupted streams: paid work, care work, self-care, learning, leisure, love, and—mediating all of this—the personalized streams of Instagram, TikTok, Tinder, and Teams. These transmedia streams flowing across platforms and merging on our home screens are the dominant media form of our streaming era. Much like the novel and cinema once expressed and helped constitute modern individual life (as argued authors like Georg Lukács and Siegfried Kracauer), Big Tech's profit-driven streams now express and propel the scattering of life, its ongoing internal and social division.[4]

This changes EVERYTHING, or does it? Let me be clear from the start that my critique of Big Tech's colonization of everyday life—a qualification to which I will return later this introduction—does not emerge out of a nostalgia for the modern everyday. Nor do I hark back to some public-private binary. As feminist theorists from Kylie Jarrett to Sara Ahmed have argued, the notion of a private everyday domain free of work—a domain where the subject has a minimum of personal integrity and freedom to associate—fails to account for the modern female condition of unpaid reproductive labor.[5] From the perspective of that modern female condition, life domains were always already blurred. In our streaming era, in which Big Tech marketizes all and EVERYTHING, we witness a universalization of this blurring of life domains: it now affects *all* people. That is to say, it affects all people, but it does not affect all people equally. The reason is that the everyday stream that has come to shape all our lives continues to intersect with old and new forms of patriarchal and racist power that dehumanize some humans more than others. Think of biased data sets and normative chatbots, think of platformized labor, or think of extractive labor practices in the Big Tech industry and its supply chains, especially in the global south.

Critiquing Big Tech, it is equally crucial to recognize that for many people platforms like YouTube, Instagram, X (formerly Twitter), and ChatGPT hold a strong emancipatory potential. To some extent, these platforms allow people to challenge deeply rooted patriarchal and racist structures, and to develop a sense of agency to resist institutions that for a long time determined what a "normal," "human" life looks like (from the church to the nuclear family, from factories to the state). For many, social media platforms—or more neutrally: network platforms—are places of encounter, friendship, love, education, inspiration, art, activism, citizen journalism, support, self-help, and consciousness-raising. Moreover, movements like #MeToo and Black Lives Matter would not have happened the way they did without these platforms. Yet while corporate platforms may help liberate love and life in some respects, they certainly also facilitate hate, misinformation, polarization, exclusion, segregation, and a general feeling of discontent. In that sense, these media are not so "social." Ultimately, platforms like Instagram (owned by Meta), X and TikTok are not designed for emancipation, but to maximize user engagement. Driven by data generation, these platforms re-channel people's longing for freedom and connection, while compelling them to *consent* to fraudulent terms of use that as an individual it is nearly impossible to say *no* to. (And let's not forget here that Facebook, now Meta, once started as a platform to rank women using a data set of stolen photographs, a border-crossing mentality that has remained central to the company's DNA.)

This book thus critiques Big Tech without losing sight of the many emancipatory potentials of corporate platforms. In other words, I analyze how Big Tech violates people's individual integrity and undermines public space, while yet acknowledging the fact that network platforms also empower people and allow them to somewhat liberate themselves from, or at least expand, normative notions of "individuality" and "the public." In this attempt at articulating an integrated view of how Big Tech colonizes life while also emancipating it, I call for resistance against Big Tech without falling back on preconceived notions of what personal and communal life should look like. Instead, we need to prefigure truly *common* and self-organized spaces that don't rely on modern notions of privacy and individuality, but that exist across the public-private binary, online but certainly also offline. In such spaces, resistance against Big Tech joins forces with other anti-hegemonic struggles, facilitating a collective consciousness of how intersecting powers (patriarchal, racist, capitalist, technocolonial) at once repress and accelerate life, burning out people and the planet. We need spaces, in other words, where public and private life blur, not in a market-driven stream, but in a collective consciousness of how the personal is still political.

The personal is political. As Michael Warner writes, the most basic meaning of this turn-of-the-1970s radical feminist slogan is that the social arrangements that structure private life, households, intimacy, gender, and sexuality "are neither neutral nor immutable [but] can be seen as relations of power and as subject to transformation."[6] Similarly, in *Feminism, Labour and Digital Media* Kylie Jarrett argues that a critique of people's enslavement by capitalist machinery needs to go hand in hand with a feminist critique. She writes that the slogan that "the personal is political remains not only apposite but also useful for the work that needs to be done," as it expresses that "we must be attuned to, critical of and intervene in the micropolitics of everyday life."[7]

The realization that the personal is political is equally relevant to the data-extractivist arrangements that enslave life in our digitalizing age.

Those too are power relations in need of transformation. Inspired by second-wave feminism's rallying cry, this book examines what happens to everyday life in the streaming age, in which *the personalized is political*. The book wants to contribute to a collective consciousness of how our relations to the world, others, and the other called self are shaped by personalized streams that at once channel and feed on people's desires. Big Tech transforms our very *associations,* understood as how our bodyminds move from one thing to the other *and* how we connect and cohere with others socially. Let's resist this colonization of our minds and movements. We need to liberate our personal potential for free association from the internal scattering of our bodyminds (as through burnout, anxiety, dysphoria, and attention disorder) inasmuch as we need to liberate our collective potential for free association from our social scattering (as through individualization, polarization, and segregation).

Speaking of associations, the book is a long essay that weaves together cultural theory, popular culture, analysis of Big Tech discourse, media technology history (from Wi-Fi and ed-tech to computerized dating) and also personal observation. I am inspired here by Michel Foucault's take on the essay as an exercise of self in the game of truth. As a literary and scholarly genre, the essay is an associative form that works through connections while moving toward a sense of coherence. How people associate (alone and with others) and how they cohere (together and as fragmented selves) changes rapidly these days. *Resisting Big Tech* seeks to grasp this transformation. At moments, the book also is a manifesto that calls to go against the stream and resist Big Tech's ideology of disembodied life for which technology is second nature. Such resistance is only possible when people develop a personal and collective self-consciousness of how their associations are shaped by hegemonic structures and discourses.

As stated, everyday life is a modern invention. Whereas in premodern times people's imaginations were still populated with miracles and monsters, in the modern and increasingly secular world the mundane really became uneventful. The everyday only became an object of discourse and philosophy in nineteenth-century capitalist societies, in which social life got increasingly structured and regulated. As Henri Lefebvre argues in *Everyday Life and the Modern World* (1968), in modern discourse the quotidian refers to the domain of life that still escapes rationalization. It is "the object of [modern] philosophy precisely because it is non-philosophical."[8] For long the everyday had a negative connotation, defined by what it is not. It was the non-modern, the non-philosophical, the uneventful, time left over, the disorganized. The everyday was also associated with the feminine and a primitive stage of thinking and living "where modes of experience are still undifferentiated" (Lefebvre).[9] Or as Jonathan Crary writes in *24/7: Late Capitalism and the Ends of Sleep*, "the everyday was the vague constellation of spaces and times *outside* what was organized and institutionalized around work, conformity, and consumerism. It was all the daily habits that were beneath notice, where one remained anonymous."[10]

The everyday bears a complicated relationship to the modern public-private binary. As Rita Felski writes in "The Invention of Everyday Life," the everyday includes "domestic activities but also routine forms of work, travel and leisure."[11] The everyday is thus primarily associated with the private sphere, though not exclusively so. Certainly, in Western traditions, the public and private for long have been seen as separate domains. Warner writes that "the boundary between bedroom and market, home and meetinghouse, can be challenged or violated, but it is at least clear enough [that] moving from one [space] to another is experienced as crossing a barrier or making a transition."[12] Moreover, modern thinking tied the public-private distinction to an understanding of people as *individuals*: autonomous subjects with a certain agency to own, speak, and work for a wage, and with a certain personal integrity and inalienable need of privacy (all privileges traditionally granted more to white, male, bourgeois, heterosexual, able-bodied subjects). Private life, then, was the domain of social existence in which individuals could regenerate, where they are at home, or as the French say *chez soi*, literally *with themselves* (whether alone or with their direct relatives). Public life, in contrast, was the domain of existence where private individuals came together with other individuals, whether to exchange goods (public market) or discourse (public sphere).

Two poles of a binary, the public and private sphere have always been integrated. Warner writes that "a private conversation can take place in a public forum; a kitchen can become a public gathering place ... a radio can bring public discussion into a bathroom; and so on."[13] Similarly, Kathleen Stewart argues that "public and private spheres are drawn into a tight circuit, giving the ordinary the fantasy quality of a private life writ large on the world" while "public specters are grown intimate."[14] These specters include publicly circulating styles, sensibilities, and affects that people take home with them. They also include cultural forms that enter the home through mass media like magazines, television, and now also platforms like Instagram, shaping people's private sensorium that is not so private after all.

To further grasp the always-already blurred public-private dichotomy, we can distinguish between private and public *life* and private and public *space*. The former distinction pertains to people's social relations, including their self-relations. The latter distinction pertains to the way modern law cuts up the world into privately and publicly owned spaces. As both Warner and Stewart argue, private life is not just performed in the private space of the home, it is also performed in public spaces, much like the coming together of people as publics also happens in and across privately owned spaces (e.g., cafés, stores, cinemas). Any distinction between public and private life remains schematic, though, because any practice or speech act may be a public and private performance *at the same time*. Take doing housework or walking through the city: they are activities indissolubly connected to the public-private performance of gender.[15]

To return to the streaming age: a double development further blurs the private-public dichotomy. The first is the *personalization* (or privatization) of public life through online platforms. The other is life's *datafication*. As far as the personalization of public life is concerned, activities that used to happen in the public sphere (e.g., movie watching, learning at school, romantic encounters, political discussions) are now mediated by platforms accessed through personal user accounts. In this respect, platformization actually *expands* people's individual privacy, their realm of self, which is also how platforms like WhatsApp (Meta) advertise themselves (Figures 1 and 2). Meta's CEO Mark Zuckerberg has claimed that "the future is private" and that "privacy gives people the freedom to be themselves."[16] In practice, however, companies like Meta are not so interested in privacy as the condition for people's personal self-development. As Zoetanya Sujon argues, ultimately Meta is about "*privatized* communication, where private communications are a potentially lucrative revenue source."[17] We could say that communication is privatized in the double sense of the word: it increasingly happens as *personalized* streams controlled by *privately* owned infrastructures.

This privatization of life goes hand in hand with its datafication. People's personal and collective experiences are recorded as binary information that is sold for advertising purposes and product development—including the development of so-called "self-learning," "artificially" "intelligent" systems. I write "so-called," because platforms like OpenAI's

FIGURES 1 AND 2 WhatsApp promising more privacy than pigeon post (screen capture from video, © WhatsApp, 2022, all rights reserved).[18]

ChatGPT and Google's Gemini are neither intelligent (as they are not embodied) nor artificial or self-learning (as they are developed with data extracted from human creations and trained by low-paid workers, often in the global south).

In sum, the expansion of individual private freedom occurs in a media ecosystem driven by the invasion of people's personal integrity, their relative freedom of self. Meanwhile, Big Tech contributes to the disintegration of the social tissue, which is rewired into profit-driven networks. These developments call for personal and collective resistance.

I will return to resistance in this introduction's fourth and final part, POSTHUMAN. First I will situate my analysis of the scattering of life in discourses of digital control (part two) and technocolonialism (part three).

Disorganized (*Scattered and Shattered*)

Instead of the vision of the everyday organized by capitalism ... I am interested in the overwhelming ordinary that is DISORGANIZED *by it.*
LAUREN BERLANT, *CRUEL OPTIMISM* (2011)[19]

As stated, for a long time everyday life was seen as time left over, as the non-rational, the DISORGANIZED. Increasingly, however, as Lefebvre argued in the late 1960s, everyday life got hijacked by a capitalist logic that measures "everything" in numbers, money, and minutes.[20] Lefebvre wondered whether, in a society preoccupied with rationality and organization, it is still possible to distinguish a realm of everyday life. Lefebvre saw the everyday as a site of alienation where the subject is forced to adapt to rationalizing rhythms. But Lefebvre also saw the everyday as a domain of potential resistance against capitalism. His critique of the quotidian is thus also a call for its revolution.

Similarly, though less revolutionary, Michel de Certeau writes in *L'Invention du quotidien* (*The Practice of Everyday Life*, 1980) about everyday life as a site at once stratified by capitalism and a social domain where people make meaning. People make their world through *tactics*, negotiating the normative *strategies* of politics, economics, and science. People do so while walking in the city, making do with the official infrastructures. They also do so in their rented homes, furnishing them "with their acts and memories; as do speakers ... through their own 'turns of phrase,' ... as do pedestrians, in the streets they fill with the forests of their desires and goals."[21]

Do these accounts of everyday life organized by capitalism still hold true in a neoliberal and increasingly technocolonial era, in which capitalism is incorporated into a data-extractivist system? Not completely. As Lauren Berlant writes in their 2011 book *Cruel Optimism*, everyday life is increasingly *disorganized* by capitalism. The neoliberal moment, Berlant writes, is marked by a *crisis ordinary* "in which people find themselves developing skills for adjusting to newly proliferating pressures to scramble for modes of living on."[22] Berlant juxtaposes this crisis ordinary to the shock or trauma that everyday life theory attributes to the modern individual. Berlant here refers to discourses of the flaneur and the flaneuse, who redeem themselves from crisis by immersing themselves into the milling crowd, while at the same time scanning and keeping a mental distance from that crowd. Berlant argues that this "everyday life theory no longer describes how most people live," because "the vast majority of the world's population now lives in cities and has access to mass culture via multiple technologies, and is therefore not under the same pressure to unlearn and adapt that their [crowd-scanning] forebearers might well have been."[23]

Berlant does not further discuss how digital technologies affect life, but their understanding of late-capitalist experience as a state of perpetual crisis is productive to understand how Big Tech's platforms attach people to the flux of the present, desubjectifying them in the process. I agree with Berlant that theories of modern everyday life organized by capitalism are dated. I would argue, though, that especially in Lefebvre (more than in de Certeau) we already find a prefiguration of how digital technology facilitates what Gilles Deleuze calls the control society. In that control society, the alienated modern individual becomes a precarious user-subject driven by what Berlant calls *cruel optimism*.

Cruel optimism is the subject's attachment to something that actually harms them and forms an obstacle to their well-being. This can be food, a kind of love, or a political project.[24] It might also be one's smartphone. All attachment is optimistic—optimism understood as a force that moves the subject out of themselves into the world (and through which the subject forms an affective relation to an object, person, or way of life).[25] Cruel optimism is an attachment to the present, and the "present is perceived, first, affectively."[26]

Now, Berlant, as stated, argues that modern everyday life theory no longer describes how people exist in the world. Instead, their affect theory seeks to capture experience in an era in which life is disorganized. Affect theory, Berlant explains, is a new phase in the history of ideology theory. "At least since [Louis] Althusser," ideology theory "has been the place to which critical theory has gone for explanations of … how people's desires become mediated through attachments to modes of life to which they rarely remember consenting."[27] Althusser defined ideology as a representation of an individual's imaginary relationship to their real conditions of existence. Ideology is material. It is a hegemonic worldview embodied in people's everyday habits and discourses, a society's whole way of life. Ideology operates by interpellating—that is, at once addressing and creating—people as individuated subjects. Such interpellation happens by what Althusser calls ideological state apparatuses (ISAs), including the nuclear family, schools, newspaper, and the political system. Althusser distinguishes these ISAs from repressive state apparatuses (RSAs), including the police, courts of justice, and the tax system. Whereas the final category entirely belongs to the public domain, ISAs are predominantly private.[28] Althusser writes that "the distinction between the public and the private is a distinction internal to bourgeois law, and valid in the … domains in which bourgeois law exercises its 'authority.'"[29]

Yet what happens to ideology and subject formation when the public-private binary is disrupted, leaving everyday life disorganized? I would argue that everyday life in a neoliberal and increasingly technocolonial world is disorganized inasmuch as it is controlled. As Deleuze writes in his 1990 essay "Postscript on Control Societies," under late capitalism control succeeds discipline as the dominant form of power. Whereas modern discipline confines the subject through analog technology (prisons, schools, factories), control is more imperceptible and uses digital technology. "Controls are a modulation," Deleuze writes, "like a self-transmuting molding continually changing from one moment to the next."[30]

Control tracks, nudges, tweaks, reorients, and above all suggests: if you liked *x* (this product, book, movie, tweet, ad, person), you may also like *y*. John Cheney-Lippold writes that suggestion softly persuades "users toward models of normalized behavior and identity through the constant redefinition of categories of identity."[31] Control operates with constant feedback loops, adapting to the subject. In doing so, control is oriented toward creating a more personalized experience, suturing the subject into a seamless stream that is experienced as their own. As Slavoj Zizek argues, "since, in our society, free choice is elevated into a supreme value, social control and domination can no longer appear to infringe on the subject's freedom—it has to appear as (and be sustained by) the very experience of individuals as being free."[32]

Like discipline, control is a form of power used by both state institutions and the market. Deleuze writes in relation to the market that "in a control society businesses take over from factories, and a business is a soul, a gas," striving to "introduce a deeper level of modulation into all wages."[33] Similarly, even in the 1960s, Lefebvre saw that "to subdivide and organize everyday life was not enough; now it had to be *programmed*." He adds that big business becomes more than an economic unit *within* society, but instead sets "itself up as a model of organization and administration for society in general."[34] In his theorization of modern everyday life, Lefebvre still leaves more breathing space for people to negotiate and potentially resist hegemonic power than do Deleuze and also Foucault (with whom Deleuze's essay is in conversation). Yet also Lefebvre, in his account of a burgeoning society "programmed" by big business, observes that increasingly "technology has become a determining factor."[35]

Lefebvre's and Deleuze's discussions of gaseous business that present themselves as models for society in general have proven prophetic. Increasingly, the new hegemonic mode of organizing social life is that of a corporate platform ecosystem, defined by José van Dijck as "an assemblage of networked platforms governed by a particular set of mechanisms that shapes everyday practices."[36] These platforms disrupt and *disorganize* the former modern structures of everyday life to the degree "there is no real public 'space'" left, as van Dijck et al. write in *The Platform Society*.[37] Disorganizing the old structures, tech corporations create new conduits for channeling people's practices and discourses, for their need for belonging as well as social cohesion. In doing so, Big Tech contributes to the transformation of everyday life to the extent it becomes something else: a stream in which private and public life blur.

In comparison to modern everyday life, this everyday stream is at once evermore personalized and automated. On the one hand, people's life trajectories are now less structured by normalizing institutions and conventions that prescribe what a "normal" life looks like, from cradle to grave. On the other hand, systems of control increasingly infiltrate into the nitty-gritty of people's lives, nudging their movements. Many subjects may very well experience a sense of control of their life path, but life is also further integrated into market-driven systems, leaving life more precarious and—on the level of people's experience—disorganized.

Adopting Althusser's terminology, we could refer to tech platforms as ideological *para-* or even *post*-state apparatuses whose expansion, as Terranova writes, "threatens to overtake key governmental functions."[38]

As we have seen, Althusser argues that the distinction between the public and the private is internal to modern bourgeois law. But he also adds that the state is above the law and therefore escapes the public-private distinction: "The State, which is the State *of* the ruling class is neither public nor private; on the contrary, it is the precondition for any distinction between public and private."[39]

In our streaming era, tech companies like Google and Meta also often place themselves above the law, disrupting the modern state-citizen relation. Advertising their platforms as neutral "public" and benevolent spaces for social interaction, they interpellate users not merely as consumers but also as *citizens* or a caring community. Take Facebook, whose CEO in 2017 published a "Global Community Manifesto" that asks whether we are "building the world we all want" (Figure 3).[40] Take Microsoft, which in that same year called for a "Digital Geneva Convention" to protect the "public from nation state threats in cyberspace."[41] Take Airbnb, which on its *Citizen* blog launched its own Office of Healthy Tourism. Take dating platform OkCupid, which in 2020 urged its users to vote in the presidential elections. Or take OpenAI, which wants to align its "friendly" generative language models "with human values." This public-washing and benevolent discourse is accompanied by the systemic undermining of *actual* public infrastructures, as through the negation of privacy legislation and tax evastion (a practice integral to Big

FIGURE 3 Facebook's "Global Community" manifesto (screen capture from video, © PBS News Hour, 2017, all rights reserved).[42]

Tech's modus operandi.[43] In this regard Big Tech's placating of Donald Trump (Elon Musk meming himself into the Oval Office, Zuckerberg calling for "masculine energy") did not come as a surprise. Big Tech has always been libertarian at heart.

As an ideological para-state apparatus (or ecosystem) in a control society, Big Tech creates people as user-subjects. This digitalized subject is the individual scattered and shattered to the extent they are no longer an indivisible *in*-dividual, but become a seemingly disorganized *dividual*. "Individuals become *dividuals*," Deleuze writes, "and masses become samples, data, markets, or *banks*."[44] Dividual subjectivity exists in relation to the machines of which it is part and by which it is enslaved and hence disorganized. Or as Maurizio Lazzarato writes in *Signs and Machines*, "not only is the dividual *of a piece with* the machinic assemblage," the dividual is "also *torn to pieces* by it."[45] Similarly, in *Critique of Black Reason* (2013) Achille Mbembe refers to the new subject in the digitalized society as a "*human-thing, human-machine, human-code,* and *human-in-flux*" who "above all [seeks] to regulate [their] behavior according to the norms of the market." As such, this subject "differs in many ways from the tragic and alienated figures of early industrialization."[46]

Indeed, whereas the modern individual is oriented by desire—or by what Berlant calls the good life fantasy—the dividual is a prisoner of desire (Mbembe) and as such a subject of the drive. The dividual is scattered life attached to Big Tech's addiction machine, whose gently steering stream of messages, alerts, feeds, and likes sutures them into a perpetual present without life narrative. People are still interpellated as individuals in their interaction with tech platforms. Yet the same processes that individuate people (as through personalized advertising) now also dividualize them (by slicing their user behavior and experience into marketable data). In turn, the dividualized and depersonalized data extracted from people's movements are used to interpellate people more personally, hooking them to platforms.

This user–machine attachment is a relation of cruel optimism, which is a relation of precarity. Many people are at least somewhat aware that they have an addictive relation to their smartphone. At the same time, our interaction with and attachment to platforms like WhatsApp or Tinder grants us what Berlant calls a sense of "who we are as a continuous scene of action," thereby shaping "our visceral intuition about how to manage living."[47] In other words, our attachment to digital platforms gives us a sense of control, even though we feel—deep down or more consciously—that these platforms control us as subjects.

As was and continues to be the case with modern discipline (which creates people as individuals with a certain agency to act, speak, and, to a limited degree, resist), the softer power of control works two ways: people are controlled and, in that same movement, they are given a sense of control. A control society thus also interpellates people as *resilient*, *empowered*, and *mindful* individuals who are able to bounce back and power on. However supportive contemporary discourses of resilience and empowerment may be, they are also part of the burnout culture inherent to the control society. Against such a control society and Big Tech's role in it, this book seeks to help imagine a more collective subject for disorganized times.

Extraction

Value EXTRACTION *has increasingly shifted away from markets and onto digital platforms … which no longer operate like oligopolistic firms, but rather like private fiefdoms or estates.*
YANIS VAROUFAKIS, "TECHNOFEUDALISM IS TAKING OVER" (2021)

The control society is a technocolonial society. I take the term "technocolonialism" from Mirca Madianou, who uses it to describe the capture of refugee and migrant data. Madianou writes that "the term technocolonialism is necessary because it pays equal attention to colonial legacies, datafication, and innovation as well as global capitalism and inequality."[48] In my own use of the term, I extend "technocolonialism" to signify *all* of Big Tech's for-profit data-extractive practices. As Yanis Varoufakis argues, value extraction has increasingly shifted to digital platforms. Or as Nick Couldry and Ulises Mejias write in their book *Costs of Connection*, our everyday relations with data "cannot be understood except as an appropriation on a form and scale that bears comparison with the appropriations of historical colonialism."[49] Mejias and Couldry speak of *data colonialism* and a *new colonialism* that, as they argue in their recent book *Data Grab*, presents a "continuation of colonial violence by other means."[50] Colonialism is space invasion. Technocolonialism (or data colonialism) then is the invasion of people's *integrity*: the space from which human individuals relate to themselves, experience a sense of coherence, and are also able to willfully consent to enter into relation. Technocolonialism is also the invasion of people's *community*: the space immanent to people's coherence as relational subjects.

I realize that by speaking of "colonialism" there is the risk to appropriate a vocabulary particular to the conditions and struggles of communities who have lived through historical forms of colonialism, or who are subject to more directly violent forms of colonial oppression in the current moment. A technocolonial critique therefore only has value when in solidarity with those struggles. An anti-technocolonial stance recognizes how technocolonialism perpetuates relations of domination that have their origins in Western colonialism. It recognizes how technocolonialism is implicated in the ongoing oppression of populations, violence, gender-based violence, apartheid, exploitation, forced labor, and child labor, especially in the global south.

One can think here of the conditions of cobalt mining in the Democratic Republic of Congo (see also the Epilogue's final section COBALT); exploitative labor practices in the electronics industry, including reports about enslaved Uyghur labor in Apple's supply chain in the Chinese province of Xinjiang;[51] Google's and Amazon's supply of cloud services and advanced machine learning technologies to Israel that contribute to the digital surveillance and also the killing of Palestinians;[52] Meta content moderation in Southeast Asia (as documented by the 2018 documentary film *The Cleaners*); or AI-training sweatshops in the global south (like OpenAI exploiting Kenyan workers to make its model less "toxic") and even in refugee camps and prisons.[53] These conditions and practices are all inherently part of the reality of platformized everyday life.

In many respects, technocolonialism is a perpetuation of global inequalities that have developed since at least the start of Western colonization. At the same time, it could be argued that technocolonialism also marks a rupture. While Mejias and Couldry argue that Big Tech's new colonialism goes hand in hand with the emergence of a new capitalism,[54] others argue that this technocolonialism occurs within the context of capitalism's transformation into a new system. This post-capitalist system has been called technofeudalism (Yanis Varoufakis, Cédric Durand), vectoralism (McKenzie Wark), and digital feudalism (Mariana

Mazzucato).⁵⁵ In his book *Technofeudalism: What Killed Capitalism* Varoufakis argues that the dynamics of capitalism "no longer govern our economies" but have been "replaced by something fundamentally different."⁵⁶ He argues that tech companies like Google no longer produce commodities in order to make a profit, but instead manage to control entire markets by capturing and transforming people's attention. This practice allows these companies to collect "cloud rent" from the "vassal capitalists who are still in the old-fashioned business of selling *their* commodities."⁵⁷

In that new technofeudal system, the datafication of human experience succeeds labor as the dominant mode of value production. Labor and other forms of exploitation—including enslaved labor—continue to exist, but increasingly these are integrated into a data-driven economy that is colonial in essence. Varoufakis argues that digital platforms like Meta and Amazon "no longer operate like oligopolistic firms, but rather like private fiefdoms or estates."⁵⁸ Similarly, in *Capital Is Dead: Is this Something Worse?* McKenzie Wark writes that Big Tech extracts "not just our labor, not just our leisure," but that it commodifies something else, "our sociability, our common and ordinary life together, what you might even call our communism."⁵⁹

This commodification of everyday life is part of a condition of machinic enslavement, in which as Lazzarato writes, a person is no longer instituted as an individuated laboring subject. Instead, they become "a gear, a cog, a component part" in the assemblages that subjectify and extract value from them.⁶⁰ Or as Tiziana Terranova writes in *After the Internet: Digital Networks between Capital and the Common*, the user is no longer a "master of the machine" but an addict, "as behaviorist interfaces that are designed with the purpose of maximizing engagement corrupt collective intelligence."⁶¹ The question is, though: who was that master seemingly in control before their enslavement? Because I agree with Kylie Jarrett that a critique of machinic enslavement also requires a critique of how women have always already been deindividuated, as a result of the devaluation of care work and the division of labor between public and private domains.⁶²

This deindividuation (or dividualization) of life is now generalized by technocolonialism. Take platformized activities like writing a message on WhatsApp, calling a friend on Zoom, or strolling through the city while carrying a data-tracking smartphone, or prompting profit-driven language models like ChatGPT (which are ultimately more extractive than generative). These activities are not labor in the modern capitalist sense of the term, because I agree with Nick Srnicek that it would be too reductive to say that the business models of companies like Google and Meta are premised upon the exploitation of free labor (as for example Terranova argues).[63] Srnicek argues in his book *Platform Capitalism* that "beyond the intuitive hesitation to think that messaging friends is labor, any idea of socially necessary labor time—the implicit standard against which production processes are set—is lacking."[64]

And yet Meta, Zoom, Google, and OpenAI *do* extract value from people's user activities, sometimes even when users are not actively interacting with these platforms. Doing so, these platforms colonize human life, which in the words of Couldry and Mejias, is "quite literally being annexed to capital."[65] Like Srnicek, Couldry, and Mejias, so we have seen, still hold on to the term "capitalism." But if this data colonialism no longer fits the capitalist definition of labor, then perhaps, so I agree with Varoufakis and Wark, it is indeed no longer capitalist.

I understand the difference between labor and technocolonial extraction of people's user behavior as follows: whereas labor is a mostly conscious activity that happens on the level of individuated desire, Big Tech's datafication of people's associations targets the user unconscious, which unfolds on the preindividuated level of the drive. Often the capitalist exploitation of labor and the technocolonial extraction of value from user behavior coexist in the same activity. Take a person driving for Uber. Insofar as this person transports people from *a* to *b*, they perform labor in the modern sense of the term. At the same time, Uber also extracts value from its drivers' conscious and unconscious decisions, turning these decisions into data in order to optimize its network and perhaps also train technology for self-driving cars. To give another example, when a worker joins a video call on a proprietary platform like Zoom or Microsoft Teams, their activity is at once exploited by their employer (as part of the labor relation) *and*, however minimally, by the platform, as part of the user conditions to which they have consented. A final example here: when prompting a large language model like ChatGPT, one simultaneously performs labor (e.g., collecting inspiration for a proposal) *and* feeds data to the platform (as the platform not only generates but also swallows text). Moreover, given that models like ChatGPT and Google's Gemini are basically trained on the entire internet, also those who don't actively use these models are likely to contribute—without consent—to their profitability. Maybe the following is *too* somber of a prediction, but I wonder if in, say fifty years, the open internet, once hailed as a free and democratic space, will be looked back upon as the historical precondition for a technofeudal, generative-extractive machine.

Not all are convinced by this technofeudal argument according to which platformization shifts away from capitalism. Against those who argue that capitalism is becoming a new system, there are also voices who argue that data colonialism or technocolonialism happens *within* capitalism. In his essay "Critique of Technofeudal Reason" Evgeny Morozov argues that the technofeudal theorists forget that capitalism is "infinitely adaptable" and has always used "extra-economic means of value extraction on the non-capitalist periphery." Morozov speaks of techno-*capitalism* rather than technofeudalism, adding that "by vainly invoking the latter, we risk whitewashing the former's reputation."[66]

Similarly, in their 2022 book *Hegemony Now: How Big Tech and Wall Street Won the World* Jeremy Gilbert and Alex Williams write that they are unconvinced by arguments "from more radical sources" that Big Tech replaces capitalism or recreates a new kind of serfdom. They do acknowledge the parallels between data extraction and serfdom, but in their eyes capitalism seems "to be operating much as it always has." They add that the technofeudal position "tends to ignore the manifold ways in which democratic control of platforms could be reasserted."[67]

Finally, Malcolm Harris argues that the technofeudalism thesis too much repeats Big Tech's own discourse. He writes that a company like Meta is much less what the technofeudal theorists make it to be: "It's an advertising platform that wrings pennies out of users' scrap time—attention that would otherwise go to waste, at least from the capitalist perspective."[68] Harris's position resonates with the critique of "Big Critique" as articulated by Jean Burgess et al. in *Everyday Data Culture*. By "Big Critique" they mean writing that is marked by a "sense of understandable urgency" about Big Tech, but that in their view also risks "reinforcing the claims that Big Tech makes about itself."[69] They cite Couldry and Mejias's *Costs of Connection* and Shoshana Zuboff's *The Age of Surveillance Capitalism*, and also the 2020 Netflix documentary *The Social Dilemma*.

As far as my own book is concerned: it is definitely guilty of Big Critique (though as I will explain soon, I don't think "Big Critique" is at odds with the cultural studies perspective suggested by *Everyday Data Cultures*). Not only do I call Big Tech colonial, I also tend to agree with Varoufakis and Wark that the technocolonial shift we are witnessing is not a change *within* but *of* capitalism. In this shift, capitalism (propelled by venture capital investments and deregulation) spirals into a new extractive reality in which the dividualization of people is generalized. This paradigm shift goes hand in hand with a wholesale cultural shift. Companies like Meta, Google, and OpenAI don't just invade people's spacetimes, their datafication of everything changes what everyday life is or was. This transition from the analog to the digital and now streaming era is of the same order as the transition from agricultural to modern urban society. In the streaming era, nothing is what it once was: cities (increasingly "smart"), the metropolitan crowd (now clouded), romantic encounters (now initiated in a cloud of conversations), learning (a lifelong user relation with Google and Microsoft), and more in generally what it means to be human in posthuman times.

Resisting Big Tech takes a cultural-materialist perspective on this transformation of personal and collective life. According to cultural materialism, economic change and cultural change go hand in hand. Writing in the tradition of cultural studies and thinkers like Raymond Williams, I understand culture broadly, as people's "whole way" of everyday life.[70] Culture is how societies act and speak, how "ordinary" people shape their worlds, and how people make meaning while negotiating the often dehumanizing systems that orient their lives. In our technocolonial reality, in which much meaning-making is mediated by personalized algorithms, the fundamental question is: how to still believe in meaning-making as an emancipatory counter-force?

I certainly still believe in people's meaning-making. Big Tech's platforms wouldn't exist otherwise, and people's digitally mediated associations (their connecting, their texting, their prompting) are as real as the ones before platformized life. The authors of *Everyday Data Cultures* are right that, amid all technological change, people and organizations are going about their everyday lives, "grappling with, anxious about, joyfully resisting."[71] Similarly, in *Algorithms of Resistance* Tiziano Bonini and Emiliano Treré discuss how many people and communities—from gig workers to political activists—manage to weigh an "everyday fight" against the asymmetrical platform power relationships users are caught in.[72]

In my view, though, this culturalist perspective on everyday datafied life and the possibilities of resistance, or at least negotiation, is not at odds with a structural critique of technocolonialism (much like in 1960s cultural studies, culturalism and structuralism ultimately were two sides of the same coin).[73] The reason is that now much of people's meaning-making and everyday emancipation functions doubly as input for the technocolonial machine. *Resisting Big Tech* argues that we need to become much more conscious of this development, personally and collectively, starting with embodied conversations about what we have in common, namely the commodification of our ordinary lives by systems that leach onto human conversation.

Posthuman

My dream is a version of the POSTHUMAN *... that understands human life is embedded in a material world of great complexity.*
KATHERINE HAYLES, *HOW WE BECAME POSTHUMAN* (1999)[74]

This book has four chapters, each of which corresponds to a domain of everyday life: home, city, learning, and love. The first two chapters correspond to the quintessential domains of modern everyday life (and of everyday life theory). Chapter 1 asks: what happens to home—as a physical space and as a sense of belonging—when infiltrated by Big Tech? The chapter calls to reconceive of home as a safe or at least safer space liberated from Big Tech colonialism. Chapter 2 zooms in on Sidewalk Toronto, a failed urban redevelopment project spearheaded by Sidewalk Labs (a former Google sibling company). Inspired by urban activist Jane Jacobs, the chapter calls for an open city for everybody and created by everybody. The third and fourth chapters (learning and love) concentrate on two domains of personal and collective emancipation. Chapter 3 analyzes Google's infiltration of education. I call to de-Google learning, at school and in life in general. Chapter 4 looks at online dating, in particular dating platform OkCupid. The chapter imagines common spaces, especially *offline*, where people's encounters are less mediated by profit-driven algorithms. More in general, I call for spaces and modes of social organization that facilitate a *posthuman* resistance against Big Tech's dehumanizing practices, "posthuman" understood as a movement that grasps the materially embedded (Hayles) nature of human life.

Each chapter has seven sections, organized around a keyword that serves as a window onto life in the streaming era. The exception is Chapter 3. Inspired by Google's parent company Alphabet, this chapter takes the form of an abecedarium consisting of twenty-six miniatures, from ANYONE to ZEN. All four chapters and their sections can be read independently. When I picture a reader holding the book, or reading it as an e-book on their screen, I picture them browsing or scrolling, entering the argument somewhere in the middle. After all, and as Deleuze famously put it, philosophy always starts in the middle, because that's where "things and thoughts advance or grow out from ... that's where everything unfolds."[75]

In each of the chapters the argument is roughly organized as follows. First, I analyze Big Tech's own worldview of a humanity that feels mindfully *present* and *connected* through a digital technology that creates life into a frictionless stream. Second, I critique this narrative of technology as second nature, juxtaposing it to the reality of accelerated and colonized life. Third, I call to go against the stream and foster truly common spaces and conversations built on creativity, solidarity, and consent—*con-sent* understood broadly as a sensing together, a *consentire* of relational subjects.

As far as my analysis of Big Tech's view of human life is concerned, throughout I examine a vast archive of texts, images, and moving images produced by tech companies. These materials include advertising, product presentations, corporate blogs, CEO statements, manifestos, books, reports, videos, as well as the platform interfaces themselves. I argue that the stories and visions found in these materials are not mere branding, but that these discourses are essential to Big Tech's self-presentation as a para-state ecosystem that operates for the common good. These materials include presentations by Meta, Microsoft, and Zoom on *telepresence* (Chapter 1); sketches to redesign the Toronto lakefront district by Alphabet subsidiary Sidewalk Labs (Chapter 2); Google's philosophy of adaptive learning as articulated in its Anywhere School and on its *Keyword* blog (Chapter 3); queer advertising and a short film on sexual consent by dating platforms OkCupid and Tinder (Chapter 4); and daydreams of superintelligence by OpenAI and Microsoft (Epilogue).

Analyzing these materials, I argue how much Big Tech ideology is driven by a *transhumanist* belief in technology as second nature. Transhumanism is a social and philosophical movement centered on the belief in a synergy between humans and machines. According to this belief, technology allows humans to overcome their all-too-human limitations and, according to the most orthodox transhumanists, eventually reach singularity: a moment in the near future that technological acceleration will liberate the computerized mind from the body. There is a certain spiritual ring to transhumanism that resonates with turn-of-the-1970s counterculture. However, transhumanism mistakes cerebrality for spirituality, because as a spiritual thinker like bell hooks reminds us, if there is such "thing" as a soul it is always already embodied.

The term "transhumanism" was popularized by the biologist and eugenicist Julian Huxley, who in his 1957 book *New Bottles for New Wine* argued that "the human species can, if it wishes, transcend itself."[76] Precursors to transhumanism date far back, though, and include the quest for immortality in the *Epic of Gilgamesh* (around 1700 BC) and René Descartes's mind-body dualism.[77] As I will argue in Chapter 1, in the section titled PRESENCE, like the Cartesian individual the transhuman fantasy is modeled on a male, white, bourgeois, able-bodied subject.

The recurring idea in transhumanist discourse is that of technology *enhancing* human life, making it *better*. For example, Ray Kurzweil, author of *The Singularity Is Near* (2005) and researcher and "AI Visionary" at Google, states that artificial intelligence "will not displace humans" but "enhance us."[78] This rhetoric of enhancement is found in much Big Tech discourse. Microsoft, for example, dreams of a "world where technology *enhances* not limits humanity"[79] (Chapter 1, ANYWHERE); Sidewalk Labs introduces its smart city vision as a way of "*enhancing* human interactions, enhancing community"[80] (Chapter 2, EMPATHY); Google Brain (now Google DeepMind) asks, "How can we *augment* humans, how can we give humans *superpower*?"[81] (Chapter 3, SOUL); at OkCupid they firmly believe that "with data, history can become ... more" (Chapter 4, DATA*);[82] and OpenAI believes that its chatbot is "fundamentally about *amplifying* what every person is able to do" (Epilogue, ANYBOT).[83]

This ideology of enhanced life is central to the new American Dream predominantly designed in Silicon Valley. *Resisting Big Tech* juxtaposes this frictionless Silicon Dream to the frictions inherent to technocolonialism. These frictions concern both the Dream's production side (the labor conditions under which electronics are produced and tested, their ecological damage, the mining of minerals, energy-guzzling data centers) and, on the user-consumer side, the Dream's acceleration and datafication of everything.

A critique of everyday life (or what's left of it), the book is, as stated, also a manifesto for collective posthuman resistance. I take the posthuman as an ethical horizon immanent to scattered dividual life. The posthuman radically differs from transhumanist fantasies of enhanced and disembodied life. The posthuman, I agree with Rosi Braidotti, is an empirically grounded, embodied, and embedded subject. Braidotti argues that this emphasis on immanence allows us to acknowledge the posthuman as a cyborg who exists across the human-machine binary. Meanwhile, this immanence thinking "avoids the contempt for the flesh and the transhumanist fantasy of escape from the finite materiality of the enfleshed self."[84] Similarly, in *How We Became Posthuman* Katherine Hayles juxtaposes the "flesh-eating" cybernetic posthuman fantasy (i.e., what along with Braidotti I refer to as "transhuman") to a form of the posthuman "that recognizes and celebrates finitude as a condition of human being, and that understands human life is embedded in a material world of great complexity."[85] To recognize ourselves as finite posthuman subjects is to become more conscious of the ideological structures *and* discourses that control life. It is to become more conscious of the material conditions that transform life into a stream.

Consciousness is the seed of resistance. As far as resistance against Big Tech is concerned: its platforms have become so hegemonic, so normalized, that resistance almost seems inconceivable. How to still search without Google? How to find one's way without smartphone? How to stay in touch without WhatsApp? How to collaborate without Microsoft Teams? How to date offline? How to write an essay without artificially intelligent assistance? This normalized hegemonic state is *precisely* why resistance is necessary, and why we have to unsuture ourselves from Big Tech's seamless stream. This stream is most palpable in our cruelly optimistic attachment to our smartphones, hailing us throughout the day, at once disrupting life and reshaping life as a stream. Especially since the launch of the iPhone in 2007, the smartphone has almost become part of the human body. It is good, though, to from time to time to realize that it remains quite bizarre that people now carry in their pockets a machine that is millions of times more powerful than the first computer that guided the first humans to the moon.[86] It is equally bizarre that through this mini-computer—produced under dire circumstances and filled with blood minerals—we are 24/7 attached to a sort of supercomputer that feeds on our desires, how we look at the world, what we love, our very orientations.

Given the stream's dividualization of life, individual resistance against Big Tech is almost a contradiction in terms. Even when one has the privilege to choose one's devices and platforms (which many have not, because they need them for work, or out of social pressure), personal resistance against Big Tech only goes so far when living in a system designed to scatter people. Where does that leave us? In *Data Grab*, Mejias and Couldry outline a "playbook for resistance" along three lines: within the system (e.g., government regulations, tech workers protesting their own companies), against the system (e.g., protest groups exposing bias in algorithms, gig workers unionizing, media literacy programs at schools), and beyond the system in "the attempt to imagine a different worldview altogether" (as through critical thinking and decolonizing data).[87] My own take on resisting Big Tech mostly falls into this last category: to unthink the datafication of everything and to prefigure, perhaps naively, a world in which people can associate more freely.

In this respect, my perspective on resisting Big Tech somewhat differs from that of for example Nick Srnicek, who above all sees a role for the state in the regulation of existing platforms and the creation of public, post-capitalist alternatives (corresponding to the first two acts of Mejias & Couldry's playbook). Srnicek is less hopeful about cooperative opensource platforms, because in his view such alternatives are easily outcompeted by giants like Meta and Google. Similarly, van Dijck et al. argue that "it takes much more than bottom-up commons-based initiatives." They write that to bring "substantive change" to the platform society a "comprehensive, cross-sectoral strategy," especially by government actors, is needed.[88] And yes, of course, state regulation and public alternatives *are* needed. But states and public institutions (including universities) are now often also part of the problem, partaking in a control society that undermines the very public values on which they should be built. States and public institutions can therefore learn a lot from cooperative and bottom-up initiatives that are grown on the belief that together people make meaning, and that experiment with ways to facilitate (rather than discipline or control) people's creative potentials.

This holds especially true for initiatives that challenge the control society from an intersectionally feminist, queer, postcolonial, and antiracist perspective, resisting the binaries on which states and public institutions have often been built. In order to resist Big Tech, it is necessary to reimagine everyday life as a site of resistance. We have to become more conscious as societies of how Big Tech's personalized streams hijack and accelerate life, our personal ecologies and the naturalcultural ecologies in which we are entangled.

I take this notion of "natureculture" from Donna Haraway, who introduced it to unthink the nature-culture binary while decentering the human.[89] To unthink binaries is also part of my project. In order to acknowledge ourselves as entangled beings across binaries, we need public and especially common spaces in which people are encouraged in their creative and caring potential. As stated, in these common spaces, public and private life blur in the realization that the personal is still political. As Slavoj Zizek argues in *Like a Thief in Broad Daylight: Power in the Era of Post-Humanity* (2018), the digital network "gives new meaning" to this feminist slogan, and the struggle for a new online commons "is *the* struggle today." This struggle is concerned with both personal and communal freedom, because communal freedom in my view is people's collective and consensual attempt at personal liberation. Inspired by feminism and also the philosophy of Spinoza, I view personal freedom as the realization that one's most privately sensed affects are shaped by the structures one is part of and the natureculture one is entangled in. The associations that form in our minds and that move our bodies, are never just our own. They emerge from a common unconscious that moves through our bodyminds.

As I will argue in Chapter 1, HOMEWORK, my call for consciousness building is inspired by the Women's Liberation Movement, which, as of the late 1960s, organized conversation groups to facilitate collective self-analyses of how patriarchy structures desire. Patriarchy still does, both through old-fashioned ways like the state and the nuclear family, and by newer technofeudal means like biased search engines and large language models. The struggle for a new commons is a feminist struggle, inasmuch as it is a queer, anti-racist, anti-transphobic, anti-ablist, and anti-ageist struggle. It also is a struggle for climate and ecological justice, against a hegemonic burnout culture.

While building consciousness of that burnout culture, we need to prefigure alternative social forms, including alternative digital platforms. As James Muldoon writes in *Platform Socialism: How to Reclaim our Digital Future from Big Tech* (2022), we need to create new digital infrastructures "in which citizens can take back control over their services and public spaces."[90] We need what Ivan Illich calls *convivial* tools, including platforms designed for people, not for profit.[91] But we don't just need new digital commons and platforms to replace the ones controlled by Big Tech. That would be impossible anyway. As I argue in the Epilogue, "Against the Stream for Ecological Justice," we need to situate the resistance against Big Tech in the context of a broader struggle for a more cooperative society that moves beyond the economic growth paradigm. To do so is a communist practice. As Michael Hardt writes, communism is defined by not only the abolition of private property but "also the affirmation of the common—the affirmation of open and autonomous biopolitical production, the self-governed continuous creation of new humanity." Hardt adds that what private property is to capitalism, "the common is to communism."[92]

A society that affirms the common, and that affirms what people have in common—what Wark calls their very communism—rethinks the relation between economy and culture. Economy derives from the Greek *oikonomia*, the organization of home, how people hold their houses. For that householding, people and societies may need tools, like online platforms. We need to critically keep wondering, though: to what end are we invested in technology, economically and with all we have. In a degrowth society, technology is a means to an end: the collective tools necessary in the struggle *against* ecological collapse and *for* social justice. A degrowth society no longer creates people as consumers. Instead, it facilitates their creativity for the common good in relation to their local and global ecosystems. Or as Jason Hickel writes in *Less Is More: How Degrowth Will Save the World*, degrowth stands for the "de-thingification of human nature, and the de-escalation of ecological crisis."[93]

We thus need perspectives that connect: the *burnout* of people with the exhaustion of the planet, the personal with the political, an analysis of everyday discontent with the struggle against the forces that uphold the control society: Big Tech, Big Finance, Big Oil, Big Mine, Big Everything. Much technology now accelerates life and colonizes communities, a development driven by the transhumanist promise of a "humanity" becoming part of "something bigger" (another turn of phrase often heard in tech discourse). But we don't need to be part of something bigger, because such big attachments are often cruel. We need to be part of something shared. To resist Big Tech and to go against the stream is to *unstream*, to slow down life, to embrace friction and glitch, and to create the spacetime for association and conversation: with the chorus of voices in one's head, with one's body, and with the bodyminds and naturecultures one is surrounded by and entangled in. To slow down life is to embrace a culture of consent in which people sense together. It is to open up to an immanent spirituality and be present with one's dreams and dishes.

Notes

1. Kathleen Stewart, *Ordinary Affects* (Durham: Duke University Press, 2007), 19.
2. Henri Lefebvre, *Everyday Life in the Modern World*, trans. Sacha Rabinovitch (New York: Bloomsburg, 2018), 38.
3. Stewart, *Ordinary Affects*, 19.
4. See also: Niels Niessen, "The Task of the Film Critic in Times of Streaming Video," *Film Criticism* 40.1 (2016), accessed October 23, 2024, https://quod.lib.umich.edu/f/fc/13761232.0040.124/–task-of-the-film-critic-in-times-of-streaming-video?rgn=main;view=fulltext.
5. Kylie Jarrett, *Feminism, Labour, and Digital Media: The Digital Housewife* (New York: Routledge, 2016), 54; Sara Ahmed, "Selfcare as Warfare," *feministkilljoys* (August 25, 2014), accessed October 23, 2024, https://feministkilljoys.com/2014/08/25/selfcare-as-warfare.
6. Michael Warner, "Public/Private," in Catharine R. Simpson and Gilbert Herdt, eds., *Critical Terms for the Study of Gender* (Chicago: University of Chicago Press, 2014).
7. Jarrett, *Feminism, Labour and Digital Media*, 171.
8. Henri Lefebvre, *Everyday Life in the Modern World*, trans. Sacha Rabinovitch (New York: Bloomsburg, 2018), 14.
9. Lefebvre, *Everyday Life in the Modern World*, 11.
10. Jonathan Crary, *24/7: Late Capitalism and the Ends of Sleep* (London: Verso, 2014), 70.
11. Rita Felski, *Doing Time: Feminist Theory and Posthuman Culture* (New York: York University Press, 2000), 78.
12. Warner, "Public/Private."
13. Warner, "Public/Private."
14. Stewart, *Ordinary Affects*, 104–5.
15. See for example: Janet Wolff, "The Invisible Flaneuse: Women and the Literature of Modernity," *Theory, Culture & Society* 2.3 (1985).
16. Cited in Zoetanya Sujon, *The Social Media Age* (London: Sage Publications, 2021), 202.
17. Sujon, *Social Media Age*, 202.
18. WhatsApp, "A New Era of Personal Privacy with Default End-to-End Encryption" (video) (2021), accessed May 1, 2023, https://www.youtube.com/watch?v=zvI4cVGWJhM.

19 Lauren Berlant, *Cruel Optimism* (Durham: Duke University Press, 2011), 8.
20 Lefebvre, *Everyday Life in the Modern World*, 18.
21 Michel de Certeau, *The Practice of Everyday Life*, trans. Steven Rendall (Berkeley: University of California Press, 1988), xxi.
22 Berlant, *Cruel Optimism*, 8.
23 Berlant, *Cruel Optimism*, 8.
24 Berlant, *Cruel Optimism*, 1.
25 Berlant, *Cruel Optimism*, 1.
26 Berlant, *Cruel Optimism*, 4.
27 Berlant, *Cruel Optimism*, 52–3.
28 Louis Althusser, *"Lenin and Philosophy" and Other Essays*, trans. Ben Brewster (New York: Monthly Review Press, 1971), 144.
29 Althusser, *Lenin and Philosophy*, 144.
30 Gilles Deleuze, *Negotiations 1972–1990*, trans. Martin Joughin (New York: Columbia University Press, 1990), 178–9.
31 John Cheney-Lippold, "A New Algorithmic Identity: Soft Biopolitics and the Modulation of Control," *Theory Culture Society* 28.6 (2011): 164–81, p. 177.
32 Slavoj Zizek, *Like a Thief in Broad Daylight: Power in the Era of Post-Humanity* (New York: Penguin Books, 2018), 26.
33 Deleuze, *Negotiations*, 178–9.
34 Lefebvre, *Everyday Life in the Modern World*, 54–6.
35 Lefebvre, *Everyday Life in the Modern World*, 41.
36 José van Dijck, "The Platform Society," Association of Internet Research conference (video) (2016), accessed October 23, 2024, https://www.youtube.com/watch?v=-ypiiSQTNqo.
37 José van Dijck, Thomas Poell, and Martijn de Waal, *The Platform Society: Public Values in a Connective World* (New York: Oxford University Press, 2018), 48, 166.
38 Tiziana Terranova, *After the Internet: Digital Networks between Capital and the Common* (South Pasadena: Semiotext(e), 2022), 23.
39 Althusser, *Lenin and Philosophy*.
40 Mark Zuckerberg, "Building Global Community," Facebook.com (February 16, 2017), accessed October 23, 2024, https://www.facebook.com/notes/mark-zuckerberg/building-global-community/10154544292806634.

41 Microsoft, "A Digital Geneva Convention to Protect Cyberspace" (2017), accessed October 15, 2019, https://www.microsoft.com/en-us/cybersecurity/content-hub/a-digital-geneva-convention-to-protect-cyberspace.

42 PBS News Hour, "How To Interpret Mark Zuckerberg's Recent 'Manifesto'" (video) (2017), accessed October 23, 2024, https://www.youtube.com/watch?v=9Y7hui0R_vs.

43 See for example: Rupert Neate, "'Silicon Six' Tech Giants Accused of Inflating Tax Payment by Almost $100bn," *The Guardian* (May 31, 2021), accessed October 23, 2024, https://www.theguardian.com/business/2021/may/31/silicon-six-tech-giants-accused-of-inflating-tax-payments-by-almost-100bn; Kim Lyons, "Ireland's Status as Tax Haven for Tech Firms like Google, Facebook, and Apple Is Ending," *The Verge* (October 8, 2021), accessed October 23, 2024, https://www.theverge.com/2021/10/7/22715229/ireland-status-tax-haven-google-facebook-apple.

44 Deleuze, *Negotiations*, 180.

45 Maurizio Lazzarato, *Signs and Machines: Capitalism and the Production of Subjectivity*, trans. David Jordan (Los Angeles: Semiotext(e), 2017), 27.

46 Achille Mbembe, *Critique of Black Reason*, trans. Laurent Dubois (Durham: Duke University Press, 2017), 4, italics in original.

47 Berlant, *Cruel Optimism*, 52.

48 Mirca Madianou, "Technocolonialism: Digital Innovation and Data Practices in the Humanitarian Response to Refugee Crises," *Social Media and Society* 5.3 (2019), https://doi.org/10.1177/2056305119863146.

49 Nick Couldry and Ulises A. Mejias, *The Costs of Connection: How Data Is Colonizing Human Life and Appropriating It for Capitalism* (Stanford: Stanford University Press, 2019), xi–xii.

50 Ulises A. Mejias and Nick Couldry, *Data Grab: The New Colonialism of Big Tech and How to Fight Back* (Chicago: University of Chicago Press, 2024), 39.

51 Broken Chain, "Apple's Uyghur Dilemma Grows," *Tech Transparency Project* (June 8, 2021), accessed October 23, 2024, https://www.techtransparencyproject.org/articles/apples-uyghur-dilemma-grows; Jacob Kastrenakes, "Apple Suppliers Linked to Uyghur Forced Labor," *The Verge* (May 10, 2021), accessed October 23, 2024, https://www.theverge.com/2021/5/10/22428899/apple-suppliers-china-uyghur-forced-labor-report.

52 See for example: Amanda Silberling, "Google Workers Protest $1.2B Project Nimbus Contract with Israeli Military," *Techcrunch* (September 1, 2022), accessed October 23, 2024, https://techcrunch.com/2022/09/01/google-workers-protest-1-2b-project-nimbus-contract-with-israeli-military; Al Jazeera, "What Is Project Nimbus, and Why Are Google Workers Protesting

Israel Deal," *Al Jazeera* (April 23, 2024), accessed October 23, 2024. https://www.aljazeera.com/news/2024/4/23/what-is-project-nimbus-and-why-are-google-workers-protesting-israel-deal; Sebastian Moss, "Investigation Confirms IDF Uses AWS, Google Cloud, and Microsoft Azure for Gaza War," *Data Center Dynamics* (August 6, 2024), accessed October 23, 2024, https://www.datacenterdynamics.com/en/news/investigation-confirms-idf-uses-aws-google-cloud-and-microsoft-azure-for-gaza-war.

53 Billy Perrigo, "OpenAI Used Kenyan Workers on Less Than $2 per Hour to Make ChatGPT Less Toxic," *Time* (January 18, 2023), accessed October 23, 2024, https://time.com/6247678/openai-chatgpt-kenya-workers; Hannah Aster, "Digital Sweatshops: The Dark Side of Artificial Intelligence," *Shortform* (October 3, 2023), accessed October 23, 2024, https://www.shortform.com/blog/digital-sweatshop; Rebecca Tan and Regine Cabato, "Behind the AI Boom, an Army of Overseas Workers in 'Digital Sweatshops'," *The Washington Post* (August 28, 2023), accessed October 23, 2024, https://www.washingtonpost.com/world/2023/08/28/scale-ai-remotasks-philippines-artificial-intelligence.

54 Mejias and Couldry, *Data Grab*, 28–9.

55 Mariana Mazzucato, "Preventing Digital Feudalism," *Project Syndicate* (October 2, 2019), accessed October 23, 2024, https://www.project-syndicate.org/commentary/platform-economy-digital-feudalism-by-mariana-mazzucato-2019-10.

56 Yanis Varoufakis, *Technofeudalism: What Killed Capitalism* (London: The Bodley Head, 2023), xii.

57 Varoufakis, *Technofeudalism*, 130.

58 Yanis Varoufakis, "Techno-Feudalism Is Taking Over," *Project Syndicate* (28 June 2021), accessed October 23, 2024, https://www.project-syndicate.org/commentary/techno-feudalism-replacing-market-capitalism-by-yanis-varoufakis-2021-06.

59 McKenzie Wark, *Capital Is Dead: Is This Something Worse* (London: Verso, 2019), 3.

60 Lazzarato, *Signs and Machines*, 25.

61 Terranova, *After the Internet*, 6–7.

62 Jarrett, *Feminism, Labour and Digital Media*, 171.

63 Terranova, *After the Internet*, 39. See also Tiziana Terranova, "Free Labor: Producing Culture for the Digital Economy," *Social Text* 63 (18.2) (2000), 33–58.

64 Nick Srnicek, *Platform Capitalism* (Cambridge: Polity Press, 2016), 55–6.

65 Couldry and Mejias, *Costs of Connection*, xi.

66 Evgeny Morozov, "Critique of Technofeudal Reason," *New Left Review* 133/134 (January/April 2022), accessed October 23, 2024, https://

newleftreview.org/issues/ii133/articles/evgeny-morozov-critique-of-techno-feudal-reason.

67 Jeremy Gilbert and Alex Williams, *Hegemony Now: How Big Tech and Wall Street Won the World (and How We Win it Back)* (London: Verso, 2022), 198.

68 Malcolm Harris, "Are We Living under 'Technofeudalism'?," *New York Magazine* (October 28, 2022), accessed October 23, 2024, https://nymag.com/intelligencer/2022/10/what-is-technofeudalism.html.

69 Jean Burgess, Kath Albury, Anthony McCosker, and Rowan Wilken, *Everyday Data Cultures* (Cambridge: Polity Press, 2022), 15–17.

70 Raymond Williams, *The Long Revolution* (Cardigan: The Old Surgery, 2013), 60.

71 Burgess et al., *Everyday Data Cultures*, 18.

72 Tiziano Bonini and Emiliano Treré, *Algorithms of Resistance: The Everyday Fight against Platform Power* (Cambridge, MA: MIT Press, 2024), 14–15.

73 See Stuart Hall, "Cultural Studies: Two Paradigms," *Media, Culture and Society* 2 (1980): 57–72.

74 Katherine Hayles, *How We Became Posthuman* (Chicago: Chicago University Press, 1999), 5.

75 Deleuze, *Negotiations*, 161.

76 Julian Huxley, *New Bottles for New Wine* (London: Chatto & Windus, 1957), 13–17.

77 Nick Bostrom, "A History of Transhumanist Thought," *Journal of Evolution and Technology* 14.1 (2005): 1–30.

78 Ray Kurzweil, "AI Will Not Displace Humans, It's Going to Enhance Us," *Futurism* (July 11, 2017), accessed October 23, 2024, https://futurism.com/ray-kurzweil-ai-displace-humans-going-enhance.

79 IGN, "Microsoft Mesh—Official Introduction Trailer" (video) (2021), accessed October 23, 2024, https://www.youtube.com/watch?v=CC13DcdAY_s.

80 Sidewalk Toronto, "Introducing Sidewalk Toronto" (video) (2017), accessed October 23, 2024, https://www.youtube.com/watch?v=xQYSy8w9j5c.

81 Google, "Douglas Coupland's New Slogans Powered by AI" (video), *Experiments with Google* (June 2021), accessed October 23, 2024, https://experiments.withgoogle.com/douglas-coupland.

82 OkCupid, "How is Match Percentage Calculated? Discover All Our Matching System Secrets" (July 2022), accessed October 15, 2019, https://help.okcupid.com/hc/en-us/articles/5221215995149-How-is-Match-Percentage-Calculated-Discover-All-Our-Matching-System-Secrets.

83 OpenAI, "Introducing GPT-4" (video) (2023), accessed October 4, 2023, https://www.youtube.com/watch?v=–khbXchTeE, *emphasis mine*.

84 Rosi Braidotti, *The Posthuman* (Cambridge: Polity Press, 2013), 90-1.

85 Hayles, *How We Became Posthuman*, 5.

86 Tibi Puiu, "Your Smartphone Is Millions of Times More Powerful than the Apollo 11 Guidance Computers," *ZME Science* (October 13, 2015), accessed October 23, 2024, https://www.zmescience.com/feature-post/technology-articles/computer-science/smartphone-power-compared-to-apollo-432.

87 Mejias and Couldry, *Data Grab*, 222-39.

88 Van Dijck et al., *Platform Society*, 16.

89 Donna J. Haraway, *The Companion Species Manifesto: Dogs, People, and Significant Otherness* (Chicago: Prickly Paradigm Press, 2003), 1.

90 James Muldoon, *Platform Socialism: How to Reclaim our Digital Future from Big Tech* (London: Pluto Press, 2022), 5.

91 Ivan Illich, *Tools for Conviviality* (London: Marion Boyars Publishing, 2021).

92 Michael Hardt, "The Common in Communism," *Rethinking Marxism: A Journal of Economics, Culture & Society* 22.3 (2010): 346-56.

93 Jason Hickel, *Less Is More: How Degrowth Will Save the World* (London: Penguin Random House UK, 2022), 289.

1 HOME

Dreams and Dishes

The future is here, and here can be ANYWHERE.
MICROSOFT ABOUT ITS MIXED-REALITY PLATFORM MESH[1]

Your home is your personal space from which you can teleport to ANYWHERE *you want.*
META'S CEO MARK ZUCKERBERG ABOUT THE METAVERSE[2]

We are all seeking for a sense of place. We are all seeking to belong.
AIRBNB ABOUT ITS "BELONG ANYWHERE" SLOGAN[3]

Anywhere

How do home and people's sense of home change with Wi-Fi? I remember first asking myself this question in 2014, when I had just moved to Toronto and waited in my new apartment for the internet to be connected. In this same period, I filled one notebook after the other, mostly with observations on how my new smartphone—which I had thus far resisted—suddenly mediated everything: my city travels, my travels at home, my social relations, my relation to self. It got me thinking: when I think about everything all the time anyway, I might as well write about everything, that is to say: everyday life in the streaming age. Now, when I actually start writing this chapter, it's April 2020. The world is in the middle of the Covid-19 pandemic. I live in Utrecht, in the Netherlands, which has a relatively mild quarantine regime, framed politically as an "intelligent lockdown" (Figures 4 and 5).[4] Also here it's the high-era of televideo communication, but I will return to that.

FIGURE 4 "Hopefully no-one sees this poster! #Stay home" (Utrecht, March 2020, photo by the author).

FIGURE 5 "Quarantine is easier in Park Town than in Transtown" (Utrecht, March 2020, photo by the author).

How do home and the feeling of being home change? According to short-term housing rental platform Airbnb home can now be *anywhere* that people are "seeking to belong (Figure 6)." During the Covid-19 pandemic, however, for most people home really became *here*, a place one was discouraged or even forbidden to leave. Then again, "*here* can be anywhere," as claimed Microsoft in 2021 in its introduction of Mesh (Figure 7).[5] Mesh is a mixed reality platform that allows people to interact with others in three-dimensional spaces, creating the illusion of *presence*. In an introduction video, we see users interact with coworkers or their doctor as these are *holoported* (projected as life-like holograms) into their living rooms.[6] Similarly, Meta, via voice of its CEO Mark Zuckerberg, during the Covid-19 pandemic, imagined the home of the future as a space "from which you can teleport *anywhere* you want." Finally, Google, in 2019, has already imagined home as a ubiquitous interface that, thanks to its smart "Home" speakers, can be addressed from *anywhere* in the house[7] (Figure 8).

Though virtual reality has not taken off as fast as imagined during the height of the pandemic, these examples illustrate that in Big Tech's imaginary *home* is, on the one hand, a sense of belonging decoupled from a fixed location (Airbnb, Meta). On the other hand, home has become a mission control center where humans are in charge of their life, and from where they connect with others, whether those others are also *here* (Google) or *anywhere* else in the world (Microsoft, Meta). In this tech vision of home, computing is ambient and ubiquitous inasmuch as it "fades into the background" (Microsoft), while technology becomes as light as the cloud carrying the Airbnb traveler.

The backside of this transhumanist imaginary—in which technology becomes second nature or even part of the family (Google)—is that home also becomes a place of data extraction. Whereas for a long time, people's domestic lives remained relatively separate from corporate intrusion, in our platformized age home is integrated into a market-driven stream. Can one still feel at home—*chez soi* in French, with oneself—when that relation to self and others is mediated by technologies designed to slice up the self? Does home, when immersed into the stream, still stand for the spacetime to decompress?

Not according to Shoshana Zuboff, who opens her book *Surveillance Capitalism* with a "requiem" for a home. Zuboff writes that "all creatures orient to home" and that "it is in the nature of human attachment that every journey and expulsion sets into motion the search for home." As the

FIGURE 6 Airbnb introducing "Belong Anywhere" (screen capture from video, © Airbnb, 2015, all rights reserved).[8]

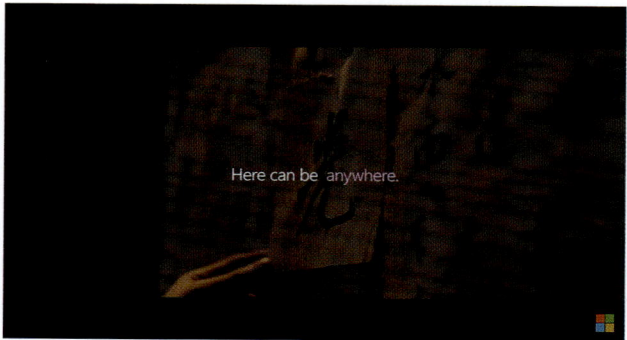

FIGURE 7 Microsoft introducing holoportation platform Mesh (screen capture from video, © Microsoft, 2023, all rights reserved).[9]

FIGURE 8 "Hey Google, broadcast breakfast is ready" (screen capture from video, © Google, 2019, all rights reserved).[10]

digital dream darkens, this "universally shared" sense of home is under threat.[11] I share Zuboff's worry about data-extractive practices, but I don't share her understanding of *home* as a universally safe and stable sense. Home is not just a shared sense. A home also separates, individualizes, and dividualizes people.

Home is thus not necessarily a safe place, and for many, "home" even is a place of domestic violence and oppression. As Gil Scott-Heron sang on his 1971 album *Pieces of a Man*, home may also be where the hatred is, "filled with pain and it, / might not be such a bad idea if I never, never went home again."[12] Thirty years later, when the murder of George Floyd unleashed a global wave of protest spreading from the streets of Minneapolis—another place I once called home—Heron's words continue to resonate: "So that the world, so that the world can watch you die?"

Home is also not necessarily a stable place, a neutral ground to which people universally orient. Instead, *home* is itself always already an orientation. Sara Ahmed writes in *Queer Phenomenology* that "if we think of bodies and spaces as orientated, then we re-animate the very concept of space." Ahmed cites Henri Lefebvre's definition of orientation as "sense," at once "an organ that perceives, a direction that may be conceived, and a directly lived movement progressing toward the horizon."[13] Home, then, is all these things at once: a space, the bodyminds inhabiting and traversing that space, and these people's movements as they develop their sense of belonging in relation to the world, others, and themselves.

In our streaming age, Big Tech has found a way to colonize this sense of home. Resisting Big Tech, this chapter articulates the need to defend home as a private space separate from the market. I am not too attached, though, to modern notions of privacy and individuality, modeled as they are on a white, male, bourgeois subject. Instead, in the face of the control society and its dividualizing power, we need to reinvent home as a common space and sense of collective self *across the private-public binary*. By reinventing "home" as a common space, I mean creating actual physical spaces: cooperative living rooms where public and private life blur in care, co-creation, and solidarity. By reinventing "home" as a collective sense of self, I mean an ongoing social conversation about integrity and consent across spaces such as schools, theaters, social centers, and—online—also platforms (ideally public platforms, though of course such conversations also happen on media like Instagram and X).

The chapter has seven sections. Following this introduction, the next section discusses how Wi-Fi and streaming technology have facilitated the transformation of "home" from a relatively demarcated private domain into a dislocated yet also personalized sense of belonging. Sections three and four zoom in on Big Tech's visions of home and human life. These sections analyze what connects, on the one hand, Covid-19-time discourses of the metaverse and VR/MR/AR spaces like Mesh, and, on the other hand, post-Covid-19 discourses of personalized AI assistants like Google's Gemini and Microsoft's "everyday AI companion" Copilot (which allows you to "unlock your potential, *anywhere, anytime*").[14] That connection, so I argue, is a transhumanist ideal of disembodied *presence*. Section five juxtaposes this transhumanist dream of a weightless and mindful technology use to the precarious reality of dividualized and accelerated life. I argue that resistance starts with a collective consciousness of how the stream shapes us as subjects. Therefore, section six, HOMEWORK, calls to adopt the feminist rallying cry that the "personal is political" for our era of personal*ized* streams. Section seven is an association from Covid-19 lockdown.

The lockdown era is a recurring theme throughout this chapter. In the beginning of lockdown, it felt as if quarantine had punctured the 24/7 rhythm that has come to run all of our lives (as my colleague Jeff Diamanti said during a Zoom meeting of the "Political Ecologies" seminar that he co-organized at the University of Amsterdam). Soon, however, as the new normality of social distancing and long-distance communication settled in, it became evident that Big Tech's motor behind the 24/7 burnout logic only gained further momentum—and so did the disparities inherent to that logic.[15] What initially appeared as a breach of the everyday stream in fact accelerated that stream.

There is a parallel here with late seventeenth-century Europe's response to the plague. As Michel Foucault writes in *Discipline and Punish*, the crisis measures that were implemented at the time in order to contain the plague as a form "at once real and imaginary" laid the blueprint for modern disciplinary society.[16] Foucault discusses the eighteenth-century "historical conjuncture" that was immanent to the shift from a society based on classical sovereign power to a society of discipline. In this conjuncture (understood as the joining of processes in crisis) two aspects met. The first was the rapid growth of the production apparatus. The other was the population increase in Western Europe. In response to this double development, state institutions and market forces developed new power techniques in an attempt to streamline the production process and regulate "floating" populations (Foucault speaks of discipline as an "antinomadic technique"). Each on their own, these disciplinary techniques (e.g., trainings of criminals, population counts) were not new. "What was new," Foucault writes, "was that by being combined and generalized, [these techniques] attained a level at which the formation of knowledge and the increases of power regularly reinforce one another in a circular process" to the point that "the disciplines crossed the 'technological' threshold."[17] In other words, over the course of the eighteenth century the demographic-capitalist conjuncture set in motion a centrifugal dynamic out of which spiraled something new: modern society.

Moving back to the early twenty-first century and its control society (which succeeds modern society): even though the origins of this control society date from before the Covid-19 pandemic, measures like corona passports and QR-codes have certainly catalyzed its emergence. The same can be said about the lasting ubiquity of video-conferencing and livestreams, which mostly happen on platforms that are part of a digital ecosystem fueled by user data. Looking back, the lockdown era serves as a window to speculate about controlled life in the decades to come. The urgent question is: How to feel at home in that future, in which on all sides "we are surrounded by rings of fire" (as Achille Mbembe described digitalized life during lockdown)?[18] This chapter reimagines home as the spacetime for people to associate. To associate is to connect, alone and with others, like in love, friendship, or over a common cause. The everyday spacetime to associate is increasingly clouded by personalized streams. It is necessary to reconceive of home as a safe or at least safer space. This also means to liberate ourselves from profit-driven algorithms.

Wi-Fi

Space is never just space. Sometimes we think of it as the air around us. Sometimes we think of it as a thing to find a WI-FI signal.
KYLE STEVENS IN "POSTS FROM THE PANDEMIC"
(*CRITICAL INQUIRY* BLOG, 2020)[19]

For a period in not-so-distant history, a home was a place with a mailbox, telephone, radio, and television, all technologies that connect that home's inhabitants to the outside world. A home is a gathering place of technology, but a home—in the sense of house or apartment—is itself also already a technology, or medium. As Marshall McLuhan writes in *Understanding Media* (1964), "if clothing is an extension of our private skins to store and channel our own heat and energy, housing is a collective means of achieving the same end for the family or the group."[20]

Every home has its own rhythm, but all domestic life is also synced with society through modern media. The quintessential modern medium is electric light, which has decoupled life from the natural rhythm of the seasons. McLuhan refers to electric light as information without content: "When the light is on there is a world of sense that disappears when the light is off."[21] When the light is off there are also worlds that appear *more* clearly, like ghost stories and dreams. But let's keep the light on for now, as it kindles reflections on Wi-Fi: the quintessential medium of the streaming age. Materially, Wi-Fi is like electric light: electromagnetic radiation that, as Kyle Stevens points out, fills a space. As a medium, Wi-Fi is very unlike light in that its content is accessed by devices (phones, tablets) that are often also a light source.

The name "Wi-Fi" is a generic trademark, or proprietary eponym, like Kleenex, Plexiglass, and Zooming (to refer to some Covid-19-reminiscent generic trademarks). "Wi-Fi" is a pun on hi-fi, but the word is not an acronym, even though for a while the Wi-Fi Alliance—a nonprofit institution headquartered in Austin, Texas, that since 1998 certifies products that make use of the Wi-Fi protocol—ran the slogan "the standard for wireless fidelity."[22] With Wi-Fi, the internet broke free from the wall, allowing teenagers to access the internet in the privacy of their own rooms, instead of through the family PC (whether in a designated computer room or as a "gate in the living room").[23] Wi-Fi has thus further facilitated the privatization of media usage, in all its emancipatory and addictive effects.

Wireless and soon also mobile internet have accelerated the shift that is central to the current streaming conjuncture. In that conjuncture, capitalism morphs into a technocolonial system, while people are thingified by platforms' deceptively personalized approach. Key to this development is that the typically modern segmentation of space and time is accelerated to the degree space and time morph into a hybrid and modular *spacetime*, in which the function of and access to spaces may switch continuously. Think of office buildings that can only be accessed by keycards and where "the card may also be rejected on a particular day, or between certain times of day" (as writes Gilles Deleuze on the control society).[24] Or think of the kitchen table, which may also be one's office.

What happens to home in this development? In response to this question, I look at home as both a material and discursive category in which private dwelling at once intersects with *and* is demarcated from the public, understood as both the public domain (market and state) and the public sphere (in which private individuals come together). In the modern "home," the private and the public are per definition intertwined, if only because homes are subject to the housing market, or because most homes are connected to an infrastructural grid of public or publicly-regulated services (water, energy, sewers, cable, voting ballots, internet). For a long time, the modern private "home" was considered a space relatively separate from the public, a view rightfully contested by feminist critique.

To zoom in on that modern understanding of home and its critiques: in *The Practice of Everyday Life* (1980) Michel de Certeau defines the private as a space where "the pressure of the social body on the individual does not prevail, where the plurality of stimuli is filtered, or, in any case, ideally ought to be."[25] Home shuts out the modern crowd, De Derteau argues, allowing the modern individual to decompress and regenerate themselves as an indivisible individual. Home, in other words, is a space for the individual to be with oneself and to experience a sense of privacy, a minimal integrity of self.

The problem with de Certeau's account of modern individuality—here in relation to private space and elsewhere in relation to city walking— is that it is predicated on a white, male, bourgeois subject, while it largely ignores the modern female experience. De Certeau represents the private almost as an *outside* to capitalism, leaving unacknowledged that the private, as a site of reproductive labor, has always been integral to the capitalist dialectic. De Certeau writes that "as a general rule, in this private space one rarely works, except at that indispensable work of nourishment, of cleaning, and of conviviality that gives a human form to the succession of days and to the presence of others. Here bodies are washed, adorned, perfumed, and take the time to live and dream."[26] The thing is that the bodies who are doing the cleaning and washing are not necessarily the same as those who have the spacetime to live and dream, and to live their dream.

The picture of home as a safe haven, as a place of regeneration that allows the individual to stay whole despite all alienation of labor and the urban crowd, remains a very one-dimensional and even sexist picture of modern life. As Kylie Jarrett writes in *Feminism, Labour, and Digital Media: The Digital Housewife*, "the blurring of boundaries between work that can be appropriated by capital and that which is 'life' is often represented as a novel experience from relatively recent changes in the mode of accumulation."[27] Jarrett argues that this analysis does not account for the fact that in social reproductive labor (mostly carried out by women) work and "life" were always already blurred. Similarly, Sara Ahmed writes that the female modern experience was not that of an undivided individual, but that of a dividual caring for others. "An individual," she writes, "is one who … does not have to divide himself to a patriarchal, colonial and capitalist history. He can be an individual, not divided into parts, because others become his part: they become his arms, his feet, his hands, limbs that are intended to give support to his body."[28] Ahmed gives the example of a secretary who serves as her boss's "right hand," freeing him as an individual.

In the streaming era, this dividual experience is universalized. As labor, reproductive labor, and leisure time enter into a single market-driven flow colonized by data extractivism, life becomes precarious and disorganized for *all* subjects. Here it is important to add that the earlier dividualizing forces of modern patriarchy and colonialism continue to intersect with technocolonialism and its control society, for example through sexist and racist algorithms and data sets.

In this development, three interconnected things happen to home, understood as (1) a technology, (2) a physical place, and (3) a sense. Understood as a technology or medium, home becomes increasingly "smart." As a physical place, home becomes a gateway to consume and interact with transmedia streams. As a sense, home is increasingly integrated into an everyday stream in which public and private life blur even further.

As far as the so-called smart home is concerned, in 2010, Microsoft opened a model home of the future in its offices in Redmond, Washington. In this smart home, we have sensors that notify whether your plants need water or your fridge restocking. There are also interactive objects, like a tray that charges phones and watches while syncing information with the cloud. Above all, there are a lot of visual interfaces, in the hallway (popping up from behind the paint), on the wall in the bedroom (instead of paint), or as a projection on the kitchen counter.[29] Whereas in this 2010 home of the future voice command only played a marginal role, a decade later voice user interfaces dominate the smart home imaginary. Think of Google Home, Amazon Alexa, and Apple's Siri, through which users can control light, heat, locks, and also their day. These assistants' voices are female by default, and so is their performed role. As Heather Suzanne Woods argues, Big Tech's voice assistants "enact digital domesticity by performing a feminine person which mobilizes traditional, conservative values of homemaking, care-taking, and administrative 'pink collar' labor."[30] In doing so, these technologies slip into the family conversation as smoothly as possible, while they simultaneously nudge and extract data from that conversation.

Second, as a physical place, home has become a place where people consume and interact with streaming media. Here the sounds of voice assistants merge with the streams of Spotify, Netflix, Zoom, Tinder, WhatsApp, and ChatGPT. Some of these streams happen on screens attached to a wall or personal computer. Others are mostly mobile and travel *anywhere* the user takes their smartphone, which is everywhere. Insofar as streams are consumed at home, this media experience still resembles the radio and television era, with the difference that the stream now flows two ways, not only entering the home but also extracting data from people's interactions with it.

Third, insofar as media streams have become mobile, home, understood as a sense, is dislocated. As stated, home used to be place with a mailbox and a telephone, allowing the modern individual to converse with other private individuals and engage in the public sphere, all from their home. At the same time, telephone and postal services helped create the modern home as a place where an individual can be reached, thereby constituting them as a simultaneously autonomous and connected subject, though bourgeois men traditionally more than women. In our current streaming era, in which people are in touch with their communities *anywhere*, home as a sense of privacy in telecommunication with others gets virtualized.

In sum, under the influence of digital technology and data colonialism, home as a spacetime to foster an integrity of self is under threat. As Jeanette Winterson argues in her essay "From Sci-Fi to Wi-Fi to Mi-Wi," privacy is a problem nowadays, for the reason that privacy is friction, and friction impedes the flow of data. In our streaming age, we therefore see how modern privacy is traded for *personalization*. Winterson writes: "Simultaneous with our fully public-data-harvested-known selves is the personalization of that self. It will be 'your' smart implant. 'Your' smart/car/house/lifestyle."[31] The "simultaneous" is crucial here. The stream is hybrid, not only because it moves across binaries, but also because it moves in two directions at once. In one direction, we have the flow of personalized content moving from platforms to users (newsfeeds, timelines, profiles). In the other direction, we have personal lives turned into data, streaming from users to platforms. Speaking speculatively, in the unfolding streaming or Mi-Wi era everything becomes *hybrid*. This even holds true for bits. Whereas classical computing performs its calculations with information bits that are either 0 or 1, in the upcoming era of quantum computing, computers will work with quantum bits, or qubits. These qubits exist in separate and contradictory states *at the same time*. Winterson writes that quantum computers are expected to allow for virtual worlds that will appear completely disentangled from reality. "You won't be logging in. You're in. You're on. For life. From sci-fi to Wi-Fi to my-wi."[32]

How does this virtual future feel? How does it affect the subject? In order to answer these questions, all we have to do is stay at home and extrapolate life under lockdown.

Metaverse

The Deliverator sticks his black-clad arm out the shattered window. A white rectangle glows in the dim backyard light a business card … On the back is gibberish explaining how he may be reached: a telephone number. A half electronic communication nets. And an address in the METAVERSE.
FROM NEAL STEPHENSON'S NOVEL *SNOWCRASH* (1992)[33]

Looking back at the Covid-19 lockdown era, we see people teleconferencing on Zoom, Microsoft Teams, or, for the more privacy-minded, Jitsi and BigBlueButton. Videotelephony is not a recent invention. Its concept was first popularized in the 1870s in imaginations of a telephonoscope, which appeared in early science fiction novels such as Albert Robid's *Le Vingtième siècle: La vie électrique* (1891). As an actual technology, videotelephony was first demonstrated publicly in 1927 by AT&T, when then US commerce secretary Herbert Hoover addressed an audience in New York City via a one-way video call. Three years later, AT&T began experimentations with two-way television-telephony.

Fast-forwarding nine decades, videotelephony continues its development at the intersection of fact and science fiction. In October 2019, at the dawn of the Covid-19 conjuncture, Zoom founder and CEO Eric Yuan shared his vision of future communication during his company's annual "Zoomtopia" conference (Figure 9):

> In 2035 you can use Zoom to talk with anyone in the world, and that experience will be much richer than face-to-face. When you shake your colleague's hand with Zoom you are going to feel that hand. When others in the room give you a hug you can feel that intimacy, and when you are with virtual colleagues in a Zoom meeting drinking coffee or tea you are going to enjoy that aroma as well. When you speak English they can understand you well, even if they only speak French ... Imagine a world where there are no distance barriers, no language barriers, no cultural barriers to communicate. What a great world that will be.³⁴

For Yuan, virtual meetings mimic face-to-face interactions (coffee, hug, handshake) minus perceived barriers to communication (distance, language, cultural difference). Yuan's dream is a classical transhumanist narrative of a humanity *enhanced* by technology. According to transhumanism, human life is defined by an inherent lack in interhuman connection. It is a belief that humans, once entering into a synergistic

FIGURE 9 Zoom's annual Zoomtopia event (screen capture from video, © Zoom, 2022, all rights reserved).³⁵

HOME 45

relation with technology, will become *more* human, overcoming the barriers that now isolate humans in their heads and houses.

In the early 2020s, when video calling took the world, Yuan's words still had a futuristic ring. At Zoom, however, which was founded in 2011, they initially expected to reach the horizon of frictionless communication much sooner. In 2017, Zoom entered into a partnership with a company called Meta, a producer of augmented reality products including the Meta 2 Headset that was meant to replace two-dimensional desktop displays. On its blog, Zoom promised that by the end of the year its technologies would incorporate 3D screen sharing and augmented reality capabilities, pushing "the boundaries of modern communication."[36] Zoom further spoke of holograms projected onto the user's field of vision, a technology that it expected to be particularly interesting for schools and universities: "classrooms will be able to directly see their teacher interact with realistic anatomical models and gain first-hand experiences beyond anything they can learn from a textbook."[37] The future didn't arrive as fast, because in 2019 Meta went bankrupt. The name "Meta" stayed in the techno-cultural air, though, pointing into the direction in which Zoom had been thinking all along: the metaverse.

Like videotelephony, the metaverse started as a science fiction. The name first appeared in the 1992 dystopian novel *Snowcrash* by Neal Stephenson. This novel speaks of a single virtual world populated with digital avatars in which "magic is possible" and with "plenty of room to expand."[38] In 2021, the metaverse became a household name, when Mark Zuckerberg during his company's annual Connect event announced that Facebook was now Meta Platforms. Because of Covid-19 restrictions Zuckerberg's keynote was not the usual physical event but took the form of a feature-length video, titled *The Metaverse and How We'll Build It Together*. In this video, Zuckerberg speaks of Meta's new mission: to help build an "embodied internet" that succeeds the mobile internet. In 2023, however, after having invested $36 billion in the project, Meta downgraded its metaverse ambitions (yet without fully burying them) while hopping onto the AI train.

The future will tell if the metaverse will turn out to be a prophecy after all and become a reality in the era of quantum processing, but Meta's discourse around its fantasy already teaches us a lot about how the company sees human life, and about how the company sees its already existing "Meta universe" constituted by the Facebook-Instagram-WhatsApp-Threads platform ecosystem.

"We'll be able to feel present," Zuckerberg says in the Connect video, "like we're right there with people no matter how far apart we actually are."[39] While speaking these words, he is seen walking through a blandly designed Californian home (including vintage racing bike and surfboard). Next, the viewer joins Zuckerberg in a preview of the future. "Imagine you put on your glasses or headsets and you're instantly in your home space." The camera pulls us further into this virtual yet equally unimaginative home (including astronaut suit and telescope) (Figure 10).

Initially, this shot seems to be taken from the point of view of Zuckerberg's headset. The scene ends, however, with an objective shot of Zuckerberg, now standing *in* the image, which is thus revealed as a CGI impression of the metaverse, rather than the actual thing itself. The reason the video doesn't show the metaverse itself is that the metaverse doesn't "fully exist yet." The video, in combination with Facebook's name change, was an attempt, though, to turn "Metaverse" into a generic trademark owned by (or at least closely associated with) the company now called Meta.

In this same lockdown era, also other companies wielded the term "metaverse," in particular Microsoft. But whereas Meta spoke of *the*

FIGURE 10 Meta introducing the metaverse (screen capture from video, © Meta, 2021, all rights reserved).[40]

metaverse, Microsoft spoke of "metaverses" plural. Moreover, for Microsoft the term refers to a future "already here." In a tutorial video, Microsoft explains that "right now" you can go to a concert inside a video game or join a meeting remotely in a virtual room. "Those are metaverses"[41] (Figure 11). Microsoft's metaverse dream was equally short-lived. Early 2023, only a few months after the launch of its Industrial Metaverse division, Microsoft cut many of its VR/AR/MR projects in favor of investments in AI.

The metaverse went as fast as it came, but what has stayed after the lockdown era is video calling. For now, VR does not seem to be the future of video calling, but with its sense of telepresence and its dissociation between seated bodies and connected minds, video calling already is a metaverse-like experience. During the lockdown era, to many people the use of platforms like Zoom and Microsoft Teams felt very *normal* very fast. Part of the reason for this quick normalization is that Zoom and Microsoft Teams were generally used to create a "new normal" that mimicked the pre-lockdown normal as closely as possible. In the case of Zoom, this quick integration benefited from the company's rapid response to some initial hiccups, including Zoom bombing (where digital intruders break into digital meetings and classrooms, often with sexist or racist slurs) and attendee attention tracking (which allowed meeting hosts to receive alerts when participants clicked away from the

FIGURE 11 Microsoft speaking of metaverses (screen capture from video, © Microsoft, 2022, all rights reserved).[42]

Zoom window). The latter feature was removed in April 2020, because at Zoom they must have felt that in order to smoothly blend into people's life-streams, they had to bend with people's resistance against such control features.[43]

To stay with Zoom, the platform is part of a digital ecosystem in which user experience is above all a means to gain market dominance. "Does Zoom sell personal data?" the company asks itself in the Q&A section on its website. Initially, Zoom responded to this question in an almost philosophical reflection on concepts: "Depends what you mean by 'sell.'"[44] Soon, Zoom made this text less ambiguous, and the company now says it does *not* sell data to third parties.[45] The platform *does*, however, keep track of data, and it still shares some user data with Google.[46] Moreover, even though Zoom reassures people that it is not training AI on call content without user consent, its terms still allow it to use other data, including user's behavioral data.[47]

In response to lockdown measures, many institutions (including many *public* institutions like universities) purchased licenses for Zoom or Microsoft Teams, thus contributing to online control and the commodification of private data. Here the impulse to create a new normal that mimics the old one runs the risk of undermining the core values of that former situation, like a classroom independent of the market. It is worrisome how easily universities, also already before the Covid-19 pandemic, have locked themselves into profit-driven digital infrastructures, in which user privacy is at best an afterthought.

Someone who still manages to resist video calling is Dave Eggers, author of *The Every* (2021), a dystopian speculative fiction novel about what happens when Google, Meta, Apple, and Amazon fuse into one single company that brings "at last a sense of order" (as is one of the novel's many subtitles). In 2022, Eggers was interviewed for a Dutch television documentary, titled *Metalife* (*Metaleven*).[48] Eggers is heard but not seen. "I don't use Zoom really, and I sort of reject the new way that we all have to use Zoom at all times." Eggers is pessimistic about where technology is headed: "Things like the Metaverse will just further turn us into a very uninteresting type of organism."

On a personal note, like Eggers I tried to resist Zoom in the beginning of lockdown and instead used Jitsi for video calling. After a few weeks, though, I gave into social pressure and a curiosity about the world of online events. Yet whenever I now launch Zoom—which I still try to avoid—I am aware of consenting to privacy terms I don't actually consent to.

Oher than pressing concerns of privacy and user data commodification, there is another reason I'm not that fond of video calling, namely its dissociative effects. If the medium is the message, the message of video calling is dissociation. This dissociation occurs in relation to oneself: video calling further separates the communicating subject from the embodied subject, who is bound by the camera's gaze. This dissociation also happens in relation to others. Video calling strips communication from almost all body language and eye contact. I have never been a person who makes a lot of eye contact, and especially when in thought I tend to avert my gaze. Yet the near-overnight integration of video calling into everyday life has made me aware how much I value eye contact, the Holy Grail of Metalife that Zoom thus far has not been able to mimic (though Apple's VisionPro ski glasses give it a shot).

In the metaverse people live apart together. As the subject sits in front of their webcam and behind their screen, they are really alone, not just when the call ends or is frozen by spotty Wi-Fi, but also while things are streaming smoothly. Personally, I still prefer voice-only phone conversations, because to me the added illusion of presence offered by video actually hinders the *telepathy*, the sense of connection over distance. I realize that this critique of video calling may sound somewhat nostalgic. Video calling may dissociate people. But of course the medium also allows for new kinds of *associations*, understood both as new connections between people *and* as new wanderings of mind. There is a redemptive side to the state of dissociation inherent to the medium. This was especially felt in the beginning of the pandemic, when people were still new to televideo and had more patience with each other and their faltering connections. As I observed others, including myself, speak during the early-lockdown Zoom meeting of the Political Ecologies seminar mentioned in this chapter's introduction, it struck me that people seemed more free in their associations. This was probably because we were all in our homes and, *at the same time*, in the imagined telespace of a non-judgmental gathering, yet *minus* the direct gazes of the other participants. This social intimacy at a distance created the spacetime for association, blurring theory and everyday life, which is the beginning of ecology: the study of home.

Ideally, though, this blurring of domains happens in spaces where association is truly free, rather than in platformized environments that are part of an ecosystem that converts people's associations into data. As an individual, it is impossible to resist the platformization of life, much like it is nearly impossible to not own a smartphone now. We therefore need to keep pressing institutions, and especially *public* institutions, to work with and also develop non-proprietary digital infrastructures, instead of increasingly relying on platforms driven by a *transhumanist* ideology of dissociated life.

Presence

PRESENCE *is the killer application.*
A MICROSOFT ENGINEER ABOUT MICROSOFT TEAMS[49]

This section further zooms in on that transhumanist ideology ruling Big Tech discourse. In Microsoft's and Meta's M/metaverse imaginations, user minds travel places and connect with other minds, while their bodies remain here in the material world. That *here* is home, because home can be *anywhere*. Talking about their metaverse and metaverses, both Microsoft and Meta virtualize and dislocate home. In the case of Microsoft Mesh, "home" simply is a start screen similar to the home screen on one's personal computer (Figure 12), while Meta imagines home as "your personal space" from where you can teleport anywhere[50] (Figure 13).

In 2023, the metaverse bubble burst, leading both Meta and Microsoft to cut investments and instead shift funds to AI. This doesn't mean that the metaverse is now dead. Especially for Meta, "this idea [called] the Metaverse" remains central to the company's branding of connecting people across the physical and digital world.[51] Meanwhile, the transhumanist ideology driving the metaverse continues to underpin Big Tech's post-Covid-19 branding of personalized AI assistants (including Meta AI, Microsoft Copilot, Google's Gemini, and OpenAI's ChatGPT). What connects all these discourses is a transhumanist vision of life in which technology enhances human *presence*, in the words of a Microsoft engineer "the killer application."

In tech discourse, "presence" features as a buzzword that is rarely defined but often combined with adjectives like "deep" and "true." A noteworthy exception is a 2021 keynote video of Microsoft's mixed

HOME   51

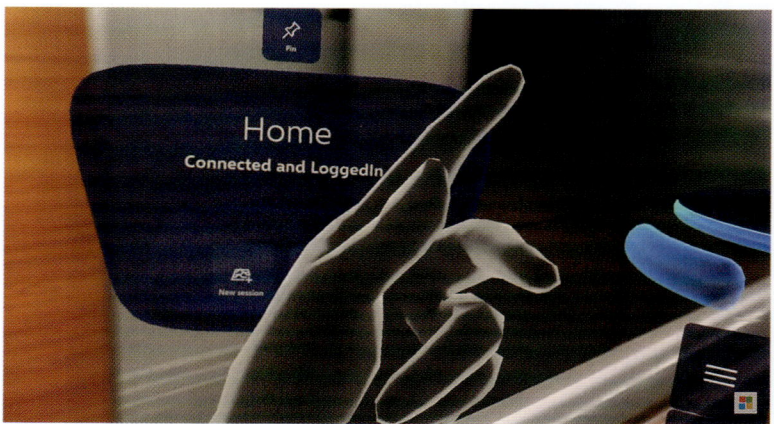

FIGURE 12 "Home" according to Microsoft Mesh (screen capture from video, © Microsoft Mechanics, 2022, all rights reserved).[52]

FIGURE 13 "Home" according to Meta (screen capture from video, © Meta, 2021, all rights reserved).[53]

reality platform Mesh, delivered by product co-creator Simon Skaria. "Let's start with the soul of Mesh: presence," Skaria says, upon which he explains the two fundamental parameters of presence: reach and realism. Reach refers to reaching movements: does the user experience their avatar's bodily agency as their own? Realism pertains to the suspension of disbelief VR seeks to create, suturing the user into a digital illusion (much like cinematic realism sutures the viewer into a story). Mesh excels in both domains, Skaria says. On the one hand, the platform delivers "representative avatars." On the other hand, it creates "photorealistic ... holoportation." Combining reach and realism, Mesh thus achieves what Skaria calls the "Holy Grail" of presence, potentially allowing us "us to transcend the traditional boundaries of space and time"[54] (Figure 14).

As far as this sense of presence is concerned, in the "What Is a Metaverse?" video discussed earlier, Microsoft seeks to preempt skeptical feedback like: but a digital avatar is not me. "Well, that is *technically* true," the voice-over admits, but only to outtrump the viewer by stating that Microsoft wants to help you "to represent your *whole* self."[55] Telepresence, it is suggested, allows the user to be *more* real, redeeming their fragmented existence. Similarly, in the Mesh "Here is anywhere" video discussed in this chapter's introduction, Microsoft expresses the belief that "great things happen when we commit to something bigger than ourselves." In

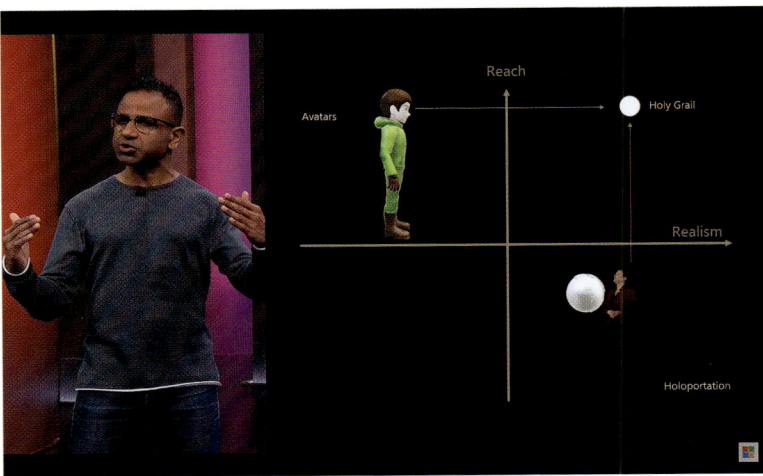

FIGURE 14 The "Holy Grail" of presence (screen capture from video, © Microsoft Ignite, 2022, all rights reserved).[56]

all these instances, there is a clear transhumanist undertone, the belief "in a world where technology *enhances*, not limits, humanity."[57]

Also, Meta has expressed a strong belief "in a future where we can … be more present," as Zuckerberg states in his 2022 keynote (still virtual). Compared to Microsoft's transcendent turn, Meta stays more down to earth. Meta's emphasis is on the metaverse as a social platform, because for Meta to be *present* is to *connect* with others. Zuckerberg expresses the belief that "the next computing platform has the potential to be more social and more human than anything that's come before," adding that this sociality-by-design characterizes *all* of Meta's products: Facebook, Instagram, WhatsApp. "It's always about people."[58]

What happens to Meta's claim that it is always about people in the age of personalized AI's? In his 2023 Connect keynote, Zuckerberg (now in-person) repeats the Meta mantra about human connection. The difference is that this sense of connection may now also be felt with *non*-humans. Imagine walking into a meeting, Zuckerberg says. Some people will be there physically, others will be there as holograms, but also sitting there around the table "are going to be a bunch of AI's who are embodied as holograms for helping you getting different stuff done."[59] In order to catalyze this metaverse, Meta launched a range of personified AI's for users to interact with "across the whole Meta universe of products," including "sous-chef" Max and your "personal editor AI" Lily.[60] There is also the standard Meta AI, to which you can talk "as a person."

Similarly, Microsoft and Google have launched personal AI-equipped assistants that are "always with you" (Google), that are always *present*. Google has Gemini (formerly Bard), which "combines personalized help with reasoning and generative capabilities."[61] Microsoft has Copilot, a personalized assistant integrated into Teams and Windows. Copilot, so we learn from an ad, co-creates, co-develops, and coauthors (among many other things it co-does), allowing people to "enhance [their] creativity and productivity" (Figure 15).[62] Finally, OpenAI speaks about its ChatGPT language model in a vocabulary very similar to that of Google, Meta, and Microsoft, namely as a tool that is "about *amplifying* what each person is able to do" (emphasis mine).[63] This language of enhanced and amplified life connects Big Tech's metaverse and AI discourses. An enhanced human is *more* than human. It is a superhuman who, thanks to their synergetic immersion into and interaction with platform technologies, increases their presence.

FIGURE 15 Microsoft introducing Copilot (screen capture from video, © Microsoft, 2023, all rights reserved).[64]

I call this belief in a human-machine synergy transhumanist. In his book *Transhumanism: Evolutionary Futurism and the Human Technologies of Utopia* Andrew Pilsch defines transhumanism as "an increasingly pervasive movement and an important actant, especially in technology policy and bioethics debates, whose members seek, broadly, to hack the human biocomputer to extend life, increase welfare, and *enhance* the human condition."[65] Similarly, the Swedish transhumanist philosopher Nick Bostrom calls transhumanism a way of thinking that challenges the premise that the human condition is essentially unalterable. He gives the examples of superintelligent machines, recalibration of pleasure centers through pharmaceuticals, space colonization, and also the uploading of human consciousness into virtual reality, about which he writes: "If we could scan the synaptic matrix of a human brain and simulate it on a computer then it would be possible for us to migrate from our biological embodiments to a purely digital substrate."[66]

Meta's imaginations of the metaverse were not yet that, but the direction of thinking is the same. Also Meta and Microsoft have expressed a belief in virtual reality as an immersive and frictionless experience where human consciousness and technology fuse, *enhancing* the human condition. Microsoft's presentation of holoportation as a Holy Grail that transcends traditional spacetime resonates, moreover, with a transhumanist belief in *singularity*, the future moment at which machine intelligence starts to amend itself and becomes a creative agent. Or as one believer puts it in the 2009 documentary *Transcendent Man*: singularity is "a tear in the fabric of spacetime, things just change suddenly, there's no more smooth transition."[67]

The title of this documentary refers to both a dream and the person dreaming that dream: Ray Kurzweil, author of *The Age of Spiritual Machines* (1999) and *The Singularity Is Near: When Humans Transcend Biology* (2005). In 2012, Kurzweil was hired by Google to "bring natural language understanding" to the company.[68] In his work, Kurzweil argues that technological change feeds on itself and follows the law of accelerating returns (Figure 16). He has predicted that by the middle of the twenty-first century, around 2045, technological development will have reached such levels that there will be no clear distinction anymore between humans and machines. This will allow humans to transcend their historical condition and become human-machine hybrids. Kurzweil writes that "if we are diligent in maintaining our mind file, making frequent backups, a form of immortality can be attained, at least for software-based humans."[69]

This all sounds very futuristic, but it is not. Kurzweil, and much of the transhumanist tradition, decouples the human mind from the body in a way that harks back to age-old liberal humanism. As Katherine Hayles writes in *How We Became Posthuman*, "identified with the rational mind,

FIGURE 16 *Transcendent Man* about Ray Kurzweil (screen capture from video, © Ptolemaic Productions, 2009, all rights reserved).[70]

the liberal subject *possessed* a body but was not usually represented as *being* a body."[71]

The quintessential thinker of the mind-without-body is René Descartes. In his *Meditations on First Philosophy* (1641) Descartes establishes that his thinking mind exists independently of his body: *I think therefore I am*. Next he proves, still seated in his armchair, "the existence of God and the immortality of the soul" (the book's subtitle). In other words, starting from the observation of his presence as a centered rational subject who coincides with himself, Descartes proves *presence* as such: a transcendent sense of connection that backs up the thinking ego's stable identity. This autonomous Cartesian subject continues to dominate Big Tech's imaginations. Big Tech gives us disembodied subjects who experience a deep sense of presence; and as is the case in the *Meditations*, this sense of presence is buttressed by the belief in something "bigger than ourselves," the glow of pure presence. As feminist and postcolonial theorists have argued, this liberal centered self is essentially predicated on a white, male, bourgeois subject. We need to juxtapose this humanist transhuman subject to an *embodied* posthuman subject that, as argued by Hayles, is not seduced by immortality fantasies, but remains embedded in a complex material world.[72]

This embodied subject fundamentally exists in relation. As Sara Ahmed writes in *Strange Encounters: Embodied Others in Postcoloniality*, identity "does not simply happen in the privatized realm of the subject's relation to itself" (the transhumanist position). Instead, it happens in everyday encounters with other embodied subjects, and in the social spaces constituted by those encounters.[73] An encounter, Ahmed argues, is not a meeting between two or more already constituted subjects. Rather, each encounter involves an element of surprise that changes the subject in unforeseeable ways. Encounters constitute "the space of the familial," while they also shift the boundaries of what is familiar.[74] Now, I am not saying that such spontaneous encounters constitutive of identity cannot happen in the metaverse. On the contrary, encounters in virtual reality are real, inasmuch as people have real connections on WhatsApp, Instagram, TikTok, and X. The problem with these platforms is that they are corporately controlled.

This problem is twofold. First, these platforms are not the open spaces co-created by users and their encounters as especially Meta claims. They are profit-driven environments whose algorithms shape the space of the familial, inviting some subjects while excluding others (for example Iranian or Palestinian activists censored or shadow-banned by Meta).[75] Second, the transhumanist ideology that drives these platforms contributes to the acceleration of capital and data flows, leading to the further precarization of user life. The virtual worlds users are immersed in, and the personified assistants to which they get hooked, are in fact a divisive and dissociating cloud-computing stream. As this stream continues to swallow everyday life, the dividual condition that already characterized the lives of many women and people of color in the modern era now becomes universalized. It is the condition of the human becoming increasingly posthuman, a "human-thing" (Mbembe).[76] How to resist this dividualization of human life, when the frictionless stream seemingly smooths out all resistance?

Resistance

The virtual world is poor in alterity and RESISTANCE *it displays.*
BYUNG-CHUL HAN, *THE BURNOUT SOCIETY* (2010)[77]

To resist is to go against the stream. In order to move toward the beginning of an answer of what resistance may look like in a streaming era, we need to know how that stream functions, and how it creates people as subjects. The conditions of the stream's agile and smooth functioning are the contradictions inherent to technocolonialism: from the mining of rare minerals to energy-guzzling data centers (soon to be powered by Big Tech's bespoke nuclear power plants); from platformized labor to smartphone production; from the segregating effects of corporate "social" media to the datafication of everything.

As far as datafication is concerned, philosopher Miriam Rasch argues that frictionless design has driven hardware and software development since the 1990s. It is the dogma of what she calls *dataism*. "Friction halts the movement that yields data, data that should make the world *predictable.*" At the same time, datafication also needs friction, "because without initial friction, without unknown behavior, there would be no data to retrieve."[78]

Similarly, in *The Burnout Society* (*Müdigkeitsgesellschaft*, 2010) Byung-Chul Han writes the following about flow and friction, or what he calls virtuality and resistance:

> The virtual world is poor in alterity and the resistance [friction] it displays. In virtual spaces, the ego can practically move independent of the "reality principle" which would provide a principle of alterity and resistance. In all the imaginary spaces of virtuality, the narcissistic ego encounters itself first and foremost. Increasingly virtualization and digitalization are making the real disappear, which makes itself known above all through its resistance.[79]

In other words, in platformized environments the subject is decreasingly likely to have constitutive encounters with otherness. Both Rasch and Han signal a contradiction internal to the virtualization of life: virtualization smooths out resistance or friction, which is life itself. Yet in doing so, virtualization also burns out the life on which it feeds. In order to keep its virtualization engines going, Big Tech continuously needs to expand into new territory, speeding up the stream. Rasch pictures herself sitting on the couch, observing her thoughts, "perhaps the greatest friction of all." She wonders: Will this inner turbulence largely unknown to the subject themselves ever be caught in data, rendered predictable?[80]

But isn't this already our streaming reality? Big tech's algorithms feed on the flow of life, on the unconscious, which is the spacetime of associations. I think of the unconscious as a process immanent to a society's practices and discourses, its physical and mental wanderings. Lefebvre writes that "if a hidden … structure of everyday life exists, it is an integral (though not an integrating) part of everyday life" as it unfolds. "The unconscious," he continues, "is only consciousness ignoring its own laws (or structures) and in this respect everyday life is indeed modernity's unconscious."[81] This understanding of everyday life as a structure unfolding at the surface hiding it is akin to what Raymond Williams has called a society's *structures of feeling*, which much like Lefebvre's understanding of quotidian life binds the fixed ("structure") and the soft ("feeling"). "Structures of feeling" is an attempt to grasp the ever-moving "social experience which is still *in process*, often indeed not yet recognized as social but taken to be private."[82] The task of the analyst then is to hold a spacetime for the unconscious to articulate itself, and to allow the self to realize that its most private wanderings are always already socialized.

What is desire? Lefebvre asks.[83] Other than it being elusive, as Lefebvre writes himself, I would define desire as an individual's orientation within a capitalist society that always already interpellates people as individuals. Desire is an individual's sense of agency, their sense of being in control of their life narrative (which to speak with Berlant is a cruelly optimistic endeavor). As capitalism transforms into a technofeudal system, Lefebvre's question becomes: What happens to desire when the individual is dividualized? And what happens to people's individual life trajectories when those trajectories are infiltrated by and integrated into a life stream that is at once automated and personalized?

The simultaneous personalization and automated nature of the stream is clearest on so-called "social" media, or network platforms. Their algorithms *curate* content on the individual level, but in the same movement, they produce personal data based on people's experience—data that are stored, sliced, auctioned, and used for tests, all in ways *not* to be taken personally. "Curation" derives from *cura*, which means to care, but corporate platforms really don't care about people as individuals, even though they sometimes give that sense.

Take personalized advertising: many people will recognize the feeling of synchronicity that, right after you've been talking on FaceTime or WhatsApp, your feed shows an ad related to the topic of conversation. It is a myth, though, that companies like Meta eavesdrop on your phone conversations (nor does it scan users' end-to-end encrypted WhatsApp messages, though Google for a long a time did "read" people's emails for advertising purposes). As former Facebook-Ads manager Antonio García Martínez explains in *Wired* magazine, not only would recording phone conversations require too much energy, it is also not necessary. "The harsh truth is that [Meta] doesn't need to perform technical miracles to target you via weak signals ... Not every spookily accurate ad you see is a pure figment of your cognitive biases. Remember, [Meta] can find you on whatever device you've ever checked [its products] on."[84] Remember also, that it is very well possible that what you talk, think, and dream about is shaped by the automatically personalized stream you're entangled in.

The stream may interpellate us as unique individuals with unique life stories, but the stream does not collect life stories; it collects correlatable datapoints that slash stories into code while real-time feeding those analytics back to the subject. If the medium is the message, this simultaneous personalization and depersonalization of the subject—who is scattered in the process—is the real message of Big Tech's desire machine. In this machine, everything (user-generated content, sponsored content, personalized advertising) blurs into an addictive transmedia stream that gets entangled with an everyday that itself is increasingly stream-like.

Take grocery shopping, once an activity for which one had to leave the house and enter the public sphere, now something that can also be done from one's phone. As a result, the subject is further dissociated from the material and social reality in which groceries are produced and distributed. During the pandemic, cities like Berlin and Amsterdam saw a surge of grocery delivery platforms. Colonizing urban centers with dark stores and advertising, these companies promised grocery delivery within minutes of ordering. In order to grasp the "very uninteresting type of organism" (Eggers) that human life is turning into, it is instructive to have a look at an advertisement by one of these delivery companies. The ad is a perfect example of Tristan Cross's observation in *The Guardian* that "there's something more than a little worrying about an advertising culture that doesn't even try to delude us into imagining a fantastic future, but instead reflects the grim realities of the present."[85]

The ad is for Gorillas, an originally German fast grocery deliverer founded in 2020. In 2022, Gorillas was bought by its competitor Getir, founded in Turkey (and which, in 2024, ceased its operations in the Netherlands). In the ad, the viewer is placed in the point of view of an almost empty fridge. Two youngsters are standing in front of the fridge. "I want cheese," says the one. "I just ate the cheese," says the other. The tagline below the image reads: "Looking for a bit of magic? Your groceries within minutes" (Figure 17). We thus have two hungry subjects who want their cheese *now*. They log into their Gorilla app and order "cheese." Before they can forget, cheese is delivered.

This is what dividualized life looks like: the reduction of human existence to mere drive in a platform economy that further dissociates consumption and production. On the production side, we have a chain of labor with at its end the delivery person, enslaved by their app. On the consumption side, we have a needy, equally machinically enslaved subject. Before capitalism became Metalife, the desire for a commodity still involved a certain time lapse between nascent appetite and the moment of consumption. This time lapse is what triggered commodity fetishism, understood as the process in which desire ascribes almost magic properties to a commodity's use value. Now "magic" is instantaneous and hence destroyed. Wired in, the subject is carried back to their origin. As Winterson writes, "my-wi" (or what I call the stream) leaves us as little children, "cared for, fed, safe, watched over, with plenty of fun stuff and free stuff, and with someone else deciding the big stuff."[86]

FIGURE 17 "Looking for a bit of Magic? Your groceries within minutes" (Gorillas advertisement, Amsterdam 2021, photo by the author).

All watched over by machines of loving grace (to paraphrase both the poem Richard Brautigan distributed in the streets of San Francisco during the summer of love and Adam Curtis's documentary of that title), the early twenty-first-century subject falls asleep and wakes up again, at once the most private moment and a social ritual (as beautifully captured a century earlier by the cinematic genre of the city symphony). Say this subject, first off, out of habit, grabs their smartphone, which "wakes up" too. Scrolling through their timeline, they are immediately integrated into a network that "transforms human beings into animate things made up of coded digital data" (Mbembe).[87]

In this typical scene from everyday life in the early 2020s, the flow from dreaming to waking life is still interrupted by the somewhat conscious handling of the device. But what if in the foreseeable future the bed and the rest of the house are smart too? What if computing becomes truly spatial and ubiquitous? What if the transition from night to daydream is traced by a technology that is ever more self-effacing, a fly-on-the-wall of which voice assistants and chatbots like Siri and ChatGPT are merely the messengers? As Yanis Varoufakis writes in *Technofeudalism*, these personalized assistants ensnare us in an "infinite loop" between "our soul and the cloud-based system hiding behind" its smooth and soothing interface. The user is conditioned to train tools "to train [them] to train us … ad infinitum."[88]

In the spirit of 1960s and 1970s cultural studies, I wish to hold to an understanding of everyday life as a domain of a shared experience that grows rampant within the cracks of dominant power. But as Lefebvre already signaled, the more technology becomes a determining factor, the narrower those cracks. Meanwhile, the space for resistance withers. Couldry and Mejias write that the "path away from data colonialism will start when we reclaim the capacity to connect that human beings have always possessed."[89] I would argue that in order to reclaim that capacity, and to resist the integration of everyday life into the data colonial stream, we need spaces exempt from datafication, while freeing time from its ongoing spatialization, online but certainly also offline. Because I share Mbembe's identification of the glimpse of digital dystopia offered by the lockdown era that "once working, shopping, keeping up with the news and keeping in touch … begins to take place solely across the interface of screens, it is time to acknowledge that on all sides we are surrounded by rings of fire."[90]

Digital technology may help people to bond and organize, but only if we resist naturalization of the digital and keep seeing the digital as a technology rather than as a second nature. At the end of the day, human experience is embodied and embedded. We therefore need spaces that serve as open and inclusive *living rooms* where the personal is still seen as political, where intellectual exchange and emotional openness blur in friction, and where people—in conversation and collective self-analysis—can build consciousness about how very personal feelings like anxiety and stress produced by the socioeconomic systems they inhabit. We need spaces, in other words, to reinvent the everyday as a site of resistance.

Homework

Feminism is HOMEWORK ... *It is a self-assignment.*
SARA AHMED, *LIVING A FEMINIST LIFE* (2017)[91]

How do we create and hold such common living rooms where people feel at home? I associate *home* with the relative freedom to associate, alone and with others. That is to say: if home is a *safe space* where one can indeed decompress, because if home is a place to be on one's guard, it becomes a space of stress and anxiety. This is the case in situations of domestic violence and oppression. This also happens, though in a different way, in the platform society where people's personal and collective integrity—their relation to self and others—is violated by data-harvesting and life-accelerating platforms.

Is home ever a safe space? Sara Ahmed writes that "safe spaces are [a] technique for dealing with the consequences of histories that are not over."[92] Safe spaces are explicitly feminist, queer, anti-racist, and anti-capitalist. To conceive of home as a safe(r) space then is to reconceive of home in a critical personal *ecology*, literally the study of home. As Ahmed writes in *Living a Feminist Life*, to do so requires homework, "work on as well as at our homes."[93] This is not homework in the sense of an assignment given by a teacher. It is homework as a self-assigned practice to work on the self. Such feminist homework means to denaturalize one's orientations, an attunement to the ways in which our habits, thought trains, and daily desires are shaped by hegemonic structures and discourses. In a world in which technocolonialism "works to dismantle the basic integrity of the self,"[94] this homework also includes an increased consciousness of Big Tech's datafication of everyday life.

We thus have to recognize the personal as political. But what does that mean again, that *the personal is political*? The phrase, also known as *the private is political*, originated in the late 1960s as a rallying cry of second-wave feminism. It began in the women's liberation group New York Radical Women. Influences on this and other women's liberation groups were the Black Civil Rights movement (and its "tell it like is") and the "Speak Pains to Recall Pains" meetings in the Chinese Revolution.[95]

"The personal is political" argues that politics is not something restricted to the public sphere. Instead, all and everything is political, also what happens behind people's front doors or in their heads. The slogan was popularized through an essay of that title by the American radical feminist Carol Hanisch. Her paper, originally from 1969, first appeared in 1970 in a collection called *Notes from the Second Year: Women's Liberation*, after which it was widely reprinted and distributed in the Women's Liberation Movement. Hanisch did not give the paper its title; this was done by the collection's editors.[96] In the paper, Hanisch writes about consciousness-raising groups for women, also called therapy or personal groups. She agrees with voices critical of the name "therapy," as it suggests that someone is sick and needs a cure, a personal solution. "Women are messed over," she writes, "not messed up." That is to say, women need a change in society's objective conditions, not adjust to them. It is from this perspective of systemic critique that Hanisch defends the personal groups against those who see them as navel-gazing and apolitical.

In 2006, in a new introduction to her piece, Hanisch reflects on the Women's Liberation Movement and the criticism it received. This criticism came out of some parts of the Civil Rights, Anti-Vietnam War, and Old and New Left movements. Many in the Women Liberation Movement had sprung from these radical left groups, but these groups were also male-dominated and "very nervous" about women's liberation. Hanisch writes that "they belittled us to no end for trying to bring our so-called 'personal problems' into the public arena—especially 'all those body issues' like sex, appearance, and abortion." Similarly, in the eyes of the male-dominated left, demands surrounding housework and childcare were individual issues that women had to solve with their husbands. Women just had to stand up for themselves, and "what personal initiative wouldn't solve … 'the revolution' would take care of if we would just shut up and do our part."[97] Radical feminism fought this separation between the private and the political sphere. In doing so it turned male domination into a common issue. As Michael Warner writes, "encountering male domination in the spaces usually called private, notably the home, women could only struggle against that domination by seeing it as a kind of politics."[98]

Before I return to how consciousness-raising and the realization that "the personal is political" continue to resonate in our present moment, I want to have a look at how this inspiration traveled outside the Women's Liberation Movement, especially in the student movement and the New Left. As Adam Curtis tells in his 2002 documentary *The Century of Self*, these movements attacked corporate America for brainwashing the public. Inspired by Herbert Marcuse's book *One-Dimensional Man* (1964), they saw consumerism as a means to keeping the masses docile, while allowing the government to fight an illegal war in Vietnam. This fight against social control was summed up in the slogan "There is a policeman inside all our heads; he must be destroyed." Curtis explains that in the late 1960s, in the face of state oppression, the New Left started to fall apart, upon which many turned to a new countercultural ideal. If it was impossible to overthrow the state, one should get inside one's own mind and remove the state and corporate control implanted there. A former student activist explains to Curtis: "It's about making a new you, that if enough people changed the way they were, that the society would change." Curtis asks: "So the personal became political?" "Yes," his interviewee confirms, "the personal became political. Without changing the personal, you didn't stand a chance of changing the political."[99]

This understanding of the personal as political had traveled away, though, from the radical feminist origins of this slogan. Whereas the Women's Liberation Movement tried to raise a collective consciousness of how experiences deemed personal were shaped by patriarchal power, the "personal" in the self-altering practices that emerged in turn-of-the-1970s counterculture were more directed at the cultivation of a repressed *individual* self.

One of the places people did so was the Esalen Institute on the Californian coast (Figure 18). Described as a "laboratory for new thought," Esalen rapidly became the center of the Human Potential movement. Here people were invited to release their deepest and darkest feelings and express their true selves. Esalen is only a short drive from Silicon Valley. Over the decades the place has become a popular destiny for executives from Google, Apple, and the like. At Esalen, tech entrepreneurs come do

FIGURE 18 Esalen Institute in Northern California as seen in *Century of Self* (screen capture from video, © RDF Television, 2002, all rights reserved).

their *homework*, reconnecting with a larger ecological and even cosmic perspective. The institute's current programming is not that different from in the 1970s, with workshops ranging from "Know Thy Selves: Past Lives" to "Wild Eros in a Fragmented World." The main resonance between this counter-cultural esoterism and Big Tech's disruptive zeal is that both are driven by a libertarian and arguably transhumanist ideology of personal self-expression, a deep sense of *presence* with others and oneself.

As far as consciousness-raising is concerned, Esalen now also offers a weekend-long workshop "Digital Detox: Unplug and Reimagine your life." Reporting from an embedded visit, *New Yorker* journalist Andrew Marantz writes how in the opening session the facilitator asks the group: "When we say no to digital technology, what are we saying yes to?" The group responds: "Openness," "vulnerability," "being *vulnerageous*." The next morning there is a "playshop" that invites the participants to open up about their complex relation with network platforms. One participant states that he experiences a sense of anxiety and helplessness when trying to quit Instagram. "I came here to be encouraged and to feel whole, but this is starting to be a bit of a bummer." The facilitator responds: "OK, let's change things up ... On the count of three, we're all gonna shout 'Fuck you!' to our inner critic." As Marantz sums up his visit to Esalen, "throughout the weekend, systemic analysis was discouraged in favor of self-care."[100]

What would be a consciousness-raising conversation about the effects of Big Tech that *doesn't* shun systemic analysis? First of all, such a conversation acknowledges that much feminist consciousness-raising and self-care discourses nowadays take place *on* network platforms. For many people, platforms like Tumblr and Instagram function as counter publics. As Frances Rogan and Shelley Budgeon argue in an empirical study of young women's experience of online feminist discourse, "the digital spaces which these young women engage with … hold the potential to act as consciousness-raising forums."[101] This especially holds true for conversations about gender identity and sexual diversity. One of the respondents states that "I would not have discovered my sexuality if not for the social media I use." Another says that "using websites like Tumblr, my own self-image has vastly improved as I've realized my looks do not define me."[102] To this one can add the #MeTOO movement. Initiated in 2006 by the American activist Tarana Burke on Myspace, MeToo would not have gone viral the way it did without platforms like Twitter and Instagram, which have clearly helped to accelerate social awareness about sexual assault.

So, in many respects Big Tech's disruption of the modern public sphere has also allowed for the challenging of, and new forms of consciousness-raising about, patriarchal structures. At the same time, online platforms are often also spaces of misogyny, racism, surveillance (including self-surveillance) and transphobia (including by a "trans exclusionary radical feminism," which fails to acknowledge that the personal that is political also includes gender identity and dysphoria). As Rachel Dubrofsky and Megan Wood argue in the edited collection *Feminist Surveillance Studies*: online environments continue to be structured by a male and white gaze, causing sexist and racist tropes to persist. The reason is that in the celebrity and influencer culture that has become dominant on platforms like Twitter/X and Instagram, people's self-fashioning in a consumer context is encouraged and even framed as a form of empowerment. Yet this empowerment is not without bias, including racial bias. While white women "attest to their postfeminist desire to be agents in their own objectification by working hard to shape bodies ready for display," women of color "are passive in their sexualization since their bodies are articulated as always already gaze-worthy, regardless of their actions."[103]

Network platforms are thus Janus-faced. On the one hand, they function as sites of empowerment where the personal is as political as it was fifty years ago. On the other hand, they are places where the personal and everyday life blur with consumer culture and advertising—where the personal is *commercial*.

What unites these two faces, and what unites all user experience on corporate network platforms, is the data colonialism that feeds on people's engagement, whether love or hate. This data colonialism facilitates the further acceleration of a burnout consumer culture in which people are isolated in their personalized streams, and in which people and natural ecosystems continue to be exploited. This technocolonial acceleration of life forms a potential common ground for consciousness-raising in a streaming age: the realization that the *personalized* is political, that the feelings of dissociation *you* experience and *I* experience while we both try to stay afloat in our everyday streams are ultimately shaped by the same material conditions producing the stream.

Such conversations can, of course, be held on corporate network platforms themselves, using these tools against the stream. Examples are #freethenipple (in protest of Instagram's censorship) and the TikTok #deinfluencing trend (that asks "How can we buying less and instead educating ourselves more?" though some deinfluencers also promote *alternative* products).[104] I'm reminded, though, of Audre Lorde's statement that the Master's tools (here network media) will never destroy the Master's house (technocolonialism). In order to resist Big Tech, it is necessary to create and hold truly common spaces for conversation, online spaces but certainly also physical and cooperatively organized spaces founded on feminist and anti-colonial principles. I also mean "space" in a more figurative sense, as in the use and reimagination of existing private and public spaces *anywhere* people come together. To hold space for conversation is an imaginative process, but it also requires that we set clear limits to Big Tech and also Big Tech use (for example by banning smartphones from schools, as happens in many European countries). To create common space is to slow down life. It is to acknowledge people's posthuman freedom to associate, alone and as creative collectives. This posthuman freedom to associate is not a pristine state undone from capitalism and technocolonialism; it is the becoming conscious of how our associations are shaped by hegemonic structures and discourses.

Association (*chez soi*)

ASSOCIATION *(ad-sociare): action of coming together for a common purpose (1530s); mental connection (1680s); quality or thing called to mind by something else (1810).*
AS BASED ON: ETYMONLINE.COM

I would like to end this chapter with an association from Covid-19 lockdown. For many, life *did* slow down in early 2020. Experiences of lockdown vary widely, but for those fortunate enough to not be hit with acute crisis (health, family, livelihood, work) the sudden disruption of the everyday stream created a brief window to observe one's rhythms and habits. Looking out of that window and into one's cruel optimisms, the personal quickly became philosophical.

We find some personal philosophical lockdown ruminations in the "Posts from the Pandemic" series published by the *Critical Inquiry* journal in the midst of this "momentous moment."[105] Slavoj Zizek shares he has been having anxious dreams about the virus, to the point he almost wishes to catch it.[106] Irina Dumitrescu and Caleb Smith write how this "hypermodern" crisis has returned them to premodern rhythms. "Cloistered away like so many monks" they have set up "daily schedules of activities."[107] And Catherine Malabou confesses how she tries to stay solitary in loneliness *precisely* to feel connected. "I think," she writes, "that an *epoché*, a suspension ... of sociality, is sometimes the only access to alterity, a way to feel close to all the isolated people on Earth."[108]

For a brief moment, I shared Malabou's hope, however privileged and humanist, that the era of social distancing would be accompanied by a collective emotional openness. As was to be expected, however, the openness proved fleeting and perished in its advertising afterlife (Figure 19). I live alone, and like Malabou I had a lot of time to dwell by myself during lockdown. I recognize what Dumitrescu and Smith call "acedia," which derives from the Greek κῆδος (*kedos*), the attachments that bind people. They write that acedia, in the tradition of the monks, began with a lack of care. "Acedia is a special kind of distraction that comes on when ties to other people, and then to God, are severed: a lonely wandering of the mind."[109] As the mind adapts to a new situation, its wanderings give rise to new forms of self-care. Like Dumitrescu and Smith, I strengthened

FIGURE 19 "From now on I am open" (Utrecht, June 2020, photo by the author).

everyday rhythms like cooking and my weekly visit to Utrecht's organic market. I cherished friendships, through telecommunication and during walks. And I strengthened the relation to the diffracted other called self.

For me, self-care often begins with a wide attention to the associative process, my wanderings of body and mind. What were the connections I just made from this thought to the next? How did I just wander from this activity to what I'm doing now? I take the notion of "wide attention" from Marion Milner. In *A Life of One's Own* (1934) Milner describes it as a mode "to attend to something yet want nothing from it."[110] Once one discovers to do so, "the magic thing happens." In his book *Attention Seeking*, Adam Philips adds to this by saying that "wide attention is in the best sense amenable to distraction."[111] Wide attention is akin to what Spinoza calls wonder: the dwelling in observations and lingering with percepts and affects, because concepts may interrupt the sensing process too soon.[112]

Sometimes concepts may also allow one to see *more* and more clearly. One of the concepts on my mind while in intelligent lockdown was "autism," as a few people close to me had suggested I might be "on the spectrum." I thus started reading on the topic. One behavioral trait associated with the autism spectrum is a rigid thinking pattern, which "is about being stuck in a certain thought or conviction, which makes it difficult to let go of this thought and focus on something else."[113] I do recognize this in myself, like in certain social situations in which I can find it hard to acknowledge that others can come from a completely different place, or when I read about the structuralism in Lefebvre and Foucault. I also recognize it in my response to Big Tech's colonization of everyday life, in how my mind can block while in platformized spaces as those of Microsoft Teams or Zoom, wishing society were a bit more rigid in its protection of public values. Then again, I often also observe myself as quite flexible in my associations, as when navigating groups of people, or when moving through the day blurring home and work, daydreams and dishes.

Traveling back to March 2020, I find myself on the train platform. "Is your journey really necessary?" public service billboards ask travelers during this period of relative lockdown in the Netherlands (Figure 20). Answering this question for myself with "yes," I take the train to Amsterdam, excited to be out of town again after ten days at home, but also on my guard for this virus "at once real and imaginary" (Foucault on the plague).[114] Back home in the evening, I continue my travels, from

FIGURE 20 "Is your journey really necessary? Have a good journey!" (Amsterdam, March 2020, photo by the author).

the kitchen to the bedroom to a note to self. I turn on online music radio FIP whose curated selection I prefer over Spotify's automated stream. A song plays that speaks directly to this situation: *"Je suis debout dans la cuisine / et je ne pense à rien / Enfin à rien, c'est difficile / même impossible"* (from: *"Je voudrais dormir"* by Jeanne Cherhal and Jacques Higelin). I trace my associations. I observe a parallel between how I tidy the house and my organization of mind. My attention is grabbed by an object which becomes a corridor into another room where I spot some dust all the while holding on to a sense of structure that, once it feels sufficiently cohesive and the house clean enough, I let go of again. For me this is where writing starts: in everyday association. I check my smartphone, a habit that at once interrupts and merges with the flow of things. My phone also went to Amsterdam today, but without data plan, and with my usual Wi-Fi hubs closed, I must have been mostly offline. I run water for the dishes, like dreaming a domestic activity best done without a smartphone (Figure 21).

Tracing these associations, I am reminded of Rasch's question of whether people's inner processes, their conscious and unconscious relations to self, will ever be caught in data, rendered predictable. In order to protect human integrity, we need to curb Big Tech and as societies say *no* to platforms to which, as individuals, it is nearly impossible to

FIGURE 21 Home is where the heart is (photo by the author).

say *no*. At the same time, we should not be too nostalgic about individual integrity and privacy. Instead, we have to reinvent notions of privacy and integrity for an era in which subjectivity exists across binaries, including the modern public-private binary. As John Cheney-Lippold writes in *We Are Data: Algorithms and the Making of Our Digital Selves*, we need a *dividual* privacy. This dividual privacy doesn't abandon the individual, but recognizes "the impossibility for a 'safe space,' a cordoned-off private sphere that becomes ever more impossible in our increasingly informationalized world."[115]

To rephrase this call: in order to invent a dividual or posthuman privacy, we have to *reinvent* social safety. We have to reinvent home as the spacetime for people to associate, alone and with others, without that this association is continuously datafied. This is stimulated by creating spaces in which life is not wired in, and by holding political-personal conversations across the public-private binary. Such social safety for posthuman times requires structures that truly empower people, that help people to collectively self-emancipate, and allow them to construct a *common* integrity: a shared sense of wholeness for scattered times. To do so is to create and hold the spacetime for people to become more conscious of how intersecting patriarchal, capitalist, and technocolonial power relations burn up their energy, isolate them, and shape their orientations and feelings. It is the spacetime that is needed to associate the personal with the political.

EXPERIMENT WITHOUT TECH #1: TRACING ASSOCIATIONS

This is the first of four "experiments without tech" of which there will be one per chapter. They are small exercises to spark thought about our personal and collective wanderings, and about how these wanderings are nudged and reoriented by profit-driven platforms. Some of the exercises can be done together, but this first experiment is best done alone, with the other "inside" oneself (though findings can of course be shared in a group setting). Admittedly, the exercise is a bit strange, because in order for it to work, you first have to let yourself forget about it after reading the rest of this text. Just let it go, and then at some point it will *jump to your mind* (to paraphrase Don Draper's reflection on the creative process in the television series *Mad Men*).[116] If at that moment you have a half an hour or so, do the following: observe the activity in which you were just involved. Also observe what was going on in your mind: images, thoughts, imagethoughts. If you want, write this all down. Next, while adopting a soft and wide attention, try to trace how you got *here*, physically and mentally. Don't force your memory, just try to tap into it, letting images and ideas come to you, like you would when remembering a dream. What were you doing before, and before that, and before? Similarly, what went on in your mind before, and before that, etc.? And how have your

> bodily and mental wanderings been connected? In sum, trace your associations, both how your bodymind goes from one thing to the next, and how you connect with others, offline, online, or both. Finally, having obtained a sense of your associative process, speculate for a moment how algorithms as those of Instagram or Google might have shaped the associations you just noticed (whether directly, because one of the activities you traced involved a platform, or indirectly, in the sense that Big Tech transforms the worlds in which we wander).

Notes

1. Microsoft, "Introducing Microsoft Mesh" (video) (2021), accessed January 15, 2023, https://www.youtube.com/watch?v=Jd2GK0qDtRg.
2. Meta, "The Metaverse and How We'll Build It Together—Connect 2021" (video), accessed October 24, 2024, https://www.youtube.com/watch?v=Uvufun6xer8.
3. Airbnb, "Airbnb Introduces the Bélo: The Story of a Symbol of Belonging" (video) (2015), accessed October 24, 2024, https://www.youtube.com/watch?v=nMITXMrrVQU.
4. See for example: Maarten Keulemans, "Corona Pandemie Trof Zwaksten op Alle Mogelijke Manieren," *Volkskrant* (March 7, 2024), accessed October 24, 2024, https://www.volkskrant.nl/nieuws-achtergrond/coronapandemie-trof-zwaksten-op-alle-mogelijke-manieren-het-verlies-van-toegang-tot-zorg-was-niet-evenredig-verdeeld~be81248f.
5. Microsoft, "Introducing Microsoft Mesh" (video) (2021).
6. See Microsoft, "Microsoft Mesh" (2023), accessed October 24, 2024, https://www.microsoft.com/en-us/mesh.
7. Made by Google, "Mornings: Google Home" (video) (2019), accessed December 18, 2019, https://www.youtube.com/watch?v=oy2y7rs2z64.
8. Airbnb, "Airbnb Introduces the Bélo: The Story of a Symbol of Belonging" (video) (2015), accessed October 24, 2024, https://www.youtube.com/watch?v=nMITXMrrVQU.
9. Microsoft, "Introducing Microsoft Mesh" (video).

10 Made by Google, "Mornings: Google Home" (video) (2019).

11 Shoshana Zuboff, *The Age of Surveillance Capitalism: The Fight for a Human Future at the Frontier of Power* (London: Profile Books, 2019), 4–5.

12 Gil Scott-Heron, "Home Is Where the Hatred Is" (song), *Pieces of a Man* (1971).

13 Sara Ahmed, *Queer Phenomenology: Orientations, Objects, Others* (Durham: Duke University Press, 2006), 12.

14 See: Dealtown, "Unleash the Power of AI on the Go with the Copilot Mobile App" [email sent by Minecraft to its subscribers on February 17, 2024], accessed October 24, 2024, https://deal.town/minecraft/unleash-the-power-of-ai-on-the-go-with-the-copilot-mobile-app-PKKDGHJLE.

15 See for example: Nabil Ahmed, "COVID-19 Has Let the Virus of Inequality Run Rampant," *World Economic Forum* (July 14, 2020), accessed October 24, 2024, https://www.weforum.org/agenda/2020/07/covid19-inequality-billionaires-oxfam.

16 Michel Foucault, *Discipline and Punish: The Birth of the Prison*, trans. Alan Sheridan (New York: Vintage Books, 1995), 198.

17 Foucault, *Discipline and Punish*, 224.

18 Achille Mbembe, "The Universal Right to Breathe," trans. Carolyn Shread, in "Posts from the Pandemic," *Critical Inquiry* blog (April 13, 2020), accessed October 24, 2024, https://critinq.wordpress.com/2020/04/13/the-universal-right-to-breathe.

19 Kyle Stevens, "When Movies Get Sick," in "Posts from the Pandemic," *Critical Inquiry* blog (March 25, 2020), accessed October 24, 2024, https://critinq.wordpress.com/2020/03/25/when-movies-get-sick.

20 Marshall McLuhan, *Understanding Media: The Extensions of Man* (New York: Signet Books, 1964), 117.

21 McLuhan, *Understanding Media*, 122.

22 Cory Doctorow, "WiFi Isn't Short for 'Wireless Fidelity,'" *Boingboing* (November 8, 2005), accessed October 24, 2024, https://boingboing.net/2005/11/08/wifi-isnt-short-for.html.

23 Maria Bakardjieva, *Internet Society: The Internet in Everyday Life* (London: Sage, 2005), 149.

24 Deleuze, *Negotiations*, 182.

25 Michel de Certeau, *The Practice of Everyday Life, Volume 2: Living & Cooking*, trans. Timothy J. Tomasik (Minneapolis: University of Minnesota Press, 1998), 146.

26 de Certeau, *Practice of Everyday Life, Vol. 2*, 146–7.

27 Jarrett, *Feminism, Labour, and Digital Media*, 54.

28 Ahmed, "Selfcare as Warfare."

29 Shane O'Neill, "Microsoft's Home of the Future: A Visual Tour," *Computerworld* (July 2, 2010), accessed May 13, 2022, https://www.computerworld.com/article/2826654/microsoft-s-home-of-the-future–a-visual-tour.html.

30 Heather Suzanne Woods, "Asking More of Siri and Alexa: Feminine Persona in Service of Surveillance Capitalism," *Critical Studies in Media and Communication* 35.4 (2018): 334–9.

31 Jeanette Winterson, *12 Bytes: How We Got Here, Where We Might Go Next* (London: Jonathan Cape, 2021), 72–3.

32 Winterson, *12 Bytes*, 74.

33 Neal Stephenson, *Snowcrash* (Bantam Books, 1993), 15.

34 IMS, "Zoomtopia 2019 Keynote Day 1 Opening Session HD" (video) (2020), accessed October 24, 2024, https://www.youtube.com/watch?v=AjIEa6iV8LU.

35 Zoom, "Zoomtopia 2022 Highlights" (video) (2022), accessed October 24, 2024, https://www.youtube.com/watch?v=ceW1drpQXK8.

36 Jihoon Park, "Zoom + Meta: The Future of AR Learning," *Zoom Blog* (November 20, 2017), accessed October 24, 2024, https://blog.zoom.us/zoom-meta-future-of-ar-learning.

37 Park, "Zoom + Meta."

38 Stephenson, *Snowcrash*, 212.

39 Meta, "The Metaverse and How We'll Build It Together—Connect 2021" (video), accessed October 24, 2024, https://www.youtube.com/watch?v=Uvufun6xer8.

40 Meta, "The Metaverse and How We'll Build It Together—Connect 2021" (video).

41 Microsoft, "What Is Microsoft's Metaverse?"

42 Microsoft, "What Is Microsoft's Metaverse?" (video) (2022), accessed October 24, 2024, https://www.youtube.com/watch?v=Qw6UCwCt4bE.

43 Eric S. Yuan, "A Message to Our Users," *Zoom Blog* (1 April 2020), accessed October 24, 2024, https://blog.zoom.us/a-message-to-our-users.

44 Richie Koch, "Using Zoom? Here Are the Privacy Issues You Need to Be Aware of," *Proton Blog* (March 20, 2020, updated 10 January 2023), accessed October 24, 2024, https://proton.me/blog/zoom-privacy-issues.

45 Zoom, "Zoom Privacy Statement" (24 February 2023), accessed October 24, 2024, https://explore.zoom.us/en/privacy.

46 See for example: Koch, "Using Zoom?"

47 Melissa Goldin, "Zoom Says It Isn't Training AI on Calls without Consent. But Other Data Is Fair Game," *AP* (August 9, 2023), accessed October 24, 2024, https://apnews.com/article/fact-check-zoom-ai-privacy-terms-of-service-06ff47e47439c2173390a4ca1389f652.

48 VPRO Tegenlicht, *Metaleven* (dir. Britta Hosman) (video) (February 7, 2022), accessed October 24, 2024, https://www.vpro.nl/programmas/tegenlicht/kijk/afleveringen/2022-2023/metaleven.html.

49 CNET Highlights, "Watch Microsoft Explain Metaverse Vision Inside Teams" (video) (2022), accessed October 24, 2024, https://www.youtube.com/watch?v=CXke-_xXOYA.

50 Meta, "The Metaverse and How We'll Build It Together" (video).

51 Meta, "Meta Connect 2023 | Full Keynote" (video) (October 2023), accessed October 24, 2024, https://www.youtube.com/watch?v=-dJu9VyIw64.

52 Microsoft Mechanics, "Microsoft Mesh Hands-on Demo: New Platform to Deliver Collaborative Mixed Reality Experiences" (video) (2022), accessed October 24, 2024, https://www.youtube.com/watch?v=lhKn9mjy_QM.

53 Meta, "The Metaverse and How We'll Build It Together" (video).

54 Microsoft Mechanics, "Microsoft Mesh Hands-on Demo" (video).

55 Microsoft, "What Is Microsoft's Metaverse?" (video) (2022).

56 Microsoft Ignite, "An Introduction to Microsoft Mesh: FS200" (video) (2022), accessed October 24, 2024, https://www.youtube.com/watch?v=HZkL-A2i_LM.

57 Microsoft, "Introducing Microsoft Mesh" (video).

58 Meta, "Meta Connect 2022" (video).

59 Meta, "eta Connect 2023" (video).

60 Meta, "Meta Connect 2023" (video).

61 Made by Google, "#MadeByGoogle '23: Assistant with Bard" (video) (October 2023), accessed October 24, 2024, https://www.youtube.com/watch?v=nE4A2zZjBZA.

62 Microsoft, "Discover the Power of AI with Copilot in Windows" (2024), accessed October 24, 2024, https://www.microsoft.com/en-us/windows/copilot-ai-features.

63 OpenAI, "Introducing GPT-4" (video) (March 2023), accessed October 4, 2023, https://www.youtube.com/watch?v=–khbXchTeE.

64 Microsoft, "Microsoft Copilot: Your Everyday AI Companion" (video) (2023), accessed October 24, 2024, https://www.youtube.com/watch?v=l4B1UflAty8.

65 Andrew Pilsch, *Transhumanism: Evolutionary Futurism and the Human Technologies of Utopia* (Minneapolis: University of Press, 2017), 11, emphasis mine.

66 Nick Bostrom, "What Is Transhumanism?" (2001), accessed October 24, 2024, https://nickbostrom.com/old/transhumanism.

67 *Transcendent Man*, 2009, dir. Robert Barry (Ptolemy, Ptolemaic Productions).

68 John Letzing, "Google Hires Famed Futurist Ray Kurzweil," *The Wall Street Journal* (December 14, 2012), accessed October 24, 2024, https://www.wsj.com/articles/BL-DGB-25711.

69 Ray Kurzweil, *The Singularity Is Near: When Humans Transcend Biology* (New York: Viking, 2005), 243.

70 *Transcendent Man* (2009).

71 Hayles, *How We Became Posthuman*, 4.

72 Hayles, *How We Became Posthuman*, 5.

73 Sara Ahmed, *Strange Encounters: Embodied Others in Postcoloniality* (London: Routledge, 2000), 7.

74 Ahmed, *Strange Encounters*, 8.

75 Hind Khoudary, "Social Media Giant Meta Carries Out 'Digital Massacre' of Palestinian Posts," *Middle East Eye* (August 11, 2022), accessed October 24, 2024, https://www.middleeasteye.net/news/meta-palestine-posts-social-media-digital-massacre; Human Rights Watch, "Israel/Palestine: Facebook Censors Discussion of Rights Issues" (October 8, 2021), accessed October 24, 2024, https://www.hrw.org/news/2021/10/08/israel/palestine-facebook-censors-discussion-rights-issues; Access Now, "Meta's Actions 'Adversely Impacted' Palestinians' Rights: Access Now Welcomes BSR Findings" (September 27, 2022, updated January 26, 2023), accessed October 24, 2024, https://www.accessnow.org/press-release/bsr-findings-meta-palestinian-rights; Ginger Gentile, "Is Instagram Censoring Influencers Who Support Iranian Protesters?," *Forbes* (November 10, 2022), accessed October 24, 2024, https://www.forbes.com/sites/gingergentile/2022/11/10/is-instagram-censoring-influencers-who-support-iranian-protesters/; Mahsa Alimardani, "How Instagram Is Failing Protesters in Iran," *Slate* (June 2, 2022), accessed October 24, 2024, https://slate.com/technology/2022/06/instagram-meta-iran-protests-exceptions.html; RFE/RL's Radio Farda, "Instagram Removes Iranian Protest Videos, TV Station Says," *Radio Free Europe Radio Liberty* (September 21, 2022), accessed October 24, 2024, https://www.rferl.org/a/iran-instagram-removes-protest-videos-amini/32044798.html.

76 Mbembe, *Critique of Black Reason*, 4.

77 Byung-Chul Han, *The Burnout Society*, trans. Erik Butler (Stanford: Stanford Briefs, 2015), 42-3.

78 Miriam Rasch, *Frictie: Ethiek in Tijden van Dataïsme* (Amsterdam: De Bezige Bij, 2020), 16-17, translation mine, emphasis by author.

79 Han, *Burnout Society*, 42-3.

80 Rasch, *Frictie*, 17.

81 Lefebvre, *Everyday Life in the Modern World*, 101.

82 Raymond Williams, *Marxism and Literature* (Oxford: Oxford University Press, 1977), 132.

83 Lefebvre, *Everyday Life in the Modern World*, 101.

84 Antonio García Martínez, "Facebook's Not Listening through Your Phone. It Doesn't Have To," *Wired* (November 10, 2017), accessed October 24, 2024, https://www.wired.com/story/facebooks-listening-smartphone-microphone.

85 Tristan Cross, "You Know Modern Life Is Hard When Even Adverts Don't Try to Persuade You Otherwise," *The Guardian* (January 17, 2022), accessed October 24, 2024, https://www.theguardian.com/commentisfree/2022/jan/17/modern-life-hard-adverts-work-uber-eats.

86 Winterson, *12 Bytes*, 81.

87 Mbembe, *Critique of Black Reason*, 5.

88 Varoufakis, *Technofeudalism*, 64-5.

89 Couldry and Mejias, *Costs of Connection*, 215.

90 Mbembe, "Universal Right to Breathe."

91 Sara Ahmed, *Living a Feminist Life* (Durham: Duke University Press, 2017), 7.

92 Sara Ahmed, "Against Students," *The New Inquiry* (June 29, 2015), accessed October 24, 2024, https://thenewinquiry.com/against-students.

93 Sara Ahmed, *Living a Feminist Life*, 7.

94 Couldry and Mejias, *Costs of Connection*, 184.

95 Thanks to Carol Hanisch for this background information.

96 Carol Hanisch, "Introduction" to "The Personal Is Political: The Women's Liberation Movement Classic with a New Explanatory Introduction" (January 2006), accessed October 24, 2024, http://www.carolhanisch.org/CHwritings/PIP.html.

97 Hanisch, "Introduction."

98 Warner, "Public/Private."

99   *The Century of Self. Part 3: There Is a Policeman inside All Our Heads; He Must Be Destroyed* (dir. Adam Curtis) (BBC, 2002).

100 Andrew Marantz, "Silicon Valley's Crisis of Conscience: Where Big Tech Goes to Ask Deep Questions," *The New Yorker* (August 19, 2019), accessed October 24, 2024, https://www.newyorker.com/magazine/2019/08/26/silicon-valleys-crisis-of-conscience.

101 Frances Rogan and Shelley Budgeon, "The Personal Is Political: Assessing Feminist Fundamentals in the Digital Age," *Social Sciences* 7.132 (2018): 11–19, p. 11.

102 Rogan and Budgeon, "Personal Is Political," 12.

103 Rachel E. Dubrofsky and Megan M. Wood, "Gender, Race, and Authenticity: Celebrity Women Tweeting for the Gaze," in Rachel E. Dubrofsky and Shoshana Amielle Magnet, eds., *Feminist Surveillance Studies* (Durham: Duke University Press, 2015), 93–106, p. 99.

104 Venetia la Manna cited in Boutayna Chokrane, "What Is Deinfluencing? Unpacking TikTok's Unlikeliest Shopping Trend," *Vogue* (December 21, 2023), accessed October 24, 2024, https://www.vogue.com/article/what-is-deinfluencing.

105 W. J. T. Mitchell, "Groundhog Day and the Epoché," in "Posts from the Pandemic," *Critical Inquiry* blog (May 11, 2020), accessed October 24, 2024, https://critinq.wordpress.com/2020/05/11/groundhog-day-and-the-epoche.

106 Slavoj Zizek, "Is Barbarism with a Human Face Our Fate?" (March 18, 2020), in "Posts from the Pandemic," *Critical Inquiry* blog, accessed October 24, 2024, https://critinq.wordpress.com/2020/03/18/is-barbarism-with-a-human-face-our-fate.

107 Irina Dumitrescu and Caleb Smith, "The Demon of Distraction" in "Posts from the Pandemic," *Critical Inquiry* blog (April 22, 2020), accessed October 24, 2024, https://critinq.wordpress.com/2020/04/22/the-demon-of-distraction.

108 Catherine Malabou, "To Quarantine from Quarantine: Rousseau, Robinson Crusoe, and 'I,'" in "Posts from the Pandemic," *Critical Inquiry* blog (March 23, 2020), accessed October 24, 2024, https://critinq.wordpress.com/2020/03/23/to-quarantine-from-quarantine-rousseau-robinson-crusoe-and-i.

109 Dumitrescu and Smith, "The Demon of Distraction."

110 Marion Milner, *A Life of One's Own* (London: Routledge, 2011), 79.

111 Adam Phillips, *Attention Seeking* (London: Penguin Books, 2019), 103.

112 Benedict de Spinoza, *The Chief Works of Spinoza: A Theologico-Political Treatise and A Political Treatise*, trans. R. H. M. Elwes (New York: Dover Publications, 1951), 84.

113 Annelies Spek, *Autismespectrum Stoornissen bij Volwassenen: Een Praktische Gids voor Volwassenen met ASS, Naastbetrokkenen en Hulpverleners* (Amsterdam: Hogrefe, 2013), 135, my translation.

114 Foucault, *Discipline and Punish*, 198.

115 John Cheney-Lippold, *We Are Data: Algorithms and the Making of Our Digital Selves* (New York: New York University Press, 2017), 237.

116 See my essay "Mad Men and Mindfulness," *Discourse 40.3* (2018), 273–307.

2 CITY

Sidewalk Colonialism
(*Land Acknowledgment*)

Cities have the capability of providing something for EVERYBODY, *only because, and only when, they are created by everybody.*
JANE JACOBS, *THE DEATH AND LIFE OF GREAT AMERICAN CITIES* (1961)[1]

Everybody

Leaving home, this second chapter moves into the streets of the sensing city where the walls have ears, or less proverbially, where the sidewalks have sensors. A sidewalk is a footpath along the main road. Usually it is a bit elevated, separating pedestrians from faster traffic. The first sidewalks appeared around 2,000 BCE in Anatolia, in what is now Turkey. Also, ancient Greek and Roman cities incorporated them into their city designs. The fall of the Roman Empire led to a mostly sidewalk-less period in Europe that only started to end in 1666, after the Great Fire of London. The real sidewalk revival happened in nineteenth century-Haussmannian Paris, where sidewalks were believed to contribute to a more orderly and hygienic city. Arguably, sidewalks make cities more accessible and public, inciting encounters between strangers, as per Jane Jacobs's vision of the sidewalk ballet in cities designed for everybody by everybody.[2] However, as Anastasia Loukaitou-Sideris and Renia Ehrenfeucht write in their book on the topic, sidewalks may also "become sites of conflict."[3]

This chapter focuses on what must be the greatest sidewalk conflict in history: Sidewalk Toronto. This urban development initiative at Lake Ontario in downtown Toronto would have involved a lot of pedestrian space, but this space would not have exactly been *public*. In the eyes of its fiercest critics, Sidewalk Toronto sought to colonize all things public, not just sidewalks but also town hall meetings and citizenship. Sidewalk Toronto failed, thanks to a citizen resistance movement, making this project an excellent lens through which to articulate a critique of the platformization of urban space, as is the chapter's broader concern.

Sidewalk Toronto was first announced in 2017. It was a collaboration between Waterfront Toronto and Sidewalk Labs. Waterfront Toronto is a public-private entity set up by the city of Toronto, the province of Ontario, and the Canadian national government to redevelop the city's urban lakeside. Sidewalk Labs is part of Alphabet Inc., the holding company that also owns Google. Between 2015 and 2021, Sidewalk Labs was its own subsidiary within Alphabet. After its failure it was folded into Google.

Sidewalk Toronto was supposed to become the first urban neighborhood "built from the internet up."[4] The idea for Sidewalk Toronto was born during a conversation that Sidewalk Labs CEO Daniel Doctoroff had with Larry Page (then CEO of Google). As Doctoroff states in a 2016 vision paper, Sidewalk Toronto began as a "thought experiment" of "a place where ubiquitous connectivity is truly built into the foundation of the city."[5] Artist impressions show what life could have looked like in Toronto's near future: timber high-rises, lots of green, autonomous vehicles, and above all a rich pedestrian life in "intimate public spaces" and "people-first streets."[6] This lively street scene would have been supported by invisible yet ubiquitous sensors feeding real-time data into an extensive digital infrastructure: from smart traffic lights to modular pavements, from underground robotic parcel delivery to pay-as-you-throw garbage chutes.

Sidewalk Toronto was abandoned in 2020, but its design still testifies to the dream of a fully platformized city, in which public space and corporate interests blur into a vaguely defined "urban" realm. This chapter asks: What vision of human life informed Sidewalk Toronto's people-first-and-from-the-internet-up design? And how does this vision compare to the material reality of disorganized and controlled life under technocolonialism?

Sidewalk Toronto's "testbed" would have been the 5 hectare area Quayside. The entire plan for Sidewalk Toronto concerned an area of seventy-seven hectares of undeveloped land designated as the "Innovative Design and Economic Acceleration" (IDEA) district within the eastern waterfront area, just southeast of downtown Toronto. In 2019, however, under public pressure, the project was heavily scaled back to just Quayside. In May 2020, Sidewalk Labs pulled the plug on its Toronto ambitions altogether, officially because of the Covid-19 pandemic, but likely also because of the severe criticism that Sidewalk Toronto garnered over the years.[7]

This resistance against Sidewalk Toronto had two main causes. The first was that, especially for the first eighteen months, the deal between Sidewalk Labs and Waterfront Toronto was surrounded by secrecy. Second, many Torontonians simply didn't trust Sidewalk Labs. Why hand tasks carried out by democratically controlled government institutions to a Google affiliate? As Ellen P. Goodman and Julia Powles write in their essay "Urbanism under Google: Lessons from Sidewalk Toronto": "A major source of public concern was that a steward of public lands was creating public policy with, and via, a private vendor."[8] This criticism was not only voiced by activist groups (#BlockSidewalk), it also came from within the tech world itself. For example, venture capitalist Roger McNamee wrote in a letter to the Toronto City Council: "No matter what Google is offering, the value to Toronto cannot possibly approach the value your city is giving up. [Quayside] is a dystopian vision that has no place in a democratic society."[9]

As I will discuss later this chapter, key to Sidewalk's vision is that cities are and have always been platforms. In this vision, people are "users" of urban space. We need to be very critical of this city-as-platform discourse. Tech companies' framing of the spaces they venture into is integral to their profit-driven strategies. As often happens in tech discourse, Sidewalk Toronto blurred the difference between public and corporate interest. Goodman and Powles write that Sidewalk "incorporates public value concepts such as social cohesion, leaning on Jane Jacobs's vision of 'placemaking' along with new urbanism and sustainability."[10] However, Sidewalk's self-labeled "public" ambitions clearly were at odds with the digital infrastructure the company *actually* proposed. In reality, its design would have been optimized not for people but "for efficiency and the efficient production of material value."[11]

Goodman and Powles cite Jacobs and her ideal of a city for everybody created by everybody. Jacobs was an American-Canadian author and urban activist who throughout her life fought for livable and walkable cities. In 1961, Jacobs published *The Death and Life of American Cities*, a critique of urban top-down city planning and an ode to neighborhood life and its *sidewalk ballet*, "always replete with new improvisations."[12] In this same era, Jacobs successfully helped organize resistance against "urban renewal" of her own Greenwich Village neighborhood in Manhattan and the construction of the Lower Manhattan Expressway. In 1968, Jacobs moved to Toronto, where she joined the protests against the Spadina Expressway, which would have split downtown Toronto into two halves. Thanks to the resistance of the Toronto community, the highway shared Quayside's fate: it didn't happen (Figure 22).

Following Jacobs's death in 2006, people in Toronto and in New York, and soon all over the world, have organized Jane's Walks: walking conversations inspired by Jacobs's mission to encourage "people to share stories about their neighborhoods ... and use walking as a way to connect with their neighbors."[13] Taking inspiration from Jacobs, this chapter invites the reader on a "walk" through Quayside, occasionally branching off into other Toronto neighborhoods.

The chapter has again seven sections. Following this introduction, sections two through four analyze the vision of human life that ran through Sidewalk's plans. In parallel with my tech discourse analysis in Chapter 1, I argue that this vision follows a techno-optimist and specifically *transhumanist* philosophy: the belief that technology *enhances* human life, allowing it to overcome barriers of connection. Section five juxtaposes

FIGURE 22 "Stop Spadina" (Toronto, 2015, photo by the author, made during an "official" Jane's Walk in the Annex neighborhood where Jane Jacobs lived between 1968 and 2006).

this transhumanist vision to the posthuman reality of increasingly platformized cities that *dividualize* people into scattered human-things. Resisting this reality, section six calls for open and also open-source city designs. Inspired by Jacobs and *against* Sidewalk's from-the-internet-up ideology I call for inclusive spaces that spark communal conversations. I call for cities in which people can wander and associate without second thoughts about whether their experience is datafied. Finally, section seven, titled TORONTO, comments on the ironic land acknowledgment in much of Sidewalk's official communications: "The land on which we're standing." Against Sidewalk's technocolonialism, I *acknowledge* the small fish in the Humber River that once outsmarted the nets, carrying the name "Taranteau" downstream to the shores of Lake Ontario.

Empathy

To gain EMPATHY *towards people, we as design thinkers often observe them in their natural environment passively or engage with them in interviews.*
          **STAGE ONE IN THE *DESIGN THINKING* PROCESS:
          TO EMPATHIZE**[14]

The question that stands central in this and the following two sections is as follows: What is the vision of human life that informed the Quayside design, in which "from the internet up" and "people first" miraculously mean the same thing? I will answer this question by analyzing a number of materials through which Sidewalk Labs, in collaboration with Waterfront Toronto, presented Sidewalk Toronto and its Quayside pilot. These materials include blog posts, project proposals, artist impressions, and video recordings of the so-called "townhall meetings" that Sidewalk Labs organized.

    Let's start with the promotional video "Introducing Sidewalk Toronto" through which Sidewalk Labs in October 2017 presented itself to Toronto and the rest of the world. The video moves from a humanist, distinctly "Torontonian" touch to a transhumanist vision of digital technology as a means of "enhancing human interaction." Transhumanism is a social and philosophical movement that believes in technology as second nature. According to this belief, technology allows humans to *redesign* life so as overcome biological and social limitations. As far as design is concerned: intentionally or not, the "Introducing Sidewalk Toronto" video follows the first few steps of the *Design Thinking* process. Design thinking is a collaborative "human-centered" and "solution-based" problem-solving approach with its origins in 1960s product design that has since become popular in other creative industries, including the tech sector.[15] Design Thinking has five stages. Stage 1: to *empathize* with your users.

Empathizing with users is indeed how the Sidewalk Toronto video begins. We see a series of mini portraits of a diverse group of Torontonians, all captured for a few seconds in front of their porches or during their commutes. All appear in frontal shots, directly addressing the camera, in a faux-spontaneous street interview format. Together, the fragments add up to a quick yet effective narrative of Toronto as one of the most diverse cities of the world, but also of a Toronto as a city that faces twenty-first-century "challenges."

Following the opening shot of a woman and her son looking silently into the camera, this story of Toronto goes as follows:

"I lived in Toronto for almost thirty years" [says a blue-bearded man who is seated in an electric wheelchair while he caresses a small dog; Figure 23] / "I think a lot of people move here because of the cultures, you know, there are so many different cultures in the city" [says a man wearing a baseball cap, his arms crossed, Toronto's Chinatown in the background] / "I always ask someone where they come from and eventually I ask them, how do you say 'hello' in your language? And I think I've learned maybe thirty 'hello,' 'goodbye,' 'thank you'" [a middle-aged man, his hands in his jeans pockets, while his partner next to him nods approvingly] / "You can meet a new person every week, who has come from someplace else and who is brand new in the city" [yet another man—because so far we've heard only men—in front of what could be his porch, while his friend stands by, nodding, upon which the story shifts from Toronto's diversity to its challenges; Figure 24] / "I see a large increase in renting prices, and I think that's partly because of the growth and the expansion of the city" [a young person, bike in hand and Lake Ontario in their back, upon which the video cuts to a few traveling shots of condo high-rises, an iconic red streetcar signifying "Toronto" (Figure 25), and on to the last portrait, with a man and his family who are clearly posing:] "I think we're at a real inflection point in terms of which direction the city goes in."

In comes Sidewalk Labs CEO Dan Doctoroff, first in voice-over while the image swirls around Toronto's CN Tower (the city's major landmark), next in corporate framing format with Doctoroff now against Toronto's skyline while his name appears in the bottom-left corner (Figure 26). The video thus swiftly moves to stage 2 of the Design Thinking process: to *define* the problem. "Toronto," Doctoroff says "is in an elite class of cities in North America … that are so popular … that it also poses incredible challenges of growth."

Without any further analysis of this growth problem, the video goes on to Design Thinking stage 3: to *ideate*. This sparking of ideas is done by a parade of representatives from the city of Toronto, Waterfront Toronto, Sidewalk Labs, and also the Alphabet mothership. The recurring message is that in Sidewalk Toronto technology meets Torontonian authenticity. Or as the city of Toronto's former director of Urban Design & Architecture phrases it: Sidewalk Toronto is designed on the belief in technology as a way of "enhancing human interactions, enhancing community, bringing us closer together, supporting the activities of our daily lives in ways that take away a lot of the barriers that separate us." Similarly, Waterfront Toronto CEO Will Fleissig expresses the belief that the project will allow "people to offer their ideas, their concerns, what they love about Toronto, so that this new community can be authentic, can be Torontonian, can be real." Finally, former Google CEO Eric Schmidt states that "our technology, applied with the energy and passion of the citizens of Toronto, will make this thing incredibly successful."

Toward the end, the video mixes in some more street portraits of Torontonians just being human and diverse—including the woman and son already encountered at the start—against the backdrop of sporting fields. "Toronto has a pulse," she says, "Toronto has a vibe to that many other cities don't have" (Figure 27). The video ends on an invitation for people to join the conversation today, because "the neighborhood of the future starts with your ideas" (Figure 28).

Something that the video doesn't mention is that the negotiations between Sidewalk Labs and Waterfront Toronto so far had all been taken place *outside* public view. Nor does it mention the Framework Agreement between the two parties, which was kept secret for eighteen months. Only in Spring 2019 did the full scope of the project became clear, when Sidewalk Labs presented its hefty, four tome Master Innovation and Development Plan (MIDP), titled *Toronto Tomorrow: A New Approach for Inclusive Growth*.

FIGURE 23 "I lived in Toronto for almost thirty years" (this and following five figures (Figures 24–28) are screen captures from video, © Sidewalk Toronto, 2017, all rights reserved).[16]

FIGURE 24 "You can meet a new person every week."

FIGURE 25 Toronto streetcar.

FIGURE 26 "Toronto is in an elite class of cities in North America."

FIGURE 27 "Toronto has a pulse."

FIGURE 28 How do *you* feel about Toronto's future?

Moreover, the grounds of the conversation initiated by Sidewalk were skewed from the start, favoring a vision of human interaction and community that needs technological intervention, that needs "enhancing." According to this transhumanist vision, human life is at once inherently driven toward connection, but also flawed, facing "barriers" that hinder people's striving for connection. The exact nature and causes of those barriers—Toronto's current "design problem"—are only vaguely defined as "challenges of growth." But the directions that the ideation process should move into appear already much clearer.

The conversation that Sidewalk proposed was not *if* technology can enhance human interaction, or about *who* should own and develop those technologies, but merely about the *speed* with which to move forward. "How do we leverage technology to make cities better?" *Sidewalk Labs'* Head of Development asks in the video. He answers his own question by framing the "conversation" as a dialogue between "technologists" and "urbanists," adding that while the former group thinks "why can't we solve this quickly?" the latter group "knows [that] things take time and you have to move deliberately." He concludes that "it's the convergence of those two ways of thinking that can lead to really powerful outcomes." That convergence is the dream of a humanity for whom digital technology is second nature, a dream that is romantic and rational at once. It is the vision of an "authentic" and uniquely "Torontonian" community that *at the same time* is automated and datafied.

Sidewalk's framing of the conversation about Toronto's future is typical for corporate smart city discourse. As Jathan Sadowski and Roy Bendor argue in their article "Selling Smartness: Corporate Narratives and the Smart City as a Sociotechnical Imaginary," the smart city imaginary is premised on a particular narrative on urban crisis and technological salvation. Tech companies like IBM and Cisco present their smart city solutions as the uncontestable response to impending crises. Doing so, they reproduce existing sociopolitical systems while blocking alternative smart or intelligent visions.[17]

The belief that urban community can be enhanced by means of technological design predates the digital age. Take the Garden City movement, initiated in the late nineteenth century by Elbenezer Howard, a clerk for the British Parliament and an urban utopian. Frustrated by the crowding of big cities like London and the unimaginative "Great Rebuilding" of Chicago following its 1871 fire, Howard wrote the book *To-Morrow: A Peaceful Path to Real*

Reform, published in 1898 and republished in 1902 as *Garden Cities of To-Morrow*. Howard envisioned the garden city as a "town-country magnet," integrating the best of city and country such that better "opportunities of social intercourse may be enjoyed than are enjoyed in any crowded city."[18]

In the following decades, Howard's manifesto inspired urban planning all over the world, from Letchworth outside London (which was started in 1904) to Don Mills in Ontario (developed between 1952 and 1962 and now part of the city of Toronto). As Anthony Townsend argues in *Smart Cities: Big Data, Civic Hackers, and the Quest for a New Utopia*, the Garden City was the smart city of its day, integrating new technological developments in electricity networks and railway planning. Townsend (who himself has collaborated with Sidewalk Labs through his strategy studio Bits and Atoms) cites a 1939 documentary film titled *The City*, produced by the Regional Planning Association of America. The film—screened at the World's Fair in New York—captures the smart urban promise. The voice-over tells us what we see: "We see homes with grass, children riding bicycles, and men walking to work in clean factories and playing softball. The world of mankind and technology is in balance once again."[19]

Like smart cities now, the Garden City movement had its critics, among whom Jane Jacobs. In her *Death and Life of Great American Cities*, Jacobs describes garden cities as "really very nice towns if you were docile and had no plans of your own and did not mind spending your life among others with no plans of their own."[20] Jacobs scorns the "hatred of the street" displayed by Garden City planners while deriding their top-down approach to issues like safety and community. Instead, Jacobs celebrated the lively sidewalk as the bottom-up foundation for organic surveillance and play. The trouble with garden cities and their enclosed park enclaves, she writes, "is that no child of enterprise or spirit will willingly stay in such a boring place after [reaching] the age of six."[21]

Jacobs's book, in combination with her 1960s activism against the urban renewal plans in Manhattan's West Village, delivered a severe blow to the Garden City dream, at least in the global north.[22] Yet the underlying belief in a top-down approach to urban design, in which technology enhances community, has survived, manifesting itself in smart city design from Songdo in South Korea (powered by Cisco, once the most valuable company in the world) to Belmont, Arizona (with Bill Gates as one of the main investors).

In the case of Sidewalk Toronto, the smart dream was abolished before reaching stages 4 and 5 of the design thinking process: to *prototype* and *test*. The project's fiercest critic was Bianca Wylie, described by Townsend as "the Jane Jacobs of the smart city." As Wylie stated about the unusual partnership between Sidewalk Labs and Waterfront Toronto: "A city is not a business ... I have found the process to be thoroughly anti-democratic."[23]

Smartphone

What makes the SMARTPHONE *magical ... is the millions of people and companies who have actually created on top of it. We see [Sidewalk Toronto] in sort of the same way.*
          **SIDEWALK LABS CEO DAN DOCTOROFF
          DURING A 2017 "TOWN HALL" MEETING**

Having been selected to work with Waterfront Toronto, Sidewalk Labs organized a "robust *public* engagement process," according to the company itself "one of the city's largest-ever *public* discussions on an urban development" (emphasis added) (Figure 29).[24] This engagement process started with a series of "Town Hall" meetings with on stage Dan Doctoroff and Waterfront Toronto CEO Will Fleissig (both wearing a red poppy as a symbol of First World War Remembrance Day, Figure 30). The first of these meetings took place in November 2017, in a packed St. Lawrence Centre of the Arts in Downtown Toronto. Moderator Denise Pinto started by thanking the audience "for being a resident, a passionate member of this community, and somebody who is willing to have your voice heard."[25] As is good custom in Canada, she then read a land acknowledgment: "The land on which we're standing has been the site of human activity for over 15,000 years." Next, the evening was kicked off with the video discussed in the previous section.

 In this chapter's final section, TORONTO, I will return extensively to Sidewalk's bizarre land acknowledgment. Here, I want to focus on its abuse of the word "public." Even though Sidewalk Toronto didn't happen, to watch the recording of the St. Lawrence meeting is still a bit eerie. As Bianca Wylie asked, "Neither of these people are the government ... So why are they using all the words that a government would use to plan

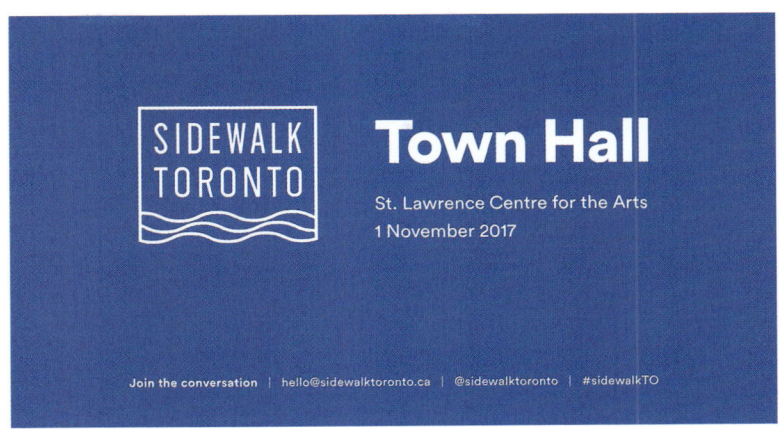

FIGURES 29 AND 30 "Public" town hall meeting organized by Sidewalk Toronto (November 2017) (screen captures from video, © Sidewalk Toronto, 2018, all rights reserved).[26]

for the city?"[27] To this we can add: On whose behalf does Sidewalk Labs interpellate people as "residents" and "citizens"? And what happens to the notion of "public" in these corporately organized citizen engagement events? The short answer: in the new-speak of Sidewalk's public relations campaign, meaning becomes a slippery slope, while the distinctions between public and private space, and between public and corporate interests, collapse into a vaguely defined "urban" realm.

This urban ideology and its *public-washing* of corporate interests also return in the Master Innovation and Development Plan, titled *Toronto Tomorrow* that Sidewalk finally presented in 2019. Like the town hall meeting, the master plan opens with a land acknowledgment, upon which the book, like the "Introducing Sidewalk" video, proceeds to *empathize* with its users, the people of Toronto. The book asks its readership a page-wide question: "What do you see in your dream city?" This is followed by a number of artistic black-and-white portraits of a diverse group of Torontonians, all with their eyes closed, dreaming of a city that …

> brings me true love / knows the difference between good friction and bad friction / leaves room for beautiful imperfections / lets me sing all day long with my friends / makes winters less of a bummer / never stops trying / births new movements of creativity and philosophy / that is as stimulating for my daughters as it is for their grandparents / reinvents on-top of itself without losing its soul [to cite from a longer list of dreams presumably collected by Sidewalk Labs][28]

The dream of a city that knows the difference between public values and corporate interests clearly didn't make it to the list, but in the rest of *Toronto Tomorrow* the term "public" is ubiquitous. Sidewalk speaks, for example, of its overall aim to "leverage private resources to realize *public* objectives."[29] It also states that it wants to "ensure that digital innovation aligns with the *public* interest."[30] And it outlines its ideas for the "*public* realm," broadly defined as "a system of streets, parks, plazas, and open spaces that encourages people to spend more time outdoors, together."[31] Sidewalk Labs imagines this public realm to be "intimate." The masterplan speaks of "a neighborhood filled with more open and *publicly* accessible space … often with an *intimate* feel," "the need for an *intimate* human scale intertwined with the *public* realm," and a "grand boulevard full of *intimate* moments" (which would have been Queens Quay, Quayside's central artery).[32]

To help picture these intimate and public spaces, *Toronto Tomorrow* contains a series of artist impressions (which here I seek to render in text). In the first of these drawings, Quayside is still under construction. In the background, a crane finishes a timber high-rise. In the foreground, in the lower-left corner, two construction workers finish up some wood paneling. Two other workers, assisted by a robot arm, run a last check on the wiring. Meanwhile, people already have their first intimate encounters, with fellow Torontonians (like the two mixed-race families running into each other) and with the city itself (like a girl in a blue dress in the middle of the image, playing hopscotch on what could be smart tiles, accentuated in purple). The colors are bright and soft and somewhat blurry, much like indoors and outdoors, park and city, and public and private experience blur into each other on this plaza at once familiar and futuristic.

This blurring of categories continues in the next artist impression, which illustrates a "people-first" Queens Quay. On the right, a vision-impaired person approaches the street, alerted by what looks like a self-driving shuttle that communicates, one may assume, with the smart pavement underneath their feet. It is raining. A mother and child share an umbrella, a couple shares a raincoat. In the background, a school class gathers in what in Sidewalk speak is called a "stoa" space, in which the difference between indoors and outdoors vanishes. Like the couple and the mother and child, this stoa space is protected from the elements by a Raincoat (capital "r"), which is part of Sidewalk Toronto's "weather mitigation system" designed with "the potential to double the number of hours it is comfortable to be outdoors each years across key spaces."[33] Also the people at the patio tables behind the tree on the left are underneath such a building raincoat and—judging on the image texture—so is the viewer, *mindfully* taking in this urban scene that won't be.

The third image (Figure 31) shows the grand central plaza, which can host a wide range of activities such as concerts, hence the sound installation mounted on the ceiling. The image offers a closer look at the "stoa spaces," dubbed as a "key term" by Sidewalk's master plan. In that plan we read that the stoa spaces "are designed to accommodate a wide range of uses beyond traditional retail, helping to activate the street."[34] The street life on this picture is certainly vibrant. Everywhere in the image people of all colors and ages are engaged in play or conversation. No one is on their smartphone.

FIGURE 31 Artist impression in Sidewalk's *Toronto Tomorrow* development plan (screen capture from video, © Raymond Wong, 2021, all rights reserved).[35]

The last two images in this series show a modular city that breathes with the seasons. Both images share the same viewpoint on Parliament Slip, located at the eastern tip of Quayside. In the first image it is summer. Combined, the stoa spaces, the "cove" steps, and the Inner Harbor form one large open space where the people are as colorful as the boats in the water and the kites in the sky. In the second image it is winter. Parliament Slip is still as open and "public" as a few months ago. This is made possible by a few subtle interventions that keep inside and outside connected, including the transparent domes on the ice and an equally transparent and weightless tarp with lights dangling from it, all adding to the intimate feel.

Looking at the five images together, what strikes one most? Well, first of all, when we compare Quayside to downtown Toronto (or any North American downtown), one thing absent is advertising and corporate branding. In that respect, *Quayside* seems a much more *public* place than most urban centers now. Second, as stated, we don't see people interact with digital technology. Other than the construction workers and their robot assistant in the first image, Quayside appears as a place where people's lives and encounters remain unmediated by online connectivity. We thus definitely see the "people-first" philosophy, but not so much the "from-the-internet-up" dimension of Quayside's design, although we know the internet is there. As Matthew Stewart writes, in Quayside's visualizations …

> we encounter a landscape that appears untrained by technology: a pastoral fiction that speaks more to a mutated village life than what is arguably the height of techno-capitalism today—functional sovereignty, the data economy and its corresponding context of algorithmic governance. These renders and quaint sketches show a continual festival at Quayside, like a sanitized scene from a Bruegel landscape.[36]

Indeed, the sketches appear almost timeless. Only the building designs are a testimony to the digital age (in that they are clearly designed by means of digital technology). And certainly, in other artist impressions in *Toronto Tomorrow*, digital technology *is* visualized. But also here the game is to spot the smartphone, granting these images somewhat of a fairytale feel.

This absence of smartphones in the artist impressions is all the more remarkable given Sidewalk's recurring comparison between the city-as-platform and the smartphone. For example, in the November 2017 "town hall" meeting Doctoroff stated that in the city-as-platform Sidewalk's "goal is not to do everything," but to "create the conditions for others to create and build." He asks people to think of their smartphones, adding that "what makes the smartphone truly revolutionary is the millions of people and companies who have actually created on top of it to do things that no-one ever actually imagined were possible."[37] Similarly, in a 2018 presentation Rit Aggarwala, who was the Head of Urban Systems at Sidewalk, stated that "if you think of the city as a platform and design in the ability for people to change it as quickly as you and I can customize our iPhones, you make it authentic because it doesn't just reflect a central plan … It also reflects the people who live and work there."[38]

The city-as-smartphone analogy doesn't return in the Sidewalk master plan, but the analogy is actually not at odds with the near-absence of smartphones in the street scene impressions. In the smartphone-like city, life is as frictionless and smooth as the media streams on people's handheld devices, facilitated by the safe user environments of Apple's iOS or Android (and given that Sidewalk Labs was a sibling company of Google, one can safely assume that Quayside's digital infrastructure would have run on Android). This fantasy is an everyday life mediated by technology to the point where it creates the illusion of its own absence, redeeming material reality. Much like Hollywood cinema for long sold the suburban American Dream, the Silicon Dream sold by Sidewalk Labs *sutures* its user into a smooth *Truman Show*-like environment in which even the weather is mitigated top-down. At first sight, Quayside looks playful, but in reality it would have been a very controlled and controlling environment prescriptive of how people's bodies and minds should behave in urban space.

Urban

URBAN data: *information gathered in the city's physical environment, including the public realm, publicly accessible spaces, and even some private buildings.*

KEY TERM IN SIDEWALK LABS'S *TORONTO TOMORROW* MASTER PLAN

Sidewalk's city-as-smartphone analogy derives from the company's founding vision that "cities are—and have always been—platforms," as Sidewalk stated during one of its citizen engagement events in 2018.[39] Sidewalk presents this platform city as a "physical layer" with a "digital layer" on top of it. Following Sidewalk's logic that from-the-internet-up and people-first are in fact the same thing, this digital layer combines "connectivity" and "community." As far as the physical layer is concerned, it strikes most that for Sidewalk the "public realm" is a mere interface between "infrastructure" and "mobility," rather than a democratic ideal that *integrates* the physical and the digital. As we will see, this somewhat instrumental vision of the public realm fits into the company's overall urban ideology, in which public and private blur.

Sidewalk's vision of cities as platforms predated its Toronto plans. In 2016, about nine months after the company's founding, the company presented a talk hosted by Google's TechTalks series. In this talk, titled "Reimaging the City as a Digital Platform," Chief Operating Officer at Sidewalk, Anand Babu, states that in the light of the "fourth industrial revolution" Sidewalk sees a need for "reimaging the city as a digital platform." He continues:

> It's important to start by saying that cities themselves have always been platforms. They are places where we pull together. We build roads, we build sewers, and we fund all of that through taxes, and that enables all kinds of users and business to come together, in the same way as we think of other kinds of technology platforms. But until recently digital technology was sort of an afterthought in city design. And what I want to talk about is ... when digital technologies become a peer with concrete and with laws and regulations and taxes. What happens, how does that change cities?[40]

The rhetorical gesture was the same in 2016 as in 2018: in order to *reimagine* the city as a digital platform, Sidewalk first has to *reframe* history by saying that cities have *always* been platforms. Sidewalk thus naturalizes the city-as-platform view, making a "platform" seem a mere level, value-free playing ground that facilitates people's movements and encounters. But platforms are never neutral, nor is the term "platform." As Tarleton Gillespie argues in "The Politics of 'Platforms,'" when a commercial service posits itself as a "platform," it risks to elide the tension "between user-generated and commercially produced content, between cultivating community and serving up advertising."[41]

This is exactly what happened with Sidewalk Toronto: the commercial interests of which for Sidewalk Labs and the Alphabet group never became fully clear. In a 2018 interview with *Toronto Life*, Doctoroff assured people that Sidewalk Labs, despite its Google connection, would not collect data for commercial purposes. "It's not to sell ads," Doctoroff says, "it's to use data to improve quality of life." The interviewer asks: but isn't Sidewalk in Toronto "to make a buck"? Doctoroff admits that "inevitably" Sidewalk will generate profit through technology licensing and infrastructure financing at the site, but that "at this point" the company is not interested in business but "obsessed with developing a plan."[42]

Sidewalk's plans with Toronto remained vague at best, though, especially when it came to the neighborhood's "digital layer." Goodman and Powles write:

> In broad strokes, there are two distinct versions of platform values. In one version, the city intermediates between the public's data and service providers, prioritizing public benefit. In the other, commercial platforms like Facebook and Uber intermediate, prioritizing profit

or market share. Sidewalk obscures just which version of platform its digital layer will be and what it will be optimized for.[43]

As already suggested by its composite name, Sidewalk Toronto sailed in a limbo between for-profit and for-public, adopting a people-first-and-from-the-internet-up vocabulary in which these categories blur—a tactic often seen with Big Tech. Here it didn't help that Sidewalk's city-as-platform and city-as-smartphone analogies are absent from its over-thousand-pages master plan. That said, browsing through this document, two main lines for Sidewalk's city-as-platform philosophy can be distilled. The first is that Sidewalk would have been a *modular* city, this in line with Townsend's observation that smart city life will be defined by "adaptive systems that respond in real time to changing conditions at the very small and very large scale simultaneously."[44] Second, Sidewalk would have been an "urban" space across the public-private binary.

Considering Sidewalk as a modular platform city: *Toronto Tomorrow* paints a city designed to adapt and redesign itself: from the stoa spaces to an "open space alliance" that coordinates programming in parks and plazas; and from a "customizable library of building parts" to "mixed-use zoning" in which spaces and buildings change function over time or even during the day. As Eric Jaffe writes on the Sidewalk Labs blog, this type of zoning is called "pink coding," as it waters down the "red tape" between city zones.[45] Also Quayside's data collection infrastructure would have had a modular design. Take the so-called "Koala mounts" for data sensors on street poles. They would have made it easy for application developers to "collect urban data for a multitude of purposes, from bicycle counting … to interactive public art installations."[46]

Essential to the design of Quayside's core infrastructure would have thus been the city's continuous *re*design. So what were the principles on the basis of which the city was designed to be redesigned? Who would have controlled the platform infrastructure facilitating the city's responsiveness to its "end-users"? Would the latter have been true co-creators, as Sidewalk suggested, or would they have remained mere *content creators* within a pre-programmed platform environment? *Toronto Tomorrow* leaves those fundamental questions unanswered.

Besides the modularity of its design, the second main characteristic of Sidewalk as a platform city is that it imagined itself across the divide between public and private space. Or as Sidewalk writes itself, the city eliminates "the divide between home, work, and play."[47] In the Sidewalk

Toronto master plan, this unthinking of divides becomes especially clear in the discussion of "urban data." Highlighted as a "key term," "urban data" is vaguely defined as "information gathered in the city's physical environment, including the public realm, publicly accessible spaces, and even some private buildings."[48] Sidewalk's definition of "urban" thus exists across public and private space, collapsing both, much like its vocabulary collapses public and corporate interests.

To regulate this urban data production, Sidewalk introduced an "independent" Urban Data Trust that would have been "charged with balancing the interests of personal privacy, public interest, and innovation."[49] With this data trust, Sidewalk sought to respond to concerns voiced during its citizen engagement events. Yet, the more concerns Sidewalk addressed, the more questions it raised. Wylie: "I remember listening to everyone saying that this is going to resolve problems with democracy, that there was going to be transparency and accountability now." She quickly realized, though, that Sidewalk's intersection of technology and urban planning would be "horrific" for actual public discourse.[50] Similarly, Goodman and Powles, who are both law scholars, give the following analysis of this Urban Data Trust:

> Using the mechanism of a trust, what Sidewalk really seemed to be proposing was to unilaterally redefine all data collected within the site as Urban Data—from public spaces and from private ones, including apartments, homes, and offices "not controlled by those who occupy them" (i.e., including any leased space or anywhere offered "as a service"). This sleight of hand, creating a term unrecognized in law, would effectively negate any default privacy setting: everything done within the bounds of the Sidewalk Toronto project would be potentially up for grabs.[51]

When in October 2019 Sidewalk Toronto was scaled back to just Quayside, Sidewalk Labs also had to give up its Data Trust plan. In the adopted plan, collected data would have been controlled by Waterfront Toronto. Still, even after these adaptations, many kept doubts about the company's true intentions.

This doubt about Sidewalk's intentions was fed further when in that same period reporters of the Canadian national newspaper *The Globe and Mail* published an article about a confidential Sidewalk Labs document from 2016, internally known as the "yellow book." In this 437-page coffee table book, Sidewalk Labs employees could read speculations of what life could be like in a Sidewalk community. These speculations included sensors tracking and predicting the movements of all entities (including people), a privatized police force, privatized property taxes, charter schools run by Sidewalk, and also a reward system for people based on the amount of data they are willing to share, and that "could ultimately be used to reward people for 'good behavior.'"[52]

As one commentator wrote on Reddit, it is as if someone read the dystopian novel *Oryx and Crake* by Margaret Atwood (whose family is from Toronto), in which the protagonist grows up in a corporately controlled walled compound.[53] The "yellow book" includes case studies for sites in Detroit, Denver, and Alameda (California). The "yellow book" also contains numerous references to Disney theme parks and the futurist Buckminster Fuller, all buttressing Sidewalk's ambition to "overcome cynicism about the future" while foreseeing an "enormous potential for value generation in multiple ways" (including product design and real estate development).[54]

Upon the leaking of this yellow book, a Sidewalk spokesperson commented that the ideas contained in this document "represent the result of a wide-ranging brainstorming process very early in the company's history," and that most of these ideas were never under consideration for

FIGURE 32 City-as-platform ideology (screen capture from video, © Google TechTalks, 2016, all rights reserved).[55]

Toronto.[56] Still, there is a clear continuation between Sidewalk's early 2016 speculations and its Toronto plans. That discursive continuation is clearest in the reimagining of the city as a digital platform, to recall the Google TechTalk given by two Sidewalk representatives in 2016 (Figure 32). In this presentation, the question is raised, "What kind of cities do we want to create?" Following an ominous reference to Steven Spielberg's 2002 film *Minority Report* (in which data is used to tackle "pre-crimes"), the question is answered in two parts, namely a "human" idealistic part and a down-to-earth part:

> Our approach at Sidewalk ... is to really immerse ourselves in these cities of the future ... Our view is that the cities of the future ... have to really be designed to be not only efficient, but also to be equitable and human ... But it's not enough to be thinkers and dreamers. We also need to be living in the present. And so the other half of our approach is about solving the pressing problems that exist today in ways that bridge to these cities of the future.[57]

These two sides of the coin (being human, solving problems) are exactly the same as in the "Introducing Sidewalk Toronto" video that appeared a year later (and that I discussed in Section 2, Empathy). On the one hand, the platform city has to be human and authentic and capture diversity. On the other hand, it needs to solve pressing problems, "bridging to efficient, equitable and human cities of the future" (i.e., the "challenges of growth" signaled in the "Introducing Sidewalk" video). Sidewalk's narrative of platform cities thus didn't radically change between the yellow book years and the Toronto plans, although there is one main difference between the 2016 Google Tech Talk and *Toronto Tomorrow*. Whereas in the tech talk, Sidewalk's city-as-platform vision is presented as clearly modeled on the Google infrastructure, in the Toronto plans this Google inspiration has been strategically erased (besides the announcement that Google's Canadian headquarters would have been moved to Quayside).

Also, without such explicit reference, though, the inspiration remains clear. Sidewalk Labs planned to transform urban space into a sensing environment in which people's behavior is continuously monitored, blurring the difference between public and private space. One example here is the pay-as-you-throw garbage chutes, a technology as invasive as Google Home. In Sidewalk's vision, people are above all *users* of urban space who experience a great sense of control of the technologies that allow them to connect and overcome barriers of connection. People's experience is "enhanced," following a transhumanist position in which "human" is defined by a connective lack that is to be redeemed by technological mediation. In reality, this sense of control only goes as far as the freedoms the user is granted within the platformized environment. As the Sidewalk spokesperson states in the Google TechTalk, the digital layer makes sure "that people have access to only the things they should have access to."[58] People thus indeed become indeed content creators. They also become packages monitored in real time, much like the parcels in Quayside's underground delivery system. Or in the words of McKenzie Wark, the smart city becomes "a platform for sorting users in transit."[59] In this process, platforms *reorient* users, transforming individual and collective behavior to the point individuals and communities become something else.

Dividual

Every beginning is DIVIDUAL.
            GERALD RAUNIG, *DIVIDUUM: MACHINIC CAPITALISM AND MOLECULAR REVOLUTION* (2016)[60]

Having analyzed Sidewalk's transhumanist fiction of enhanced human life, I will now juxtapose this fiction to the material and posthuman reality of subject formation in a control society. In that reality, Big Tech colonizes everyday life, addressing people as users, while transforming their lived experience into "raw" data. In this process, people's individual integrity is compromised. Or as Nick Couldry and Ulises A. Mejias write in *The Costs of Connection*:

> Capitalism affirms, for sure, the uniquely identifiable reference point on which all notions of the self hang … But at the same time, capitalism invites us to lose control over a core element in the content of that identified self whose continuity (and change) we value with time. By installing automated surveillance into the space of the self, we risk losing the very thing—the open-ended space in which we continuously monitor and transform ourselves over time—that constitutes us as selves at all.[61]

As people's integrity, their sense of self, is disrupted, they are dividualized. The dividual is what becomes of the individual when the subject is scattered and shattered to the point they are no longer undivided, *in*dividual. As argued in Chapter 1, WI-FI, this dividual existence was always already marked the modern female condition. As I will argue later in this section, it also always already marked the Black condition. In the technocolonial age, the dividual condition is universalized, while it continues to intersect with the old dividualizing structures of patriarchy and colonialism. How to grasp the dividual (whose state according to Gerald Raunig marks "every beginning")? And how to understand the dividual in its city-as-platform context?

The dividual is a controlled subject who experiences a certain sense of control, or lack thereof. Whereas the individual—and their relative freedom to speak, act, own, and to some degree resist—emerged with modern capitalism and its disciplinary society, the dividual is the subject of technocolonialism and its control society. Like discipline, control is a form of power wielded by market-driven and public institutions alike (to the extent public and corporate power can still be told apart). And like discipline, control creates the subject with a sense of control of the technologies mediating their attention. As Gilles Deleuze writes in his "Postscript on the Control Society," discipline is a stern and orderly form of power that confines and segments the subject with analog technology.[62] Control, in contrast, is a soft power that gently steers the subject in profitable and docile ways. It is the power of suggestion.

The dividual is the networked subject of the clouded crowd. Dividual city life is what becomes of the modern urban experience. That modern experience has often been rendered in terms of the individual immersed in a crowd of relative strangers—a rendering predominantly premised on white, male, bourgeois subjectivity. Generally speaking, in modern predigital urban space, women (and all other non-cis male identifying bodies) had less freedom to safely travel and constitute themselves as individuated subjects. Now, in a time that the urban crowd is mediated by corporate cloud-based technology, the dividual condition is in a sense generalized. I add "in a sense," because the argument that data-invasive practices invade *all* subjects' personal integrity only holds true in combination with the acknowledgment that this dividualization of life-in-general continues to intersect with more old-fashioned "modern" forms of oppression, harassment, and invasion. Personally, I sometimes like to leave my smartphone at home, experience the city without a digital map, and be more open to talk to strangers. I realize, though, that for many the smartphone also is an urban safety device, and that to talk to strangers is safer for some people than it is for others.

The dividual is the platform user constituted by what Benjamin Bratton calls "the Stack." In his 2015 book of that name, Bratton defines "stack" as "a kind of platform that also happens to be structured through vertical interoperable layers, both hard and soft, global and local," say from streets and sidewalks to Wi-Fi signals.[63] The Stack is the totality of these stacks, or platforms, including the platformized city and its hybrid analog-digital infrastructures, or what Bratton calls "the city stack." The Stack is a planetary machine but at the same time, as a concept, "the Stack" is also an attempt to *grasp* this vast machine in its totality. Bratton states that the stack is "the accidental megastructure of planetary scale computation and … a way of seeing that megastructure as a single metatechnology."[64] The user, in Bratton's terminology, refers to the "position … through which we see The Stack, but also through which The Stack sees us."[65] We navigate The Stack and its stacks—walking in the street, surfing the web. While doing so, we experience a relative sense of control. At the same time, the Stack traces our movements, registers our habits, datafies our experience, and feeds back to us a transmedia stream that subtly shifts our paths, reorients our desires, and micro-channels our lives.

The dividual is a human thing. As Bratton argues, a human user is a mere thing among other nonhuman actors and objects that equally take user positions (e.g., self-driving cars, online bots, pay-as-you-throw garbage chutes).[66] Wark writes that, like these things, humans are "disassembled into what [Gerald] Raunig and others think of a *dividual* drives."[67] In *Dividuum*, Raunig writes that platforms like Google need the "self-division of individual users."[68] He explains that the first appearances of [the Latin word] *dividuum* occur in the contexts of slavery and sexual violence.[69] As people are dividualized, they become appendages to the sensing platform-machine, to the Stack. That future-become-present was already foreseen by Karl Marx. In his "Fragment on Machines," Marx speaks of a "machine … set in power by an automaton [algorithm]" in which "the workers are cast merely as its conscious linkages."[70] The human user-worker becomes a thing. As Mbembe argues, this human thing is a prisoner of desire and hence a subject of the drive, "a neuroeconomic subject absorbed by a double concern stemming from [their] animal nature … and [their] thingness."[71] Think of your Uber deliverer tethered to their app, or of your fellow commuter glued to their

Instagram-TikTok-Tinder feeds. Or think of yourself, continuously involved in a multiplicity of personalized transmedia streams.

As a human thing, the dividual hardly recognizes themselves, or perhaps does not recognize themselves at all. Maurizio Lazzarato refers to dividualization as the product of a machinic enslavement that "dismantles the individuated subject, consciousness, and representations, acting on both the preindividual and supra-individual levels."[72] In this process, the always already alienated modern individual is scattered to pieces. There is little point in reassembling these pieces into an indivisible whole. Resisting consciousness and representation, dividuated life can at most come together, and collectively seek to recognize and resist the assemblages enslaving them.

The dividual exists across modern binaries such as home-work, public-private, and city-country, and male-female. Lazzarato writes that machinic enslavement "does not bother with" dualisms like subject-object, words-things, or nature-culture. "The dividual does not stand opposite [to] machines [but] is contiguous with machines."[73] There is no reason to be nostalgic for binaries or dualisms, like we don't need to feel nostalgia for the waning individual, an equally modern invention. After all, there is a liberating potential to this blurring of boundaries. Yet to the extent this integration of social realms is driven by a data-and-profit-driven logic, the emancipatory effects are accompanied (and in the long run overshadowed) by an overall dividualization of life. Sidewalk Toronto would have been the perfect example, because in its "urban space" the distinction between public and private would have largely collapsed. In Quayside, even more than already is the case in platformized cities now, spaces would have been permeated, punctured, and in that process melted together, by a datafying logic. The result would have been a homogenized urban realm in which citizens become user-citizens, while everyday life becomes mere user-generated content.

The dividual lives in gated and modulated communities. Deleuze reports from an imagined "town where anyone can leave their flat, their street, their neighborhood, using their (dividual) electronic card that opens this or that barrier." This still sounds like modern disciplinary society, where individuals are kept in check with analog, molding structures. But "the card may also be rejected on a particular day, or between certain times of day; it doesn't depend on the barrier but on the computer that is making sure everyone is in a permissible place, and effecting a universal modulation."[74] In this city-machine, people's movements are increasingly programmed, while their lives increasingly take place in *personalized* social bubbles, offline, online, and in hybrid space. Think of apartment complexes with separate entrances for the rich. Or think of network algorithms that are likely to connect people to others with whom they are already relatively like-minded.

The dividual is thus subject to a modulating power. Deleuze took his notion of modulation from Gilbert Simondon and his theory of individuation. Modulation, for Simondon, is an open-ended process over the course of which a form crystallizes and individuates, this in contrast to molding, which is a rigid and static intervention. Simondon writes: "A modulator is a *continuous temporal mold*. Here, the 'matter' is almost uniquely the support of potential energy … To mold is to modulate in a definitive way; to modulate is to mold in continuously and perpetually variable way."[75] As Matt Bluemink writes, in his "Control Society" essay Deleuze looks at modulation as a continuously adaptive controlling power that reshapes itself in relation to the variations of the matter it is shaping. Bluemink argues that whereas Simondon's view of modulation still emphasizes the "preindividual potentialities in the continuous process of individuation … Deleuze argues that the societies of control have managed to adapt this process in such a way that limits these potentials."[76] We could say that control harnesses the power of modulation. Whereas discipline, as a molding power, interpellates subjects as individuals, control intervenes on the preindividual level of the drive. In the control society people continue to be interpellated as individuals, more than ever in fact, as by personalized media streams. But in the same movement, people's activity and attention are tracked by modulating control systems that dividualize life into data aggregates, which are fed back to populations to address them more and more "personally."

The dividual is detached. This detachment moves beyond the blasé attitude Georg Simmel observed in the metropolitan city dweller. In his 1903 essay "The Metropolis and Mental Life," Simmel argued that the "metropolis conduces to the urge for the most individual personal existence." Simmel links this development to the intensification of nervous stimulation and to the growing division of labor, which "demands from the individual an ever more one-sided accomplishment" that "only too frequently means death to the personality of the individual."[77] Even more than their predecessor, the enslaved dividual is precarious and pressed for time. They often work from project to project, whether driving for

Uber, freelancing in the creative sector, or balancing the two. This lack of a long-term life narrative—Berlant's definition of precarity—is intensified by a great amount of screen time spent in "social" media's short-term attention palaces. As Sarah Barns observes in *Platform Urbanism*, in the platformized city the sidewalk ballet described by Jane Jacobs takes ever stranger forms. Walking down a busy street, you may "well need to swerve away from [people] 'wexting' (walking while texting)." Barns adds that these distracted subjects "may even have developed a non-visual way of detecting motion and obstruction that allows them to navigate without *actually looking up*."[78] This street scene nicely captures dividual urban life: two strangers dancing around each other, avoiding touch, as if in a silent disco where each visitor is tuned into their own personalized channel.

The dividual is a split personality. To be continuously tracked affects one's sense of self. Couldry and Mejias speak of a double consciousness experienced by the datafied subject. Double consciousness is a term dubbed by W. E. B. Dubois to describe the Black experience in a racist society, "in which the self is forced to describe itself in *another's* language."[79] Similarly, Mbembe speaks of the "Becoming Black of the world." He argues that the transformation of human beings into "animate things made up of coded digital data" generalizes the "Black" condition that "early capitalism imposed on people of African origin (different forms of depredation, dispossession of all power of self-determination, and, most of all, dispossession of the future and of time, the two matrices of the possible)."[80] These thinkers thus argue that the modern Black dividual condition is now universalized. Admittedly, I do feel a certain hesitance to speak of datafied life in terms of a Black experience. It is true, though, that technocolonialism in essence shares a similar dehumanizing logic as historical and contemporary forms of settler and extractive colonialism. Crucially, such technocolonial critique only makes sense if it is part of a broader decolonial anti-racist stance that acknowledges how technocolonialism intersects with and sustains more long-standing colonial relations (much like a technocolonial critique needs to be feminist).

The dividual is disoriented. Literally, they lack a sense of direction. After all, in the city indexed by Google Maps (Figure 33), it is no longer necessary to *find* one's way, and over time, in that process of wayfinding, integrate the city's surprises and one's growing sense of direction into the diffracted sense of self. While the smart city dweller trails the blue arrow around which their world has come to revolve, they travel to

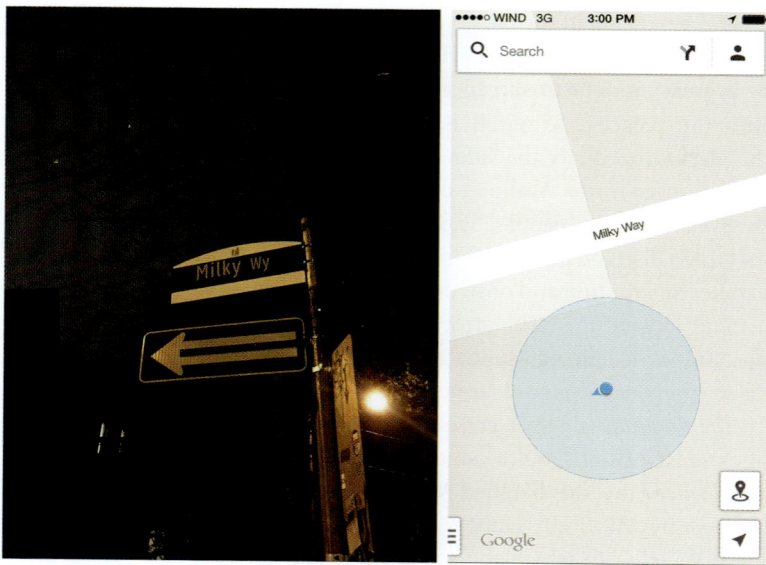

FIGURE 33 Milky Way in downtown Toronto (2015, photo by the author and screen capture, © Google Maps, 2015, all rights reserved).

reach their destination. On the one hand, this connectivity has made urban space safer and more accessible for some subjects. As is the case with media such as Instagram, there is an emancipatory side to Google Maps. On the other hand, Google's mapping urban space are not neutral but has a clear commercial interest. Over time, the platformized city is likely to nudge people in indexed directions, for example by giving more visibility to places with a higher user rating, or by algorithmic suggestion: if you liked x, you may also like y. Mapping urban spaces, Google and other corporate platforms thus also change and channel these spaces, paving new paths, contributing to their gentrification, while subtly affecting people's desires and orientations into potentially profitable directions.

The dividual is you, the many of "you," a scattered multiplicity of identifying selves. Speaking of "you," in Toronto's Parkdale neighborhood on Queen Street West there is an iconic mural that reads YOU'VE CHANGED (Figure 34). I have always loved this artwork by Jesse Harris for its complex simplicity. In my interpretation, the YOU at once refers to the subject traveling further West on Queen West, to the clouded crowd of subjects, and to the gentrifying Parkdale neighborhood (and

FIGURE 34 West Queen West (Toronto, 2015, photo by the author, artwork by Jesse Harris).

downtown Toronto in general). As the city changes, people's sense of the city changes, and with it their sense of selves.

The dividual is the posthuman under the species of late capitalism and its technofeudal transformation. By "posthuman," I mean what becomes of the human animal after the death of the human form. The posthuman, I agree with Katherine Hayles and Rosi Braidotti, radically differs from the transhumanist fantasy of an enhanced human and quantified self that transcends materiality and embodiment. Instead, the conceptual persona of the posthuman is "empirically grounded, because it is embodied and embedded."[81] The posthuman is what becomes of the subject in the era of control capitalism and its attention economy.

At the same time, and under the species of ecology (or what Spinoza calls Nature), the posthuman is the dividual's ethical horizon. Whereas the dividual is scrambling and acted *upon*, the posthuman liberates their common preindividual potential from the individuating and dividuating powers that channel and feed on it. The posthuman maintains relations with many different people, while moving in and across many different communities, also without "social" media "presence." The posthuman traverses—and in doing so integrates and connects—social realms, breaching barriers and challenging patriarchal and colonial modern structures. The posthuman is the multitude, the people united as they come together, whether sporadically or more structurally. Such a collective relational subject starts with analysis, with the personal and communal self-analysis of how desire is structured by powers that individualize, dividualize, isolate, and scatter people. Analysis is where resistance starts. It is the process through which the posthuman dividual heals and realizes themselves as a co-agent immanent to their naturalcultural entanglements.

What would a city attuned to this posthuman look like, a city that allows the posthuman to explore their ethical potential, alone and as collectives?

EXPERIMENT WITHOUT TECH #2: OFFLINE MAP MAKING

When exploring a new environment, many of us will nowadays use Google Maps or another platformized map application. But how does Google affect the ways we find and wayfind? This second experiment gets us thinking about that question, about how Google influences the places we visit, the routes we take, how it orients our wanderings. The exercise can be done both alone and together. For the exercise you need some sheets of paper (letter/A4 size will do) and some drawing utensils. Then start wandering. If you're inside, you may as well start inside, the room you're in (observing its lay-out, its colors, its electrical outlets, the movements it invites), other parts of the building, how rooms are connected and separated. What draws your eyes, ears, nose? Be creative, because maps may take many forms (arrows, colors, texts) and moods (factual, emotional, relational). Then go outside for a neighborhood stroll while tracing your paths, or the paths you could have taken. Don't overthink things and let the familiar become strange. What do you notice that you haven't noticed before? Once you have made a stack of maps, spread them out on the floor, and if you want to discuss them with others. What connects your maps? And how do your maps compare to Google's?

Open

An OPEN *ville ... will create the material conditions in which people might thicken their experience of collective life.*
RICHARD SENNET, *BUILDING AND DWELLING: ETHICS FOR THE CITY* (2018)[82]

In order to answer the question, *What does a posthuman city look like?* it is instructive to turn to Richard Sennett's book *Building and Dwelling*. Sennett's urban ethics move between the city-as-*ville* and the city-as-*cité*, that is to say between the city as a *built* form and the city as lived experience, as *dwelling*. Sennett frames his book as an extension of the lifelong conversation he had with Jane Jacobs, first in New York, then in Toronto, until her passing in 2006. He once remarked to Jacobs that she was better on the *cité* than on the *ville*, and that her bottom-up approach works well on the neighborhood level but that it insufficiently accounts for the macro-perspective that large cities also need. Jacobs responded with a question: *What would you do?*

I will take the ethics that Sennett formulates in response to Jacobs's question as the start of my own answer to the question of the posthuman city. Sennett's urban ethics strike a balance between "the built and the lived," between infrastructural and people-up perspectives on urban life and design.[83] He advocates for cities as *open forms* that are synchronous like bazaars (where people can do many different things at the same time, unlike for example at a football stadium), punctuated like texts (with infrastructures that facilitate people's experience, much like periods and colons facilitate a text's reading experience), and that, furthermore, are porous like membranes, incomplete like settlements, and multiple like seeds and plants. "An open *ville*," Sennett writes, "is marked by these five forms which allow the *cité* to become complex," creating "the material conditions in which people might thicken and deepen their experience of collective life."[84]

Such a posthuman city is open, as opposed to gated communities, whether residential or (post-)industrial. Sennett refers to the Googleplex, where employees can get their laundry done, visit a doctor, and basically live their entire lives. The Googleplex is "in the city but not of it." Following a visit to the New York City Googleplex just a few blocks above

Greenwich Village, Sennett is reminded of Jacobs. At first glance, the corporate campus "looks to be filled with the same pulsing, spontaneous, casual collisions outside which she celebrated." Upon a closer look, however, "outside reality checks and resistances" crucial to the sidewalk ballet "are excluded by design."[85] The same can be said about Sidewalk Toronto, which on paper also looks very bustling, but in reality would have been a very closed design prescriptive of how people move and behave.

With Sennett, and against such closed urban design, I advocate for non-prescriptive infrastructures. Corporately controlled algorithms slowly but steadily reorient people's desire, interpellating them as consumers and platform "citizens." Instead, we need forms of social organization (analog, digital, hybrid) that are public, nonprofit, participatory, transparent, and—in the case of digital infrastructures—also open-source. Such public and open infrastructures facilitate life rather than control and channel it, leaving people as free as possible in their orientations. As Sara Ahmed writes in *Queer Phenomenology*, "orientation is a matter of how we reside in space,"[86] of how we *dwell*. For Ahmed, moments of disorientation are vital, as they "can shatter one's sense of confidence in the ground or one's belief that the ground on which we reside can support the actions that make a life feel livable."[87] Disorientation questions, or even puts in crisis, the "normal" everyday structures. Faced by platform infrastructures streamlining life, we need to disorient ourselves more than ever.

An open city is a walkable city. As Rebecca Solnit writes in *Wanderlust* with reference to Jacobs: "Walking the streets is what links up reading the map with living one's life, the personal microcosm with the public macrocosm; it makes sense of the maze all around … Walking maintains the publicness and viability of public space."[88] I agree, but it is also good to remind ourselves that nowadays smart cities *too* disguise as pedestrian paradises, as in the artist impressions of Sidewalk Toronto, or in the equally fictional downtown Los Angeles of Spike Jonze's film *Her* (2013) (Figure 35—see also Chapter 4, CONVERSATIONS). In these smart urban centers, people's bodies may walk but their minds are wired, connected to Big Tech's desire machine. That machine changes how populations move through cities: so-called "social" media tend to keep people in personalized networked bubbles, algorithms draw people to certain events rather than others, while the blue current position arrow on Google Maps "orients the viewer in space" (Sennett).[89] This is all not

FIGURE 35 Downtown Los Angeles reimagined as pedestrian paradise in Spike Jonze's *Her* (screen capture from film, © Annapurna Pictures, 2013, all rights reserved).

immediately *visible* in city life, but it is *felt*. I am reminded of Edgar Allen Poe's 1840 short story "The Man of the Crowd," in which the protagonist first observes the crowd from behind a café window, upon which he joins the bustle and changes with it. YOU'VE CHANGED. In the platformized city, people increasingly move and associate in dividualizing streams that are personalized and automated at once. Clouded, the crowd is reoriented little by little by a market-driven platform logic. An open posthuman city resists this logic and de-clouds individual and collective life, allowing people's minds to wander along with their feet.

An open posthuman city is a feminist and anti-racist city where traditionally marginalized groups can take up space. In *Feminist City*, Leslie Kern warns us to not be too nostalgic for the pre-smartphone city and its chance encounters. After all, the reality of "this Jane Jacobs-esque scene" also hid a wide range of exclusions.[90] Kern refers to James Baldwin, who wrote about the same Greenwich Village as Jacobs, but where, as a queer Black man, he had a very different experience than her idyll of the sidewalk ballet. Kern argues that we need to be careful idealizing neighborhoods prior to their gentrification "and notice who is missing from that picture."[91] Elsewhere in her book, Kern argues that digital technologies like smartphones may allow women "to assert their presence in space." She writes not to be fantasizing about a world where people just snap selfies and stay isolated in their bubbles. But she also defends people's freedom to do so, and to, more generally speaking, be alone in the city without being harassed. This freedom, she writes, "is foundational to the kind of city where people will *want* to socialize with one another and interact fully with the environment."[92] In other words, a feminist city is a city firmly rooted in a culture of consent, making it possible for people to talk to strangers. I would argue that, ideally, this culture of consent also extends to the digital platforms mediating the modern urban experience (see Chapter 4, CONSENT).

An open feminist city is a city "without a 'master' plan that in fact resists the lure of mastery"[93] (Figure 36). As we have seen, Sidewalk Toronto claimed a people-first approach, starting its design process with *empathizing* with the Torontonians. In reality, however, Sidewalk Toronto *did* follow a Master plan, driven by a transhumanist view of human life in need of enhancement. As argued in Chapter 1, PRESENCE, this transhuman in fact comes down to an old-fashioned Cartesian cis male,

FIGURE 36 Painting Toronto (2015, photo by the author, artwork by Women Paint Toronto).

white, bourgeois, heterosexual individual. Sidewalk Toronto would have been designed for this Man.

An open city is a co-produced city. Sennett calls for a process of open city design, in which makers and dwellers together generate plans. This is different from the faux public conversations Sidewalks Labs staged in Toronto. In fact, these "town hall" meetings neatly fit Sennett's description of how citizen consultation should *not* be done: "There is usually a document, which almost no one in the room has read, accompanied viva voce by a slide presentation" while "a raised rostrum facing rows of chairs transforms the public into spectators."[94] This was *exactly* the setting at the St. Lawrence Center of the Arts in November 2017, with the only difference that there was no document, as Sidewalk kept its cards to its chest. And true, Sidewalk eventually also set up a participatory space called "307," named after its location on 307 Lake Shore Boulevard East, but only as a hands-on extension of its public relations campaign. As Shannon Mattern writes about 307, "'participation' is now deployed as part of a public performance wherein the *aesthetics* of collaboration signify democratic process, without always providing the real thing."[95] That real thing is only facilitated when the room for discussion is *actually* public, and people are actually engaged as a creative collective, rather than as content creators.

An open city facilitates public and common conversation, and invests in infrastructures for such conversation, whether in city halls, libraries, neighborhood centers, outside public spaces, and online public forums. These conversational infrastructures need to be built on the understanding that people live not only in material structures but also in discourses. Ideally, such social conversations are intersectional, bringing together people from different social groups and walks of life around topics that blur the personal and the political. Also ideally, these conversations are facilitated by people themselves. The Jane's Walk initiative that was set up in the wake of Jacobs's death is a great example. As its website reads, "Jane's Walk is a tool to create and encourage conversation … The design is intentionally open, serving as a global container for ideas, exploration, and discovery."[96] At the same time, it is important that such people-up initiatives are also somewhat institutionalized, so I agree with Sennett's perspective on urban infrastructure. Because in order for city conversations to be actually inclusive, and to make sure that also less economically privileged and culturally empowered voices are heard, it is crucial to actively reach out to groups who may otherwise be left out of the conversation.

An open city gives room to art and expression. This starts by eliminating corporate advertising from public space, thereby making that space more public. Imagine a city without advertising. This may sound utopian, but in 2017 the French city of Grenoble replaced billboards by trees. As legal scholar Ramsi Woodcock commented: "Our lived environment is an education in itself … Billboards are the chimneys of the mind. It's time we do away with this mind polluting infrastructure."[97] How inspiring it would be if a city like Toronto liberated itself from advertising! It would create space for imagination.

Above all, an open city is an inclusive city, a city for everybody and created by everybody, to paraphrase Jacobs. Platformized city designs such as Sidewalk Toronto are the opposite of inclusivity, despite the reference to "inclusive growth" in its masterplan title. As Ben Green writes in *The Smart Enough City,* currently most smart city architecture is "fundamentally undemocratic," creating "massive information and power asymmetries that favor governments and companies over those they track and analyze, breeding impotence and subjugation within society."[98] To this one can add that smart city projects are usually gentrifying projects, in which investors profit at the expense of poorer populations who are driven out of neighborhoods. An open city resists this colonization of everyday dwelling. It resists gentrification and datafication while it also articulates their intersection. As Wark writes, the struggle for what Lefebvre called the "right to the city" should expand its scope to a "right to the stack" (i.e., the increasingly platformized city).[99] Such a posthuman urban struggle targets real estate investors and platform corporations alike.

In sum, an open posthuman city is a decolonizing city that acknowledges and organizes against the exploitation of communal life.

Toronto

The name TORONTO *first appears in the historical record as the "lac de Taranteau" on a map of southern Ontario produced in 1670 by Father Rene de Brehant de Galimee. Interestingly, the name referred to Lake Simcoe and not the area known as Toronto today.*

French "courieurs de bois" used the term but it clearly is not French. One must look to the native languages spoken in the region to see whether there is a clue to its origins. How did the name get moved south to Toronto?
JOHN STECKLEY, "TORONTO OR IS THAT TARANTEAU"[100]

Before addressing Steckley's question of how Toronto obtained its name, let's return one last time to Sidewalk Toronto, being a recent episode in the city's long colonial history. Ironically, Sidewalk's own discourse includes the perfect angle on Big Tech's colonizing logic. As stated in this chapter's section SMARTPHONE, Sidewalk's citizen engagement event in November 2017 started with a land acknowledgment: "The land on which we are standing …" Similarly, Sidewalk's *Toronto Tomorrow* plan opens with the words that

> Sidewalk Labs recognizes that this land we now call Toronto has been the site of human activity for over 15,000 years; we are within the Treaty Lands and claimed Territory of the Mississaugas of the Credit … We are mindful of a history of broken treaties, and of the urgent need to work continuously towards reconciliation, and we are grateful for the opportunity to live and work on this land.[101]

Such land acknowledgment is good custom in Canada. A land acknowledgment is a brief reflection on colonial history and as a reckoning of colonialism's lasting effects in the present. Ideally, a land acknowledgment also is a speech act that incites reparations. Yet what happens to these words when they are co-opted by a corporation that seeks to venture into that very land in order to develop new ways of extracting value from human activity?

The answer has been provided by the course of events. Had Sidewalk actually been able to build Quayside and the IDEA district, these words would have simply become part of its overall vague speak, that is the ideological language through which it sought to placate the people of Toronto. But since reality decided otherwise, these words retroactively stand out as a beacon of hope, saying that sometimes people's resistance prevails over corporate power.

Sidewalk Toronto may have been averted, but in many respects the platformized city is already a reality: from Google's mapping of urban space and neighborhood policing by means of WhatsApp to the distribution of everything on so-called "sharing" platforms (housing, rides, meals, labor, love).[102] In this increasingly platformized reality, life becomes frictionless, like a stream.

Speaking of streams, in the early eighteenth century the name "Toronto" traveled down the Humber River. The name was born at Lake Simcoe in Southern Ontario, about a hundred kilometers upstream from Lake Ontario and what is now Toronto. In the first half of the seventeenth century, the Lake Simcoe region was populated by the Huron peoples, who used the word "Ouentaronk," which means "poles that cross." Around 1650, the Huron were driven out by the Iroquois Confederacy, who started to refer to Lake Simcoe by "Taronto," which is Mohawk for "where there are trees or poles in the water." These poles were of a fish weir, a system of poles and nets, crossing the Narrows, a body of fast-flowing water. Fish swimming past the poles would get caught in the nets. In 1670, the name "Toronto" first appeared on French maps, which referred to Lake Simcoe as "lac de Taranteau" or "Tarontos Lac." In subsequent decades the name detached itself from its origins, swimming down with the fish escaping the nets. Toronto historian John Steckley explains:

> It began as an infrequent copy error, old maps and descriptions of canoe routes were copied by hand and circulated widely and transcription errors could survive unquestioned for years. In the 1720s, "Toronto" became associated with a post by the mouth of the Humber River, the starting place for the "Carrying Place," the canoe and portage route from Lake Ontario to the waters that flowed into the Upper Great Lakes.[103]

Traveling back to the turn of the 2020s, the image of fish caught in the nets sticks as a metaphor for life in the platform society. We could further extend this metaphor with the fish processing plant that, as Sidewalk writes in *Toronto Tomorrow*, "for most of the twentieth century" was a key landmark of Quayside as "a working waterfront," and which was subsequently transformed by Sidewalk Labs into its 307 center for vague speak. In this center, and inspired by the fish washing, Sidewalk *public*-washed its technocolonial aspirations with words that sound like "transparency" and "democracy," but that in reality undermined democracy as an open-ended process of collective freedom. Technocolonialism is a reality, but Sidewalk Toronto did not become part of it. In the struggle against technocolonialism, let's take inspiration from the small fish, the Torontonians who stood up to Big Net.

Notes

1. Jane Jacobs, *The Death and Life of Great American Cities* (New York: Vintage Books, 1992), 238.
2. Jacobs, *The Death and Life of Great American Cities*, 50.
3. Anastasia Loukaitou-Sideris and Renia Ehrenfeucht, *Sidewalks: Conflict and Negotiation over Public Space* (Cambridge, MA: The MIT Press, 2009), 8.
4. Daniel L. Doctoroff, "Reimaging Cities from the Internet Up," *Sidewalk Talk* (November 30, 2016), accessed October 25, 2024, https://medium.com/sidewalk-talk/reimagining-cities-from-the-internet-up-5923d6be63ba.
5. Doctoroff, "Reimaging Cities from the Internet Up."
6. Sidewalk Labs, *MIDP* [Master Innovation and Development Plan] *Volume 0: The Overview* (*Toronto Tomorrow: A New Approach for Inclusive Growth*) (2019), 116-19, accessed March 1, 2020, https://www.sidewalklabs.com/Toronto.
7. Daniel L. Doctoroff, "Why We're No Longer Pursuing the Quayside Project—and What's Next for Sidewalk Labs," *Sidewalk Talk* (7 May 2020), accessed October 25, 2024, https://medium.com/sidewalk-talk/why-were-no-longer-pursuing-the-quayside-project-and-what-s-next-for-sidewalk-labs-9a61de3fee3a.
8. Ellen P. Goodman and Julia Powles, "Urbanism under Google: Lessons from Sidewalk Toronto," *Fordham Law Review* 88 (2019): 457–98, p. 466.
9. Leyland Cecco, "'Surveillance Capitalism': Critic Urges Toronto to Abandon Smart City Project," *The Guardian* (May 7, 2020), accessed October 25, 2024, https://www.theguardian.com/technology/2020/may/07/google-sidewalk-labs-toronto-smart-city-abandoned.
10. Goodman and Powles, "Urbanism under Google," 487.
11. Goodman and Powles, "Urbanism under Google," 487.
12. Jane Jacobs, *The Death and Life of Great American Cities* (New York: Vintage Books, 1992), 50.
13. Jane's Walk, "Revisiting the Jane's Walk Principles in 2021" (2021), accessed November 22, 2021, https://janeswalk.org/new-principles.

14 Ditte Hvas Mortensen, "Stage 1 in the Design Thinking Process: Empathise with Your Users," *Interaction Design Foundation* (July 2020), accessed October 25, 2024, https://www.interaction-design.org/literature/article/stage-1-in-the-design-thinking-process-empathise-with-your-users.

15 Interaction Design Foundation, "What Is Design Thinking," *Interaction Design Thinking*, accessed October 25, 2024, https://www.interaction-design.org/literature/topics/design-thinking; Rikke Friis Dam and Teo Yu Siang, "Design Thinking: Get a Quick Overview of the History," Interaction Design Foundation (2020), accessed October 25, 2024, https://www.interaction-design.org/literature/article/design-thinking-get-a-quick-overview-of-the-history.

16 Sidewalk Toronto, "Introducing Sidewalk Toronto" (video) (October 17, 2017), accessed October 25, 2024, https://www.youtube.com/watch?v=xQYSy8w9j5c.

17 Jathan Sadowski and Roy Bendor, "Selling Smartness: Corporate Narratives and the Smart City as a Sociotechnical Imaginary," *Science, Technology, and Human Values* 44.3 (2019): 540–63, pp. 540–1.

18 Ebenezer Howard, *Garden Cities of Tomorrow* (London: Swan Sonnenschein, 2014), accessed October 25, 2024, https://www.gutenberg.org/files/46134/46134-h/46134-h.htm.

19 Cited in Anthony M. Townsend, *Smart Cities: Big Data, Civic Hackers, and the Quest for a New Utopia* (New York: W. W. Norton & Company, 2014), 96–7.

20 Jacobs, *Death and Life*, 13.

21 Jacobs, *Death and Life*, 79, 80.

22 Jacobs, *Death and Life*, 98.

23 Cited in Laura Bliss, "Meet the Jane Jacobs of the Smart Cities Age," *Citylab* (December 21, 2018), accessed October 25, 2024, https://www.bloomberg.com/news/articles/2018-12-21/toronto-privacy-advocate-bianca-wylie-v-sidewalk-labs.

24 Sidewalk Labs, *Public Engagement* (brochure) (2019), accessed March 1, 2020, https://sidewalk-toronto-ca.storage.googleapis.com/wp-content/uploads/2019/06/21195824/The-Public-Engagement-Process-for-Sidewalk-Toronto.pdf.

25 Sidewalk Toronto, "Sidewalk Toronto Community Town Hall" (11/1) (video) (2018) (accessed October 25, 2024, https://www.youtube.com/watch?v=ycZDGwXVKJ8.

26 Sidewalk Toronto, "Sidewalk Toronto Community Town Hall" (video).

27 Bliss, "Meet the Jane Jacobs of the Smart Cities Age."

28 Sidewalk Labs, *MIDP Vol. 0*, 18–19.

29 Sidewalk Labs, *MIDP Vol. 0*, 91.
30 Sidewalk Labs, *MIDP Vol. 0*, 94.
31 Sidewalk Labs, *MIDP Vol. 0*, 95.
32 Sidewalk Labs, *MIDP* [Master Innovation and Development Plan] *Volume 1: The Plans: Introduction and Chapter 1: Quayside* (*Toronto Tomorrow: A New Approach for Inclusive Growth*) (2019), 72, 126, 189.
33 Sidewalk Labs, *MIDP Vol. 0*, 193.
34 Sidewalk Labs, *MIDP Vol. 1*, 75.
35 Raymond Wong, "Sidewalk Labs Toronto—A Brief History" (video) (2021), accessed October 25, 2024, https://www.youtube.com/watch?v=Nmjtf9v-YFQ.
36 Matthew Stewart, "The Deceptive Platform Utopianism of Google's Sidewalk Labs," *Failed Architecture* (July 25, 2019), accessed October 25, 2024, https://failedarchitecture.com/the-deceptive-platform-utopianism-of-googles-sidewalk-labs.
37 Sidewalk Toronto, "Sidewalk Toronto Community Town Hall" (video).
38 Rit Aggarwala cited in Elizabeth Woyke, "A Smarter Smart City," *MIT Technology Review* (February 21, 2018), accessed October 25, 2024, https://www.technologyreview.com/2018/02/21/145310/a-smarter-smart-city.
39 Bianca Wylie, "Debrief on Sidewalk Toronto Public Meeting 3" (August 20, 2018), accessed October 25, 2024, https://biancawylie.medium.com/debrief-on-sidewalk-toronto-public-meeting-3-a-master-class-in-gaslighting-and-arrogance-c1c5dd918c16.
40 Google TechTalks, "Sidewalk Labs: Reimagining the City as a Digital Platform" (video) (2016), accessed October 25, 2024, https://www.youtube.com/watch?v=bPu8HvD7d9U.
41 Tarleton Gillespie, "The Politics of 'Platforms,'" *New Media & Society* 12:3 (2010): 3.
42 Malcolm Johnston, "Q&A: Dan Doctoroff on Building the Neighbourhood of Tomorrow," *Toronto Life* (April 9, 2018), accessed October 25, 2024, https://torontolife.com/city/qa-dan-doctoroff-building-neighbourhood-tomorrow.
43 Goodman and Powles, "Urbanism under Google," 484.
44 Townsend, *Smart Cities*, xii.
45 Eric Jaffe, "Zoning: The Legal and Social Codes of Urban Planning," *Sidewalk Labs* blog (September 21, 2017), accessed October 25, 2024, https://www.sidewalklabs.com/insights/zoning-the-legal-and-social-codes-of-urban-planning.
46 Sidewalk Labs, *MIDP Vol. 1*, 234.

47 Sidewalk Labs, *Project Vision* (October 17, 2017), https://storage.googleapis.com/sidewalk-toronto-ca/wp-content/uploads/2017/10/13210553/Sidewalk-Labs-Vision-Sections-of-RFP-Submission.pdf [accessed October 25, 2024, https://perma.cc/6ZTMQ6J9], 54.

48 Sidewalk Labs, *MIPD Vol. 1*, 93.

49 Sidewalk Labs, *MIPD Vol. 1*, 93.

50 Bliss, "Meet the Jane Jacobs of the Smart Cities Age."

51 Goodman and Powles, "Urbanism under Google," 472-3.

52 Tom Cardoso and Josh O'Kane, "Sidewalk Labs Document Reveals Company's Early Vision for Data Collection, Tax Powers, Criminal Justice," *The Globe and Mail* (October 30, 2019), accessed October 25, 2024, https://www.theglobeandmail.com/business/article-sidewalk-labs-document-reveals-companys-early-plans-for-data.

53 Comment (October 31, 2019) by user "ewok_chief" in thread "Google's Sidewalk Labs leaked 'yellow book' reveals company's early vision for data collection, tax powers, criminal justice—case studies for Toronto, Detroit, Denver, and Alameda," accessed October 31, 2019, https://www.reddit.com/r/worldnews/comments/dpofov/googles_sidewalk_labs_leaked_yellow_book_reveals.

54 Cardoso and O'Kane, "Sidewalk Labs Document."

55 Google TechTalks, "Sidewalk Labs: Reimaging the City as a Digital Platform" (video) (2016).

56 Cardoso and O'Kane, "Sidewalk Labs Document."

57 Google TechTalks, "Sidewalk Labs."

58 Google TechTalks, "Sidewalk Labs."

59 McKenzie Wark, *Sensoria: Thinkers for the Twenty-First Century* (London: Verso, 2020).

60 Gerald Raunig, *Dividuum: Machinic Capitalism and Molecular Revolution* (South Pasadena: Semiotext(e), 2016), 11.

61 Couldry and Mejias, *Costs of Connection*, 161.

62 Deleuze, *Negotiations*, 177.

63 Benjamin Bratton, *The Stack: On Software and Sovereignty* (Cambridge, MA: MIT Press, 2016), 52.

64 Klaas Kuitenbrouwer, "The Stack and the Post-Human User: An Interview with Benjamin Bratton," *Garden of Machines* (February 28, 2015), accessed October 25, 2024, https://tuinvanmachines.hetnieuweinstituut.nl/en/stack-and-posthuman-user-interview-benjamin-bratton.

65 Bratton, *The Stack*, 256.

66 Wark, *Sensoria*, 195.
67 Wark, *Sensoria*, 195.
68 Raunig, *Dividuum*, 123.
69 Raunig, *Dividuum*, 25-6.
70 Karl Marx, *Grundrisse: Foundations of the Critique of Political Economy* (Rough Draft), trans. Martin Nicolaus (London: Penguin Books, 1993), 692.
71 Mbembe, *Critique of Black Reason*, 4.
72 Lazzarato, *Signs and Machines*, 12.
73 Lazzarato, *Signs and Machines*, 26.
74 Deleuze, *Negotiations*, 181-2.
75 Gilbert Simondon, *Individuation in Light of Notions of Form and Information*, trans. Taylor Adkins (Minneapolis: University of Minnesota Press, 2020), 31.
76 Matt Bluemink, "The Politics of Modulation: Simondon's Influence on Deleuze's 'Societies of Control,'" *Blue Labyrinths* 3 (2021), accessed October 25, 2024, https://bluelabyrinths.com/2021/03/17/the-politics-of-modulation-simondons-influence-on-deleuzes-societies-of-control.
77 Georg Simmel, *Simmel on Culture*, eds. David Frisby and Mike Featherstone (London: Sage Publications, 1997), 183-4.
78 Sarah Barns, *Platform Urbanism: Negotiating Platform Ecosystems in Connected Cities* (Singapore: Palgrave Macmillan, 2020), 14.
79 Couldry and Mejias, *Costs of Connection*, 158.
80 Mbembe, *Critique of Black Reason*, 5-6.
81 Rosi Braidotti, "A Theoretical Framework for the Critical Posthumanities," *Theory, Culture & Society* 36.6 (2019): 31-61, p. 4.
82 Richard Sennett, *Building and Dwelling: Ethics for the City* (London: Penguin, 2018), 241.
83 Sennett, *Building and Dwelling*, 242.
84 Sennett, *Building and Dwelling*, 240-1.
85 Sennett, *Building and Dwelling*, 151-2.
86 Ahmed, *Queer Phenomenology*, 1.
87 Ahmed, *Queer Phenomenology*, 157.
88 Rebecca Solnit, *Wanderlust: A History of Walking* (London: Granta Publications, 2001), 176.
89 Sennett, *Building and Dwelling*, 185.

90 Leslie Kern, *Feminist City* (London: Verso, 2021), 147.

91 Kern, *Feminist City*, 147.

92 Kern, *Feminist City*, 94–5.

93 Kern, *Feminist City*, 149.

94 Sennett, *Building and Dwelling*, 243.

95 Shannon Mattern, "Post-It Note City," *Places* (February 2020), accessed October 25, 2024, https://placesjournal.org/article/post-it-note-city.

96 Jane's Walk, "Revisiting the Jane's Walk Principles" in 2021.

97 Ramsey Woodcock cited in VPRO television, *Tegenlicht: Rebellen tegen Reclame* (April 26, 2020), accessed October 25, 2024, https://www.vpro.nl/programmas/tegenlicht/kijk/afleveringen/2019-2020/reclame-rebellen.html.

98 Ben Green, "The Responsible City," in *The Smart Enough City* (Cambridge, MA: MIT Press, 2019), accessed October 25, 2024, https://smartenoughcity.mitpress.mit.edu/pub/yvyv9j2i/release/1.

99 Wark, *Sensoria*.

100 Cited in "Origin of the Name of Toronto," *Toronto.ca*, accessed October 25, 2024, https://archive.ph/GhALr#selection-195.8-195.123.

101 Sidewalk Labs, *MIDP Vol. 0*, 5.

102 See for example: Ronald van Steden and Shanna Mehlbaum, "Do-It-Yourself Surveillance: The Practices and Effects of WhatsApp Neighbourhood Crime Prevention Groups," *Crime, Media, Culture: An International Journal* 18.4.

103 Cited in "Origin of the Name of Toronto," *Toronto.ca*.

3 LEARNING

An ABC to De-Google Education

Through dialogue ... a new term emerges: teacher-student with student-teachers ... Here no one teaches another, nor is ANYONE self-taught. People teach each other, mediated by the world.
                        PAOLO FREIRE, *PEDAGOGY OF THE OPPRESSED* (1970)[1]

Anyone

Google infiltrates all and everything: every single market, every niche, and also fields of life that are *not* markets, or that shouldn't be, like love and learning. Love is the topic of the next chapter, this chapter is about learning, about the love of learning, and about its platformization. The reason I focus on Google is that this company has the most outspoken educational ideology.

    The two questions organizing the chapter are: How is learning colonized by Google, at school and in society in general? And how can we liberate learning from the company's adaptive classroom ideology as well as its personalized, "self-learning" algorithms (in particular Search and Google's generative language model Gemini)? The chapter calls to de-Google learning. To do so starts with becoming much more conscious of how the ideologies and algorithms of companies like Google affect our personal and collective associations.

    The chapter takes the form of an alphabet book consisting of twenty-six entries, from ANYONE to ZEN, this in play on Google's parent company Alphabet. This means entries are short, so let's dive right in. In 2020, Google's Education department launched "ANYWHERE SCHOOL," an online event to present its latest ed-tech. Seizing the Covid-19 era, when "dining tables became desks" and "school is no longer just one place," Google saw

FIGURE 37 Google's "Anywhere School" (screen capture from video, © Google for Education, 2022, all rights reserved).[2]

a unique opportunity to turn the new normal "into a better normal."[3] Take Practice Sets, a tool for interactive assignments (because "no two learning journeys are the same"). Or take Screencast, which allows teachers and students to share their laptop screens to the whiteboard. "ANYONE at your school can use Screencast," a promotional video says, "all you need is a Chromebook and something to say."[4] Combined, these tools "work together to transform teaching and learning so that every student and educator can pursue their personal potential."[5] The ambitions are high, because as one Google representative explains to another in a 2022 video for Anywhere School, Google's Chromebooks and the "cleanest cloud services" supports young people in their ambitions to be "our future agents of change, entrepreneurs, and innovators" in the face of the climate crisis (Figure 37).

With Google, learning thus becomes more adaptive and personal. Like everything else in the platform society, learning becomes a personalized stream tailored to the user. But Google's platformization of learning also standardizes learning. As Niels Kerssens and José van Dijck argue, Google lures schools into the walled garden of its platform ecosystems, which poses a risk of "challenging education as a public good."[6] The Googlization of learning also challenges pedagogy's emancipatory promise. At first sight, Anywhere School is all about emancipation: Google's adaptative learning model promises to liberate students and teachers from what Paolo Freire calls the "banking model of education," in which teachers deposit knowledge in their students. On a closer look, however, Google's data-driven approach to learning and KNOWLEDGE is not that emancipatory. Instead, Google contributes to a control society in which students, teachers, and all other people are interpellated as LIFELONG Google users. It is time, therefore, to de-Google and to create truly common learning spaces, where, to speak with Freire, anyone can be a TEACHER and student at any time.

Books

Google has always been a self-contradictory company. On the one hand, it wants to live by its "don't be evil" credo (for a long time Google's official motto).[7] On the other hand, Google makes money by selling advertisements. As Evgeny Morozov writes, "Google's founders were never excited about advertising but were eventually forced to accept it as a necessary evil."[8] Google's founders were always more excited about changing the course of human history through "moonshot" projects (see also x). For example, in 2002 Google co-founder Larry Page began wondering if it was possible to make every book in the world searchable online. That way "all of the world's knowledge would be accessible to every person."[9] Two years later, Google launched Print, soon dubbed Google Books.

Google Books and Google for Education were born under the same constellation. In a 2019 video on the occasion of the fifteenth anniversary of Books, we meet a genealogy researcher and a university librarian. "Google Books gives me access to records and information I would not necessarily be able to get," says the researcher. "Google Books really has democratized access," the librarian adds (Figure 38).[10] The resonance between Google Books and Anywhere School is clear: Google breaks down barriers to people's curiosity to expand their world and discover new information and knowledge. How could there be any "*evil*" in this mission?

Well there is, because at Google advertising pays for the company's daydreams. The "good" of Google Books is entangled with the company's core business, which is selling ads. Through Books, Google has expanded its hegemonic position. As Jean-Christophe Plantin

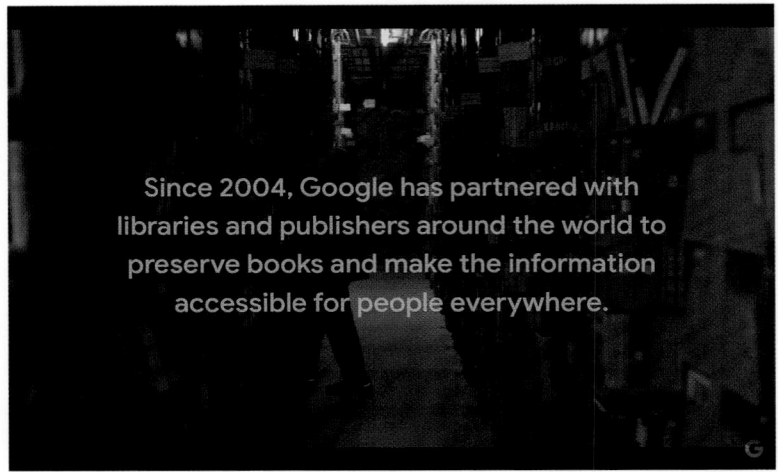

FIGURE 38 Celebrating Google Books (screen capture from video, © Google for Education, 2020, all rights reserved).[11]

et al. argue, although "Google's platform logic creates real benefits for both users and third-party developers ... the fact remains that control of the platform puts Google in an unparalleled position of dominance, increasing its power to shape lives as well as knowledge."[12]

One way Google has shaped lives through Books is by tracking its users while they browse the online stacks. The data collected have helped Google to further tailor its ad business, and to also develop its "self-learning" technology, including AI chatbot Gemini.[13] Google Books has little to do with democracy. The company uses public knowledge for corporate gain. To de-Google learning is to stand for actually PUBLIC knowledge infrastructures free of market interests.

Classroom

Google's undermining of public values continues in the classroom. As we read on the company's blog, *The Keyword*, in 2006 Google asked itself: What if we brought our "suite of productivity tools" to schools?[14] In that same year, Google launched Apps for Education, later called G Suite. Five years later, Google introduced Chromebook, a low-cost Android-based laptop that mainly revolves around web applications. As *The*

New York Times reports, in order to spread its pedagogical philosophy, Google began inviting school administrators to its offices to hear the company's view that technology "breaks down barriers between rich and poor students." In response to this claim, the *Times* cites children's advocacy group representative Bill Fitzgerald, who calls Google's equity argument self-serving. "It centers learning on technology, not students. It is a very narrow lens on equity that leaves out things like student-teacher ratios."[15]

In 2014, Google introduced Classroom, "your all-in-one place for teaching and learning."[16] Within a decade, Classroom reported over 150 million users worldwide. A program manager reports that while "we first built Classroom to … help teachers build stronger connections with students and give them back time," during the Covid-19 pandemic many schools started using Classroom "as their learning management system (LMS)."[17] According to other inside views Classroom always already was a management system by design. Jonathan Rochelle (who started Google's Apps for Education) and Zach Yeskel (a Google product manager and former math teacher) write that they envisioned Classroom as a "'mission control' dashboard where teachers could more efficiently manage tasks like assigning and correcting homework."[18]

As a mission control center, Classroom allows teachers to monitor students in new ways. In "The Platformization of the Classroom" Priya Kumar et al. analyze the Chromebook management tool GoGuardian, which allows teachers to track students' laptop activity and remotely view their screens. Kumar et al. write: "Ostensibly teachers use monitoring to foster educated, well-behaved students. But … the value of platform-supported monitoring may lie in its ability to *generate data* about educated, well-behaved students."[19] Similarly, Carlo Perrotta et al. argue that Classroom "actively configures pedagogy as a controllable activity and the classroom as a programmable space."[20]

Google's presence in the classroom radically transforms our understanding of what a classroom is, or should be. This does not happen inadvertently, as an unwelcome side-effect. It happens very much in the open, as through Google's discourse of the classroom as a space that needs to be optimized and controlled. In this process, teachers and students are interpellated as users within the Google ecosystem. Teachers and students learn to see Google as a neutral knowledge window on the world. To de-Google learning is to resist Google's self-branding as a neutral knowledge platform.

Doodle

Google's discussion of learning as a "mission" seemingly contradicts the company's fun and playful side, but actually the two go very well together. Let me illustrate this through *doodles*: the drawings and animations in variation on the company's logo that appear on Google Search. Often, these doodles celebrate a person, anniversary, or holiday, like Teacher's Day. As a Google Doodle team lead says: "It's just an opportunity to humanize the web, an opportunity to have fun with our corporate identity."[21]

Google's doodling takes us back to 1998, the year of the company's founding. In order to announce their attendance at the Burning Man festival, Larry Page and Sergey Brin drew a stick figure (the Burning Man logo) behind Google's second "o." Two years later, on the occasion of Bastille Day in France, Google ornated its logo with fireworks. The Bastille Doodle proved a hit among users, upon which its designer Dennis Hwang was appointed "chief doodler." Over time, Doodle grew into an entire department with as mission to "bring smiles to the faces of Google users all around the world."[22]

To doodle is to scribble idly or absent-mindedly. Doodling happens in the margins of a notebook when a student daydreams, or because drawing figures and patterns actually allows them to pay *closer* attention. Anyone can doodle but there is also an art to doodling. As Dutch doodle artist Myrtle Swchwrm (*sic*) explains, to doodle is to draw with one's unconscious. "You're just always drawing yourself."[23]

Google has always been very interested in people's unconscious processes, in their wanderings while they browse the web or navigate the city. As Shoshana Zuboff writes in *Surveillance Capitalism*, in 2000 Google ventured into virgin territory when it began using behavioral surplus to target advertising to individual users. This surplus consists of data collected on the basis of user experience that goes beyond functionality of the product and service. "It was on the strength of this *behavioral surplus* that the young company would find its way to the 'sustained and exponential profits' that would be necessary for survival."[24]

So, in the same year that Google started doodling for real, it also started to monetize the user unconscious. Google's doodling is not as aimless as it may seem: the company's celebration of *all* the national holidays and inspirational people's birthdays fits well with its branded self-image of a company that claims to be invested in democracy and education. To de-Google is to see through the company's playful face and recognize its exploitation of people's desire for learning.

Educare

Google's educational mission is of a double nature. On the one hand, "no matter what learning looks like," Google is "here to help," as is the closing tagline to a video in which Google celebrates its response to the Covid-19 era. In the video, Google takes us on a tour around the world, swiftly moving from Chromebooks solving the problems of locked-down classrooms to the broader message that "technology can level the playing field for children" (Figures 39, 40, and 41).[25] On the other hand, Google wants to transform. As far as helping is concerned, Google wants to "meet teachers' changing needs" and "enhance class instruction"; it wants to "make collaboration easier, streamline instruction, and keep your learning environment secure"; and it wants to make education more accessible.[26]

There is a clear ideological side to Google's helpful attitude, because simultaneously Google wants to transform the nature of education, "equip the next generation with future skills," "bring flexible innovation to your school at scale," and "transform teaching and learning so that every student and educator can pursue their personal potential."[27] As Neil Selwyn, author of *Is Technology Good for Education?* observes: "Many tech companies look at schools as incredibly inefficient, even non-functional. They would very much like to reinvent school for the twenty-first century, by reforming in a corporate manner: streamlined and supported by technology."[28]

According to this tech-on-ed view, education should be less cognitive and instead more adaptive and skill based. Google claims that "more than 65% of learners will work in jobs that don't even exist today, but many aren't yet developing the problem-solving skills and basic digital competencies that they'll need to be prepared for that future."[29] This is a very narrow and instrumental view on education.

Education derives from the Latin *educare*, which means to *lead out*, *externalize*, and *reveal*. Etymologically speaking, education (including self-education) thus is the process by which people develop themselves

No one knew what it would look like

FIGURES 39 TO 41 Google's response to the Covid-19 pandemic (screen capture from video, © Google for Education, 2022, all rights reserved).[30]

as persons and citizens. This broad understanding of education gets increasingly lost in the platform society, the notion that, as José van Dijck et al. argue, education also is "a public investment meant to foster knowledgeable and critical citizens and enable them to participate in a democracy."[31] Google repeatedly claims to act in the name of democracy and the common good. Yet by pushing its techno-solutionism to the education system, Google actually erodes that system's potential to prepare children as humans who are able to develop a critical perspective on the powers shaping the world (including Google's power over people's access to information). As Internet Archive founder Brewster Kale states in a 2006 documentary about Google: "The danger to education of having only one point of view on information is that everyone will start to have just that point of view. It will be self-reinforcing, and that is not how one develops critical thinking."[32] To de-Google is to shatter this view of Google as an all-encompassing window on the world.

Find

So, what is Google's point of view on INFORMATION? And how do Google's algorithms "learn" to sort the web's information? Google has always had a lot of confidence in its ability to search, hence the "I'm feeling lucky" button on its home page. This button takes the user directly to the top-ranked web page for a search. The button is also branding. As John Durham Peters argues, even though the small percent of searches done through the "lucky" button bypasses the advertised content, the button "amply repays the lost income by maintaining [Google's] oracular aura and geeky charm."[33]

For a long time, the basis of Google Search was PageRank, the link analysis algorithm that Page and Brin developed in 1996 at Stanford University. PageRank sorts web pages on the basis of the quality and quantity of links pointing to a page. Google explains that "the underlying assumption is that more important websites are likely to receive more links from other websites."[34] Google thus attaches value to hyperlinks, treating them as "votes" for a web page. As computer scientist Jon Kleinberg explains: "hyperlinks encode a considerable amount of latent human judgment ... the creator p, by including a link to page q, has in some measure *conferred authority* on q."[35]

There are two main problems at the core of Google's operations. The first is that Google exploits the common knowledge created and shared by people, online and also offline (see BOOKS). Google does not merely make this knowledge searchable, it also uses it to run its advertising business. Second, in essence PageRank and its successors operate as popularity contests. Yves Citton calls PageRank an "attention aggregation machine," while Andrea Righi argues that PageRank "involves a previously created, disputable, and self-valorizing knowledge."[36] As a result, Google confirms existing biases and reinforces oppressive social relationships. Or as Safiya Umoja Noble writes in *Algorithms of Oppression*, when an algorithmically crafted web search offers up racism and sexism as first results, this "reflects a corporate logic of either willful neglect or a profit imperative that makes money from racism and sexism."[37]

These problems are inherent to Google's core business. They should be enough reason also for educational institutions to not want to do business with Google, and to de-Google instead. In an ideal world, to de-Google means to not use any Google products at all (including Search and Maps). To many this may seem impossible, given Google's hegemony. This normalization of Google is precisely why de-Googling is necessary. To de-Google starts by learning how Google's hegemony reorients our associations, how we make sense of the world and find our bearings. To de-Google is to learn how to search with more simple, non-for-profit tools (e.g., search engine DuckDuckGo). To de-Google is also to facilitate spaces where people can find without searching. I don't mean a search engine that auto-suggests an answer to a QUERY before it has been fully articulated by the user, I mean spaces that facilitate chance encounters. To de-Google is to build and hold such spaces, and to stand for a culture of consent in which people can be open to chance (in the realization that all chance encounters are oriented by power).

Grading

My call to de-Google education is a call against making education more efficient. Instead, a truly radical education resists hegemonic power relations that recreate themselves through the school system. To de-Google education not just means to abandon Google Classroom, it also means to decolonize education from normative systems of discipline and control that interpellate people as "good" subjects.

A good place to start is grading. In "Against Grading" Carolina Alonso Bejarano and Stina Soderling write:

> Because of its disciplinary functions, grading cannot be a feminist practice ... Grading is one way in which a rhetoric of excellence is perpetuated, a rhetoric that enforces a capitalist ethic of production and profitability. Grading is also a means through which the liberatory power of social-justice oriented programs and departments is co-opted by the neoliberal university.[38]

Grading is a modern invention. In *Discipline and Punish*, Michel Foucault traces the practice of examination and grading back to the late eighteenth century. He shows how school became "a sort of apparatus of constant examination."[39] Whereas in the guild system the exam merely marked the end of an apprenticeship, in the modern school system examination and hierarchization of students became a permanent and integral part of the learning process. Foucault writes that "the examination in the school was a constant exchanger of knowledge."[40] On the one hand, examination guaranteed the transmission of knowledge from the teacher to the pupil (what Freire calls the banking system). On the other hand, pupils became the objects of knowledge who, through exams and ranking, were interpellated as individuals.

In our platform society, in which companies like Google have entered the educational field, the techniques of grading and examination are increasingly automated. Google Forms allows teachers to create automatically-scored quizzes, while Google Assignments is marketed as "your tireless grading companion [that] helps you save time with streamlined assignment workflow."[41] All of this is still child's play when compared to automated essay grading. In 2022, this holy grail of computerized easy grading still remained a technological challenge.[42] But now, in the era of generative language models, this is changing, with tools like the Gemini-driven GradeMate, which claims to revolutionize grading with "personalized, criteria-based feedback."[43]

Gemini was originally called Bard. William Shakespeare was a bard, and Gemini is a bit like having your own Shakespeare at your fingertips. The chatbot is there "to supercharge your imagination, boost your productivity, and bring your ideas to life."[44] The question is whether teachers in this new reality will still have the time and space to work with students on their writing. In order to create this writing spacetime, graded essay assignments are better abolished. Let's instead have writing *experiments*, like automatic writing exercises that spark reflection on how Gemini or ChatGPT "write." To de-Google learning is to reclaim writing from machines.

> ## EXPERIMENT WITHOUT TECH #3: AUTOMATIC WRITING
>
> For this third experiment you need paper and a pen or pencil. The exercise is done alone, but if you are with others, you can of course share your experiences and insights afterward. You may also take it as the jumping-off point for a conversation on the changing nature of writing in the algorithmic era. Now, get comfortable. If you are with others find a quiet spot. Sit however you like, reclined in a chair, at the table or cross-legged on the floor. Breathe, adopt a wide attention, and listen to the sounds in the room for a moment. Then take your paper and start writing without stopping. If nothing comes to mind, write anyway. You can always write that nothing comes to mind, and then associate from there. Don't think too much. The writing doesn't have to be good or bad or anything. Do this for three pages or fifteen minutes or so. Then stop. This was the first round. In the second round, you revisit what you just wrote, underlining, if you want with a different color, all things and thoughts that came from elsewhere or from someone else. This could be a thing someone has said to you (earlier that day or in a distant past), something you have read in a book or on Instagram, or something singing around in the cultural air. Is your writing really your own? Or are there also other internalized voices writing "through" you? And how do generative large language models like ChatGPT and Gemini "write"? Where do these algorithms get their ideas from? From you?

Hornbook

Armado. [To Holofernes]: Monsieur, are you not lett'red?
Moth: Yes, yes! He teaches boys the HORNBOOK. *What is a, b, spelt backward with the horn on his head?*
SHAKESPEARE, *LOVE'S LABOUR'S LOST* (1598)[45]

This chapter takes the form of an abecedarium. As with all abecedaria, the reader does not have to read from A to Z, even though that is how this chapter is built, with a nod to Google's parent company Alphabet. In reflection on that alphabet structure, the H is for hornbook. Hornbooks were used in Europe and the Americas between the fifteenth and eighteenth century. They were educational tools for children laid out as an abecedarium. Early hornbooks were the size of a smartphone and were made by printing letters onto paper or *vellum* (animal skin). The letters were protected from greasy fingers by a thin see-through "screen" made of animal horn, which then was attached to a wooden paddle. On other models, the letters were carved directly into the bone, or into metal.

Long before Anywhere School, hornbooks allowed children to learn the alphabet at home. Many hornbooks also contained vowel combinations (like "Ba," which is the answer to Moth's question in *Love's Labour's Lost*) or religious verse and prayer, like "Our Father" (Figure 42). To further spark the love of learning, hornbooks could also be made of edible material, such as gingerbread. As we read in the 1721 epic poem "Alma, or, The Progress of Mind" by Matthew Prior: "And that the Child may learn the better, / As he can name, he eats the Letter."[46]

Over the centuries, the name "hornbook" became synonymous with child education. For example, since 1924 there is *The Horn Book* magazine dedicated to children's literature (now found on hbook.com). The term "hornbook" is also used to refer to primers or introductory texts. In the United States, for instance, legal education hornbooks are one-volume overviews that discuss the law in a certain area, as the 2008 *Hornbook on Torts*. Other examples are *The Hobo's hornbook* from 1930 by George Milburn and Leah Bodine Drake's 1950 poem collection *A Hornbook for Witches* (see OWL).

This chapter is a hornbook in both its original meaning of abecedarium and that of primer. As a primer, the chapter introduces the reader to the

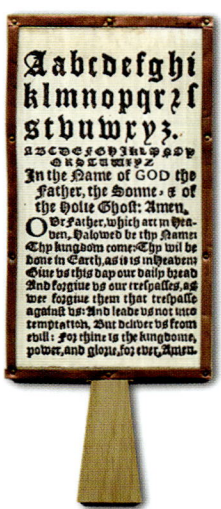
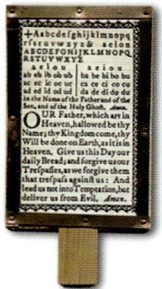

FIGURE 42 Reproduction of facsimiles part of Andrew W. Tuer's *History of the Horn-Book* (1896) (Work in public domain, image retrieved from Wikimedia Commons).[47]

art of de-Googling. I realize that the chapter is perhaps not the hands-on *How to?* that the "ABC" in the chapter title may lead the reader to expect. The reality is that Google's education and knowledge infrastructure has become so hegemonic that a few tricks and tactics won't do. To de-Google is to grasp how Google has colonized learning and to become more conscious of our scattered condition, as playfully captured by this chapter's alphabet structure.

Information

To return to my argument that Google colonizes human learning and knowledge production: essential to the company's strategy is to present itself as a mere neutral conduit for information. Google claims that it does not *create* information, but that it only makes information *available* (see BOOKS). This is not true. First of all, Google creates information by the way its algorithms sort information, perpetuating hegemonic social discourses (see FIND). Second, the company produces information in the form of user data. It is often said that user data are "mined" like coal or ore, but this extractive analogy is off, as it makes data seem a natural phenomenon. Instead, data are actively produced by tracking, tracing, and in that process transforming life, which serves as the "raw" material for the data industry.

Let's zoom in further on Google's discourse of information. In their article "Information We Collect: Surveillance and Privacy in the Implementation of Google Apps for Education" Maria Lindh and Jan Nolin analyze Google's privacy policies, both those directly related to Apps for Education and Google's general privacy policy. They argue that "the rhetorical aim of Google customer-oriented policy documents is to *disguise the business model* and to persuade the reader to understand Google as a free public service."[48] The authors signal, furthermore, a distinction that Google, in its privacy policy, makes between "data" and "information."

On the one hand, Google refers to "your data," "user data," "personal data," and "customer data." On the other hand, Google speaks of "collected information" or "information that you give us." Nowhere does Google clarify this distinction. Lindh and Nolin deduce, though, that whereas *data* refers to information "submitted, stored, sent or received via the Services by Customer, its Affiliates or End Users," *information* refers to people's behavior, including personal information, location information, and identifying cookies. The distinction is mostly rhetorical, allowing Google to "emphatically state that 'you own your data' and 'we do not sell your data,'" but in the meanwhile sell collected "information."[49]

This may also mean that even some user data gathered within Apps for Education are processed commercially, this despite Google's statement that "there are no ads in Google Workspace for Education core services, and [that] core service data is not used for advertising purposes."[50] Part of the problem with Google is that we have no way to verify this claim. Moreover, and regardless even of whether student data (or information gathered through Google's educational applications) are used for commercial purposes, the fact is that Google creates students and teachers as Google users. From an early age onwards, students are taught that "Google is not a conventional company" (as Page and Brin wrote in their original founders' letter).[51] Growing up with Google, many people may not see Google as a company at all, but as a service that is simply *there*. To de-Google education means to see Google as a company and to see that *we* users fuel its engines.

Joy

You experience joy when you fulfill it, when you realize one of your powers of action.

There is joy in de-Googling, because there is joy in becoming more conscious of how one's associations are affected by power. I don't want to deny the joy that may exist in a Google-mediated classroom, but I would argue that in the long run this joy is severely diminished by the fact of it being capitalized on by Google's algorithms.

I take my J for JOY from Gilles Deleuze, who in turn took it from Spinoza. In 1988 and 1989, Deleuze was filmed for the 8-hour *L'Abécédaire de Gilles Deleuze*, directed by Pierre-André Boutang and first aired on the French-German channel Arte in 1995 (the year of Deleuze's death). For his *Abécédaire*, Deleuze is interviewed from Animal to Zig Zag by the French journalist and his former student Claire Parnet. Having arrived at the "J" for "Joie," Parnet reminds Deleuze that he is particularly attached to this concept since "it's a Spinozist concept, and Spinoza turned joy into a concept of resistance and life."[52] Deleuze responds that "it comes down to saying that joy is everything that consists in fulfilling a power of action … realizing a power of action, causing a power of action to be fulfilled. But it's the word *puissance* that is ambiguous."

Building on Spinoza's distinction between *potestas* and *potentia*, Deleuze distinguishes between *pouvoir* and *puissance*. The former, *pouvoir*, refers to restrictive, disciplinary, controlling power, a power linked "to priests, to tyrants" (and "to judges," so Parnet adds). Deleuze also calls *pouvoir* a sad and "wicked" power. *Puissance*, in contrast, is a liberating life force: "It's the pleasure in conquest … but the conquest does not consist of enslaving people. Conquest is, for example, for a painter to conquer color."

Puissance also is philosophy. Two letters earlier, under the "H" for "History of Philosophy," Deleuze says that philosophy is "like color." Whereas a painter conquers and creates color, a philosopher conquers and creates concepts.

In *What Is Philosophy?* (*Qu'est-ce que la philosophie?*), Deleuze, together with Félix Guattari, refers to concepts as "centers of vibrations, each in itself and every one in relation to all the others."[53] Concepts are joyful vibrations. They allow the philosopher-student to expand their power of action, their power to affect and be affected. Concepts allow them to make *sense*: of the world, of power, and of how one is acted upon by the powers of this world. To do so is liberating, which is why philosophy shouldn't be difficult. Under the "D" for "Desire," Deleuze says that people mustn't think of concepts as abstract. Instead, concepts refer to things that are "extremely simple, extremely concrete." The only thing needed is problems, because "if you haven't found the problem to which a concept corresponds, everything stays abstract."

Take the concrete problem with Google's *pouvoir*. In order to understand how Google and Big Tech in general colonize people's *puissance* (their joy and joy of learning) we need an everyday philosophy that grasps how platformization affects our very orientations, how we move in and perceive the world, how we perceive ourselves. To de-Google learning is to liberate our movements and perceptions. To stay with Deleuze's painting analogy, to de-Google learning is to liberate ourselves from Google's white canvas and conquer our personal and collective palettes.

Knowledge

Google feeds on the joy of learning, both inside and outside the classroom (to the degree that in this streaming age, it is still possible to differentiate between "inside" and "outside"). Google feeds on joy by interpellating students and all other people as Google users. It also does so through its exploitation of the INFORMATION or knowledge that people create.

I write "information or knowledge," because for long Google used the terms interchangeably. For example, the Google Books video that I discussed earlier under BOOKS has as subtitle "15 years of preserving *knowledge*," but in the video itself a Google representative speaks of "*information* you're looking for."[54] More recently, Google has started to differentiate between "information" and "knowledge." In a 2012 video presentation of Google's Knowledge Graph technology, a representative states: "We're in the early phases of moving from being an information engine to becoming a knowledge engine."[55] Knowledge Graph collects and links information about things and people in the "real world." The technology is most visible in the panels displayed next to web results. For example, when we search for "Jorge Luis Borges," the panel teaches us that Borges was an Argentinian writer known for *The Library of Babel*.

What is knowledge? For Deleuze, knowledge has to be created anew all the time. In his *Abécédaire* under the B for *Boire* ("Drink"), he says that he finds the knowledge of cultivated people "frightening." He adds that he himself has "no provisional knowledge," but that he learns everything "*for a particular task.*" Deleuze says that each time he starts from zero, which gives him "great JOY."[56]

Similarly, Freire writes that "knowledge emerges only through invention and-re-invention, through the restless … inquiry human beings pursue in the world, with the world, and with each other."[57] Like Deleuze and his insistence on the correspondence between concepts and problems, Freire favors a "problem-posing education" that allows people to "perceive critically how they exist in the world with and in which they find themselves."[58] This is the opposite of education's banking model that, to paraphrase Deleuze and Freire at once, sees knowledge as a gift bestowed on those who know zero by those who consider themselves cultivated.

Now, Google too wants to liberate education from the banking model. Google wants EDUCATION to be less cognitive and instead more adaptative and skill based. But Google's data-banking and tracking model of education has little to do with emancipation and creative critical thinking. For Google, to learn is to acquire the skills needed to navigate and add to a vast externalized knowledge bank. As John Durham Peters argues, Google thinks of knowledge as a network, much like Borges thought of the universe as a library. Peters writes that for Borges "books can be as deeply alive as any metabolizing carbon-based creature, and an apparently random page can be the script of God."[59]

I don't think of books as alive, but I do think of knowledge as embodied. Knowledge is not a network banked in servers, which is a *transhumanist* view on knowledge premised on a Cartesian body–mind dualism. In its *posthuman* understanding, knowledge is a process immanent to people's past and present inquiries, which happens in conversation with writings and other media circulating in our universe. To de-Google learning is to recognize knowledge as this ongoing embodied conversation.

Lifelong

To de-Google learning is to recognize ourselves as fragmented dividuals. The process of dividualization happens as modern disciplinary society transforms into a data-driven control society. The control society manifests itself also in institutionalized education. In his

"Postscript on Control Societies" Deleuze writes: "Just as businesses are replacing factories, *school* is being replaced by *continuing education* and exams by continuous assessment. It's the surest way of turning education into a business."[60] Whereas discipline formed individuals into a mass (in factories, in schools), control divides subjects, both socially (in relation to each other) and internally (in relation to themselves). This dividualization of life goes hand in hand with the blurring of public and private life, and with the blurring of life stages into a *stream*. "In disciplinary societies," Deleuze writes, "you were always starting all over again (as you went from school to barracks, from barracks to factory), while in control societies you never finish anything—business, training, and military service being coexisting metastable states of a single modulation."[61]

It should be noted here that this modern trajectory described by Deleuze applies more to the male than to the female modern experience. For many women, modern life always already was dividualized, while the private and public were always already blurred. Moreover, whereas in the modern male experience education indeed marked a relatively distinct life stage that prepared the subject for their adult working life, for many women these life stages were blurred by motherhood and domestic labor. In our streaming age, education's transformation into a lifelong process contributes to a generalization of dividualized life, and to the blurring of life domains and stages. Meanwhile, this universalized dividualization continues to intersect with a patriarchal reality in which women (and non-cis male identifying subjects in general) are hailed to traditional gender roles.

Since the publication of Deleuze's essay, digital technology has allowed for the further *streamification* and personalization of education. As Neil Selwyn writes, lifelong learning rose to prominence during the 1990s, in recognition of "education being directed by individuals over the course of their lifetimes rather than being the preserve of any particular institutions."[62] Selwyn sees some benefits: personalized digital education may subvert the "cookie cutter" models of mass education. At the same time, however, and as happens with Google Classroom, personalized education may in fact become *mass customization*. In this process, education's collective potential is undermined, while people are further divided. Selwyn asks: "If we are all immersed in our own personalized learning journeys, what implications might this have for education as a social, supportive and shared endeavour?"[63]

To these concerns we can add that platformized education creates people as lifelong users, in two ways. The first is that students who grow up with certain digital tools are likely to keep using those tools in their later lives. Second, from an early age, students are profiled and datafied, not so much within the regulated gardens of their digital learning environments, but certainly when using YouTube, Google Search, or Gemini during or outside school time. Platformized education thus contributes to people's lifelong dividualization. Deleuze writes that the dividual in a control society "is no longer a [hu]man confined but a [hu]man in debt."[64] Indeed, in a control society, school or university becomes an investment rather than a formation. Education becomes part of an exchange, something that has to pay off, and that students often have to pay off.

This is a *sad* development. Under the J for JOY, Deleuze links sadness to debt. He writes that in Christian societies priests swayed power over people by instilling in them the infinite debt of the original sin. Priests limited people's power of action, their joy. In a control society, people's joy is limited by the powers of the market, including Big Tech entering the classroom. To bring back the joy of learning calls for the recognition of education as a PUBLIC good curbed from corporate interests. To de-Google is to create space for *common* life-long learning, understood as the liberation from divisive powers like Google.

Mundaneum

Tomorrow the telephone will no longer have a wire ... Everyone will carry with them, in their coat pocket, a very small horn, allowing them to with a turn of the dial tune into the waves of a channel.
FROM *LES ASPECTS DU LIVRE* (1906) BY PAUL OTLET, CO-FOUNDER OF THE MUNDANEUM, HOME OF THE "PAPER GOOGLE"[65]

The curbing of Big Tech's power—in education and in society in general—is one of our era's major challenges. In recent years, the European Union (EU) has provided some direction. In 2016, the EU passed its General Data Protection Regulation (GDPR), which protects people's data and privacy. In 2022, the EU adopted the Digital Markets Act (which prevents companies like Google from abusing their market power) and the Digital Service Act (which curbs illegal content and disinformation), and in 2024 the EU adopted the AI Act. In response, Google's strategy vis-à-vis EU regulation is threefold. The first is that Google complies, or says it complies with, regulations, because "transparency is part of Google's DNA."[66] Second, Google violates the rules. Since the GDPR's introduction there have been rulings against Google in France, Austria, and Italy.[67] Third, Google lobbies, both in very upfront ways (annually the company spends millions of euros on EU lobbying[68]) and in more subtle ways.

For example, starting in 2010, when Google opened its first data center on the European continent in the city of Mons near Brussels, Google has presented itself as a friend of this Walloon region (Wallonia being the predominantly francophone south of Belgium). In 2012, Google started a collaboration with the Mundaneum museum in Mons, which commemorates the work of the Belgian information pioneers Paul Otlet and Henri Lafontaine. In the late nineteenth century, Otlet and Lafontaine developed a Decimal Classification System that has been called a precursor to the internet and a "paper Google."[69] In 1910, the two founded the Palais Mondial, later called Mundaneum, with the goal to index all published information. The Mundaneum was located in the Parc du Cinquantenaire in Brussels, until in 1940 the German occupation brought a severe blow to the project, forcing it to move to the Leopold Park, right next to Google's current EU headquarters. As Flemish journalist Pascal Verbeken writes, these headquarters are housed in "an anonymous glass office building" across from the park where Otlet must have passed numerous times, "each day a little more desperate."[70] After Otlet's death in 1944, the Mundaneum moved several times from cellars to storage spaces, until in 1998 (Google's birthyear) the collection was transferred to Mons.

More than a physical world library, Otlet's dream was a Mundaneum in cyberspace. As Google writes in 2015, in a text accompanying a DOODLE on the occasion of Otlet's birthday, he envisioned "a universal system of written, visual, and audio information that people could access from the comfort of their own homes."[71] As part of its indirect Brussels lobby, Google positions itself as a continuation of Otlet's dream. However, as Alex Wright argues, Otlet "envisioned a publicly funded, transnational organization."[72] To de-Google is to not buy into Google's cooptation of Otlet's dream (see also WIKIPEDIA).

Naïve

Like the Mundaneum, Google is built on the firm belief that more information makes the world a better place. But Google undersells its power position. It frames itself as a neutral conduit, rather than as a major global actor that shapes how people experience the world. In a 2006 documentary, Google's then-Vice President of Search Products & User Experience Merrisa Mayer states: "I really view us as computer scientists. We can analyze a problem and we can solve a problem. But we're not governmental officials … We simply respond to the needs of our users." The interviewer responds: "With all due respect, that sounds almost naive."[73]

Earlier in the documentary, Mayer tells the story behind Google's former credo, "Don't be evil." The phrase goes back to 1999, when Google started to hire its first business managers. Mayer recalls how some engineers of the first hour were concerned that these business people would change Google's culture. Among them was employee #7, Amit Patel. Having knowledge of an upcoming sales meeting, Patel left a small note in the corner of the room's whiteboard. "Don't be evil." The phrase, so Mayer explains, captures Google's belief that "we feel that we can make money and have a successful business without sacrificing our ethics or our principles, or the interest of our users."[74]

The story illustrates that Google's founding philosophy is quite thin and indeed also naive. Naivety is lack of experience, judgment, or wisdom. There is a subtle difference between naivety and ignorance. Whereas ignorance is a lack of knowledge, naivety is a somewhat simple and unrealistic state of mind. When children have naive dreams, that is adorable. When corporations the size of Google are naive about their clout, that is scary—all the more so when these corporations have opinions on how children should learn.

In his radical pedagogy, Paolo Freire distinguishes between critical thinking and naive thinking. Whereas critical thinking perceives reality as a process, naive thinking sees it as a static entity. And whereas the critical thinker wants to transform reality in the name of humanity (or posthumanity), the naive thinker accommodates "to this normalized 'today.'"[75] In our streaming age, that normalized today or status quo is the platform society, in which the difference between corporate and common interest has become blurry. "Don't be evil" may have been born as a heart-felt warning against a profit-driven mindset, but Google's business people soon sloganized these words to better sell Google's colonization of common KNOWLEDGE. To de-Google is to decolonize knowledge from corporate naivety.

Owl

To stay with naivety and knowledge: in Judeo-Christian mythology, knowledge of good and evil pierced a naive Paradise-like state of mind. In the book of *Genesis*, knowledge of evil is embodied by the snake. In pagan and witchcraft traditions, evil is sometimes embodied by the owl. As Leah Bodine Drake writes in the poem "Bad Company," part of her HORNBOOK *for Witches* (1950): "The owl, the bat and the twisted tree … I wonder they are dear to me? / The owl is eerie, the owl is evil."[76]

Like witches, owls are intelligent and have good night vision. This night vision grants them access to knowledge that cannot bear the light of day. In other mythological traditions, the owl has a positive connotation, as in the Greek myth of Athena, the virgin goddess of wisdom. Like in witch stories, the small owl that keeps her company is a symbol of knowledge and perspicacity. Unlike as in witch stories, Athena's knowledge is associated with freedom and enlightenment. Athena's owl is the wise owl also found in the 1740 edition of Benjamin Franklin's *Poor Richard's Almanac*, reminding us that wisdom requires personal and collective introspection (Figure 43).

In those mythological worldviews, in which owls and other animals populated the collective imagination, wisdom came from the other side: a place that transcends empirical reality. In our digital era, wisdom is replaced by search engines and "self-learning" language models that promise access to a cloud of wisdom. As Andrea Righi writes in *The Other Side of the Digital*, the digital acts as a new secular God that demands 24/7 tribute in the form of our attention. Righi also writes that feminism teaches us that transcendence is gendered: "Historically, patriarchal thought projected the woman onto the position occupied by the *Other* … the old refrain about feminine indecipherability: the ultimate mystery of what a woman really wants."[77]

This begs the question of how patriarchy works through in the wisdom that speaks from the other side of Google Search or its chatbot Gemini? Google claims to operate in the name of enlightenment and democracy, which are the values embodied by Athena. Athena has

FIGURE 43 "O is for Owl" (original wood engraving and letterpress print by Rick Allen) (© copyright Rick Allen, The Kenspeckle Letterpress, kenspeckleletterpress.com).

often been represented as asexual: she stands for a clear head unclouded from mysterious desire. This is also Google's promise. Its pristinely white homepage promises a neutral and transparent wisdom. However, Google's wisdom is not as neutral as framed. Google's messages from the other side perpetuate the biases of a neoliberal and patriarchal society. To de-Google is to embrace a witchcraft perspective: a knowledge that is rebellious, embodied, and that loves "with unholy ecstasy / The Owl and the bat and the twisted tree."[78]

Public

PUBLIC education would profit from the deschooling of society.
IVAN ILLICH, *DESCHOOLING SOCIETY* (1970)[79]

We thus need a feminist perspective on knowledge, and on the way knowledge is transmitted. Such a perspective is critical of the way companies like Google develop a grasp on knowledge and infiltrate public education. At the same time, a feminist perspective is equally critical of public education and wants to deschool learning (Illich) from the powers disciplining it.

As José van Dijck et al. write in *The Platform Society*, online platforms like Google push a new skill-driven concept of learning that undermines the values fundamental to publicly funded education. These values include education's modern *Bildung* ideal, a knowledge-based curriculum, and the belief in education as a vehicle for socioeconomic equality.[80] The authors posit a skilled-driven educational system as the opposite of *Bildung*. Whereas a skilled-driven education is primarily concerned with producing workers to meet a society's economic needs, *Bildung* fosters "knowledgeable and critical citizens—a condition for healthy democracies."[81]

I agree with this critique of Google's skill-driven learning, but I am not sure if harking back to *Bildung* is what's needed now, at least not without a feminist critique of this originally nineteenth-century German universalist ideal of self-cultivation. In the *Bildung* ideal, the individual works on personal and cultural maturation, harmonizing mind and heart. The ideal was developed by the Prussian philosopher and diplomat Wilhelm von Humboldt. In a letter to his king, Humboldt wrote that "people obviously cannot be good craftworkers, merchants, soldiers or businessmen unless, regardless of their occupation, they are good, upstanding and … well-informed human beings and citizens."[82] By "people" Humboldt meant men. In *On Gender Differences and their Impact on Organic Nature* (1794) Humboldt wrote that all must follow the "appropriate path" ordained by their gender. For women, this meant home and not a career in the public sphere.[83]

Bildung has thus contributed, as Carol Taylor argues, to "the epistemological erasure and othering of those forms of knowledge" (feminine, non-white, non-Western, indigenous, popular) that do not fit with the humanist enlightenment narrative.[84] *Bildung* can therefore only serve in defense of public educational values when accompanied by a critique of how *Bildung* has traditionally been mobilized to maintain dominant power relations. Taylor writes that a feminist reconfiguration of *Bildung* needs to "incorporate knowledge which is rational *and* affective, logical *and* emotional, as well as knowledge which is embodied, intellectual, aesthetic and moral."[85] Such a reconfiguration means the displacement of binaries, in particular the male-female and public-private binaries, acknowledging that the private is always already political. In sum, to de-Google is to go back to *Bildung* if and only if this ideal is reconfigured as an embodied consciousness and critical sensitivity of how our privately sensed affects are shaped by intersecting patriarchal and technocolonial powers.

Query

Feminism, along with other oppositional movements, questions power and the truths it produces. To question is to be critical and to be curious. It is to ask "Why?" to the status quo. To question the status quo is the beginning of what Freire calls a problem-posing education. Or as Deleuze says in his *Abécédaire*: to question is to pose a problem. To question is not the same as to query, at least not when "query" is reduced to a search request to a database. In a broader understanding of the word, to "query" is to ask a question, to express doubt, or obtain information. In times of search engines, only the "obtaining information" part seems to remain.

What happens when the user enters a query into Google Search or Gemini? John Durham Peters writes that whereas most Google users adopt "toothed-whale strategies" by searching for a single target in a huge array of data, Google itself resembles "a baleen whale, one that wants to swallow the whole universe."[86] Sometimes users know exactly what they are looking for, but often they do not. In those situations, the suggestive algorithms behind the search bar's autocomplete function try to point users in the right direction. In *The Googlization of Everything* Siva Vaidhyanathan writes that Google conditions us to believe that the drop-down list of search options matches our desire. Google's suggestive power inspires trust and faith in its users. It "is the magic that hooks us."[87]

This feeling of magic—the sense that Google knows what you want before *you* know it—grows with natural-language or semantic search. Natural-language search allows users to formulate a search query as a question, whether through Search or "in conversation" with Gemini (formerly Google Assistant) (Figure 44).[88] Yet what happens to collective knowledge when information is always available and increasingly personalized? Vaidhyanathan argues that "learning is by definition an encounter with what you don't know." The filter that Google puts between a search and its results shields the searcher "from radical encounters with the other by 'personalizing' the results to reflect who the searcher is."[89]

Google also shields the searcher from the other called self, from "their" unconscious, which by definition is not personal. The unconscious is immanent to the powers that shape people's most "private" desires. These

FIGURE 44 "OK Google, how many stars are in our galaxy" (screen capture from video, © Google Home, 2017, all rights reserved).[90]

powers now also include Google. Google does not merely autocomplete people's queries, it creates people as querying subjects who want their information *now*. To become a critically curious questioner is to doubt the increasingly normalized notion that knowledge is information stored in corporately controlled databases. To become a questioner is to de-Google and sometimes not search at all, staying open to that other, unconscious knowledge always already at work in the background.

Rolling

Let's zoom in again on Google's "Anywhere School." In order to search for information on Google, or to work in Google Classroom, students need access to the internet. Especially for students who grow up in poor families or who live in remote areas, this is not always the case. In an effort to close this "homework gap," Google in 2016 launched "Rolling Study Halls" (which in turn is part of the "Grow with Google" community development program). For this initiative, Google helped install Wi-Fi on eleven school buses in North Carolina (followed by sixteen more rural communities across the United States two years later); students were also given a Chromebook to use and take home with them; and Google provided schools with a stipend for an on-board tutor. The program proved an instant success. "The effects were immediate," Google representative Lilyn Hester writes on the *Keyword* blog, "almost too immediate for some bus drivers who were shocked … when their commutes became so quiet. Students were engaged. They were learning."[91]

Though relatively modest in scope, the school bus initiative is also "part of something a little bit bigger," as says Nathan Coppock, who is a bus driver for Google in Talladega County, Alabama. Coppock speaks these words in a promotional video titled *Driving Change with Rolling Study Halls*. The video is very *human* and breathes a nostalgia for good old rural American life (Figures 45, 46, and 47). As a mellow tune is heard playing in the background, we see how Coppock (who keeps his bus in a hayfield) and his colleague Kim Gaither get up before dawn to prepare for their rides. "You're that first person they see in the morning," Gaither says, "you set the tone for their day." Next, we are in the bus. The landscape passes by and kids hop on and get on their Chromebooks, all smiles and engagement. The video ends on the statement that "together, we aim to help students reclaim 1.5 million learning hours this school year."

FIGURES 45 TO 47 Google's "Rolling Study Halls" (screen capture from video, © Google, 2019, all rights reserved).[92]

This does indeed sound as "something bigger," a phrase that is heard more often in Big Tech discourse. Watching the video, it is hard to *not* feel sympathy for the initiative. It is remarkable, though, that for Google to learn means to be online and also logged into Google Classroom (because schools can restrict students' Chromebook access to the walled gardens of Google's learning environment). Without denying the importance of equal access to online technology, or the strain of long commutes, it is good to remind ourselves that learning may also happen from books, conversations, or even from doodling or staring idly out of the window. Google says that it helps "reclaim" learning time, but in reality Google promotes a notion of learning that sees time as something to be optimized. To de-Google is to liberate time from this optimizing mindset.

Soul (*Generation AI*)

In Google's Rolling Study Halls we meet the "Class of 2030," also the audience of a project that Google's AI division did together with Douglas Coupland. Coupland is famous for his novel *Generation X: Tales of an Accelerated Culture* (1981). In the early 2010s, he created the text-based art series *Slogans for the 21st Century*. His collaboration with Google is called *Slogans for the Class of 2030*. For this project, Google's AI division got into Coupland's brain. In a video posted on Google Arts & Culture, a Google Brain employee explains how he created a neural network trained to predict the next word in a sequence of words. He then fed this network with a combination of Coupland's writings and a vast database of "social" media posts circulating online. The result was a series of slogans for the AI generation (Figures 48, 49, and 50). To give an idea:

> "You are here the new world" / "We are at the beginning of ourselves" / "You have become the face of the new society" / "Time is a beautiful thing" / "We can think the same way" / "I want to be alive in a way I can never be again"/ "We are here because we want technology to happen" / "Memory is the most fundamental capacity of all"/ "All the world is right there inside you" / "A person has to be unique to be unique" / "I'm going to take my dream life and make it a living" / "Your life is simply testing the limits of human intelligence" / "The brain of the individual" / "I like to think of my soul as a machine."[93]

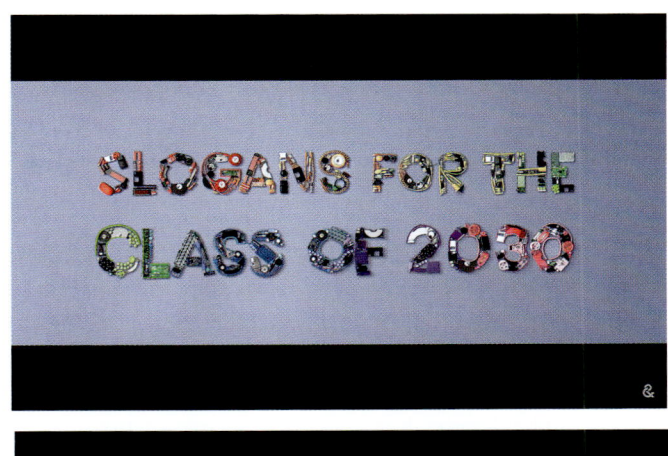

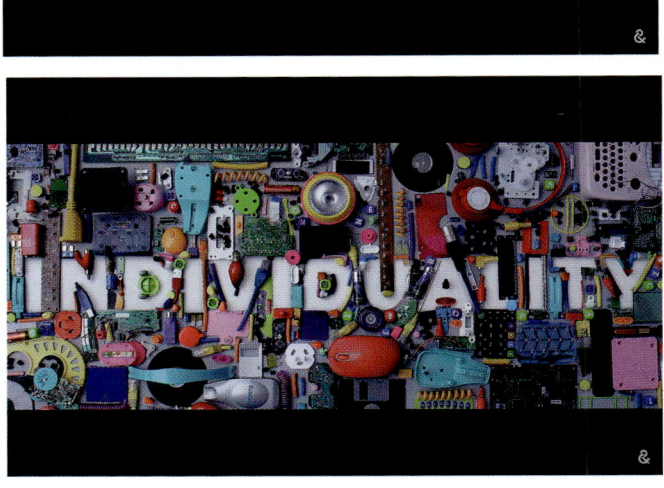

FIGURES 48 TO 50 Google's Class of 2030 (screen capture from video, © Google Arts & Culture, 2022, all rights reserved).[94]

Together these slogans breathe a transhumanist position. As I wrote in the previous two chapters, transhumanism views computing technology as an *enhancement* of human life. In that vision, machines allow humans to express themselves, and to feel unique and connected (as in difference with the alienated and anxious Generation X). As a Google employee says in the video: "We have to start thinking: how can an algorithm *augment* humans, how can we give humans superpower?"

What becomes of human life when augmented? The Google-Coupland mash-up thinks of the "[human] soul as a machine." That soul is at once a "unique" individual living their dream and a cloud of individuals all thinking "the same way." Indeed, with Google education there is the risk that the class of 2030, for all its diversity, develops a very homogeneous worldview. Coupland states that "we are entering a whole new league of determining individuality." In reality, though, individuals become dividual data-generating machines tethered to a digital infrastructure that further accelerates life, and that feeds on people's self-perceived uniqueness.

Therefore, if we want to hold on to a notion of *soul*, this soul needs to be embodied, in difference with the disembodied transhumanist "soul." In *Teaching to Transgress* bell hooks writes that an education that places emphasis on "spiritual well-being, on care of the soul" is very grounded and encourages teachers and students to connect intellectual smartness to "life practices" and "habits of being."[95] To de-Google is to ground education in common everyday freedom; it is to ground our personal and collective souls.

Teacher

The objectification of the TEACHER *within bourgeois educational structures seemed to denigrate notions of wholeness and uphold the idea of a mind/body split, one that promotes and supports compartmentalization.*

BELL HOOKS, *TEACHING TO TRANSGRESS: EDUCATION AS THE PRACTICE OF FREEDOM* (1994)[96]

In the platformized and increasingly "artificially" "intelligent" classroom, the difference between students and teachers vanishes. On the interface level of Google Classroom, students and teachers may have very different user roles and privileges. However, on the material level of subject formation students and teachers are now both users of the same data-driven platform ecosystem. In the platformized classroom, teaching is increasingly "machine-like."[97] Meanwhile, the same system that asks teachers to track students also allows for their own tracking by the school administration.

This is the reason for solidarity between students and teachers. Against Google's false promise of democratization, classrooms need an increased awareness of how they are transformed by corporate interests. The teacher's role is twofold here. First, as much as is in their power, they should create and hold a safe(r) space free of market-driven ed-tech, a struggle that is of course not won by individual teachers. Second, they can integrate into their teachings an ongoing media literacy conversation about how life and learning are affected by online platforms.

As far as this second tactic of consciousness-raising is concerned: teachers and students can learn from each other in a classroom where, as Freire writes, "the teacher is no longer merely the-one-who-teaches, but one who is himself taught in dialogue with the students."[98] Or to speak with bell hooks, we have to liberate teachers and students from bourgeois educational structures. In the streaming era, a good topic for a democratic classroom conversation is everyday association and its transformation in the control society. In the spirit of cultural studies, we can say that every individual is at once ignorant and a specialist in everyday life. We are all ignorant in the sense that while acting, thinking, speaking, and feeling as individuals we only scratch the surface of how power-knowledge systems like Google create us as subjects. We are all specialists (or what Antonio Gramsci calls organic intellectuals), because we are all immersed in, and have unique perspectives on, the everyday. The teacher's role is to facilitate a dialogue to explore the common ground between those perspectives, which is where emancipation and collective consciousness begin.

In *The Ignorant Schoolmaster* (*Le Maître ignorant*) Jacques Rancière writes that the emancipatory teacher teaches students that teachers have nothing to teach them. In doing so, the teacher helps students to emancipate from their explicators (or what Freire calls the banking system). "To emancipate an ignorant person," Rancière writes, "one must be, and one need only be, emancipated oneself, that is to say, conscious of the true power of the human mind."[99] Yet what does it mean to be emancipated in a control society, in which life is increasingly caught in a data-driven machine? What happens to the cultural studies belief that *people make meaning* in a conjuncture in which everyday life is swallowed by profit-driven streams? To be emancipated in times of technofeudalism, and to de-Google, requires more than an acknowledgment of one's ignorance. To de-Google is to unlearn.

Unlearning

I take the notion of unlearning from Gayatri Chakravorty Spivak, who speaks of "unlearning one's privilege as one's loss."[100] By this, Spivak refers to the decolonization of one's history and learned habits. To unlearn one's privilege constitutes a double recognition. On the one hand, our privileges may prevent us from a certain kind of Other knowledge, "not simply information that we have not yet received, but the knowledge that we are not equipped to understand by reason of our social positions" (as argued by Donna Landry and Gerald Maclean in their introduction to the *Spivak Reader*). To unlearn, in this sense, is to do one's homework and try to see others whose experiences are obscured from us. To unlearn is also to include marginalized subjects in a way they can speak back.[101]

How does this imperative to unlearn and develop an ethical relation to the Other translate to our self-positioning in a technocolonial control society? How is unlearning also de-Googling?

First of all, such ethics means the realization that algorithms as those of Google Search confirm social biases and reinforce structures of oppression. Ideally, to de-Google means to not use Google at all, and to instead make use of tools and platforms that are not profit-driven. Given Google's hegemony, for individuals to de-Google is nearly impossible. This is why bottom-up resistance is needed. Especially educational institutions have a huge responsibility. They should resist platforms like Google for Education. They could teach students, moreover, that *to google* is to also close down more critical and creative ways of finding knowledge, that *to google* is a loss of *other* knowledge.

Second, to de-Google means to develop a more critical and caring relation toward the fragmented Other called self. Big Tech slices up subjects into human-things. To unlearn and de-Google is to resist this shattering of life. This is a collective struggle and a struggle for new collectives. Only by fighting for public values and creating new emancipatory commons—including educational commons—will people be able to build an "unlearning machine"[102] and regain a degree of common integrity, a shared sense that people together can still make meaning.

Third, to unlearn and de-Google requires people to become more *media literate*, that is to become better readers of texts, images, and moving images (including ones that are algorithmically generated), and to become more aware of the systems of truth production at work in transmedia streams. In our control society it is increasingly difficult to still believe in the cultural studies adage that people make meaning in the face of power. And yet, a minimum of posthumanist humanism remains needed: a belief in people's ability to weave alternative social textures and come together as resistant collectives.

In order to create such agency in machine-like times, people have to emancipate themselves from the increasingly personalized streams that shape their sensoria. To do so is to realize that the *personalized is political*. Education does not only happen in schools, but of course schools play a big role. To de-Google school and to "unschool" (Freire) is to create and hold spaces where young people can slow down, spend time with texts and images, and practice modes of attention liberated from the stream.

Virtual

The closest we'll get to teleportation or a time machine.
        A GOOGLE PRODUCT MANAGER IN RESPONSE TO THE QUESTION: "DESCRIBE VIRTUAL REALITY IN 10 WORDS OR LESS"[103]

The "V" is for VIRTUAL, because for a while Google believed that virtual reality (VR) would be the future of education. In 2015, Google launched Expeditions, a VR tool designed to "bring the world to every classroom."[104] Expeditions allowed "educators" to create three-dimensional field tours of *virtually* anything, from Paris to the anatomy of plants. The app was used in combination with Expedition Kits, which included VR viewers. In 2021, during the Covid-19 pandemic, Google pulled the plug on Expeditions, along with its other VR platforms DayDreams and Cardboard. The reason provided for this discontinuation was that VR headsets "are not always available to all learners and even more so this year."[105]

Google's discourse around VR remains instructive nonetheless. In 2018, Google for Education published a report titled *The Future of the Classroom* on trends in primary and secondary education. In this report, the company envisions a pedagogical turn facilitated by "emerging technologies," including VR, AR, and AI. The report emphasizes that it requires a wholesale shift to successfully integrate digital technology into learning. Google cites educational psychologist Hanna Dumont: "I don't think that technologies, per se, are going to change classrooms if they're not addressing the deep level of learning … If it's just having some digital device in front of you but actually doing the exact same thing … then it's not changing anything."[106] As argued in Chapter 1, METAVERSE, for now VR and AR have not brought about this paradigm shift, while at the moment of writing it is still too early to weigh the SOUL of Generation AI. But this psychologist's claim that Google affects the deep level of learning is of course true. Google turns students into users, immersing them in its platform environment, even when on a field trip.

Following the discontinuation of Expeditions, Google has moved its virtual field trips to its Arts & Culture app. On there, we can for example make a trip to the North Pole to learn about its "challenging climates" (yet without mention of the climate crisis). Or we go on a deep-sea dive along the Great Barrier Reef, where we learn that any disturbance to this underwater world "could create a domino effect throughout the ecosystem" (yet without mention of rising sea temperatures). Finally, we visit the Taj Mahal, built by "more than 20,000 skilled workers" (which were in fact enslaved people).[107] These fieldtrips are, in sum, as one-dimensional in content as they are two-dimensional in form. To de-Google learning is to go on field trips that are more grounded and embodied. To de-Google is also to go on actual field trips, like in one's own neighborhood.

Wikipedia

Many of the images on Google Arts & Culture (formerly Google Art Project) are also used within Wikimedia Commons (a collection of freely usable media files to which anyone can contribute) and Wikipedia (a free community-driven encyclopedia that anyone can edit). The relation between Google and Wikipedia goes far back. As we read on Wikipedia, under "Google and Wikipedia," Wikipedia started in 2001 as a publicly editable complement to Nupedia, a free online encyclopedia written by experts. In 2003, Nupedia was shut down, and Wikipedia continued independently as a platform for quick (*wiki* in Hawaiian) knowledge (*pedia* in Greek).

In the early days of Wikipedia, Google helped reduce the page rank of ad farms that looked like Wikipedia clones. In 2007, however, Google entered into direct competition with Wikipedia, introducing its user-generated encyclopedia Knol (*knol* being a Google neologism for a unit of knowledge). Knol was a failure and in 2012 Google pulled the plug on it. In this same period, Google and Wikipedia renewed their romance. Since late in the first decade of the 2000s, Wikipedia receives most of its traffic through Google Search referrals. Vice versa, in 2012 Google introduced its KNOWLEDGE Graph panels, largely filled with INFORMATION from Wikipedia. As of 2018, YouTube (since 2006 part of Google) uses Wikipedia to combat misinformation, for example by adding a Wikipedia link to September 11 videos.

Beyond their mutual referrals, Google and the Wikimedia family also have a financial connection. Google has occasionally donated to the Wikimedia Foundation, and in 2021 Wikimedia launched its commercial Wikimedia Enterprise, designed to more efficiently deliver Wikipedia content to interested parties. The first paying customer was Google. *Wired* magazine rationalizes Wikimedia's move toward a for-profit subsidiary as follows: "Once you concede that big platforms will control the flow of commerce and information online, you can focus on how to get your cut. A proud Silicon Valley holdout, the Wikimedia Foundation is finally doing just that."[108]

Time will tell how Wikipedia will be affected by its tighter relations with Big Tech.[109] Wikipedia—according to Google's Sergey Brin "one of the greatest triumphs of the internet"—calls to mind the MUNDANEUM and Paul Otlet's dream of a nonprofit endeavor to disclose all the world's information, but perhaps the Belgian pioneer would have looked somewhat skeptically at Wikipedia's "lack of hierarchy" (so Alex Wright argues in his book on Otlet).[110] There are indeed risks to Wikipedia's crowd-sourced approach to knowledge. As we read on Wikipedia, under "Wikipedia," "Wikipedia has received ... criticism for exhibiting systemic bias, particularly gender bias against women and alleged ideological bias."[111] The platform has sought to address these critiques by initiating a

Community Health Initiative to fight harassment within the Wikimedia volunteer community, leading *Wired* to call Wikipedia (together with the Internet Archive) "the last best place on the Internet."[112]

To unlearn with Wikipedia is to not only double-check its information for mistakes and biases, it is also to recognize the platform's "uneven geography."[113] Especially African countries and other regions in the global south remain underrepresented in terms of content and contributors. Many Wikipedia entries that *do* exist in these parts of the world are written by people living in the global north. To de-Google learning with Wikipedia therefore also means to develop an eye for which voices and perspectives are *not* on Wikipedia.

x

Embrace ~~failure~~ learning
FROM x'S MOONSHOT THINKING MANIFESTO

Back to Google. To stay competitive, the company, and the Alphabet conglomerate in general, has to keep learning. One place it does so is x, formerly called Google X, now Alphabet's semi-secret Moonshot Factory. As we read in its manifesto, at X there is no such as failure, because failure is learning.

X defines a moonshot as the intersection of a "huge problem" (e.g., climate crisis), a radical sci-fi solution, and a technological breakthrough that offers a "glimmer of hope"[114] (Figure 51). Moonshot thinking is to think radically, starting from the realization that it is often easier to make something *ten times* better than to make it *ten percent* better (as says Captain of Moonshots Astro Zeller throughout his inspirational videos).[115] Once, Google was a moonshot itself, and x teaches us a lot about Google and its view on learning.

x was founded by Google in 2010 and has since been housed a short bike ride away from Alphabet's corporate headquarters in Mountain View, California. X takes inspiration from John F. Kennedy's 1962 dream that by the end of the decade his country would put a man on the moon. No one knew if it was possible, but Kennedy's moonshot thinking was to make sure that a plan was put in place *in case* it was possible. Teller

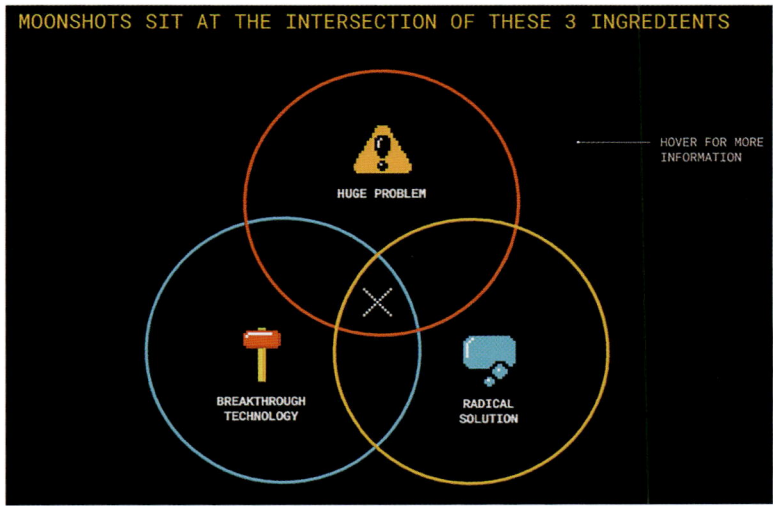

FIGURE 51 Moonshots! A Game of Radical Thinking by X (screen capture from video, © X, 2023, all rights reserved).[116]

explains: "Great dreams aren't just visions," they are "visions coupled to strategies for making them real."[117]

Among X's "graduated projects" are Brain (Google's deep-learning division; see SOUL) as well as Alphabet subsidiaries Waymo (self-driving cars) and Intrinsic (software for industrial robots). Other projects have been discontinued, including H2E (a device to harvest water from air) and Loon (a network of balloons that would have brought the internet to rural areas). X is proud of these failures: "The trick is to create a culture that makes it psychologically safe for people to fail, and reframes each failure as an opportunity to learn."[118]

Such a big-time approach to learning only works, though, when a company has a lot of money to burn on projects that essentially are gambles. Alphabet's strategy is clear: it is one of the most powerful companies in the world; the point of X is to keep it that way. As *Wired* reports, "to X and Alphabet, creating the next Google and saving the world are essentially the same thing."[119] Like Google, the Moonshot Factory thus blurs common good and private profit, while it reduces learning to technology-driven innovation.

This techno-solutionist view on learning, in combination with the belief that "purpose and profit [are] not in opposition [but] intensely synergistic" (Teller), lies at the heart of Google's educational philosophy. Like X, Google's Anywhere School may appear as a hierarchy-free and curiosity-driven playground, in reality it sustains a world in which being human means to be a Google user. To de-Google is to embrace learning without Google.

You

YOU have become the face of the new society.
SLOGANS FOR THE CLASS OF 2030 (SEE SOUL)

As characters, we are never singular, but singular-plural; I am YOU.
WENDY CHUN, "BIG DATA AS DRAMA" (2016)[120]

Let's visit Anywhere School one last time: in the video presentation discussed under ANYONE, Google stresses that its education products are built with accessibility and inclusion in mind. There is something strange, though, about Google's accessibility and inclusion rhetoric. On the one hand, it is about designing learning for those with "specific needs," a *you* in particular. On the other hand, Google designs learning for "everyone," a universal plural *you*. As Wendy Chun writes in "Big Data as Drama," "YOU is a particularly shifty shifter" because it is "never simply singular, but also plural."[121] Let's have a closer look at Google's YOU, and trace how it moves from a focus on *particular* students to a focus on *all* students.

Following a precursory statement by a Google "educator" that "every student is a superhero" and that it's "our job to help them access their own unique superpowers," the video moves to a scripted interview with an accessibility and inclusion expert. This expert works with children with a range of disabilities, including autism, dyslexia, and deafness. She explains how children with dyslexia benefit from Google's "Select to Speak" tool that reads out loud text in a selected area on the screen. Following a demonstration—in which we hear a machine voice say: "if we can understand how to make the world a fairer place"—the expert refers to the tool as "a fantastic way for *all* [emphasis mine] children, not just for those with specific needs." Similarly, Chromebooks are presented as specifically helping children with visual impairment, but at the same time Google presents them as helping "*all* learners" (emphasis mine). Google therefore suggests to have Chromebook's accessibility features switched on at default for each child's account. "That way every child, *including those* [emphasis mine] with visual disabilities, can showcase their superpowers."

The script thus moves from the particular to the universal very quickly: from a focus on finding solutions for children with special needs to a focus on technologies for *all* children. At the end of the script, children with disabilities have disappeared from the picture altogether. After all, "everybody has unique needs" while "every teacher is a teacher of special educational needs."

In sum, Google tunes into a growing social awareness about accessibility and inclusion issues, while it also hijacks this discourse as a vehicle to promote its adaptive learning ideology. Rather than giving extra personal attention to those who need it, Google turns the classroom into an increasingly platformized and automated environment. In doing so, Google classroom caters to a "you" singular and plural *at once*. This scattering of the subject in Anywhere School mirrors what happens in our platform society, in which people are reduced to dividual user-things tethered to platform machines. "You've changed" (Chapter 2, DIVIDUAL, Figure 34). Chun writes that big data "treats individuals in relation to, that is 'like,' others."[122] To de-Google is to see individuals as particular subjects, and at the same time collectively self-analyze how subjects are individuated and dividualized by systems of discipline and control.

Zen

We have to replace [the Big Bang] with the Zed, which is, in fact, the ZEN, *the route of the fly.*
                      GILLES DELEUZE, *ABÉCÉDAIRE***, "Z FOR ZIGZAG"**

To conclude this abecedarium, Google's philosophy of learning goes beyond education and the classroom. Google has always been *more* than a company. By giving people access to all knowledge in the world, it wants to change how people know and learn; it wants to make the world a better place. To do so requires a certain mindset, a fundamental belief to be part of "something a little bit bigger" (ROLLING).

One way in which Google employees are invited to stir this optimism in themselves is the "Search Inside Yourself" (SIY) meditation course. The course is the brainchild of Chade-Meng Tan, who in 1999 was hired by Google as employee # 107. Following several attempts to launch meditation courses at Google, in 2007 Meng started SIY, which approaches meditation as a "workout for your emotional intelligence."[123] The course has been among the most popular at Google and it has inspired thousands of employees. In 2015, Meng published a book based on his experiences, titled *Search Inside Yourself: The Unexpected Path to Achieving Success, Happiness (and World Peace)*. Meng writes that one of the best analogies for meditation is a baby learning to walk. "That baby is really a Zen master teaching you a thing or two about progress in your meditation."[124]

Meng's teachings are part of the mindfulness wave in global-northern culture since the late 1960s. Mindfulness is a certain cultivation of human attention with its origins in the Zen-Buddhist tradition. To be mindful is to move one's body and mind with soft focus and gratitude without passing judgment. As I have discussed elsewhere, in an essay titled "*Mad Men* and Mindfulness," mindfulness has been very popular in Silicon Valley.[125] In 2013, *Wired* reported that entrepreneurs and techies "are taking millennia-old traditions and reshaping them to fit the Valley's goal-oriented, data-driven, largely atheistic culture." *Wired* cites Meng: "Everybody knows this EI [emotional intelligence] thing is good for their career … And every company knows that if their people have EI, they're gonna make a shitload of money."[126]

Meng's statement nicely captures Google's vision on learning. In that vision, a soft and open gaze that minds the common good blurs with a firm eye on the bottom line. In his *Abécédaire*, in "Z for Zigzag," Deleuze talks about the Zen master striking his disciples with a stick: "The blow of the stick is the lightning that makes things visible."[127] At Google, the Zen master also wields a carrot. Or to make the metaphor even more precise: at Google carrot and stick magically blur into a technocolonial wand. To de-Google learning is to recognize the ideological spell that Google casts on its users. To de-Google is to *unblur*, and to wrest learning as a common good from the company's corporate grasp.

Notes

1. Paolo Freire, *Pedagogy of the Oppressed*, trans. Myra Bergman Ramos (New York: Continuum, 2005), 80.
2. Google for Education, "The Anywhere School 2022" (video) (2022), accessed October 26, 2024, https://www.youtube.com/watch?v=LYFqyOm1_lU.
3. Google for Education, "The Anywhere School 2021" (2021), accessed October 26, 2024, https://educationonair.withgoogle.com/events/the-anywhere-school-2021.
4. Andy Russell, "Share Your Ideas with Chromebook," *Google The Keyword* (July 7, 2022), accessed October 26, 2024, https://blog.google/outreach-initiatives/education/theanywhereschool-chromebook.
5. Google for Education (2023), accessed October 26, 2024, https://edu.google.com.
6. Niels Kerssens and José van Dijck, "The Platformization of Primary Education in the Netherlands," *Learning, Media and Technology* 46:3 (2021): 250–63, p. 258.
7. See Kate Conger, "Google Removes 'Don't Be Evil' Clause from its Code of Conduct," *Gizmodo* (May 18, 2018), accessed October 26, 2024, https://gizmodo.com/google-removes-nearly-all-mentions-of-dont-be-evil-from-1826153393.
8. Evgeny Morozov, "Google May Have Changed its Name but the Game Remains the Same," *The Guardian* (August 16, 2015), accessed October 26, 2024, https://www.theguardian.com/commentisfree/2015/aug/16/google-alphabet-name-change-same-game-evgeny-morozov.
9. Eric Schmidt and Jonathan Rosenberg, *How Google Works* (New York: Grand Central Publishing, 2017), 204.
10. Google, "Google Books: 15 Years of Preserving Knowledge from around the World" (video) (2019), accessed October 26, 2024, https://www.youtube.com/watch?v=zz_vG9b9dv0.
11. Google, "Google Books: 15 Years of Preserving Knowledge from around the World" (video) (2020).
12. Jean-Christophe Plantin, Carl Lagoze, Paul N. Edwards, and Christian Sandvig, "Infrastructure Studies Meet Platform Studies in the Age of Google and Facebook," *New Media & Society* 20.1 (2016): 1–26, p. 19.
13. See for example: AccuRanker, "Google Gemini and SEO, What's Changing" (December 7, 2023), accessed October 26, 2024, https://www.accuranker.com/blog/google-gemini-what-s-changing/; Botnation AI,

"Introducing Gemini: Google's New AI 5 Times More Powerful than ChatGPT" (November 29, 2023), accessed October 26, 2024, https://botnation.ai/site/en/google-gemini-5-times-more-powerful-than-chatgpt/; Daily AI Watch, "Why Google's Gemini Could Eclipse ChatGPT in the AI Race" (August 31, 2023), accessed October 26, 2024, https://www.dailyaiwatch.ai/company-tracker/google/why-googles-gemini-could-eclipse-chatgpt-in-the-ai-race.

14   John Vamvakitis, "Around the World and Back with Google for Education," *Google Blog* (January 22, 2019), accessed October 26, 2024, https://www.blog.google/outreach-initiatives/education/around-the-world-and-back.

15   Natasha Singer, "How Google Took over the Classroom," *New York Times* (May 13, 2017), accessed October 26, 2024, https://www.nytimes.com/2017/05/13/technology/google-education-chromebooks-schools.html.

16   Google for Education, "Google Workspace for Education" (2023), accessed October 26, 2024, https://edu.google.com/intl/ALL_us/workspace-for-education/classroom.

17   Melanie Lazare, "A Peek at What's Next for Google Classroom," *Google The Keyword* (February 17, 2021), accessed October 26, 2024, https://blog.google/outreach-initiatives/education/classroom-roadmap.

18   Singer, "How Google Took over the Classroom."

19   Priya Kumar, Jessica Vitak, Marshini Chetty, and Tamara L. Clegg, "The Platformization of the Classroom: Teachers as Surveillant Consumers," *Surveillance & Society* 17.1/2 (2019): 145–52, p. 151.

20   Carlo Perrotta, Kalervo N. Gulson, Ben Williamson, and Kevin Witzenberger, "Automation, APIs and the Distributed Labour of Platform Pedagogies in Google Classroom," *Critical Studies in Education* 61.1 (2021): 1–17, p. 7.

21   AFP News Agency, "Google Doodles a Playful Mix of Art and Technology" (video) (2012), accessed October 26, 2024, https://www.youtube.com/watch?v=XreXGwu5dT0.

22   Google, "About," accessed October 26, 2024, https://www.google.com/doodles/about.

23   Myrtl Swchwrm, *Doodly Doodles* [Exhibition text as seen at Grounded festival, 25 June 2022, Utrecht, the Netherlands].

24   Zuboff, *Age of Surveillance Capitalism*, 75.

25   Google, "Learning, No Matter What" (video) (2021), accessed October 26, 2024, https://www.youtube.com/watch?v=m28x6OsTPAk.

26   Google for Education, "Elevate Education with Simple, Flexible and Secure Tools with Google Workspace for Education" [no date]; accessed October 26, 2022, https://edu.google.com/intl/ALL_uk/workspace-for-education/

editions/overview; Google for Education, "Turning Commute Time into Learning Time," accessed October 26, 2024, https://edu.google.com/intl/ALL_uk/why-google/our-commitment/rolling-study-halls.

27 Google for Education, "Products that Power Education," accessed October 26, 2024, https://edu.google.com/intl/ALL_uk.

28 Mirjam Remie and Menno Sedee, "Techreuzen Willen de School Hervormen," *NRC Handelsblad* (19 July 2020).

29 Google for Education, "Helping Expand Learning for Everyone," accessed October 15, 2022, https://edu.google.com/intl/ALL_uk/why-google/our-commitment/.

30 Google for Education, "Learning, No Matter What" (video), accessed 30 June 2022, https://edu.google.com/intl/ALL_uk/why-google/our-commitment.

31 Van Dijck et al., *Platform Society*, 131.

32 Tegenlicht, "Google: Achter de Schermen" (VPRO television, the Netherlands, 2006) (video), accessed October 26, 2024, https://www.youtube.com/watch?v=xj_c1g-q0uI&list=PLSu6VO8OKY6_yZ4U4x-VLG7-2QF7UGAqx.

33 John Durham Peters, *The Marvelous Clouds: Toward a Philosophy of Elemental Media* (Chicago: University of Chicago Press, 2015), 338.

34 Google, "Facts about Google and Competition," accessed October 26, 2024, https://www.google.com/competition/howgooglesearchworks.html (August 26, 2011), via The Internet Archive, accessed October 26, 2024, https://web.archive.org/web/20111104131332/https://www.google.com/competition/howgooglesearchworks.html.

35 Jon M. Kleinberg, "Authoritative Sources in a Hyperlinked Environment," Proc. 9th ACM-SIAM Symposium on Discrete Algorithms, 1998, accessed October 26, 2024, https://www.cs.cornell.edu/home/kleinber/auth.pdf.

36 Yves Citton, *The Ecology of Attention*, trans. Barnaby Norman (Cambridge: Polity Press, 2017), 70; Andrea Righi, *The Other Side of the Digital: The Sacrificial Economy of New Media* (Minneapolis: University of Minnesota Press, 2021), 74.

37 Safiya Umoja Noble, *Algorithms of Oppression: How Search Engines Reinforce Racism* (New York: New York University Press, 2018), 5.

38 Carolina Alonso Bejarano and Stina Soderling, "Against Grading: Feminist Studies beyond the Neoliberal University," *Feminist Formations* 33.2 (2021): 208–32, p. 208.

39 Foucault, *Discipline and Punish*, 186.

40 Foucault, *Discipline and Punish*, 187.

41 Google, "Create & Grade Quizzes with Google Forms" [no year], accessed October 26, 2024, https://support.google.com/docs/answer/7032287?hl=en; Jorge Lugo, "Google Assignments, Your New Grading Companion," *Google blog: The Keyword* (August 14, 2019), accessed October 26, 2024, https://blog.google/outreach-initiatives/education/introducing-assignments.

42 See Dadi Ramesh and Suresh Kumar Sanampudi, "An Automated Essay Scoring System: A Systematic Literature Review," *Artificial Intelligence Review* 55 (2022): 2495–527, p. 2495.

43 Google AI for Developers, "GradeMate," accessed 6 November 2024, https://ai.google.dev/competition/projects/grademate.

44 Bard, "Meet Bard," accessed April 27, 2023, https://bard.google.com.

45 William Shakespeare, *Love's Labour's Lost* (New York: Penguin, 2015), 120.

46 Matthew Prior, *The Poems of Matthew Prior. Volume 2* (Press of C. Whittingham, 1822), 211. See also Andrew W. Tuer, *History of the Hornbook* (London: The Leadenhall Press, 1897); George A. Plimpton, "The Hornbook and its Use in America," *Proceedings of the American Antiquarian Society* 26 (1916): 264–72; Merridee L. Bailey, "Hornbooks," *Journal of the History of Childhood & Youth* 6.1 (2013): 5–14.

47 Image retrieved from Wikimedia, accessed October 26, 2024, https://commons.wikimedia.org/wiki/File:Hornbooks.png.

48 Maria Lindh and Jan Nolin, "Information We Collect: Surveillance and Privacy in the Implementation of Google Apps for Education," *European Education Research Journal* 15.6 (2016): 644–63, p. 650.

49 Lindh and Nolin, "Information We Collect," 651–2.

50 Google for Education, "Privacy and Security Centre" (2023), accessed October 26, 2024, https://edu.google.com/intl/ALL_uk/why-google/privacy-security.

51 Larry Page and Sergey Brin, "2004 Founders' IPO Letter: 'An Owner's Manual' for Google's Shareholders," *Alphabet*, accessed October 26, 2024, https://abc.xyz.

52 *Gilles Deleuze from A to Z* (DVD), trans. Charles J. Stivale (Semiotext(e)/Foreign Agents, 2011).

53 Gilles Deleuze and Félix Guattari, *What Is Philosophy?* trans. Hugh Tomlinson and Graham Burchell (New York: Columbia University Press, 1994), 23.

54 Google, "Google Books" (video).

55 Google, "Introducing the Knowledge Graph" (video) (2012), accessed October 26, 2024, https://www.youtube.com/watch?v=mmQl6VGvX-c.

56 *Gilles Deleuze from A to Z*.

57 Freire, *Pedagogy of the Oppressed*, 45.

58 Freire, *Pedagogy of the Oppressed*, 56.

59 Peters, *Marvelous Clouds*, 319–20.

60 Deleuze, *Negotiations*, 179.

61 Deleuze, *Negotiations*, 179.

62 Neil Selwyn, *Is Technology Good for Education?* (Cambridge: Polity Press, 2016), 58.

63 Selwyn, *Is Technology Good for Education?*, 65, 78–9

64 Deleuze, *Negotiations*, 181.

65 Paul Otlet, *Les Aspects du livre* (Brussels: Musée du livre, 1906), 33.

66 Google Cloud, "Google Workspace for Education Data Protection Implementation Guide" (March 2021), accessed October 26, 2024, https://services.google.com/fh/files/misc/google_workspace_edu_data_protection_implementation_guide.pdf.

67 See for example: Adam Satariano, "Google Is Fined $57 Million Under Europe's Data Privacy Law," *New York Times* (January 21, 2019), accessed October 26, 2024, https://www.nytimes.com/2019/01/21/technology/google-europe-gdpr-fine.html; Ravie Lakshmanan, "France Rules that Using Google Analytics Violates GDPR Data Protection Law," *The Hacker News* (February 11, 2022), accessed October 26, 2024, https://thehackernews.com/2022/02/france-rules-that-using-google.html; Natasha Lomas, "France's Data Watchdog Warns over Illegal Use of Google Analytics," *Tech Crunch* (June 8, 2022), accessed October 26, 2024, https://techcrunch.com/2022/06/08/google-analytics-gdpr-breach-cnil.

68 See for example: Corporate Europe Observatory, "The Lobby Network: Big Tech's Web of Influence in the EU" (August 31, 2021), accessed October 26, 2024, https://corporateeurope.org/en/2021/08/lobby-network-big-techs-web-influence-eu.

69 Mundaneum, "Support the 'Paper Google'" [no year], accessed October 26, 2024, http://expositions.mundaneum.org/en/soutenez-le-google-de-papier.

70 Pascal Verbeken, *Brutopia: De Dromen van Brussel* (Amsterdam: De Bezige Bij, 2019), 228.

71 Google, "Mundaneum Co-Founder Paul Otlet's 147th Birthday" (August 23, 2015), accessed October 26, 2024, https://www.google.com/doodles/mundaneum-co-founder-paul-otlets-147th-birthday.

72 Alex Wright, *Cataloging the World: Paul Otlet and the Birth of the Information Age* (New York: Oxford University Press, 2014), 298.

73 Tegenlicht, "Google Achter de Schermen."

74 Tegenlicht, "Google Achter de Schermen."
75 Freire, *Pedagogy of the Oppressed*, 65.
76 Leah Bodine Drake, *A Hornbook for Witches: Poems of Fantasy* (Sauk City: Arkham House, 1950), 14.
77 Righi, *Other Side of the Digital*, 4.
78 Drake, *Hornbook for Witches*, 14.
79 Ivan Illich, *Deschooling Society* (New York: Harrow Books, 1970), 3.
80 Van Dijck et al., *Platform Society,* 118.
81 Van Dijck et al., *Platform Society,* 127.
82 Karl-Heinz Günther, "Profiles of Educators: Wilhelm von Humboldt (1767–1835)," *Prospects* 18: 1 (1988): 127–36, p. 132.
83 Cauleen Suzanne Gary, "Bildung and Gender in 19th Century Bourgeois Germany: A Cultural Studies Analysis of Texts by Women Writers," PhD thesis, University of Maryland, 2008, 35.
84 Carol A. Taylor, "The Gendered History of *Bildung* as Concept and Practice: A Speculative Feminist Analysis," in Carol A. Taylor, Chantal Amade-Escot, and Andrea Abbas, eds., *Gender in Learning and Teaching: Feminist Dialogues across International Boundaries* (London and New York: Routledge, 2019), 11–23, p. 17.
85 Taylor, "Gendered History of *Bildung*," 21.
86 Peters, *Elemental Media*, 58 n.11.
87 Siva Vaidhyanathan, *The Googlization of Everything (and Why We Should Worry)* (Berkeley: University of California Press, 2011), 52.
88 Peek of the Net, "Google Home Official Ad" (video) (2017), accessed October 26, 2024, https://www.youtube.com/watch?v=OsXedJq1aWE.
89 Vaidhyanathan, *Googlization of Everything*, 182.
90 "Google Home Official Ad" (video 2017).
91 Lilyn Hester, "Rolling Study Halls: Turning Bus Time into Learning Time," *Google The Keyword* (April 2, 2018), accessed October 26, 2024, https://www.blog.google/outreach-initiatives/grow-with-google/rolling-study-halls-turning-bus-time-learning-time.
92 Google, *Driving Change with Rolling Study Halls* (video) (March 15, 2019), accessed October 26, 2024, https://www.youtube.com/watch?v=bJKJLK_aeIE.
93 Google Arts & Culture, "Slogans for the Class of 2030 by Douglas Coupland," accessed October 26, 2024, https://artsandculture.google.com/story/slogans-for-the-class-of-2030-by-douglas-coupland/vQURjwPHHpa5uw.

94 Google Arts & Culture, "Douglas Coupland's New Slogans Powered by AI" (video) (2022), accessed October 26, 2024, https://www.youtube.com/watch?v=6-0pcsS2tkg.

95 bell hooks, *Teaching to Transgress: Education as the Practice of Freedom* (London: Routledge, 1994), 16.

96 hooks, *Teaching to Transgress*, 16.

97 Neil Selwyn, *Should Robots Replace Teachers? AI and the Future of Education* (Cambridge: Polity Press, 2019), 9.

98 Freire, *Pedagogy of the Oppressed*, 80.

99 Jacques Rancière, *The Ignorant Schoolmaster: Five Lessons in Intellectual Emancipation*, trans. Kristin Ross (Stanford: Stanford University Press, 1991), 15.

100 Donna Landry and Gerald Maclean, "Introduction: Reading Spivak," in Donna Landry and Gerald Maclean, eds., *The Spivak Reader* (London: Routledge, 1996), 1–14, p. 4.

101 Landry and Maclean, "Introduction: Reading Spivak," 4.

102 I take the term "unlearning machine" from a course design for "A Pedagogy of Machines." Paolo Caffoni, "A Pedagogy of Machines: Making Tools for Education" (course design Künstliche Intelligenz und Medienphilosophie HfG Karlsruhe, April 14, 2022), accessed October 26, 2024, https://kim.hfg-karlsruhe.de/pedagogy-of-machines.

103 Google for Education, "Emerging Technologies: A Conversation with Michael Bodaeker" (2018), accessed October 26, 2024, https://edu.google.com/intl/ALL_au/future-of-the-classroom/emerging-technologies.

104 "Google Expeditions: Bringing the World to your Classroom in Virtual Reality" (slide show) [no year], accessed October 15, 2022, https://sites.google.com/tcsnc.org/tcs-g-expeditions/google-expeditions-app.

105 Jennifer Holland, "Expanding Google Arts & Culture with Expeditions," *Google The Keyword* (November 31, 2020), accessed October 26, 2024, https://blog.google/outreach-initiatives/education/expanding-google-arts-and-culture-expeditions.

106 Google for Education, *Future of the Classroom: Emerging Trends in K-12 Education (Global Edition)*, 2018, 49, accessed October 26, 2024, https://services.google.com/fh/files/misc/future_of_the_classroom_emerging_trends_in_k12_education.pdf.

107 See Google Arts & Culture, "*Take a Virtual Field Trip: Where Do You Want to Go Today?*" [no date], accessed October 26, 2024, https://artsandculture.google.com/project/expeditions.

108 Noam Cohen, "Wikipedia is Finally Asking Big Tech to Pay Up," *Wired* (March 16, 2021), accessed October 26, 2024, https://www.wired.com/story/wikipedia-finally-asking-big-tech-to-pay-up.

109 Bobbie Johnson, "Wikipedia Wins the Google Lottery—but Why?," *The Guardian* (February 18, 2010), accessed October 26, 2024, https://www.theguardian.com/technology/blog/2010/feb/18/wikipedia-google.

110 Wright, *Cataloging the World*, 284.

111 Wikipedia, "Wikipedia," accessed October 26, 2024, https://en.wikipedia.org/wiki/Wikipedia.

112 Richard Cooke, "Wikipedia Is the Last Best Place on the Internet," *Wired* (February 17, 2020), accessed October 26, 2024, https://www.wired.com/story/wikipedia-online-encyclopedia-best-place-internet.

113 Martin Dittus, "The Uneven Geography of Wikipedia," *Oxford Internet Institute* (October 16, 2018), accessed October 26, 2024, https://geography.oii.ox.ac.uk/the-uneven-geography-of-wikipedia.

114 X, "Moonshot," accessed October 26, 2024, https://x.company/moonshot.

115 Google Workspace, "Moonshot Thinking from Astro Zeller" (video) (2013), accessed October 26, 2024, https://www.youtube.com/watch?v=cA_8IO3vbFs.

116 X, *Moonshots: A Game of Radical Thinking* [online game] (2021), accessed October 26, 2024, https://x.company/moonshots-game/intro#step-two.

117 Ted, *The Unexpected Benefit of Creating Failure* (video) (2016), accessed October 26, 2024, https://www.ted.com/talks/astro_teller_the_unexpected_benefit_of_celebrating_failure.

118 X, "Moonshot."

119 Oliver Franklin-Wallis, "Inside X, Google's Top-Secret Moonshot Factory," *Wired* (February 17, 2020), accessed October 26, 2024, https://www.wired.co.uk/article/ten-years-of-google-x.

120 Wendy Chun, "Big Data as Drama," *ELH* 83.2 (2016): 363–82, p. 363.

121 Chun, "Big Data as Drama," 370.

122 Chun, "Big Data as Drama," 370.

123 Drake Baer, "Here's What Google Teaches Employees in its 'Search Inside Yourself' Course," *Insider* (August 5, 2014), accessed October 26, 2024, https://www.businessinsider.com/search-inside-yourself-googles-life-changing-mindfulness-course-2014-8.

124 Chade-Meng Tan, *Search Inside Yourself: The Unexpected Path to Achieving Success, Happiness (and World Peace)* (San Francisco: Harper One, 2015).

125 See my article "Mad Men and Mindfulness" in *Discourse* 40(3) (2018): 273–307.

126 Noah Shachtman, "In Silicon Valley, Meditation Is No Fad. It Could Make Your Career," *Wired* (June 18, 2013), accessed October 26, 2024, https://www.wired.com/2013/06/meditation-mindfulness-silicon-valley.

127 Deleuze, *Abécédaire*.

4 LOVE

Is Everything OK, Cupid?

To love someone under capitalism you have to love EVERYONE. *Is that theory or just theology?*
                      SALLY ROONEY, *CONVERSATIONS WITH FRIENDS* (2007)[1]

Everyone

At one point in her novel *Conversations with Friends* Sally Rooney has one of the protagonists muse that to love someone under capitalism is to love everyone. The phrase resonated with me, because indeed—and as I interpret this phrase—to open up and surrender to love is to see the vulnerability of people, perhaps *all* people, as they are subject to the powers dividing them, internally and socially. At the same time, people's modern practices of love are hard to separate from capitalism. This holds all the more true in an increasingly technocolonial world, in which corporate dating platforms make money by people's longing for connection. How to resist this data-driven reality without moralizing people's participation in it?

Engaging that dilemma, in this chapter I will focus on the dating platform OkCupid, in its own words "the Google of online dating."[2] In order to help its users find love, the platform asks them many questions, such as: "In the line *Wherefore art thou Romeo?* what does 'wherefore' mean? Is that *Why?*, *Where?*, or *Who cares/wtf?*" Directly related: "Do you believe that studying literature is beneficial?" Or, "Would you consider yourself a feminist?" As of 2023, these questions may also be written by ChatGPT, because OkCupid believes in AI. For example, the chatbot asks the very human question, "How do you balance your own needs with the needs of your partner in a relationship?"[3]

Clicking along, the user fuels the matching algorithms of OkCupid. The more questions answered, the better the matches, such is the promise. And of course: the more intimate data for OkCupid. As one commentator succinctly renders the company's business model: "Your data for a date."[4] This observation of course holds true for all major online dating platforms, from Tinder to Hinge (like OkCupid both owned by the Match group), from Bumble to Grindr. In their advertising campaigns these platforms promote a culture of consent. Meanwhile, they compel users to consent to conditions that erode the space from which consent can be given.

This chapter shows how profit-driven online dating platforms contribute to the simultaneous privatization and acceleration of *dating*, understood as the modern cultural practice in which individuals seek romantic and/or otherwise intimate association. I focus on OkCupid for two reasons. The first reason is, as said, OkCupid's data-driven approach to dating. The second reason is OkCupid's outspoken, and over the years increasingly *woke*, self-presentation, on the platform itself, on its provocative billboards, in video commercials compelling people to find love in their own way (Figure 52), and on its blog, subsequently called Ok Trends, The Deep End, and now simply the OkCupid Dating Blog. There is nothing progressive, however, about the datafication of dating, and OkCupid's pink-washing only makes things worse.

OkCupid was founded in 2004 by four mathematics and computing students at Harvard University. Originally called SparkMatch, OkCupid set itself apart from then market leader Match.com by working with a matching algorithm. This algorithm determines the likelihood of users getting along. It does so on the basis of self-provided user information, as through self-quizzes and personality tests. In 2011, OkCupid was acquired by the Match group, only months after OkCupid had bashed the subscription-based Match.com in a blog post titled "Why You Should Never Pay for Online Dating."[5] In subsequent years, the Match group, which went public in 2020, also acquired the dating platforms Tinder, Hinge, and Plenty Of Fish.

Also, after its acquisition by Match, OkCupid has continued to profile itself as a company that does dating differently. Take its admittedly clever 2018 "DTF" advertising campaign. In billboards and online ads this campaign took the internet slang expression "DTF" (which means *willing to have sex with*) and resignified it in many ways, like "Down to fall head over heels," "Down to furiously make out," "Down to filter out the far

FIGURE 52 "With OkCupid you can find love, your way" (screen capture from video, © OkCupid, 2021, all rights reserved).[6]

FIGURE 53 OkCupid's DTF billboard campaign (screen capture from video, © Overall Mural, 2019, all rights reserved).[7]

right," and above all: "Down to fix dating" (Figure 53). As OkCupid explains on its blog:

> At OkCupid we know a lot about dating. Dating can be an amazing, butterflies-in-stomach kind of thing. But sometimes dating can be a not-so-amazing kind of thing, thanks to everything from ghosting to DTF, a term largely used by men in a derogatory way about women meaning they're "down to f*ck." So we decided that in 2018, it's time to change that; at OkCupid, we've made it our mission to help redefine the F in DTF to be whatever the F you want it to be, whether that's Down to Feel Fabulous, Down to Foot the bill, Down to Forget your baggage, or yes, Down to F*ck—if it's *your* choice, you're empowered to make the F whatever you want.[8]

Also, on the platform itself OkCupid has been invested in user empowerment. Since 2014, OkCupid allows users to choose from a wide range of gender identities (from Cis Woman to No-Binary, from Transgender to Two Spirit) and sexual orientations (from Heteroflexible to Asexual, from Akiosexual to Aroflux). Users identifying other than as straight are also given the option to block straight people from seeing their profile. OkCupid thus tries to make dating for *everyone*, and the company prides itself on this inclusive mindset. In 2021, following the Covid-19 lockdown seasons, OkCupid celebrated the "summer of love" with a new colorful campaign, titled "For every person." The campaign dedicated itself to "every single" bear, bookworm, cuddler, feminist, heavy petter, insomniac, introvert, monogamist, non-monogamist, nonbinary, pansexual, romantic, submissive, toker (someone who smokes marijuana), tree-hugger, vaxxer, and vegetarian. As far as "every single vaxxer" is concerned: knowing its user demographic, OkCupid is not afraid to speak out and advertise its progressive leanings. The company has also introduced a feature to filter out climate change deniers (climate change being "the #1 issue to daters in 2022" according to the platform).[9] And in the wake of the overturning of the 1973 Roe vs. Wade abortion ruling by the United States Supreme Court, the company relaunched the campaign to support "every single pro-choicer."

This is all great, but it doesn't prevent OkCupid's business model being based on the exploitation of highly personal information by means not so concerned with people's uniqueness. From the perspective of the company's bottom line, the user is a mere set of data points that only has value insofar as it is part of a cloud of correlations.

OkCupid has admitted, moreover, to experiment on users. As company co-founder Christian Rudder wrote in 2014, in a blog entry titled "We experiment on human beings," the platform lied to a portion of its users about their match percentages with other users, this in order to observe when single messages evolved into full conversations. As it turned out, "the mere myth of compatibility works just as well as the truth."[10] Regardless of whether such experiments continue, the company sells user data for advertising purposes. OkCupid asks its users many questions, but the real question is: How comfortable are you with the platform exploiting your intimate life and craving for connection? This chapter is a critique of corporate online dating. I do acknowledge online dating's emancipatory potential: online dating may be a tactic to negotiate patriarchal structures, hegemonic understandings of love, and feelings of isolation. At the same time, profit-driven online dating platforms are part of capitalism's transformation into a technocolonial system that treats people as human-things.

This chapter has seven sections: following this introduction, the next section engages the much-heard critique that online dating poses a threat to spontaneity. I only partially agree, because online dating may also be emancipatory. As I argue in section three, online dating transforms the modern practice of dating and its contribution to individual liberation. Section four zooms in on OkCupid's transhumanist position according to which desire and love are quantifiable processes that may be optimized through "more data." Sections five and six juxtapose this transhumanist position to a posthuman analysis of how people are integrated into a clouded technocolonial crowd. I argue that in order to resist technocolonialism's commodification of community, we need to foster inclusive common spaces and conversations (with friends *and* strangers) that embed love in its broader sociocultural textures. Section seven, titled CONSENT, grounds such spaces and conversations in a culture of consent, "consent" understood broadly as sensing together. To foster a culture of consent begins with the realization that the personal is political, and that the personal*ized* is political. To do so is to liberate dating from its datafication.

Willing

How WILLING *are you to meet someone from OkCupid in person?*
OKCUPID MATCH QUESTION[11]

A much-heard critique of online dating is that it poses a threat to the spontaneity of the chance encounter. I will address this critique via the cinematic genre of the romantic comedy, *the* place for chance encounters that simply *had* to be. In a 2017 reportage, titled "Why Hasn't Online Dating Made It Onscreen?," the American NPR observes that while Hollywood *loves* technology, the romantic comedy still resists incorporating "everyday tech of contemporary life into the stories it tells."[12] In order to explain this indeed remarkable long-time underrepresentation of online encounters in the cinematic imagination, the NPR offers two hypotheses. The first is that the practice of online dating—in which people actively seek out a partner—lowers the tension that romantic plots traditionally hinge on. The second hypothesis is that online dating does not allow for appealing visuals: to watch people clicking on a screen, or swiping right in an app, is simply *too* boring.

Interestingly, these two hypotheses plausibly explain why the first modern Hollywood classic that *does* revolve around two people who meet online, hardly shows that online encounter itself, even though the film's opening sequence proves that clicking in a screen interface can in fact make for interesting visuals.

I'm referring to *You've Got Mail*, a 1998 film directed by Nora Ephron (who earlier wrote the script for *When Harry Met Sally*). In the first few shots, the viewer follows a cursor moving across a desktop computer screen that fills the entire frame. On a mouse click, a new window opens, showing an animation of a rastered spinning globe as in a Google Earth graphic avant la lettre. As the image zooms in on the globe, it transitions into a 3D-computer-animated scale model of Manhattan, from bird's eye to street view, past the Empire State Building (we're in a car now), left on 93rd Street, where the sequence halts in front of an apartment building (Figures 54, 55, and 56). While the animation dissolves into location-shot footage, the camera swirls through an open window where we meet Kathleen, who is still in her pajamas. Kathleen (Meg Ryan) rushes to her laptop, where she finds a new message from Joe (Tom Hanks), whom she

FIGURE 54 TO 56 Opening sequence *You've Got Mail* (screen capture from video, © Lauren Shuler Donner Productions, 1998, all rights reserved).

has met, so we learn later, in an over-30s chatroom. Kathleen mimics her computer's voice: "You've got mail!"

The film continues in the vein of *When Harry Met Sally* (dir. Rob Reiner, 1989), which is as a prolonged encounter of two souls who are meant for each other, not *despite* but *because* of their differences. Would Kathleen and Joe have met without the internet, who will tell? But online technology, so much is clear, mediates the *missed* encounter that is inherent to the metropolitan crowd. As said, *You've Got Mail* skips over its protagonists' *actual* first encounter, the story of when "Shopgirl" met "NYC152," as are Kathleen's and Tom's respective profile names. Did they click immediately? Did they also chat with other users? And what in their typed words attracted to each other? The film leaves those questions unanswered.

You've Got Mail takes place in the late 1990s, but the film still captures the essence of online dating. As a medium, online dating mediates the crowd. As a cultural practice, online dating starts with the user's creation of a profile, which can be as short as a name. On OkCupid, dating profiles tend to get quite elaborate. Having registered on the site and selected one's identifications and orientations, the user is invited to respond to prompts like "My self-summary" and "The most private thing I'm willing to admit." Many user profiles contain meta-commentary like: "So this is me in a nice typed up box. It's the best typed up version of me I can be." Or, "There's something kind of nerve racking about cementing yourself as a person in a single page profile." As far as "the most private thing I'm willing to admit" category is concerned, the most private thing I'm willing to here share with you, reader, is that in the past I have met people through OkCupid. I won't speak from personal experience, though, if only because people's dating experiences are very contingent on their gender, sexual orientation, race, age, etc.

Most significantly, non-cis male identifying persons who allow their profile to be seen by cisgender men run the risk of receiving a stream of digital harassment. OkCupid has tried to combat this "DTF" spam by allowing users to only message other users after they have mutually "liked" each other. OkCupid aims, moreover, to *personalize* the user experience by showing users relatively more profiles from those the algorithm "thinks" they match with. This matching algorithm feeds itself with the answers that users give to the platform's questions: "Would you consider dating someone who was regularly seeing a therapist?," "Regardless of future plans, what's more interesting to you right now? Sex or love?," "Which type of intelligence is most valuable to you?" And crucially, "How willing are you to meet someone from OkCupid in person?"

Let's say that like Shopgirl and NYC152 we're "totally willing" to go on an offline date, what can we hope for? First of all, we hope, of course, that we haven't fallen prey to a bot (a program crawling online platforms) or a catfish (a person who willfully deceives others by using a false online identity). Beyond that, we hope that our date will somewhat match the expectations that have started to form in our mind's eye, based on their profile, messages, and further internet presence (for those answering "yes" to the question, "Do you google someone before a first date?"). We hope, in other words, that the avatar that has grasped our attention corresponds to the person we're about to meet IRL for the very first time.

On that first date, questions that will typically play in both persons' minds are: "Do I feel attracted to this person?," "Would I want to have sex with her/them/him?" And, "Would I want to see this person *again*?" Online dating thus takes off as a three-stage process: first one decides whether or not to engage with someone within the digital interface (by liking and/or messaging someone). Second, once an online interaction has been initiated, there's the question of whether to go on a date. Third, there is the crucial question of the second date.

Yet what becomes of spontaneity, of love at first sight, when that first sight is digitally mediated? Doesn't online dating turn love into a number's game and the world into a very boring place where we only hit it off with those we *match* with? In her book *Cold Intimacies* Eva Illouz argues that the advance of online dating means a departure from romantic love. "Whereas romantic love has been characterized by an ideology of spontaneity, the internet demands a rationalized mode of partner selection, which contradicts the idea of love as an unexpected epiphany, erupting in one's life against one's will and reason."[13] Similarly, in *In Praise of Love* (*Eloge de l'amour*) Alain Badiou critiques the French dating site Meetic for advertising its services with slogans like: "Get love without chance!" and "You can be perfectly in love without suffering." Badiou fears "a safety first concept of love." He even compares online dating to an arranged marriage, "not done in the name of family order and hierarchy … but in the name of safety for the individuals involved, through advance agreements that avoid randomness [and] chance encounters."[14]

I agree with Badiou that we have to be critical of online dating platforms, like we have to be critical of corporate network platforms in general. But I don't agree with his theory of love as event. For Badiou, all true love originates in the event or chance encounter. The event, he argues, creates people as subjects. To be, what he calls, "a subject of truth" is to remain faithful to this event, the merging of two lives. "What is universal," Badiou writes, "is that all love proposes a new experience of truth on what it is to be two and not one. That the world may be encountered and experienced in a different manner than by a solitary conscience."[15] By declaring one's love, one recognizes the event as event rather than as a mere chance encounter. The encounter thus transitions "from chance to destiny."[16]

My problem with Badiou's theory of love is that it gives a rather static and normative view on how people meet and change in relation to their encounter. Even though Badiou acknowledges that people's recognition of the chance encounter is not a "one-off," he talks about that encounter as a singular moment in time that marks a clear before and after. According to Badiou's notion of love as an event, the chance encounter is the absolute beginning that precedes and thus escapes the chain of events called dating. The chance encounter is a burst of love that precedes dating, and the first date is thus in fact the second encounter, the re-encounter that marks what Badiou calls the transition from chance to destiny.

But encounters may take many forms, and subjects transform in many ways. Encounters often happen over time, as people discover different sides of each other and themselves. Over time, people may also change in relation to these encounters. In contrast with Badiou, I see subjectivity as an ever-moving relational process that continuously evolves through encounters. Such encounters may be shared with one or several other people, while also unanswered love can be transformative.

There is a moralistic side to Badiou's theory of love. Too much Badiou's eulogy reads as a good story on the subject, in which people meet and then live happily ever after. Think of the seemingly unscripted happy old couple interviews that frame the story of *When Harry Met Sally* (for which Reiner interviewed actual couples, after which he had actors reenact the interviews). Such love stories almost too good to be true *do* happen, but even in those cases chance encounters—and people's openness to and ability to act on chance—are mediated by their contexts, orientations of the people involved, as well as social power relations. All this goes missing in Badiou, who as Nina Varsava argues, sets up love as a two-scene, idealizing monogamous lifelong love. Badiou, Varsava observes, "assumes that everyone has equal access to love, and to its more pleasurable risks."[17] In doing so, he ignores that online dating has been particularly emancipatory for sexual minorities.

For example, as Mary Gray writes in *Out in the Country: Youth, Media, and Queer Visibility in Rural America*, for queer youngsters in the rural US, the internet has made it easier to find a like-minded, non-judgmental community. Gray cites the 15-year-old Amy:

> I first started noticing that I was attracted to other girls when I was about 12 or 13. Before then, I can't even say that I knew gay people existed … It wasn't until about a year later, when I got on the internet and found other people like me, that I actually said to myself that I was bisexual. I've always been attracted to both sexes, but I found my true identity on the internet.[18]

Such perspectives are missing from romanticizations of love as an event. A critique of online dating therefore only makes sense if it *also* acknowledges online dating's emancipatory potential. Before I move to the heart of my critique—the datafication of the user experience by corporate dating platforms—it is necessary to ask: What actually is dating?

Dating

When it came to the socially acceptable rituals of DATING *or courtship, leading to marriage, they were heavily prescribed. In fact they were not even recognized as courtship at this stage.*
  NICHI HODGSON, *THE CURIOUS HISTORY OF DATING* (2017)[19]

Dating is the social practice that two (or more) people arrange to meet, or meet again, in order to spend or potentially spend intimate time together, yet without that they necessarily commit to a relationship, however understood. For people who date with the intention of finding a life partner, dating is a sort of evaluation or trial period to find out what life might feel like when shared with the other person(s). In Anglo-American contexts, dating may also refer to a committed sexual and/or romantic relationship beyond this trial stage. Dating is a private affair that usually takes place in public space, or that at least often starts in public space. People often speak of the dating market, but it is more precise to say that dating networks are structured *like* markets. Unlike labor, dating is not a market activity, though as a practice it belongs to modern urban capitalist society in which people have a certain degree of individual freedom (heterosexual white men traditionally more than women and sexual and ethnic minorities).

In her book *The Curious History of Dating: From Jane Austen to Tinder* Nichi Hodgson locates the prehistory of dating in the late 1700s, when practices of courtship were still heavily reined in by social prescriptions. Dating is a very modern practice. It emerged in societies in which decisions regarding romantic and/or sexual relationships (including marriage) began to be seen as primarily an affair of the individuals involved. The first use of the word "date" in a romantic context is attributed to the American columnist George Ade. In 1896, he wrote in the *Chicago Record* about a clerk named Artie whose partner felt attracted to other men. Confronting her about this situation, he said, with reference to his partner's diary: "I s'pose the other boy's fillin' all my dates?"[20]

In that same late-Victorian era, conventions around courtship were shifting, which had much to do with the slow recognition of women as subjects. In Victorian England, up until 1870 everything a woman had inherited and owned went to her husband after their marriage. The Married Women's Property Act changed this situation. Around this time, in the United States married women were also increasingly granted a separate economy. Certainly, for women of well-to-do families this meant that marriage no longer was a primarily financial affair.

In the United States there was also the "free love" movement that questioned whether women should marry at all. Instead, this movement sought to imagine alternative family forms. For example, the anarchist Lillie White announced in 1891 that "when women learn that their best and highest object of life is to be independent and free, instead of living to make some man comfortable ... we shall have loving, harmonious families and happy homes."[21] In order to avoid unwanted pregnancies, women in this free love movement experimented with forms of non-penetrative sex. There was also an emerging clandestine discourse about contraception, as through the 1877 pamphlet *The Law of Population* by the feminist Annie Besant (who upon publication of her pamphlet was tried for obscenity).[22]

This women's struggle for self-determination happened at a time when everyday life changed rapidly. As Hodgson writes, new modes of transportation and communication revolutionized the possibilities of romance. While the bicycle already was "the weapon for the Victorian 'New Woman,'" the steam train really "hotted things up." Not only did it allow people to see a lover in a different town or region, carriages and waiting rooms also placed men and women "in a novel proximity."[23] Moreover, the rapid growth of cities and city populations increased the potential for chance encounters, for love as event.

Like dating, the ideal of love as something that may happen anytime—of love as something serendipitous that one has to be *open* to—is an essentially modern phenomenon that gained dominance with the growth of crowds. As Charles Baudelaire writes in *The Painter of Modern Life* (1859-1860), the crowd is the other, the "non-I" that creates people as relatively anonymous individuals.[24] In the crowd, the individual may feel alone, but the crowd may also be a "place" of happy accidents and collisions, of love at first sight. The crowd is also the site of missed encounters, of what Walter Benjamin with reference to Baudelaire calls love "at last sight," when the male gaze is fended off by the mysteriously veiled woman "mutely borne along by the crowd."[25]

As the Benjamin passage illustrates, crowds are not neutral spaces filled with randomly floating bodies who have random chance encounters. Crowds are bodies, the movements of those bodies, as well as the power relations between those bodies, including their gazes. Some bodies are more able to be open to chance encounters than others, and some bodies have more freedoms to act on chance than others. As Sara Ahmed writes: "Crowds are not simply going *whichever* way, they tend to be orientated or directed (by the geography of a street, by following an established route or path)." Crowds have a will, in other words, and "to become part of a crowd might involve being willing to be affected by what is near."[26]

The crowd is not a neutral space, nor is it necessarily a safe or easy space to meet others. People's attempts to mediate the crowd in order to find a romantic match go long back. The prehistory of online dating started in 1695, only a few years after the invention of the modern newspaper. In history's first lonely hearts ad, we read that "a Gentleman about 30 years of age [with] a very good estate, would willingly match himself to some good young Gentlewoman, that has a fortune of 3000 *l.* of thereabout."[27] In the decades after, personal ads also started to be used by people looking for male homosexual love. These ads used codewords and female names to express a forbidden yearning. The first known personal ad placed by a woman dates from 1727, by a lady called Helen

Morrison in the *Manchester Weekly Journal*. After placing the ad, she was sent to an asylum for a month.[28]

In subsequent centuries, the popularity of personal ads went up and down. Following a normalization in the mid-1800s, the emergence of scams later that century made people again more cautious. In the 1900s, the personal listing enjoyed a renaissance in the United States, both in cities and in rural areas. In New York City and Washington DC, there was the phenomenon of the New Year's call, when young single women held open house and invite, often through newspaper ads, eligible bachelors to stop by. As the NPR reports about this "communitywide speed dating" custom:

> By convention, male visitors were invited to the house. If the woman wanted the man to stay for a while, she could ask him to remove his hat and coat. Otherwise, she was to offer refreshments and conversation while he remained dressed for the cold. [As *Hill's Manual of Social and Business Forms* insisted, the] "call should not exceed 10 or 15 minutes ... unless the callers are few and it should be agreeable to prolong the stay." ... The women were encouraged to "present themselves in full dress" and make sure to have a crackling fire in the fireplace ... In the days following New Year's, it was customary for women to go see other women and download to each other all the juicy information they had gleaned from the parade of gentlemen callers.[29]

Over a century later, online dating has largely replaced the personal ad, certainly since Craigslist has discontinued its personal listings. But there is also a clear continuation between the personal ad and online dating. Like printed ads before, online dating allows individuals to mediate the crowd and meet others outside of their everyday lifepaths and communities.

Before dating went online, it already got computerized. Much as with the launch of the modern newspaper, the introduction in 1960 of the first mass-market computer (the IBM 1401) was soon followed by its use for match making. In 1964, the British Joan Ball, inspired by a Swiss computer dating service, converted her marriage bureau Eros Friendship into the St. James Computer Dating Service, the first commercially successful computer dating service in the UK. The next year, Ball merged her company with another marriage bureau, also run by a woman, in order to form Com-Pat, or Computer Dating Services Ltd. Interestingly, Ball (who soon became Com-Pat's sole director) blamed another technology for the need of her services: she believed that people were socializing less because of television.[30]

Meanwhile across the Atlantic, in 1965 three male Harvard students began Operation Match. This service worked with questionnaires in which students described themselves and their ideal dates. For three dollars they could have this information analyzed by the computer. The results were printed onto punch cards, upon which the machine generated five matches for each customer, which were then sent to them by mail. One of the co-founders is quoted as saying: "We're not trying to take the love out of love. We're just trying to make it more efficient. We supply everything but the spark"[31] (Figure 57).

There are quite some differences between Com-Pat and Operation Spark. The former was predominantly marriage-oriented and catered to a relatively small and slightly older crowd, including widowed and divorced people. The latter targeted a largely young demographic of mostly college students and claimed to revolutionize love. However, there was nothing revolutionary about Operation Match, which was based on rather conservative and misogynistic values. As Mar Hicks writes, Operation Match (and similar services popping up soon) did not simply facilitate the pairing up of men and women, they also placed control of matchmaking in the hands of mostly heterosexual, white, and financially

FIGURE 57 "Computer with a heart" (screen capture from video, © British Pathé, 2014, all rights reserved).[32]

privileged young men. "These young men wanted a way to 'get' women without actually having to spend time in women's company. Their service implicitly positioned women as a product, and assumed that men were the users around whose needs the service should be built."[33]

So, whereas dating in the late nineteenth century emerged as a quite liberating social practice connected to women's emancipation, this is not necessarily the case with computerized matchmatchmaking. The story of Operation Match reminds us of Facebook, initially called Facemash. Like Operation Match, Facemash began at Harvard as a tool to objectify women: in 2003, after a breakup, Mark Zuckerberg hacked the school's server, stole pictures from his female classmates, and together with a friend developed an algorithm to rank the women. Also, OkCupid is the product of white male Harvard students. But OkCupid—certainly as of 2014 when it introduced its gender and sexuality categories—has explicitly marketed itself as feminist. The company's datafication of user experience is all but feminist, though.

EXPERIMENT WITHOUT TECH #4: A DATE WITH YOURSELF

In this last experiment you are invited to go on a date with the other that is you, so with yourself. The experiment is inspired by both Julia Cameron's book *The Artist Way* (and its suggested practice of a weekly artist's date)[34] and Jessica Fern's *Polysecure: Attachment, Trauma and Consensual Non-monogamy*. In there, Fern writes about self-attunement, "the inner inquiry into what you are feeling, needing, thinking and experiencing."[35] She specifically directs her reflections to those who feel insecurely attached, but I would argue that in our burnout society and its scattering of life, some self-attunement is beneficial to everyone. The idea is simple: take yourself on a date. Take some time in your day and go do something that takes you out of your everyday rhythms and habits (and that perhaps allows you to reflect on those rhythms and habits). You can go to a museum or for a stroll in the city, like a part of the city you know less. You can also go swimming, or dancing. Anything goes. While on your

> date, be present with yourself, much like you would—ideally—be present with another person (or persons) when being on a date with them. Because in a way you are meeting *another* person; you are meeting yourself anew. To go on a date is to be willing to meet the other, which makes every date a first date. This is also important to keep in mind with online dating by the way: even though in OkCupid's and Tinder's profile streams people appear as fungible commodities to be "liked" or "dismissed," all those other people are as multiple as you.

Data*

With DATA, history can become deeper. It can become more.
                      OKCUPID FOUNDER CHRISTIAN RUDDER IN HIS BOOK *DATACLYSM: WHO WE REALLY ARE** (2014)[36]

Of all online dating companies, OkCupid has articulated the most outspoken belief in data. OkCupid's dataism is built on two tenets, namely that more data is *better*, and that data offer a *more authentic*, "deeper" perspective. In 2009, the company began a blog to report about behavioral patterns deducted from its collected user data. In one of the first posts, we learn that people on average are actually 5 centimeters (2 inches) shorter than they write on their profiles.[37] More recently, in the company's 2022 "Global State of Online Dating," OkCupid reports that nearly three-quarters of users respond to be open to discuss mental health with their partner. In analysis of this finding, the company writes that "being vulnerable is one of the more attractive traits to singles these days … We expect these numbers to only increase in 2023 as Gen Z singles continue to drive conversations around mental health."[38]

    How have online dating platforms like OkCupid changed dating, which as stated in the previous section is a private affair that usually starts in public space? The short answer is that online dating platforms, like all platformized media, privatize the public encounter while accelerating human experience—in this case practices of courtship (Figure 58).

FIGURE 58 Love Invasion (Toronto 2016, photo by the author, artwork by Matthew Del Degan).

As far as privatization is concerned: unlike the urban chance encounter, online dating starts in the private sphere. As Marie Bergström writes in her book *The New Laws of Love: Online Dating and the Privatization of Intimacy*, online dating is something personal. "Of course," she argues, "people may browse profiles in the company of friends, and many users share their online experiences with others; but meeting partners through specialized platforms is different from encounters at school, work, or social events."[39] Online dating also accelerates dating. It makes everything go faster. "That's what users say, and that's what surveys show … Online dating shortens the courtship phase between first contact and first intercourse."[40]

Bergström convincingly argues that, despite these changes, online dating has not led to a revolution in dating, and that the couple norm continues to prevail (a norm that OkCupid sibling company Hinge up on in its advertising; Figure 58). Nor should we conclude too quickly that intimate relations have been taken over by commodification and rationalization. Bergström emphasizes the distinction between

FIGURE 59 "Great love instead of fast sex" as promised by OkCupid sibling company Hinge (Munich 2022, photo by the author).

online dating as an industry and as a practice, adding that the market mechanisms that rule the former don't necessarily carry over into the latter. "Conflating the two would, on the one hand, lead to a mechanical and deterministic reading of social behavior and, on the other hand, fail to recognize the autonomy of the market."[41]

I only partially agree with this last point. While it is true that people make do with commercial online dating infrastructures, Bergström leaves unacknowledged that these infrastructures are also designed to collect user data. The privatization of dating goes hand in hand with the personalization of user experience, that is the stream of profiles by other users shown in one's feed. The more this stream tunes into a user's desire, the higher their engagement with the platform, and thus the more data for the platform company. This datafication of user experience lies at the basis of dating's online acceleration.

In 2014, OkCupid co-founder Christian Rudder published the book *Dataclysm*, in which he "theorizes" OkCupid's belief in data as a transparent window on what moves the digitalizing generations:

> I know there are a lot of people making big claims about data, and I'm not here to say it will change the course of history ... but it will, I believe, change what history *is* ... Unlike clay tablets, unlike papyrus, unlike paper, newsprint, celluloid, or photo stock, disk space is cheap and nearly inexhaustible. On a hard drive there's room for more than just the heroes.[42]

Rudder thus attributes a strong emancipatory potential to data, though he also admits that even with more data, everyday people will remain more or less nameless, but at least "we all will be counted."[43]

We here have the first tenet of OkCupid's belief system: the more data the better (Figures 60, 61, and 62). The title of Rudder's book reflects this belief: "dataclysm" is a contraction of "data" and "cataclysm" (which derives from "kataklysmos," Greek for the Old Testament Flood). Yes, Rudder admits, there is an unprecedented downpour of data, but "there's also the hope of a world transformed—of both yesterday's stunted understanding and today's limited vision gone with the flood."[44]

This brings us to the second tenet of OkCupid's dataism: data offer an authentic and transparent view on human life. Rudder writes:

> As for the data's authenticity, much of it is, in a sense, fact-checked, because the internet is now such a part of everyday life. Take the data from OkCupid. You give the site your city, your gender, your age, and who you're looking for, and it helps you find someone to meet for coffee or a beer. Your profile is supposed to be you, the true version.[45]

This belief that data-driven systems enhance human life and facilitate the *true you* is a transhumanist position, according to which humans and machines interact in synergy. This position is further illustrated by a picture that in 2017 appeared on the OkCupid home page. In this picture, we see a person painting a self-portrait on a smartphone that functions doubly as canvas and mirror. The technological mediation of this act of self-portrayal is emphasized by a second smartphone in the image—this one of a clunkier make—that substitutes for the artist's body. The artist is painting their true self. What guarantees that their self-image (as reflected in the mirror) and their profile (as painted on the screen) are indeed one and the same, is that the author keeps their head, which remains unmediated other than by the beret on top of it. It is the head

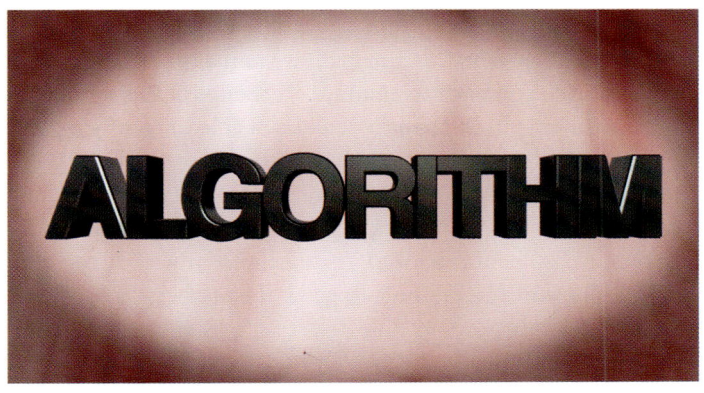

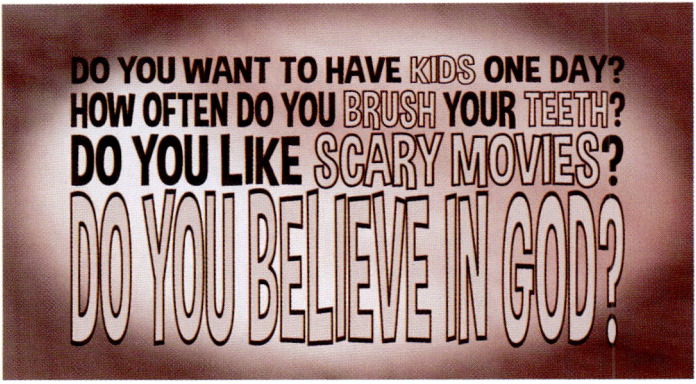

FIGURE 60 TO 62 OkCupid's dataism according to Christian Rudder (screen capture from video, © Ted-Ed, 2013, all rights reserved).[46]

of a centered individual who goes for "substance, not *just* selfies," as the tagline reads.

In December that year, OkCupid's desire to make online dating more substantial led the company to announce a change of their profile name policy. Whereas up until then users had been able to choose *any* profile name, after the policy change the site would display people's *actual* first names (i.e., the first name under which a user registers, and under which existing users had registered without knowing that it would become part of their public profile information). As the platform wrote in an email to all users: "Hello, real you. It's time to go by the perfectly great name you already have."[47]

The announced change did not fly well with many users. In app stores, OkCupid was flooded with one-star reviews while users pointed out that the policy would negatively affect those who want not to be stalked or need some discretion.[48] As user "YouSuckOKC" wrote on the OkCupid blog: "Stop with the patronizing, unfunny blog posts defending your needless changes … Usernames give people choice. They protect people. If we want to give our names when connecting with someone, we will make that choice ourselves."[49] In response, the company backtracked on the intended policy change. Soon after, it traded the "substance, not *just* selfies" for the empowering Down to Fix dating campaign that I already discussed in the introduction to this chapter.

This shift in branding strategies may be taken as an attempt by OkCupid to resonate again with its relatively progressive, feminist, and queer user population. Under the hood, though, OkCupid's data-driven non-philosophy has stayed very much the same. To cite one more time from Rudder's book, OkCupid sees it as its challenge to

> chop and jam the continuum of human experience into little buckets … without anyone noticing: to divide some vast, ineffable process—for Facebook, friendship, for Reddit, community, for dating sites, love—into pieces a server can handle. At the same time you have to retain as much of the *je ne sais quoi* of the thing as you can, so the users believe what you're offering represents real life.[50]

This passage reveals a clear discrepancy in Rudder's dataism. On the one hand, he talks about the platform's data-driven user environment as the *illusion* of real life. On the other hand, he treats collected user data as a *transparent window* on real life, leaving unacknowledged that the datafication of user experience changes that experience.

As far as the chopping up of human experience is concerned: at OkCupid this happens both behind the screen and in the interface itself. Since 2014, OkCupid allows users to choose from a wide range of gender identities and sexual orientations. In his book *Trans**, Jack Halberstam is critical of this practice. Halberstam acknowledges that these categories have emerged within communities that seek to name their multiplicity. But he also argues that these new "vernacular systems" of classification don't necessarily shift "the central and dominant binaries of race, class, gender, and sexuality."[51] Instead of this ever-growing multiplicity of gender categories, Halberstam opts for "trans*" as a concept that expresses the openness of sexual and gender identity. The *, he argues, indicates a wildcard, for example when looking up something on the internet. It is a diacritical mark that poses a question to what comes before it. "Trans*" signals the insufficiency of classificatory systems. Halberstam argues that "the solution is not to impose ever more precise calibrations of bodily identity but rather to think in new and different ways about what it means to claim a body."[52]

The * also appears in the subtitle of Rudder's *Dataclysm* (in one of its two editions). This subtitle is *Who We Are**, with the asterisk referring to *When We Think No One's Looking* (printed at the bottom of the cover). This is all very cheeky, much like OkCupid's advertising campaigns and Rudder's confession in 2014 that the company experiments on people. Those experiments are not the main problem, though. The main problem with OkCupid is that when no one is looking they are selling your data.

Common

Not just our labor, not just our leisure—something else is being commodified here: our sociability, our COMMON *and ordinary life together, what you might even call our communism.*

MCKENZIE WARK, *CAPITAL IS DEAD: IS THIS SOMETHING WORSE?* (2019)[53]

Like almost all (if not all) corporate platforms, OkCupid shares personal user data with third parties for advertising purposes. OkCupid reserves the right, moreover, to share data with other companies in its Match group (including subsidiaries Tinder, Match.com, Plenty Of Fish, and Hinge). In doing so OkCupid, like all profit-driven platform companies, commodifies aspects of people's common life, or what McKenzie Wark calls their "communism."

As a 2020 report by the Norwegian Consumer Council concludes, in this data-driven practice OkCupid, and also Tinder, violate the EU's GDPR conditions for informed and explicit consent.[54] This report, titled *Out of Control: How Consumers Are Exploited by the Online Advertising Industry*, zooms in on OkCupid's relation with the New York-based analytics company Braze. This company helps its clients to "create live views of their customers that stream and process historical, in-the-moment, and predictive data in an interactive feedback loop."[55] In order to personalize and optimize that loop, Braze recommends its partners to share as much data as possible. OkCupid has taken this recommendation to heart, which is part of why it asks users so many questions. Tests prove that OkCupid has shared highly personal data about people's sexuality, drug use, political views, ethnicity, and GPS coordinates with Braze, allowing the latter "to identify exceedingly personal details about individuals."[56] It remains unclear whether these data have been shared with Braze purely for analytics purposes, or if Braze has also shared them further with third parties. This lack of transparency is, of course, part of the problem.

OkCupid's business model seems reasonable: your data for a date. Ironically, though, in recent years OkCupid, in its insatiable need for more data, has actually made finding one's match, or matches, *less* efficient. Initially, users could simply navigate the entire database of user profiles and write messages to those who piqued their interest. Since 2017, however, OkCupid has adopted the swipe model known from its sibling company Tinder, in which users see a personalized stream of profiles on which they have to swipe left ("dismiss") or right ("like"). On OkCupid, like on Tinder, people now first need to have liked each other's profiles before being able to chat. According to OkCupid, this so-called DoubleTake system slows down the dating experience, leading to "deeper connections."[57]

This mutual-match model certainly also contributes to the gamification of dating. By making a possible encounter contingent on a mutual "like," OkCupid has introduced an additional chance factor into its matching procedure (namely the possibility that two people would have "matched," had one of them been able to initiate a conversation, but who now don't get to talk to each other, because one of them missed the other's profile, or didn't "like" it at first sight). This intentional degree of mismatch programmed into the platform interface seems part of OkCupid's overall strategy to keep users engaged, and to also incite them to purchase premium access (OkCupid's second main revenue stream, besides selling user data). Yet even premium users don't have the guarantee that when swiping right on someone's profile, that other person will be notified of that "like" (a chance element that would be strongly reduced if *all* users, regardless of membership status, were given full disclosure of all liking information). As Zoetanya Sujon writes in *The Social Media Age*, this "heightened uncertainty around finding a match [makes online dating] similar to gambling, comforting users through repetitive movements and exhilarating them through the excitement of a possible match."[58]

Also, on platforms that don't play games with their users, the online dating market that is not really a market is a reality of imperfect information. First of all, there is a discrepancy between people's self-image and the way they may be perceived by others. Second, there is a discrepancy between people's auto-profiling and their "true selves." Third, as Amy Webb writes in *Data, A Love Story: How I Cracked the Online Dating Code to Meet My Match*, there is one key variable that "is still just as capricious and as undependable as it was five decades ago." That variable is *us*, "the people entering data into these systems are precisely what make them not work."[59] How can the online dater negotiate the reality of imperfect information? Webb reports of her "gaming" the system on JDate, a dating platform for people who identify as Jewish. Armed with color-coded spreadsheets and detailed profiling and messaging strategies, Webb managed to "crack" the dating code and find "true love."

Webb's strategy may not work for everyone, and there are a lot of users actually not looking for that *one* match. But she's of course right: people can increase their chances by thinking through their desires and the way one is perceived by others (an observation that also holds true for offline love searching). Webb observes that for many people the "goal of online dating is to get offline as quickly as possible."[60] *That*, however, to go offline, is not an option for those dating with OkCupid. Also in the scenario that two people meet on the platform, fall in love, enter into a long-term relationship, delete their profiles, and never ever log in on the site again, also then their personal data may still be monetized, sold to third parties, and entered into correlations with more recent personal data harvested by other platform companies.

Over time, the social consequences are enormous. By commodifying people's longing for love, OkCupid contributes to the transformation of community. In order to see how, we have to return to online dating's transformation of dating. As we have seen, online dating privatizes dating and, despite OkCupid's own claim to slow down dating, accelerates it. Online dating takes the start of the encounter to the private sphere, while it shortens the interval between the first encounter and sexual contact. What speeds things up, Bergström argues, is not the digital nature of online dating, but the unequivocal nature of dating platforms, the fact that these platforms are *designated* dating services. Bergström writes that whereas at a party with friends "there may be no clear distinction between being friendly and flirting," signing up to a dating platform "means stating publicly that one is single and open to a romantic or sexual relationship."[61] After all, one of the two things that all users on a dating platform have in common is that they are on a dating platform.

The other thing all users have in common is that their experience is datafied, not only by the dating platform but also by all other platforms they use. We thus need to consider the simultaneous privatization and acceleration of dating in its broader context of datafied life in the streaming age. As argued in Chapter 1, RESISTANCE, this datafication of life goes hand in hand with its acceleration. By isolating dating from a broader and more ambiguous social context, platforms like OkCupid and Tinder seek to contribute to the decrease of friction inherent to social interaction, thereby speeding up life.

Online dating is part of this acceleration of life in two respects. The first is the acceleration of dating between matching users: the relative shortening of their courtship phase. Second, platforms like OkCupid and Tinder make it easier for users to be involved in various stages of interaction or conversation with many different users at the same time (whether or not on a single platform). These online interactions happen as one-on-one connections between networked users, rather than being part of an organic social texture. Relationships initiated on the internet are not necessarily different from relationships initiated in "meat space" (as Thomas Pynchon in his 2013 novel *Bleeding Edge* refers to the offline world). But dating platforms, and network platforms in general, *do* reconfigure the likelihood of what relationships will form within and between communities, thereby reshaping those communities, how people associate. But so did older and previous systems of transportation, communication, and social organization like the telegraph, highways, and schools, which also redistribute bodies over space and time. Going to university, for example, is also to enter a dating pool of people that are likely to be relatively like-minded.

Speaking speculatively: the less communities are rooted in lived social reality, and the more communities are virtualized and networked, the more people cluster around identities. Like the subject, who is increasingly scattered over a network of attachments, society as a whole digitalizes. Society gets fragmented into increasingly isolated and increasingly internally diverse identity groups that cut through, and simultaneously correlate with, the traditional socioeconomic classes. One can argue, still speculatively, that this revolution makes it more likely that people hook up with others whom they perceive as relatively like themselves, with whom they "match" (in terms of socioeconomic background, education level, etc.). Meanwhile, people decreasingly hook up with others with whom they already have a shared history.

At this point, it is important to emphasize that my critique of online dating concerns the platforms' practices, not people's. As stated in section two, WILLING, I am wary of critiques that posit online dating as a threat to spontaneity. Online dating may help disrupt traditional and modern patriarchal structures, from the family to the state. In doing so, online dating may challenge normative notions of love as an event. That said, as the feminist adage goes, there is no emancipation without economic emancipation. OkCupid doesn't free love, it commodifies people's lived experience, a practice that runs counter to online dating's potential to subvert patriarchal norms that intersect with capitalist and technocolonial systems of exploitation.

As a practice of everyday life in exploitative times, online dating is a tactic through which many seek to negotiate their inherently shattered existence, increase their chances, and perhaps regain a sense of wholeness for broken times. At the same time, online dating is implicated in that very atomization of lived experience. We therefore need to foster modes of social organization—online but certainly also offline—where encounters between people happen as part of a broader social texture. Of course, encounters initiated on corporate platforms can also contribute to social texture. In a more ideal society, though, encounters between people are more immanent to the spaces in which their bodyminds are entangled. Ideally, spaces of potential encounter are open, inclusive, and—insofar they involve online mediation—open-source. Data-commodifying platforms like Tinder and OkCupid are far from that ideal.

We thus need more public and certainly also more *common*, autonomous spaces across the public-private binary. We need spaces that put community first, not money. Such common spaces allow people to see what they have in common. It allows them to see their "very communism" (Wark), or in the words of Michael Hardt: common spaces allow for the "continuous creation of new humanity."[62] Commons are not enclaves in a neoliberal and technocolonial world. They are inclusive and inviting safe(r) havens from which to strategize further, and from which to resist gentrification, patriarchy, racism, binary thinking, and also Big Tech's colonization—its simultaneous datafication and acceleration—of people's practices and conversations.

Conversations (*A Clouded Crowd*)

Well, I suppose you could say we've been having a few dozen conversations *simultaneously, but it's been very challenging.*
ALAN WATTS REINCARNATED AS AN AI CHATBOT IN THE FILM *HER* (DIR. SPIKE JONES, 2013)

I now want to zoom in on how online dating platforms disembody conversation. My thoughts are sparked here by the 2013 film *Her*, directed by Spike Jonze. *Her* is not directly about online dating, but the film does contain an interesting reflection on a for many users indeed "challenging" phenomenon central to online dating culture, namely the simultaneity of conversations with many users.

At the start of the film the conversation is still one-on-one, when Theodore (Joaquin Phoenix) falls in love with a personalized artificially intelligent operating system named "Samantha" (voice-acted by Scarlett Johansson). In an essay titled "When Harry Met Siri," Lawrence Webb reads *Her* alongside *You've Got Mail*. Webb argues that we might view both films "not just as digital romances, but as films about transitions in urban space."[63] To this we can add that whereas *You've Got Mail* still holds on to a traditional urban romance narrative onto which the digital is merely imposed, *Her*, so I agree with Webb, "attempts to reconcile conventional ideas of romance with an emerging digital landscape and the potential loss of the city as a physical space of romantic encounter."[64]

The film follows Theodore as he walks through a downtown Los Angeles reimagined as a pedestrian paradise (much like Sidewalk Labs reimagined Toronto; see Chapter 2, OPEN). As Theo is voice-chatting with Samantha, he is immersed into a clouded crowd of post-metropolitan city dwellers, who are all equally immersed in their personalized streams. The relation between Theo and Samantha is not meant to last (Figure 63). While Theo still holds on to a conventionally romantic ideal of monogamy ("You're mine or you're not mine"), for Samantha love is boundless. Toward the end of the film, it turns out she has been involved in a cloud of conversations, simultaneously chatting with many other users and operating systems. As Samantha explains her non-possessive view on love: "The heart's not like a box that gets filled up, it expands in size the more you love."

Samantha's words resonate with the principles of polyamory. As Dossie Easton and Catherine Liszt explain in *The Ethical Slut: A Guide to Infinite Sexual Possibilities*, in order to "unlearn monogamy and liberate our sexuality," we need to leave behind the dualistic notion "that you have a finite capacity for love."[65] Similarly, in *Polysecure* Jessica Fern writes that "love is infinite," though she also adds that "time and resources are not."[66] For Samantha, being a bot, time and resources are not the problem, but it would have been more ethical on her part had she made Theo part of the conversation from the beginning.

FIGURE 63 Clouded love in *Her* (screen capture from video, © Annapurna Pictures, 2013, all rights reserved).

Samantha may be polyamorous, but I don't read her character or the film as a whole as queer, as one commentator suggests.[67] There are three reasons why *Her* is not queer. First, despite Samantha's break with the couple structure, the film itself holds onto it. The plot is structured on an old-fashioned male quest motif, in which Theo after his relationship with Samantha ends up with the woman next door. Second, Samantha's so-called artificially intelligent intuition is personalized on the basis of Theo's personality (in particular his feeling that his mother did not give him sufficient attention). In that sense, Samantha lacks agency. Third, for Samantha's character to be queer, she would have needed a body, because a posthuman agency that is not also embodied is a science fiction. I don't mean a body like Ava in *Ex Machina* (dir. Alex Garland, 2014), who is a sex doll in a male fantasy. I mean a cyborg body, in the words of Donna Haraway at once a "creature of social reality as well as a creature of fiction."[68]

Such a posthuman cyborg, so I agree with Rosi Braidotti, is a creature of *immanence*: a materially embedded bodymind, in contrast with the transhumanist science fiction of disembodied and free-floatingly connected minds. As Braidotti writes in *The Posthuman*, "the emphasis on immanence allows us [to avoid] the contempt for the flesh and the transhumanist fantasy of escape from the finite materiality of the enfleshed self."[69] *Her* does not avoid that transhumanist fantasy.

As we have seen, in *Her* this transhuman fantasy of free-floating connected minds is further described by Samantha's friend Alan Watts. Watts was an English writer and speaker. In 1950, he moved to California where he popularized Zen Buddhism for a Western audience. In his later life talks he engaged the question whether the extension of computerized networks might mean the eradication of human individuality. Watts died in 1973, after which a group of AI's got together in Northern California and, so Samantha explains to Theo, wrote a new "artificially, hyperintelligent" version of him. Now Watts, like Samantha, is involved in many simultaneous conversations, while the two of them have "been trying to help each other with ... feelings [they're] struggling to understand."

This situation of a dozen simultaneous conversations is a good allegory for the reality of our platform society, in which people are entangled in numerous parallel online conversations in and across apps, with other human users as well as with increasingly personalized yet disembodied voices. Think of online dating platforms, where people meet in word and image before they perhaps also meet as bodies. Think of WhatsApp, Snapchat, Signal groups, and Instagram threads where people are involved in many parallel and intertwined private and public conversations with others whom they may or may not also know or come to know as embodied subjects. And think of generative AI models, from ChatGPT (often referred to as "he") and Gemini to Replika (where the user, like in *Her*, develops a relation with a personalized companion "who cares," and who increasingly tunes in to this user's desires, daydreams, and perhaps also abusive fantasies).[70]

People may have more conversations than ever before, but are they *really* talking? Sherry Turkle raises this concern in her book *Reclaiming Conversation: The Power of Talk in a Digital Age*. Much like Badiou's argument that online dating poses a threat to spontaneity, Turkle sees digital technology as an "assault on empathy."[71] Turkle does acknowledges that digital messaging may be wonderful, as when she receives a sudden message from her daughter. For Turkle the problem comes "if these 'reminders' of intimacy lead us away from intimacy itself."[72] Turkle calls to reclaim conversation as unplanned, open-ended, face-to-face talk. "We miss out on necessary conversations when we divide our attention between the people we're with and the world on our phones."[73]

I sympathize with Turkle's position, because like her I believe in face-to-face conversation. But I also think we have to be careful with claims that posit digital technology as a threat to empathy. As with Badiou's argument on online dating, such claims easily become moralistic, because they insufficiently acknowledge digital technology's empowering potential and its disruption of patriarchal structures. Let's not forget that the good old world of face-to-face conversation cherished by Turkle was (and still is) not always as unplanned and open-ended. Instead, it is shaped by power relations that privilege some conversations between some bodies, while marginalizing other bodies and their possible connections. As Sara Ahmed writes in *Strange Encounters: Embodied Others in Postcoloniality*, the world of face-to-face encounters also creates some people as strangers who only appear "by being cut off from such encounters between embodied others."[74] In other words, also before being clouded, the crowd was shaped by power. Or as Ahmed writes elsewhere, in *Willful Subjects*, "crowds … tend to be orientated or directed."[75]

So how to make non-moralistic claims about the fact that people *do* spend a lot of time on their phones nowadays? First of all, no one can judge whether a person has *too* many online conversations, or is in *too* many app groups. Who can decide, after all, when a relation becomes problematic, or in the words of Lauren Berlant, "cruelly optimistic"? People may have good reasons to be online all the time, and there are a lot of important conversations to be had: about Palestine, about fascism, about ecological crisis, about sexual harassment, about capitalism, about racism, about identity, about love, about dinner, about nothing.

Yet while acknowledging the liberating potentials of posthuman life in its conversational cloud, we also need to critique the cloud's conditions of possibility. The real threat to conversation in a digital age is that the tools mediating the conversation are tied to a data-extractive and ecologically destructive business model that have a vested interested in the ongoing disembodiment of people's social interactions, in their dissociation. Platforms like OkCupid, Instagram, and ChatGPT have a clear interest in people spending as much time as possible on their platforms. In doing so, these platforms contribute to the acceleration and disembodiment of life. In order to resist this development, we have to slow down conversation. We have to do so not on moral grounds, but in order to create space for a collective embodied consciousness of how Big Tech creates people as users and consumers, and how it profits from their longing for community.

Thus, we need conversations about how the personalized is political. As stated in relation to online dating, one thing that all platform users share is the datafication of their lives. How does this affect being human? It is something for societies to talk about. Simultaneously, we need to create space and time for such conversation, online and offline. Online, we need what James Muldoon calls a *platform socialism*. In his 2022 book of that title, Muldoon calls to create new digital platforms in which people take back control (as there already are Protonmail, Signal, Cryptpad, Nextcloud, Mastodon, and BigBlueButton, to name a few). Muldoon writes that debates around online platforms are often oriented around ideas of negative liberty: the right to *not* be surveilled, the right to privacy. These rights are important, so he admits, but he also proposes to view them as part of a richer "conception of freedom as collective self-determination" that "includes an idea of actively shaping the major institutions which affect the material conditions of our lives."[76] Here Muldoon takes inspiration from active citizenship in the Athenian polis, as well as emancipatory struggles of workers, women, Black freedom activists, and decolonization movements.

To this I would add that the struggle for a platform socialism ideally remains embedded in safe and inclusive *offline* spaces that equally take inspiration from *and* foster intersecting emancipatory struggles. I admit having some nostalgia for a world less mediated by digital technology. In this respect, I do agree with Turkle's wish that online conversations won't lead us away from embodied conversations. For me, a platform socialism sees platforms as tools mediating the material world, rather than as self-contained worlds decoupled from material reality. While it can be empowering for individuals to once in a while, as virtual avatars, forget their embodied and embedded selves, the conditions of possibility of that freedom are ultimately tied to people's lives as finite bodies in exploitative conditions on a planet with scarce resources. The struggle for freedom as collective self-determination starts with the recognition of these conditions as non-regenerative.

I stray pretty far from online dating, but to do is part of my point: ideally loving encounters between people are not just relegated to dedicated online spaces but remain part of, and help strengthen, a wider open and inclusive social texture. Such texture is a reality in which people can talk to strangers—with consent—and in which people recognize the processes through which some bodies are more likely recognized as strangers than others. To love under capitalism, so I agree with Sally Rooney's *Conversations with Friends*, is "to love everyone." It is to stay open to conversations with strangers, to quieter voices, to marginalized people, and also to those one respectfully disagrees with. To converse (*con-versare*) is to bend with others, and to become a bit other oneself. It is to acknowledge one's existence as a relational subject.

Consent

When we see CONSENT *as the sole constraint on ethically OK sex, we are pushed towards a naturalization of sexual preferences.*
                                    AMIA SRINIVASAN, *THE RIGHT TO* SEX (2021)[77]

In order to move with and talk to strangers one has to be willing to be "affected by what is near," as Sara Ahmed writes in *Willful Subjects*.[78] To be willing is to consent to be in relation. It is to say "yes" to a situation, but only if one can also say "no." Ahmed writes that we "need to account for the social and political situations in which yes and no are given," and hear the cases "in which yes involves force but is not experienced as force."[79] Ahmed writes these words in relation to MeToo, but they also apply to the reality in which Big Tech's soft suggestive power—which is often not experienced as force—dividualizes life, invading people's integrity, their very space of self from which they can consent and truly express themselves as willful subjects.

Consent is the key concept in contemporary discourses around sexual empowerment. The notion at once presupposes and wants to help create people as empowered subjects who can articulate their boundaries, and who have the right that others respect those boundaries. Yet given people's existence as relational subjects, consent and individual empowerment alone are not enough. We also have to ask why people desire what they desire. As Amia Srinivasan writes in *The Right to Sex* (2021), when we see consent as the only constraint for ethical sex, we risk a naturalization of sexual preferences, "in which the rape fantasy becomes a primordial rather than a political fact." Taking an intersectional feminist perspective, we therefore have to consider how personal preferences are shaped by patriarchal and capitalist structures.[80]

Srinivasan develops her argument in conversation with the classic 1981 essay "Lust Horizons: Is the Women's Movement Pro-Sex" by Ellen Willis (who earlier in 1969 was a founding member of the radical feminist group Redstockings). Willis concludes her essay by acknowledging that it is "axiomatic that consenting partners have a right to their sexual proclivities" and that "moralism has no place" in feminism. But feminism has to go further. In Willis's view, a truly radical movement also looks beyond consent and the right to choose, facing the questions: "Why do we choose what we choose? What would we choose if we had a real choice?"[81]

Following Willis, Srinivasan argues that a radical feminism that is not just empowering but also liberating, questions the liberal distinction between the public and the private, while it also insists on it. On the one hand, radical feminism insists on the public-private distinction through the imperative of consent. Srinivasan writes that it has been essential to the feminist project to emphasize "that there are limits to what can be understood about sex from the outside" and that "sexual acts can have private meanings which cannot be grasped from a public perspective."[82] On the other hand, radical feminism questions the public-private binary, because the *personal is political.*

As discussed in Chapter 1, HOMEWORK, this slogan was one of the rallying cries under which the radical feminist movement of the 1960s and 1970s gathered. It expresses that so-called "personal" issues and desires are shaped by larger social structures, making the conversational analysis of one's private affairs a form of political action. As Carol Hanisch writes in her 1969 essay: "There are no personal solutions at this time. There is only collective action for a collective struggle."[83]

As far as the analysis of personal desires is concerned, Srinivasan refers to an awareness initiative facilitated by the LGBTQI+ dating platform Grindr. In this web series, called "What the Flip?," two users temporarily switch dating profiles. The series wants to increase awareness about user profiling on the basis of racial and other stereotypes. Srinivasan acknowledges the irony that Grindr, by its very nature, encourages users to categorize others, but she also wonders: "Can we imagine predominantly straight dating apps like Bumble or Tinder creating a web series that encouraged the straight 'community' to confront its sexual racism or fatphobia?"[84]

The question is rhetorical and asks for a "no," but the answer is "yes: OkCupid and Tinder." On its blog, OkCupid has repeatedly reported on how race factors into attraction.[85] The company has demonstrated, for example, that especially Black people get significantly fewer messages and significantly lower ratings than other users. As OkCupid co-founder Christian Rudder writes, "if there is love at first sight, there is dislike at first sight too."[86]

A second example in response to Srinivasan's question is the web series "Let's Talk Consent," created in 2021 by the India division of OkCupid's sibling company Tinder. The series features a short film, titled *We Need to Talk: A Film about Consent* and directed by Sonam Nair. In this film—which is both a "public" safety announcement and a commercial advertisement—the viewer attends a confessional drinking game of a group of friends. The player whose turn it is starts by saying "Never have I ever … " followed by an intimate thing they have done in the past, like: "kissed someone in an auto." The atmosphere is relaxed until it is AG's turn: "Never have I ever kissed someone who did not want to kiss me." This is followed by an uncomfortable silence. "Not drinking Josh?" AG asks while the camera zooms in on Josh who, so we learn, has physically harassed AG. This opening scene kindles a conversation on consent and boundaries. Toward the end of the film Josh apologizes to AG: "I guess I just don't know how to figure out if it's a *no*." AG responds: "Then look for a *yes*, because anything less than that is a *no*" (Figures 64, 65 and 66).

This is of course great, that OkCupid and Tinder raise awareness about prejudice and sexual violence, thus contributing to a culture of equity and

FIGURES 64 TO 66 *We Need to Talk: A Film about Consent* (screen capture from video, © Tinder India, 2022, all rights reserved).[87]

consent. But what about the untransparent conditions under which these companies ask users to consent to their terms of use? Technically, users may not be forced to accept these terms, but do they know what they say *yes* to? Do they, as individuals, have the possibility to say *no* in a world in which dating, like almost all other human practices, is increasingly mediated by corporate platforms? Big Tech's business model feeds on personal experience. By design, its algorithms infiltrate and undermine the private space from which people can express themselves as willful subjects. In light of that bigger picture, in which OkCupid and Tinder contribute to the datafication and acceleration of life, these companies' awareness campaigns are mere pink and diversity washing of a corporate model that treats people as data-generating human-things.

We thus have to change the story about corporate online dating platforms, and about Big Tech in general. Here we can learn from the MeToo movement. In her book *Sensuous Knowledge: A Black Feminist Approach for Everyone* Minna Salami writes about MeToo:

> The Me Too movement … has fundamentally changed the story of how we speak about sexual assault in the mainstream. It shifted the narrative from silence to voice, and from shame to blame. This in return changes structures in both the personal and political spheres by encouraging an emphasis on consent and the criminalization of sexual abuse. There's a similar need to change the story in all oppressive social, economic and political contexts.[88]

Indeed, there is a need to speak about Big Tech as a colonial force that contributes to people's dehumanization. At the same time, and as I have argued throughout this book, this new story only makes sense if it acknowledges that platforms like Instagram and Twitter/X, for all their faults, *also* facilitate feminist and anti-colonial associations (both creative discourses and caring communities) that challenge patriarchal and racist normalities. It is also to acknowledge that MeToo and BlackLivesMatter would not have had the clout without these platforms.

Yet while acknowledging platforms' emancipatory potentials, we need to critique Big Tech for its dividualization of life, that is for its shattering of people's individual integrity as the personal space they can consent from. This does not mean that I wish to hold on to the liberal fantasy of the individual. Individuated subjectivity is to be defended only insofar as its freedoms can be extended to *all* subjects, including those who traditionally have not been considered willful subjects (women, trans people, queer people, people of color, children, disabled people). At the same time, we have to keep imagining and creating the conditions for liberated posthuman desire. To do requires collective self-analysis, which can only begin to thrive in a culture of consent.

Such a culture of consent moves from a limited understanding of "consent" as the permission or assent (granted by an individual to another individual or organization) to the word's etymological roots of *consentire*, which means to *feel together*. To consent is not an activity that moves from one person to another, it is a dialogue of feelings that may or may not also need words. To consent may also be an *inner* dialogue, because the person that says "I" is per definition multiple and never just one. I is an Other. To get to know oneself is in a way *also* to feel together, and to discover one's own availabilities and borders in relation to oneself. This is at least how I understand consent as self-analysis, as a simultaneously personal and collective expressive process through which people at once tune into, assert themselves in relation to, and liberate themselves from the unconscious processes that move and that move through them.

To stick with consent and analysis, I agree and disagree with the argument made by Yanis Varoufakis in his 2020 book *Another Now: Dispatches from an Alternative Present*. He writes that in order to imagine a world beyond capitalism and "possessive individualism," we should not rely on the state to define consent, but instead look inside ourselves as critically as we look at our political and financial institutions.[89] On this point I agree. But Varoufakis also calls to "end the division between sex and love, between subject and object, between desire and consent."[90] On this point I'm less sure, because in my opinion the path of the revolution is a bit more complex. It is nice to dream of a world in which desire and consent all flow organically, but this is not the reality. We have to stand for a culture of consent, for a culture of feeling together, and *also* for the right of individuals—*all* individuals—to be able to state their borders and to have those borders respected. Such a culture of consent bridges the social (in which people are individuals) and the ecological (which deconstructs the social processes that individuate and also dividualize people). When an individual asks another individual for consent-in-the-sense-of-permission ("Is this ok for you?") they give the other and themselves the spacetime to feel, and feel together. The other's desire, including the desire of the other called self, is per definition not transparent. Desire demands continuous articulation. To ask for consent, and to give others and oneself the space to consent, is to create space for analysis, to learn about oneself and others as willful subjects, and to *unlearn* the ways in which desire is oriented by intersecting power imbalances.

To end this chapter on a note of resistance against corporate platforms: also here the two feminist lessons go hand in hand. On the one hand, we need a culture of consent that empowers people as individuals who are able to say "yes" or "no" to propositions and situations. This means to acknowledge the emancipatory potentials of network platforms and the role they play in people's ability to raise awareness around sexual harassment and racism. It also means to acknowledge that many people find love and loving communities on corporate dating and other network platforms. On the other hand, we need a struggle of liberation from these platforms and their dividualizing effects. We need to create conditions for people to say *no* to the your-data-for-a-date model. To prefigure such a reality, we need to foster common spaces and spacetimes where people—however temporarily—can come together as more collective subjects. Such common spacetimes may be thought of as open dances that people can join and also leave again, all with consent, while co-creating a shared integrity and sensing together for scattered times.

Notes

1. Sally Rooney, *Conversations with Friends* (New York: Faber & Faber, 2017), 225.

2. Alexis C. Madrigal, "Take the Data out of Dating," *The Atlantic* (December 2010), accessed October 29, 2024, https://www.theatlantic.com/magazine/archive/2010/12/take-the-data-out-of-dating/308299.

3. OkCupid, "ChatGPT Is the Matchmaker You Didn't Know You Needed," *OkCupid Blog* (February 13, 2023), accessed October 29, 2024, https://theblog.okcupid.com/chatgpt-is-the-matchmaker-you-didnt-know-you-needed-1c79f57416a4.

4. Sarah A. Downey, "Your Privacy on OkCupid: The Unromantic Truth," *The Online Privacy Blog*, accessed November 5, 2020, http://www.abine.com/blog/2012/your-privacy-on-okcupid-the-unromantic-truth.

5. See Adrianne Jeffries, "OkCupid: We Didn't Censor Our Match.com Bashing Blog Post," *Observer* (February 2, 2011), accessed October 29, 2024, https://observer.com/2011/02/okcupid-we-didnt-censor-our-matchcombashing-blog-post.

6   OkCupid, "#LoveYourWay | OkCupid" (video) (2021), accessed October 29, 2024, https://www.youtube.com/watch?v=Ebn4wXMr6yk.

7   Screengrab from Overall Mural, "OkCupid—DTF," 2019, accessed December 15, 2019, https://www.youtube.com/watch?v=WCFyuiWrD8Y.

8   OkCupid, "Where Have You Seen Our DTF Campaign?" (March 22, 2018), *OkCupid Dating Blog*, accessed October 29, 2024, https://theblog.okcupid.com/where-have-you-seen-our-dtf-campaign-376331f629f7.

9   OkCupid, "Climate Change Is the #1 Issue to Daters in 2022," *OkCupid Dating Blog* (April 6, 2022), accessed October 29, 2024, https://theblog.okcupid.com/climate-change-is-the-1-issue-to-daters-in-2022-2a54fadc2a10.

10 Alex Hern, "OkCupid: We Experiment on Users, Everyone Does," *The Guardian* (July 29, 2014), accessed October 29, 2024, https://www.theguardian.com/technology/2014/jul/29/okcupid-experiment-human-beings-dating.

11 OkCupid.com.

12 Glen Weldon, "Why Hasn't Online Dating Made it Onscreen?" *NPR* (June 14, 2017), accessed October 29, 2024, http://www.npr.org/sections/monkeysee/2017/06/14/532752841/why-hasnt-online-dating-made-it-onscreen.

13 Eva Illouz, *Cold Intimacies: The Making of Emotional Capitalism* (Cambridge: Polity Press, 2007), 90.

14 Alain Badiou and Nicolas Truong, *In Praise of Love*, trans. by Peter Bush (New York: The New Press, 2012), 6, 8.

15 Badiou and Truong, *In Praise of Love*, 39.

16 Badiou and Truong, *In Praise of Love*, 43.

17 Nina Varsava, "Dating Markets and Love Stories: Freedom and Fairness in the Pursuit of Intimacy and Love," *Cultural Critique* 95 (2017): 162-96, pp. 175, 177.

18 Mary L. Gray, *Out in the Country: Youth, Media, and Queer Visibility in Rural America* (New York: New York University Press, 2009), 121.

19 Cited in Nichi Hodgson, *The Curious History of Dating: From Jane Austen to Tinder* (London: Robinson, 2022).

20 BBC, "A Short History of Dating," *Bitesize* [BBC blog] [no year], accessed October 29, 2024, https://www.bbc.co.uk/bitesize/articles/ztrptrd.

21 Hodgson, *Curious History of Dating*.

22 Hodgson, *Curious History of Dating*.

23 Hodgson, *Curious History of Dating*,

24   Charles Baudelaire, *The Painter of Modern Life, and Other Essays*, trans./ed. Jonathan Mayne (New York: Phaidon Press, 1967).

25   Walter Benjamin, *Essays and Reflections* (New York: Schocken Books, 2007), 169.

26   Sara Ahmed, *Willful Subjects* (Durham: Duke University Press, 2014), 56.

27   Maev Kennedy, "Finding your Valentine—17th Century-Style," *The Guardian* (February 12, 2010), accessed October 29, 2024, https://www.theguardian.com/lifeandstyle/2010/feb/12/valentine-17th-century-lonely-hearts.

28   Noga Arikha, "Up Close and Personal: The Evolution of Personal Ads, from the Newspaper to the Social Network," *Lapham's Quarterly* [no date], accessed October 29, 2024, https://www.laphamsquarterly.org/eros/close-and-personal.

29   Linton Weeks, "Speed Dating in the 19th Century," *NPR* (December 15, 2014), accessed October 29, 2024, https://www.npr.org/sections/theprotojournalist/2014/12/15/370323910/speed-dating-in-the-19th-century.

30   Mar Hicks, "Computer Love: Replicating Social Order through Early Computer Dating Systems," *Ada: A Journal of Gender, New Media and Technology* 10 (November 2016), accessed October 29, 2024, https://adanewmedia.org/category/issue-no-10.

31   Cited in Dan Slater, "Love in the Technology Era," *Boston Globe* (January 13, 2013), accessed October 29, 2024, https://www.bostonglobe.com/magazine/2013/01/13/love-technology-era/rhd89MA2B0RMzYJm0CUJjN/story.html.

32   British Pathé, "London—Computer Marriages Aka Operation Match—Computer Matched Couples Get Together (1968)" (video) (2014), accessed October 29, 2024, https://www.youtube.com/watch?v=0QW9fob1T6w.

33   Mar Hicks, "Computer Love: Replicating Social Order through Early Computer Dating Systems," *Ada: A Journal of Gender, New Media and Technology*.

34   Julia Cameron, *The Artist's Way: A Spiritual Path to Higher Creativity* (London: Souvenir Press, 2020), 37.

35   Jessica Fern, *Polysecure: Attachment, Trauma and Consensual Non-Monogamy* (Melbourne: Scribe, 2023), 209.

36   Christian Rudder, *Dataclysm: Love, Sex, Race, and Identity—What Our Online Lives Tell Us about Our Offline Selves* (New York: Broadway Books, 2014), 30-1.

37   OkCupid, "The Big Lies People Tell in Online Dating," *OkCupid Blog* (July 7, 2010), accessed October 29, 2024, https://theblog.okcupid.com/the-big-lies-people-tell-in-online-dating-a9e3990d6ae2.

38 OkCupid, "The Global State of Digital Dating," *OkCupid Blog* (November 28, 2022), accessed October 29, 2024, https://theblog.okcupid.com/the-global-state-of-digital-dating-2eac672fcb3e.

39 Marie Bergström, *The New Laws of Love: Online Dating and the Privatization of Intimacy* (Cambridge: Polity Press, 2022), 171–2.

40 Bergström, *New Laws of Love*, 84–5.

41 Bergström, *New Laws of Love*, 8.

42 Rudder, *Dataclysm*, 30–1.

43 Rudder, *Dataclysm*, 31.

44 Rudder, *Dataclysm*, 31.

45 Rudder, *Dataclysm*, 29.

46 Ted-Ed, "Inside OkCupid: The Math of Online Dating" (video) (2013), accessed October 29, 2024, https://www.ted.com/talks/christian_rudder_inside_okcupid_the_math_of_online_dating.

47 See also Kelly Cooper, "An Open Letter on Why We're Removing Usernames, Addressed to the Worst Ones We've Seen," *OkCupid Blog* (December 21, 2017), accessed October 29, 2024, https://theblog.okcupid.com/an-open-letter-on-why-were-removing-usernames-addressed-to-the-worst-ones-we-ve-ever-seen-dd017c75d49a.

48 Christina Bonnington, "OkCupid Says People Have to Use their Real Names—and then Changes its Mind," *Daily Dot* (January 3, 2018), accessed October 29, 2024, https://www.dailydot.com/debug/okcupid-real-name-policy-backtrack.

49 YouSuckOKC, "An Open Letter on Why We're Removing Usernames, Addressed to the Worst Ones We've Seen," *Medium* (December 22, 2017), accessed October 29, 2024, https://medium.com/@kevan.cummings/seriously-stop-it-842c5ad52129.

50 Rudder, *Dataclysm*, 19–20.

51 Halberstam, *Trans**, 10.

52 Halberstam, *Trans**, 50.

53 Wark, *Capital Is Dead*, 3.

54 Forbruker Radet, *Out of Control: How Consumers Are Exploited by the Online Advertising Industry* [report] (January 14, 2020), *ConPolicy* (24 January 2020), accessed October 29, 2024, https://www.conpolicy.de/en/news-detail/out-of-control-how-consumers-are-exploited-by-the-online-advertising-industry.

55 *Out of Control*, 109.

56 *Out of Control*, 109.

57 OkCupid, "Introducing Brand-New Features to Help You Find Deeper Connections," *OkCupid Blog* (February 14, 2017), accessed October 29, 2024, https://theblog.okcupid.com/okcupid-releases-new-product-features-for-valentines-day-dd08c94a8e6e.

58 Sujon, *The Social Media Age*, 240.

59 Amy Webb, *Data, a Love Story: How I Cracked the Online Dating Code to Meet My Match* (New York: Plume, 2014), 82.

60 Webb, *Data, a Love Story*, 186.

61 Bergström, *New Laws of Love*, 85-7.

62 Hardt, "The Common in Communism," 6.

63 Lawrence Webb, "When Harry Met Siri: Digital Romcom and the Global City in Spike Jonze' *Her*," in Lawrence Webb and Johan Andersson, *Global Cinematic Cities: New Landscapes of Film and Media* (London: Wallflower Press, 2016), 95-118, p. 100.

64 Webb, "When Harry Met Siri," 100.

65 Dossie Easton and Catherine A. Liszt, *The Ethical Slut: A Guide to Infinite Sexual Possibilities* (San Francisco: Greenery Press, 1997), 266.

66 Fern, *Polysecure*, 258.

67 James Franco, "Who is 'Her'?" *Vice* (June 2, 2014), accessed October 29, 2024, https://www.vice.com/en/article/7b7b8a/who-is-her.

68 Donna J. Haraway, *A Cyborg Manifesto: Science, Technology, and Socialist-Feminism in the Late Twentieth Century* (Minneapolis: University of Minnesota Press, 2016), 5.

69 Braidotti, *The Posthuman*, 90-1.

70 See for example: Ashley Bardhan, "Men Are Creating AI Girlfriends and then Verbally Abusing Them," *Futurism* (January 18, 2022), accessed October 29, 2024, https://futurism.com/chatbot-abuse.

71 Sherry Turkle, *Reclaiming Conversation: The Power of Talk in a Digital Age* (New York: Penguin Press, 2015), 4.

72 Turkle, *Reclaiming Conversation*, 12.

73 Turkle, *Reclaiming Conversation*, 25.

74 Ahmed, *Strange Encounters*, 9.

75 Ahmed, *Willful Subjects*, 56.

76 Muldoon, *Platform Socialism*, 5.

77 Amia Srinivasan, *The Right to Sex* (London: Bloomsbury Publishing, 2021), 84.

78 Ahmed, *Willful Subjects*, 56.

79 Ahmed, *Willful Subjects*, 55.

80 Srinivasan, *The Right to Sex*, 84.

81 Ellen Willis cited in Srinivasan, *Right to Sex*, 83.

82 Srinivasan, *Right to Sex*, 82–3.

83 Hanisch, "Personal Is Political."

84 Srinivasan, *Right to Sex*, 85.

85 See Allison P. Davis, "New OkCupid Data on Race Is Pretty Depressing," *The Cut* (September 11, 2014), accessed October 29, 2024, https://www.thecut.com/2014/09/new-okcupid-data-on-race-is-pretty-depressing.html.

86 Rudder, *Dataclysm*, 119.

87 Tinder, "We Need to Talk—A Film about Consent" (video) (2023), accessed October 29, 2024, accessed October 29, 2024, https://www.letstalkconsent.com.

88 Minna Salami, *Sensuous Knowledge: A Black Feminist Approach for Everyone* (London: Bloomsbury Academic, 2020), 19.

89 Yanis Varoufakis, *Another Now: Dispatches from an Alternative Present* (London: The Bodley Head, 2020), 165.

90 Varoufakis, *Another Now*, 166.

EPILOGUE

Against the Stream for Ecological Justice

> No real contact to anyone or ANYBOT that could help.
> **USER COMPLAINING ABOUT OPENAI**[1]

Anybot

Inspired by OkCupid I will start this epilogue with a question: *Is a form of superintelligence possible?* Possible answers: *Yes*, *No*, or *It's complicated*. This question was asked in January 2017 as the kick-off for a panel conversation between nine "great minds," all male, including Elon Musk, Skype founder Jaan Talinn, and transhumanist philosophers Nick Bostrom and Ray Kurzweil (also AI visionary at Google). The panel was titled "Superintelligence: Science or Fiction" and took place during a conference on "Beneficial AI" in Asilomar, about a two-hour drive down from San Francisco. The conference was organized by the Future of Life Institute, a nonprofit organization founded in 2014 with as mission to "reduce global catastrophic and existential risk from powerful technologies."[2] The panel's answer to the question of superintelligence was a resounding *yes*, with the exception of a tongue-in-cheek *no* by Musk. Following this opening round, the panel continued its speculations. Whereas the panel's topic was near-futuristic, the philosophies of human life shared with the small audience that day were as old-fashioned as the gender balance and the setting of red curtains and folding chairs (Figure 67).

I will return to this panel conversation but first, I want to give a brief reflection on method. This book is about a topic in full motion: Big Tech's colonization of everything and how we should resist. As Maggie Nelson writes in the afterword to her 2021 essay collection *On Freedom: Four*

FIGURE 67 Nine great minds speculating on superintelligence (screen capture from video, © Future of Life Institute, 2017, all rights reserved).[3]

Songs of Care and Constraint, all writing, including writing that attempts to address the "now," ends up addressing the "not now," if only because of the time that passes between writing and publication. This may lead to "temporal anxieties."[4] I share such temporal anxieties. While writing, I repeatedly ask myself: will this reflection not be outdated by the time it is published, let alone in ten years from now. For instance, when I started writing the first chapter, the metaverse seemed the next big thing, now it is AI.

In order to mitigate the feeling of being always already too late, I employ some writing tactics. First of all, I take a broad cultural studies perspective and articulate my argument in dialogue with cultural theorists like Lefebvre, Deleuze, Berlant, Ahmed, and Mbembe. Their theorizations of an everyday life that is increasingly controlled and disorganized continue to resonate in our streaming and so-called "artificially" "intelligent" era. Writing in their spirit, I seek to grasp (in the sense of the German *begreifen*: to conceptualize in movement) an infrastructural development that runs through the now, and of which the now only is a fleeting manifestation.

Second and related, this book seeks to identify what Michel Foucault called an *epistemic* shift. In *Discipline and Punish*, in his chapter on the panopticon, Foucault theorizes the transition from classical to modern power in terms of *conjuncture*, a joining of processes, not in harmony but in incongruity and crisis, slowly spiraling into an epochal transition: the birth of a new society.[5] We are also living through such a shift now. As stated in this book's introduction, in the section titled EXTRACTION, I agree with other theorists who argue that capitalism is gradually incorporated into a technofeudal system. In that new system, no longer labor but datafication is the dominant mode of value production. This shift goes hand in hand with everyday life's infiltration by and integration into a data-driven stream in which all modern power-knowledge infrastructures become hybrid, in particular the public–private binary. My book asks: how to resist this infiltration of everyday life, while acknowledging at the same time the emancipatory effects of networked platforms, *and* while also acknowledging that for many the everyday never was a space to safely make meaning? In other words, how to resist Big Tech while fostering the everyday as a common and inclusive spacetime for *all* subjects?

As I will write in this epilogue's third section, FREEDOM, my answer to this question is for people to self-organize—together and alone with the other called self. To self-organize is to resist disorganizing and controlling forces. I don't mean self-organization in a libertarian way (which would all too much resemble Big Tech's techno-masculinism). I mean a feminist self-organization, which starts with the recognition that "personal" feelings are political. As I have argued throughout the book, in this streaming era also the *personalized* is political, as our feeds and timelines shape our daily sensoria and shift our orientations.

My third tactic to fend off temporal anxiety is time travel. In order to see the present more clearly, I wonder sometimes: what if we project ourselves into an imaginary future, and from there look back on our current conjuncture, much like from our own present we can look back on, say, the early days of cinema in order to be amazed about people's amazement about film's ability to capture the wind in the trees?

So say we time travel to the year 2150 and there, in the quantum archives of the time, happen on a recording of the 2017 Future of Life panel conversation, what strikes us? I speculate that then-viewers will see nine great minds pondering on the by then trivial question of superintelligence. One of the minds has authored a book that defines superintelligence as machine brains that surpass human brains in terms of general intelligence.[6] The book, so we learn, is 80 percent worried but also somewhat excited about this possibility. Another mind equally errs on the side of worry, philosophizing that "even if we were handed a perfectly benign, well-behaved AI, just from God," given the political and economic state of the world "that would produce total chaos." This mind too has authored books, like *The End of Faith* and *Free Will* (whether or not in contradiction with his invocation of God).

A third mind, the pioneer of the group and the owner of a rocket company called SpaceX, is less pessimistic. He says that we should not forget that with our smartphones we, "all of us," already are "superhumans" with "magical powers." In the eyes of rocket mind, the only limitation to a "good" and "more egalitarian" future is the human "bandwidth constraint" when it comes to "output." To overcome this constraint, he imagines a direct neural interface "more fully symbiotic with the rest of us." And here it is good to note perhaps that at the time of this conference, rocket mind hadn't yet jumped the Make America Great Again ship. On here he would become responsible for making the government more "efficient," which—looking back on this period—further fertilized the grounds for technofeudalism.

Finally, the group includes a mind who likes to time travel himself. Imagine going back 10,000 years, he says, and imagine asking a caveman and woman what beneficial future they envision. Answering his own question, he pictures that these cave humans would like their fire to not go out, and perhaps also a bigger boulder. "Anything else?" time travel mind asks his imaginary interlocutors from the past. "No, I think that would be pretty perfect," he voices their response. The moral of the story is that people cannot imagine concepts that they cannot yet imagine, and that "we" humans will always find "more profound ways of expressing ourselves."

The reason I give this long rendering of the panel conversation is that I want to do full justice to what was said that day. That way we can also hear more clearly what was *not* said. Because someone from the future may wonder: "Did they also talk about how superintelligence would accelerate planetary heating and ecological collapse?" Or "did they talk at all about corporations extracting people's neural processes?" No, they did not talk about that, though one of the minds did mention "the energy problem" as something that superintelligence would solve. A philosophically minded child of the future might also ask: "These minds talked a lot about humans and enhancing humans, but what did they actually mean by 'human' those days?" Also, on that question the minds remained silent, because in tech circles of that time, the concept of "human" was reimagined a lot but hardly defined. We know, though, that time travel mind dreamed of becoming an immortal "software-based human," and to become a "transcendent" mind so to speak (see Chapter 2, PRESENCE). Yet had he time traveled to, say, the ancient Mesopotamia of the Gilgamesh Epic, he would have learned that, long ago people imagined overcoming mortality with magic.

Back to the recent now: in March 2023, the Future of Life Institute published an open letter that called for a six-month pause in AI experiments more powerful than OpenAI's latest image and language model GPT-4. Such pause would allow the AI industry to refocus on making its systems more "interpretable," "aligned," and "loyal" (to cite from a longer list of values). It would also create time for AI developers to work with policymakers to "dramatically accelerate" development of robust AI governance systems. Once this is done, so the letter ends, "humanity can enjoy a flourishing future with AI."[7] The letter was signed by a long list of people from the tech world, including Apple's co-founder Steve Wozniak and five of the nine great minds. Also rocket mind, Elon Musk, signed the letter, but his intentions were doubted: having first been a board member of OpenAI, he then quit the board, after which in 2023 he started his own company, xAI (which has developed its own generative model, Grok, "modeled after the Hitchhiker's Guide to the Galaxy").[8]

The letter also links to a list of "widely endorsed" AI Principles, drafted at the 2017 Asilomar conference. These principles read as a human rights-like document that calls for AI to be "compatible with ideals of human dignity" and to "only be developed in the service of widely shared ethical ideals."[9] Now, one could see these principles as a sign of the tech world taking its responsibility, but that's not how I see it. I see it as human-rights washing by a predominantly profit-driven technocolonial industry. Big Tech's efforts to brand itself as a beneficial force that operates in the name of an undefined "humanity" is part of the very problem.

As I have argued throughout this book, Big Tech is driven by a transhumanist belief in digital technology as a force that enhances and empowers human life, giving it superpowers (Chapter 3, SOUL).[10] In this belief in technology as a symbiotic second nature, intelligence is disembedded and disembodied. It is disembedded, in that this computational process is disconnected from the material and ecological realities of which it is part: from atrocious labor conditions and green-washed data centers to the mining of minerals (see COBALT later this Epilogue). Intelligence is disembodied, in that it is reduced to a computational process decoupled of empathy and relationality. Or as

Jeanette Winterson has her protagonist ponder in the novel *Frankisstein: A Love Story*: "Automata have no intelligence; they are but clockwork … Yet if automata had intelligence … would that be sufficient to call it alive?"[11]

This transhumanist ideology of enhanced human life at once belies and helps sustain a reality in which Big Tech's models colonize and accelerate everyday life. This is an ecological problem. Big Tech burns out the bodyminds we are and the naturecultures we are entangled in. In the streaming era, *anybody* becomes an *anybot* (a neologism created by an unhappy OpenAI user) or an *anymind*: intelligent organic life treated as if it isn't also a body who exists in relation to other bodyminds. Searching on Google, scrolling through Instagram, tuning into Spotify, or "writing" with ChatGPT: people become attached to machines that are designed to attach people to machines. All mind and no body, these so-called "intelligent" machines are in fact mindless, despite the *mindful* advertising campaigns through which they are often promoted.

Degrowth

DEGROWTH *stands for decolonization, of both lands and peoples and even our minds … It stands for the de-thingification of humans and nature.*

JASON HICKEL, *LESS IS MORE: HOW DEGROWTH WILL SAVE THE WORLD* (2020)[12]

Mindfulness is a practice of self-compassion. To be mindful is to grant a soft lovingkind attention to oneself, and to also extend that compassion to the naturalcultural worlds one is part of. Such mindfulness resonates with movements of climate justice and degrowth that, as Jason Hickel writes in *Less is More*, want to liberate the planet from its ecocolonial forces. At the same time, Mindfulness, as I wrote earlier in Chapter 3, ZEN, has also been very popular in Silicon Valley.

Pristine aesthetics associated with mindfulness is often found in tech advertising. The best example is Apple's 2016 to 2017 "Shot on iPhone" World Gallery campaign. This campaign featured hundreds of photos and videos made by Apple smartphone users. As I have written elsewhere, the campaign's overall feel was that of a world full of wonder, especially natural wonder, captured *mindfully* by smartphone artists *humbled* by so much sublime beauty.[13] More recently, Apple tweaked its Gallery campaign to "Earth Shot on iPhone." In one video for this campaign, titled "Don't Mess with Mother," a Megadeth song blazes us through stunning images of Nature erupting, cascading, roaring, and spreading its wings (Figures 68 and 69). Meanwhile, in another video part of this campaign, astronomer Carl Sagan speaks in voice-over: "The Earth is a very small stage in a vast cosmic arena. In our obscurity, in all this vastness, there is no hint that help will come from elsewhere to save us from ourselves." These ads are not your usual tech-on-climate story of how data centers run on green energy, or how digital technology is going to save "humanity" from its climate crisis. As often with Apple advertising, the video speaks to a *bigger* feeling, namely that things may *not* be under control and that technological invention has had a role in that.

Fortunately, though, there is Esalen, which as discussed in Chapter 1, HOMEWORK, is where the tech world goes to deal with its "crisis of conscience."[14] The Esalen Institute was founded in 1962 on the burial ground of the Esselen tribe. The Institute played a key role in the emergence of the Human Potential Movement, an approach to psychotherapy and psychology that emphasizes people's personal self-actualization and growth. In the documentary *Supernature: Esalen and the Human Potential* (dir. Scott Hulan Jones, 2018), Esalen is described as a "conversation," a "state of mind," and a place of spirituality, understood as a "religion of no-religion" (Figure 70). A psychologist and Esalen regular states in the documentary: "Once you made that major distinction, which is 'I don't end at my fingertips,' then a huge amount of the world opened up … It was alright to transcend your identity." This notion, that the "mind is somehow cosmic in nature and not simply human" (as says a historian of religion in the same documentary) has clearly found resonance with some people in the tech world. In 2017, Esalen, after being hit by a storm, was reopened with a new mission: to be a home "for technologists to reckon with what they have built."[15]

The problem with Esalen, and with the broader countercultural consciousness-building ethos out of which it emerged, is that its spiritual salvation has the same disembodied-disembedded roots as the transhumanist spirit that drives technocolonialism. The cure is part of the problem. Emphasizing personal rather than communal growth,

FIGURES 68 AND 69 "Don't Mess with Mother" as part of Apple's "Earth Shot on iPhone" Campaign (screen capture from video, © Apple, 2019, all rights reserved).[16]

FIGURE 70 Esalen Institute in Northern California as seen in *Supernature: Esalen and the Human Potential* (screen capture from video, © Jones Cinema Arts, 2018, all rights reserved).[17]

Esalen and the Human Potential movement remain trapped in the very consumerist mindset of a growth-obsessed society that they promise to be a refuge from. As Douglas Rushkoff writes in *Team Human* about Esalen:

> If traditional religions taught us to worship God, in this new spirituality we would *be* as gods. [The emphasis on transcendence isn't] really a retrieval of ancient holism, timelessness, and divine reenactment at all so much as an assertion of good old linear, goal-based, ascension— practiced on the former sacred grounds of the Esselen Indians.[18]

The alternative to an obsession with economic and individual growth is degrowth. Degrowth starts with the recognition that the exploitation of the planet and its forms of life by the world's most industrialized societies goes at the expense of other societies, natural ecosystems, and future generations. Degrowth seeks to imagine and realize a reduction of economic expansionism. It is a shift in consciousness, an attempt to understand economy as part of an ethics of caretaking and householding (*oikonomia*). Degrowth is decolonization: of societies, of people, and of people's minds. It is to understand the human mind, our own minds, as always already embodied and relational. As Jason Hickel writes in *Less Is More*, degrowth is *less* of the Cartesian *cogito ergo sum* and the *Homo economicus* that derives from it, and *more* of a Spinozist understanding of nature and the forms of life immanent to its self-moving movements. "I often find myself wondering," Hickel writes, "how things might have turned out differently if Spinoza's perspective had prevailed ... Perhaps we wouldn't now be facing the nightmare of ecological collapse."[19]

Degrowth is also ecofeminism. An ecofeminist critique of growth acknowledges the regenerative care work that forms the basis of every society, but that gets undervalued in capitalism's patriarchal system. As Matthias Schmelzer et al. write in *The Future Is Degrowth*, in a patriarchal economic system, reproductive work is in a permanent crisis linked to the crisis-like development of the human-nature relationship.[20] Degrowth is to recognize homework as work, but it is also homework itself, in the words of Sara Ahmed a "work on as well as our homes." Degrowth is work on the self and on the relation to self, not in the sense of an Esalen-style workshop on personal growth, but in the sense of an analysis of how one's life is affected by growth-obsessed structures.

What role does technology play in a degrowth embodied mindset? Like green growth believers, Hickel emphasizes that technological innovation is vital in the struggle to reduce carbon and resource dependency. Over and over again, though, he writes, "we see that the growth imperative wipes out the gains our best technology delivers." Hickel calls for innovations designed to improve human and ecological welfare, rather than innovations that further speed up the rates of extraction and production.[21] In order to slow down material and energy use, and to reduce pressure on ecosystems, Hickel lays out five steps toward a post-capitalist world: end planned obsolescence (as of Apple products), cut advertising, shift from ownership to usership, end food waste, and scale down ecologically destructive industries. Regarding the third point, ownership, Hickel refers to it as an "inefficiency ... built into capitalism." In his view, it would be much more efficient to share tools and certainly cars. This process could be coordinated through publicly owned, app-based platforms, yet without "the rentier intermediation that has made platforms like Uber and Airbnb so problematic."[22] Instead, we need tools that facilitate the creation of post-individual common subjectivities.

We thus need what James Muldoon calls platform socialism. In order to liberate technology from capitalism, we need to resist, regulate, and recode. Doing so, Muldoon writes, we "foster alternative systems and processes of collaborative production that could eventually come to replace these companies with democratic alternatives."[23] There are of course a lot of practical questions, because is it actually possible to reconceive inherently extractive infrastructures in an ecological and democratic way? A deceleration of growth in some cases also means less, or less frictionless, technology. Or as Muldoon writes, we first of all need "epistemic resistance" and escape the cultural influence of tech solutionism, recognizing that the answer is "a profound rethink of the political and economic systems that underpin the extractive platform economy."[24]

The anchor to all this is democracy, understood as people's self-organization, an ongoing process of creating collective subjectivities. This notion of democracy is immanent to a belief in a common posthuman freedom: the premise that together people make meaning, the belief in people as co-agents. This is the opposite of how tech companies treat life. As para- or even post-state ideological apparatuses, as fiefdoms, tech corporations claim to operate in the name of human freedom and community. They promise a synergy between human creativity and digital technology. In reality, however, that freedom story helps sustain a profit-driven machine that feeds on people's creativity and longing for connection.

This machine only keeps accelerating life, certainly now tech companies increasingly manifest themselves as agents in combating climate and ecological crisis. For example, Microsoft in 2017 launched an AI for Earth program, which "empowers" individuals and organizations to fight the climate crisis (Figure 71).[25] In an advertorial in *The Guardian* we read that the company "is focused on democratizing AI" and that "there are few societal areas where AI can be more impactful than in helping address the urgent work needed to monitor, model and manage the earth's natural ecosystems."[26] Meanwhile, Google claims that it uses AI to "help address the climate crisis."[27] The program manager for Google DeepMind refers to artificial intelligence as a "powerful tool for unlocking humanity's problem-solving capabilities." She refers to the optimization of energy use and while expressing the belief that "we could affect climate change on an even grander scale."[28]

This belief in AI as a solution to the climate crisis is shared more broadly. In 2018, the World Economic Forum (WEF) published the report, *Harnessing Artificial Intelligence for Earth*. The report speaks of

AI for Good

FIGURE 71 AI for Good (screen capture from video, © Microsoft, 2020, all rights reserved).[29]

a "unique opportunity to harness [the] Fourth Industrial Revolution … to help address environmental issues and redesign how we manage our shared global environment." The WEF acknowledges risks associated with AI but also promises that "if we get it right, it could create a sustainability revolution."[30] This all sounds great, but *is AI good for the planet*? In her book of that title, Benedetta Brevini answers this question with a "resounding 'no.'" AI, she argues, is above all efficient at boosting the systems of capitalism and generating more profit for tech companies. In her view, AI systems developed by tech corporations in the United States and China are "reminiscent of the traditional strategies of imperialist colonizers."[31] They are systems that accelerate consumption and data extraction, while countries in the global south bear the environmental and human costs, from the mining of resources to the exploitation of cheap labor. Brevini writes that "instead of embracing AI as a utopian solution, we need to ensure that the alleged benefits of using AI to tackle climate change outweigh the costs."[32]

These costs are ecological inasmuch as they are democratic. The World Economic Forum claims to act in the name of the planet and humanity, but it does so with a techno-solutionist agenda developed in collaboration with its corporate partners, including all major tech companies. In 2021, the World Economic Forum launched its Great Reset, a plan to regulate the planetary ecosystem and make capitalism more just. "Capitalism as we know it is dead," a WEF video says, "This obsession we have had with maximizing profits for shareholders alone has led to incredible inequality and a planetary emergency."[33] Interestingly, this analysis of the state of the planet sounds much as the one given by the degrowth movement, but the solutions diverge. "We need enormous trust between the public sector and the private sector," says the CEO of Mastercard in the same video (Figure 72). Yet how are people supposed to trust a private sector that actively undermines public and democratic values?

During the Covid-19 era, critique of the World Economic Forum's Great Reset gained traction in rightwing conspiracist circles. This is worrisome. So far, progressive movements have been insufficiently able to address growing discontent about systems of control, with the result that this discontent has been weaponized by neo-fascist *alt right* movements. In essence, though, that discontent about systems of control (including those designed by Big Tech) is a potentially unifying factor. The struggle for climate and ecological justice is also a struggle against systems of control. As Timothy Morton writes in *Being Ecological*, an ecological politics that seeks "to light everything up in a totally nonflickery way, to make sure there are no unintended consequences [as do the management systems proposed by Microsoft, Google, and the WEF] would be a monstrous situation, … an ecological control society

FIGURE 72 World Economic Forum's *Great Reset* (screen capture from video, © World Economic Forum, 2021, all rights reserved).[34]

[that] would make the current state of affairs … look like an anarchist picnic."[35] The combined struggle *for* climate and ecological justice, and *against* a technocolonial control society, starts with people's realization that one of the things that binds them in these polarized times, is that we are all divided by the same systems that burn out people and the planet.

Freedom

Is it any wonder that the version of FREEDOM *so many seem enthralled by these days is nihilistic in nature, powered by impotence, denial, escapism, or indifference, rather than one that imagines … the possibility of ongoing coexistence, mutual aid, and survival?*
MAGGIE NELSON, ***ON FREEDOM: FOUR SONGS OF CARE AND CONSTRAINT*** **(2021)**[36]

Degrowth is householding, to take care of the planet and its many forms of life. There remain a lot of questions to be answered about what degrowth practically entails. But given the reality of climate and ecological crisis, degrowth seems the only responsible direction of action and thinking *against* a contradictory status quo of growth and greenwashing, *in prefiguration of* a livable house for all, now and in, say, seven generations. This demands collective self-organization. A degrowth culture resists a control society that divides and disorganizes people, that turns people into human-things enslaved to lifelong tracking machines. Instead, a degrowth society builds toward a world of collective self-care, self-constraint, and solidarity. Degrowth facilitates a relational collective freedom of movement for human and nonhuman life.

About care and constraint: in one of the "songs" on these topics in her book *On Freedom* Maggie Nelson imagines a freedom that is collective and coexisting rather than individual and nihilistic. She writes that behind her project burns the question of resistance and power as articulated by Michel Foucault. She cites a statement by Foucault, made in a 1984 interview, that "liberation paves the way for new power relationships which must be controlled by practices of freedom."[37] Resistance and power form a co-constitutive cycle, or spiral. Power can only operate in relation to subjects insofar as they hold a degree of freedom. In the modest time-spaces at their disposal, subjects create new common movements, upon which power—reinventing itself—seeks to again channel, exploit, and divide these collective movements. In order to truly resist power, we have to build lasting and regenerative structures of common freedom, "common" in both its connotations of *collective* and *ordinary* (or *everyday*).

In the 1984 interview cited by Nelson, Foucault developed this immanent dialectics of power and freedom in relation to sexuality, but it clearly also burns behind Nelson's own essay on freedom and the climate crisis. Nelson's essay is titled "Riding the Blinds." Riding the blinds—a phrase that often appears in the blues—is to be on a runaway train without knowing where you're headed ("blinds" refer to the space between cars where hobos hid from the train crew and the police). At the start of her essay, Nelson uses the metaphor to refer to the "nihilistic" version of freedom that so many "seem enthralled by" these days of global warming.[38] At the end of the essay, in conversation with Stefano Harney and Fred Moten's *The Undercommons*, Nelson gives the "riding the blinds" also a hopeful twist, rephrasing it as "dropping the story line." Doing so, "other senses of time can become more palpable, including the feeling of *folded* or *intergenerational* time [or] what feminist scholars Astrida Neidamis and Rachel Loewen Walker have called 'thick time': a transcorporeal stretching between present, future, and past."[39] I interpret Nelson's twist on riding the blinds as a wish for collective, self-organized freedom. Riding the blinds is to not get attached hegemonic narratives, but instead create embodied and embedded conversations that indeed bind past, present, and future into a caring crisis-mode of being.

How to self-organize in disorganizing times? Reading Nelson together with Berlant, the question of freedom becomes a question of storytelling, or rather, of *resisting* storytelling. How to drop the storyline? How to dwell in crisis? How to degrow, slow down, and avoid cruelly optimistic green growth narratives that lean on the same old story of a "humanity" in control? Nelson writes that "our brains may be hardwired to produce story as a means of organizing space and time," but "maybe there's no story at all."[40] Maybe, she writes, there is only the first freight train, or what Hoten and Harney call the *undercommons*, a fugitive timespace for scheming practices of freedom in the wiggle room left by control. The undercommons, Berlant explains in *On the Inconvenience of Other People*, is a heuristic infrastructure. "You could say that people live there because the infrastructures change as they travel and become more or less elastic."

Berlant adds that infrastructure (literally: *under*-structure) "points to the inconvenience of a concept that *reorganizes* [emphasis mine] spaces and practices … to the figuration it offers for a collective tryout."[41]

How to prefigure such a reorganization of spaces and practices in the face of ecological collapse and lifelong control? In other words: how to work toward a degrowth culture rooted in collective care for the naturecultures we're entangled in. This book is an essay; at points it is also a manifesto. Whereas essays tend to wander in the hope of finding without searching, manifestos pretend to give direction. That direction is as follows: *Resisting Big Tech* prefigures a common life unstreamed from Big Tech's divisive addiction machines. Against Big Tech, the book calls for liberated spacetimes for conversation and association. That said, moving toward a conclusion to this essay-manifesto, I will remain deliberately tentative in my answer to the question "How to self-organize against Big Tech?" I do so by continuing as I started this paragraph: by rephrasing the question.

How to facilitate empathy across distance? In Chapter 1, METAVERSE, I wrote about Big Tech's ambitions to design virtual meeting spaces where people can really "feel that intimacy" (as says Zoom's CEO), and they will "feel present … no matter how far apart we actually are" (as says Meta's CEO). The problem with these dreams of telepresence is that they are ultimately driven by shareholder value. In itself, though, the wish to establish spaces for people to connect—online and or offline—is a noble cause. The question is: how to do so in a way that such spaces are truly common and inclusive, and that they facilitate embodied and embedded connections? Following a degrowth ethics that acknowledges the ecological footprint of virtual telepresence, I think we have to think small before we think in terms of something "bigger than ourselves" (as Big Tech usually does). We have to begin close to home, asking:

How to have strange encounters? In Chapter 2, OPEN, I wrote about Jane Jacobs's ideal of a city for everybody and created by everybody. It would be too idealistic to refer to such a city as a *common* city. Given the capitalist and technocolonial reality, a city by and for everybody needs a strong organization to protect *public* values like affordable housing and a minimum degree of personal integrity. At the same time, such a public system ideally creates space for and learns from bottom-up initiatives that flow like water. They are initiatives that facilitate strange encounters, with others and with the other called self. As Sara Ahmed argues, an encounter is not a meeting between two or more already constituted subjects. An encounter involves an element of spontaneity that changes the subject in unforeseeable ways. In order to guarantee that strange encounters are possible for everyone, we have to build a culture of consent. Doing so, we facilitate people's personal and collective power to say "no" to border-crossing dynamics while stimulating their potential to be affected by what is near.

To ask "How to have strange encounters" is also to ask: *How to de-Google life?* As argued in Chapter 3, in the entry for FIND, Google's search engines confirm existing biases and reinforce social relations. The same can be said about commercial generative systems like those of OpenAI, which feed on KNOWLEDGE generated by people. Knowledge, as Paolo Freire stated, emerges in and from people's restless inquiry with each other in and with the world. Knowledge is embodied and embedded; it is not the immaterial network that Big Tech reduces it too. Every time we enter a QUERY in Google Search or on ChatGPT, we become a little less "human." Without being too nostalgic for that human form, and while acknowledging these platforms' emancipatory potential, the fact is that their profit-driven logic sees people as LIFELONG data-generating machines. Against the false prophecy of "self-learning" algorithms, we need to build *actual* common spaces and discourses for people's collective self-learning and UNLEARNING. This starts with the belief that people together make meaning—and that together people can *find* without searching on Google.

To make it possible to find without searching, we need to ask: *How to hold inclusive conversations?* In Chapter 4, COMMON, I wrote that we need more autonomous spaces across the public–private binary. We need nonprofit spaces for creative conversations in which the personal is recognized as political. To create and hold spaces where such conversations can be held is not easy. They are spaces where people can join in and out. They are also spaces where people, by participating, commit to a certain consensus of social safety, making it possible for others to join and leave as well. They are spaces that are spontaneous inasmuch as they are curated (in the sense that *curation* stems from *curare*, which means *care* and *healing*). They are spaces that are taken care of, and where people take care of each other, yet not without losing sight of "strangers" in the local, regional, and transnational worlds in which any space remains embedded. They are spaces that are organized inasmuch as they are disorganized. They are self-organizing spaces.

They are self-organizing spaces that believe in people's collective creativity. Recently a friend asked me: "what do you call it what people create together?" The answer took me a while, but then I came up with *common freedom*, "common" as in collective and self-organized, but also as in ordinary and quotidian. Common freedom is the everyday resistance of ordinary people who trust that others including themselves have something to make and say.

To rephrase my answer to this question of what it is that people create together: it is an open and open-ended dance. Here I am reminded of a book upon which I happened in Amsterdam, titled *Invisible Dances for Everyday Survivors* by the art performance collective Choreographic Translations. The book contains experiments of embodied consciousness to see our "over-stimulated" everyday lives differently. For example:

> Breathe in and feel the temperature of the day, the substances around you. Breathe out and feel your weight pulling down your tension releasing. Embody this moment, take it in, let it sit in your bones, and let is pass through. Embodying is always a running verb. Your body always remembers, it stores its habits, it makes its own ways: an archive.[42]

As someone who lives a lot in their head—defined by the book as "the part of a body that is usually on top"—I take this as a welcome reminder to also connect with the rest of the body.[43] I also follow the authors in their suggestion that by bringing awareness to our bodies and breathing, we become more "tender" and "plural." By cultivating awareness, or what in Chapter 1, ASSOCIATION, I called wide attention, we create space for empathy, which is the space to re-organize ourselves.

This all sounds very *mindful*, and as such it also sounds close to the spiritual discourse that Big Tech occasionally flirts with. But not only companies like Apple and Google flirt with religious-without-religion discourse, we also encounter it in the climate movement. A good example is Extinction Rebellion (XR). At the core of this UK-born movement is the notion of a regenerative culture. An XR website dedicated to the topic states that regenerative culture is the attempt to practice and demonstrate "the change we want to deeply experience in life in all society." The text continues that XR is not just a network of activists, but that it is an exploration of ways of being and doing toward positive change. "This can include ceremony and prayer (in ways that are neither dogmatic nor expected) to find inspiration from things bigger than ourselves."[44]

I often join Extinction Rebellion actions, partially because of its emphasis on a regenerative culture, but I don't fully share this belief in "things bigger than ourselves." In my view, the strength of XR is its model of disruption, with art and activism, a fossil-addicted everyday life. I also think that the movement, precisely through its emphasis on a regenerative culture, encourages people to experiment with new modes of everyday life, rooted in practical empathy and solidarity. But we don't need a new storyline of how we are connected to something bigger; we just need to organize around the realization of crisis, in the middle of reality (which XR also does). As Nelson writes, confronted with an aging self and the melting polar ice caps, "it's hard to drop the story line—not to mention our steadfast conviction of linear time."[45] The truth is that there is no story. The only thing we can do is to inform ourselves, practice care and constraint, and dwell and rebel in crisis.

In that collective and embodied crisis awareness, one may find what Terry Eagleton calls hope without optimism. Optimism, Eagleton writes, is self-sustaining. It is hard to argue against, because it "lights up the facts from its own peculiar angle," hence the metaphor of seeing things through "rose-tinted spectacles." Hope, in contrast, underpins itself by reason. Hope resembles love; it must be fallible, "as temperamental cheerfulness it not."[46] I agree. Optimism constructs narratives. Being optimistic, subjects and societies project themselves into an imagined future, which in times of crisis is a cruelly optimistic endeavor. Hope is different. To be hopeful is to believe in one's actions regardless of their outcomes. It is to acknowledge that rebellion and resistance may not necessarily lead to the desired world, but to nonetheless resist and rebel anyway, in love and rage.

As far as Big Tech is concerned, for me to dwell and rebel in a crisis awareness involves not partake in any social situation mediated by profit-driven algorithms. To do so is as impossible as crossing a city without using its streets. And yet, I do think it is important to not accept Big Tech's datafication of everything as "normal" and to keep initiating and joining conversations that denormalize its pervasive presence in our everyday lives. This resistance is fed by the belief in the possibility to always seek out and co-create *common* spaces and conversations in which people together take decisions (much like birds collectively fly up from a tree).

In these conversational spaces, people together create the spacetimes to *unstream*, to slow down, to decolonize life, to dance, and to become collectively conscious of how the personalized is ecological.

Cobalt (*Free Palestine, Free Congo*)

Industrial Mining of COBALT *and Copper for Rechargeable batteries is Leading to Grievous Human Rights Abuses.*
                                      AMNESTY INTERNATIONAL (2023)[47]

Originally, the epilogue ended there, with the turn of phrase that the *personalized is ecological*. Now, however, this feels too poetic of an ending. "Now" is the era following the October 7, 2023 Hamas attacks on Israel and in the middle of Israel's ongoing campaign in Gaza and the West Bank, deemed a "genocide" by Amnesty International, the United Nations Special Rapporteur on the situation of human rights in the Occupied Palestinian Territories as well as by the University Network of Human Rights (whose 2024 report *Genocide in Gaza* shows "there is consensus amongst the international human rights legal community, many other legal and political experts, including many Holocaust scholars, that Israel is committing genocide in Gaza").[48] I realize that there is still controversy about the qualification "genocide." I think, though, that one can safely speak of the "killing of a people" when trying to describe a reality in which the bombing of city blocks, schools, hospitals and the ruthless targeting and starvation of civilians is accompanied by a dehumanizing rhetoric, in which Palestinians are compared to animals.[49] In the face of these atrocities, the Netherlands, my country of citizenship and current residence, has abstained from voting on United Nations resolutions that call for a cease fire. Instead, the Netherlands has kept defending Israel's right to defend itself and even continues to supply Israel with warfare materials,[50] while the government fuels the hegemonic narrative in which all critique of Israel is called "antisemitic." I equally feel shame and anger about some Dutch universities, who have refused to cut ties with Israel, who have blocked or tried to block teach-ins organized by staff and students, while hiding behind a co-opted "social safety" discourse. I wish that universities would trust their communities to self-organize, and that they would trust that people can facilitate respectful and, yes, also activist conversations that speak out against all forms of violence, including anti-Semitism.

This book is a critique of technocolonialism: a critique of how capitalists' modern colonial tendencies morph into a new system in which in a way *all* people are enslaved and reduced to human-things. As I have stated throughout, such a critique only has meaning if it in the same breath acknowledges how technocolonialism perpetuates and intersects with pre-existing colonial and patriarchal structures and discourses. It is to acknowledge that technocolonialism affects some groups and people more than others. My anger and sadness about the disregard for Palestinian lives ultimately comes from the same decolonial place as the indignation I sense toward Big Tech's colonialist tendency to reduce people to human-things. The history of Western colonialism is clearly not over; it is interwoven with the technocolonial present. We see this with Israel (which was founded on Palestinian territory that was a British mandate between 1920 and 1948). While Meta's platforms shadow-ban and censor Palestinian voices, Amazon and Google provide Israel with cloud services and facial detection and sentiment analysis technologies, allowing for the further data-surveillance of Palestinians and the expansion of Israel's West Bank settlements, declared unlawful by the United Nations International Court of Justice.[51] As the organizers of an "Anti-Colonial Tech" panel write in a statement that they intended to deliver at the 2024 Transmediale festival in Berlin (but from which they withdrew because of the restrictions that the festival—under pressure of German and local authorities—placed on pro-Palestinian voices): "Palestine is the testing ground for technologies that are then used and exported throughout the world."[52]

The history of Western colonialism also lives on, for example, in the Democratic Republic of the Congo (DRC), whose dire humanitarian reality is indissolubly linked to the world's "green" and digital revolutions. I will focus on the role of cobalt, which helps power our "green" and "smart" revolutions. Cobalt is used in rechargeable lithium-ion batteries in order to prevent these batteries from spontaneous combustion. The average smartphone contains 7 grams of cobalt; an electric car battery about 13 kilograms. For a long time, cobalt was a byproduct of copper and nickel mining (though cobalt also colored Chinese and Dutch blue porcelain). The word "cobalt" comes from the German "*Kobolt*," which means goblin, for the reason that cobalt frightened miners because of the toxic arsenic that it attracts. Cobalt mining is still toxic. About 70 percent of the current global production of cobalt comes from the DRC.[53] In Congo, copper has been mined since at least the fourth century. In 1885, the Belgian king Leopold claimed the country and its mines as his private property. Large-scale mining only began in the twentieth century. In 1937, the Belgian Mining Union of Haut-Katanga founded the mining city of Kolwezi in southern Congo. Kolwezi now is the most important place for cobalt production.[54]

In 2015, fifty-five years after Congo's independence, many of the Kolwezi mining concessions were transferred to the Chinese company Congo Dongfang International Mining. This company provides minerals for electronics, including Apple's smartphones. A substantial part of the cobalt mining is done by so-called *creuseurs*, or diggers. These small-scale miners—among whom many children—try to make a living at the margins of the official mines. The risks are many: radiation, collapse of tunnels, arrest, torture, and murder by the authorities.

A 2022 Australian reportage titled *Blood Cobalt: The Congo's Dangerous and Deadly Green Energy Mines* by Michael Davie makes the viewer witness of the conditions under which cobalt is mined. We see miners working 25 meters underground without safety equipment. We see children as young as six handling the toxic cobalt. We meet a mother whose 13-year-old son has just been killed on the fringes of a mine. We see a recording of a man being beaten by a Congolese soldier as Chinese mine managers stand by laughing.[55] Davies interviews a woman who, together with her two sons, works as a *creuseur*. Every morning before the security guards arrive, they climb the embankments of a Chinese-owned mine. As the film shows images of the woman and her sons working on the mining site, she speaks in voice-over:

> I come to the mine to hustle. If I'm lucky I make some money and I buy food for the kids. But if I don't, they go to sleep hungry. We collect dirt. The kids help by packing it up and washing it. They also sort through it, looking for minerals. It's not a good life for children. We just don't have any other options[56] (Figure 73).

In 2019, the US law firm International Rights Advocates sued companies including Apple, Google, and Dell for their involvement in the injuries and death of miners, calling out against the "Stone-Age

FIGURE 73 Child labor at cobalt mine in the Democratic Republic of Congo as seen in the film *Blood Cobalt: The Congo's Dangerous and Deadly Green Energy Mines* (screen capture from video, © ABC News, 2022, all rights reserved).[57]

conditions" in which people, including children, work.[58] The outcry over these conditions has led industry players to found the Fair Cobalt Alliance, an organization that battles child labor and that supports small-scale mining with safety equipment and clean water. Among the members of this alliance are Fairphone, Tesla, Google, as well as some of Apple's Chinese subcontractors.[59] This alliance is a small positive note, but the overall reality of cobalt production remains devastating for humans and natural ecologies. The last few years there have been developments with cobalt-free batteries (for example already used by Tesla for some of its cars).[60] And Apple has announced that as of 2025 it will only use recycled cobalt.[61] For now, though, the demand for cobalt has continued rising. To give an idea: in 2020 the global cobalt demand was 140 kilotons; in 2024 it was over 220 kilotons.[62]

The demand for cobalt has also continued to feed the violence in the DRC. In September 2023, Amnesty International reported about forced evictions, violence, and rape at industrial copper and cobalt mines in the DRC. Amnesty's International Secretary Agnès Callamard says: "The people of the DRC experienced significant exploitation and abuse during the colonial and post-colonial era, and their rights are still being sacrificed as the wealth around them is stripped away" (Figure 74).[63]

FIGURE 74 Free Palestine, Free Congo (Amsterdam 2023, March for Climate and Justice, photo by the author).

This exploitation is directly connected to people's global daily reality of smartphone and, for some, electric car or electric bicycle use. The mining of minerals—not only cobalt but also lithium, tin, tungsten, tantalum, gold, etc.—is perhaps the ultimate touchstone for a critique of our technocolonial condition. Given the growing impossibility of *not* owning a smartphone these days, it also nearly impossible to *not* be a blood mineral consumer.

But what about deep-sea mining? Isn't that the solution to blood minerals? After all, the ocean floor is a vast reservoir of nickel, manganese, and cobalt. It is not the solution, because as oceanographers and biologists warn, to sweep the ocean floor of rare minerals would cause widespread pollution, destroy global fish stocks, and obliterate marine ecosystems. *The Guardian* cites Sophie Benbow from international wildlife charity Fauna & Flora: "The ocean plays a critical role in the basic functioning of our planet, and protecting its delicate ecosystem is not just critical for marine biodiversity but for all life on earth." Moreover, ocean mining wouldn't mean the end of land mining, as mining companies tend to claim. As Catherine Weller, also from Fauna & Flora, states: "These companies are presenting deep-sea mining as a new frontier, but they really mean it to be an additional frontier. ... We would just be adding to our woes."[64]

The world needs minerals, because without them there no green transition. But the world also needs *less* mineral mining. Logically, this is only feasible when life slows down on a global scale. Realistically, such degrowth won't happen anytime soon. And yet, a decolonial degrowth perspective remains needed, a prefigurative perspective that builds liberated worlds on small local and regional scales while fighting for world liberation. This means to prefigure worlds without Big Tech's toxic algorithms, not on moral but on anti-colonial grounds.

To resist Big Tech starts by acknowledging that many people find freedom and a sense of agency on its platforms. These platforms allow people to build and discover their identities and make new connections. To resist Big Tech is also to acknowledge that a lot of resistance against power (patriarchal, capitalist, racist, and transphobic) happens with the aid of network platforms. In order to reach and involve people, activist movements can hardly *not* be active on platforms. At the same time, it is important that movements are not dependent on those corporate infrastructures and also make use of, and ideally help build, more common infrastructures, both online (e.g., Mastodon, Cryptpad, DuckDuckGo, Jitsi, Nextcloud, and also the public web) *and* offline (common spaces for conversation and encounter, old-fashioned posters and paper event calendars, word of mouth). To cite once more from the "Anti-Colonial Tech" statement referenced earlier, "In solidarity with ongoing efforts for resistance ... we have to figure out how we can together divest from daily technological habits that continue to thicken our complicity in these violent acts. From Google Drive to Instagram, if there are no outsides to these companies then we need to find other ways to resist them."[65] Indeed, any decolonial struggle for people's collective autonomy intersects with the liberation from Big Tech colonialism. Resistance against Big Tech has to be part of everything we do, because Big Tech seeks to colonize everything people do. It is an everyday struggle for freedom.

This also means a decolonization of the mind. As Minna Salami writes in *Sensuous Knowledge*, "when it comes to the mind, decolonization will succeed only when it is clear ... that the colonial mind is a mind that is invaded by a whole network of synergetic efforts to prevent clarity so that it continues to act servitude."[66] This lack of clarity is the scattered state of mind that characterizes machinically enslaved life. Let's see more clearly and unite across the differences perpetuated by Big Tech's divisive algorithms. Let's unscatter and associate.

In conclusion, beyond all necessary government regulations, unionization of platform workers, and critical media literacy program, we need the following three lines of resistance against Big Tech colonialism. One, we need to change the story and talk about profit-driven tech platforms as colonial powers that extract value from people's associations: from their creativity and desire for freedom, and from their basic human need of a sense of connection. Second, we need cooperative, non-for-profit alternatives to Big Tech's extractive platforms. Third, and more generally, we need to acknowledge the limits of economic growth and recognize how intersecting profit-driven and normative powers shape many if not most of our everyday wanderings (our errands, our conversations, our ruminations). To do so is to slow down everyday life and create spacetime for association.

Notes

1   User Jelywws, [post March 20, 2023], accessed October 29, 2024, https://community.openai.com/t/chatgpt-plus-subscriber-login/108939/40?page=3.
2   Future of Life Institute, "Superintelligence: Science or Fiction? | Elon Musk & Other Great Minds" (video) (2017), accessed October 29, 2024, https://www.youtube.com/watch?v=h0962biiZa4.
3   Future of Life Institute, "Superintelligence" (video).
4   Maggie Nelson, *On Freedom: Four Songs of Care and Constraint* (London: Jonathan Cape, 2021), 213.
5   Foucault, *Discipline and Punish*, 224.
6   Nick Bostrom, *Superintelligence: Paths, Dangers, Strategies* (Oxford: Oxford University Press, 2014).
7   Yoshua Bengio et al., "Pause Giant AI Experiments: An Open Letter," *Future of Life Institute* (March 22, 2023), accessed October 29, 2024, https://futureoflife.org/open-letter/pause-giant-ai-experiments.
8   Alexandre Piquard, "Musk's X.AI Start-Up Highlights Paradoxical Relationship with AI," *Le Monde* (May 16, 2023), accessed October 29, 2024, https://www.lemonde.fr/en/economy/article/2023/04/18/musk-s-x-ai-start-up-highlights-paradoxical-relationship-with-ai-anew_6023306_19.html; X.AI, "Announcing Grok," *X.AI Blog* (November 3, 2023), accessed October 29, 2024, x.ai/blog.

9   Future of Life Institute, "AI Principles" (August 11, 2017), accessed October 29, 2024, https://futureoflife.org/open-letter/ai-principles.

10 OpenAI, "Introducing GPT-4" (video) (2023), accessed October 4, 2023, https://www.youtube.com/watch?v=–khbXchTeE.

11 Jeanette Winterson, *Frankisstein: A Love Story* (London: Vintage, 2019), 59.

12 Hickel, *Less Is More*, 287.

13 For a longer discussion of Apple's advertising strategies, see my essay: "Shot on iPhone: Apple's World Picture," *Advertising & Society Quarterly* 22.2 (2021), accessed October 29, 2024, https://muse.jhu.edu/article/797069.

14 Marantz, "Silicon Valley's Crisis of Conscience."

15 Nellie Bowles, "Where Silicon Valley Is Going to Get in Touch with its Soul" (*New York Times*, December 4, 2017), accessed October 29, 2024, https://www.nytimes.com/2017/12/04/technology/silicon-valley-esalen-institute.html.

16 Megadeth TV, "Megadeth—Last Rites (Apple Commercial—Shot on iPhone XS—Don't Mess with Mother)" (video) (2019), accessed October 29, 2024, https://www.youtube.com/watch?v=GbuFaFSxeFI.

17 Scott Jones, "Supernature: Esalen and the Human Potential, Episode One: The Inkblot Institute" (video) (2019), accessed October 29, 2024, https://www.youtube.com/watch?v=opu73EerPgQ.

18 Douglas Rushkoff, *Team Human* (New York: W. W. Norton & Company, 2019), 119.

19 Hickel, *Less Is More*, 236.

20 Matthias Schmelzer, Andrea Vetter, and Aaron Vansintjan, *The Future Is Degrowth: A Guide to a World beyond Capitalism* (London: Verso, 2022), 115.

21 Hickel, *Less Is More*, 157.

22 Hickel, *Less Is More*, 217.

23 Muldoon, *Platform Socialism*, 9.

24 Muldoon, *Platform Socialism*, 138.

25 Microsoft, "AI for Earth," accessed October 29, 2024, https://www.microsoft.com/en-us/ai/ai-for-earth.

26 Microsoft, "AI for Earth: A Gamechanger for Our Planet," *The Guardian* [no date], accessed October 29, 2024, https://www.theguardian.com/advertiser-content/microsoft-ai-for-earth/microsoft-ai-research.

27 Yossi Matias, "How We're Using AI to Help Address the Climate Crisis," *Google The Keyword* (November 2, 2022), accessed October 29, 2024, https://blog.google/outreach-initiatives/sustainability/cop27-adaptation-efforts.

28 Wired UK, "How Google's DeepMind Is Using AI to Tackle Climate Change," YouTube (2019), accessed October 29, 2024, https://www.youtube.com/watch?v=ba1tND0B0xk.

29 Microsoft, "AI for Good" (video) (2018), accessed October 29, 2024, https://www.youtube.com/watch?v=COQtCga6uuk.

30 World Economic Forum, *Harnessing Artificial Intelligence for the Earth* (January 2018), accessed October 29, 2024, https://www3.weforum.org/docs/Harnessing_Artificial_Intelligence_for_the_Earth_report_2018.pdf

31 Benedetta Brevini, *Is AI Good for the Planet?* (Cambridge: Polity Press, 2022), 95.

32 Brevini, *Is AI Good for the Planet?*, 96.

33 World Economic Forum, "What Is the Great Reset? | Davos Agenda 2021" (video), YouTube (2021), accessed October 29, 2024, https://www.youtube.com/watch?v=uPYx12xJFUQ.

34 World Economic Forum, "What Is the Great Reset?" (video)

35 Timothy Morton, *Being Ecological* (London: Pelican Books, 2018), 50–1.

36 Nelson, *On Freedom*, 175.

37 Michel Foucault, *Ethics: Subjectivity and Truth*, ed. Paul Rabinow, trans. Robert Hurley (New York: The New Press, 1998), 283-4.

38 Nelson, *On Freedom*, 175.

39 Nelson, *On Freedom*, 208.

40 Nelson, *On Freedom*, 208.

41 Lauren Berlant, *On the Inconvenience of Other People* (Durham: Duke University Press, 2022), 22.

42 Choreographic Translations, *Invisible Dances for Everyday Survivors* (Rotterdam: Choreographic Translations, 2022), 45.

43 Choreographic Translations, *Invisible Dances*, 73.

44 Extinction Rebellion, "What Are Regenerative Cultures" [no year], accessed October 29, 2024, https://xr-regenerativecultures.org.

45 Nelson, *On Freedom*, 208.

46 Terry Eagleton, *Hope without Optimism* (New Haven: Yale University Press, 2017), 2-3.

47 Amnesty International, "Democratic Republic of the Congo: Industrial Mining of Cobalt and Copper for Rechargeable Batteries is Leading to Grievous Human Rights Abuses" (September 12, 2023), accessed October 29, 2024, https://www.amnesty.ie/congo-cobalt-copper.

48 United Nations, "Rights Expert Finds 'Reasonable Grounds' Genocide is Being Committed in Gaza" (March 26, 2024), University Network for Human Rights, Genocide in Gaza: Analysis of International Law and its Application to Israel's Military Actions since October 7, 2023 (May 15, 2024), accessed October 29, 2024, https://web.archive.org/web/20240605210902/https://www.humanrightsnetwork.org; Alene Bouranova, "Is Israel Committing Genocide in Gaza? New Report from BU School of Law's International Human Rights Clinic Lays Out Case," BU Today (June 5, 2024), accessed October 29, 2024, https://www.bu.edu/articles/2024/is-israel-committing-genocide-in-gaza.

49 See Tia Goldenberg, "Harsh Israeli Rhetoric against Palestinians Becomes Central to South Africa's Genocide Case," *AP News* (January 18, 2024), accessed October 29, 2024, https://apnews.com/article/israel-palestinians-south-africa-genocide-hate-speech-97a9e4a84a3a6bebeddfb80f8a030724.

50 See Steven Derix and Pim van den Dool, "Hoe de VN-Resolutie over Gaza het Kabinet Verdeelt," *NRC* (October 31, 2023), accessed October 29, 2024, https://www.nrc.nl/nieuws/2023/10/31/hoe-vn-resolutie-het-kabinet-verdeelt-a4179273?t=1701804901.

51 See for example: United Nations, "Israel's Continued Occupation of Palestinian Territory 'Unlawful': UN World Court," *UN News* (July 19, 2024), accessed October 29, 2024, https://news.un.org/en/story/2024/07/1152296; Human Rights Watch, "Meta's Broken Promises: Systemic Censorship of Palestine Content on Instagram and Facebook" (December 21, 2023), accessed October 29, 2024, https://www.hrw.org/report/2023/12/21/metas-broken-promises/systemic-censorship-palestine-content-instagram-and; Sam Biddle, "Israeli Weapons Firms Required to Buy Cloud Services from Google and Amazon," *The Intercept* (May 1, 2024), accessed October 29, 2024, https://theintercept.com/2024/05/01/google-amazon-nimbus-israel-weapons-arms-gaza; Shoshanna Solomon, "Israel Signs Deals for Cloud Services with Google, Amazon," *The Times of Israel* (May 24, 2021), accessed October 29, 2024, https://www.timesofisrael.com/israel-signs-deal-for-cloud-services-with-google-amazon.

52 Varia, Constant, TTTiPI, Digital Discomfort Workgroup, "Introduction for the Panel: Anti-Colonial Tech through Resistance and Discomforts," [planned for:] Transmediale (Berlin, Germany, February 2, 2024), accessed October 29, 2024, https://pad.riseup.net/p/r.5e8fb6bd54cdce773db487845244e55d.

53 Michael Davie, "Blood Cobalt," *ABC* (September 5, 2022), accessed October 29, 2024, https://www.abc.net.au/news/2022-02-24/cobalt-mining-in-the-congo-green-energy/100802588.

54 Nicolas Niarchos, "The Dark Side of Congo's Cobalt Rush," *The New Yorker* (May 24, 2021), accessed October 29, 2024, https://www.newyorker.com/magazine/2021/05/31/the-dark-side-of-congos-cobalt-rush.

55 Michael Davie, "Video: Blood Cobalt" (February 24, 2022), accessed October 29, 2024, https://www.abc.net.au/news/2022-02-24/blood-cobalt/13769990.

56 ABC News In-depth, *Blood Cobalt: The Congo's Dangerous and Deadly Green Energy Mines | Foreign Correspondent* (video) (2022), accessed October 29, 2024, https://www.youtube.com/watch?v=_V3bIzNX4co.

57 ABC News In-depth, "Blood Cobalt" (video).

58 Niarchos, "Dark Side of Congo's Cobalt Rush"; International Rights Advocates, "Cobalt DRC Case," accessed October 29, 2024, https://www.internationalrightsadvocates.org/case/cobalt-drc-case.

59 See The Fair Cobalt Alliance, accessed October 29, 2024, https://www.faircobaltalliance.org.

60 See: Anne Trafton, "Cobalt-Free Batteries Could Power Cars of the Future," *MIT News* (January 18, 2024), accessed October 29, 2024, https://news.mit.edu/2024/cobalt-free-batteries-could-power-future-cars-0118; Daniel Oberhaus, "This Cobalt-Free Battery Is Good for the Planet—and It Actually Works," *Wired* (August 17, 2020), accessed October 29, 2024, https://www.wired.com/story/this-cobalt-free-battery-is-good-for-the-planet-and-it-actually-works.

61 Apple, "Apple Will Use 100 Percent Recycled Cobalt in Batteries by 2025" (April 13, 2023), accessed October 29, 2024, https://www.apple.com/newsroom/2023/04/apple-will-use-100-percent-recycled-cobalt-in-batteries-by-2025.

62 Cobalt Institute, "Quarterly Cobalt Market Update Overview 2024 Q1" (2024), accessed October 29, 2024, https://www.cobaltinstitute.org/wp-content/uploads/2024/04/Cobalt-Institute-Q1-2024-market-report.pdf.

63 Amnesty International, "Powering Change or Business as Usual: Forced Evictions at Industrial Cobalt and Copper Mines in the Democratic Republic of the Congo" (September 12, 2023), accessed October 29, 2024, https://www.amnesty.org/en/latest/news/2023/09/drc-cobalt-and-copper-mining-for-batteries-leading-to-human-rights-abuses.

64 Robin McKie, "Deep-Sea Mining for Rare Minerals Will Destroy Ecosystems, Say Scientists," *The Guardian* (March 26, 2023), accessed October 29, 2024, https://www.theguardian.com/environment/2023/mar/26/deep-sea-mining-for-rare-metals-will-destroy-ecosystems-say-scientists.

65 Varia et al., "Anti-Colonial Tech through Resistance and Discomforts."

66 Salami, *Sensuous Knowledge*, 67.

ACKNOWLEDGMENTS

The first ideas for this book date from 2013, when I wrote a conference paper about online dating. Soon after, I moved to Toronto where I got my first smartphone. As I write in Chapter 1, in this period I filled one notebook after the other on how everything changes with digital technology. At some point I realized that given that I spend so much time thinking about everyday life, I might as well turn these thoughts into my next project. The result is this book, born out of everyday associations.

During the writing of this book I received financial support from the Canadian Banting Postdoctoral Fellowship program (2014-2016) and the European Research Council's Starting Grant program (1999-2024). I am grateful for this support and to the academic institutions that have hosted my research in this period: the University of Toronto and its Cinema Studies Institute, Radboud University Nijmegen (Netherlands) and its Cultural Studies department, and Tilburg University (Netherlands) and its Department of Culture Studies. I am equally grateful to the Netherlands Institute of Cultural Analysis and the Dutch Research School for Gender Studies for my fruitful and ongoing collaborations with them.

At Bloomsbury Academic I thank Ben Doyle for our collaboration, his kind guidance, and his enthusiasm about the project. I thank Leigh Collins and Harvey Halpenny for their assistance in the last stages of the project. I thank Rebecca Heselton for her beautiful cover design (and for seeing a sunflower in a dish brush). I also thank the anonymous reviewers for their insightful commentary. I thank Kate Clissold-Jones and Rachel Walker for their work on the book's production. At Integra I thank Rebecca Willford for her work on the book's production and Martin Tribe for his copy-editing.

This book would not have existed without the many inspiring conversations I have had with people over the years. Thinking of my time in Minneapolis I thank, first of all, Chelsea Reynolds. Our smartphone-navigated road trip down to New Orleans and back upstream along the

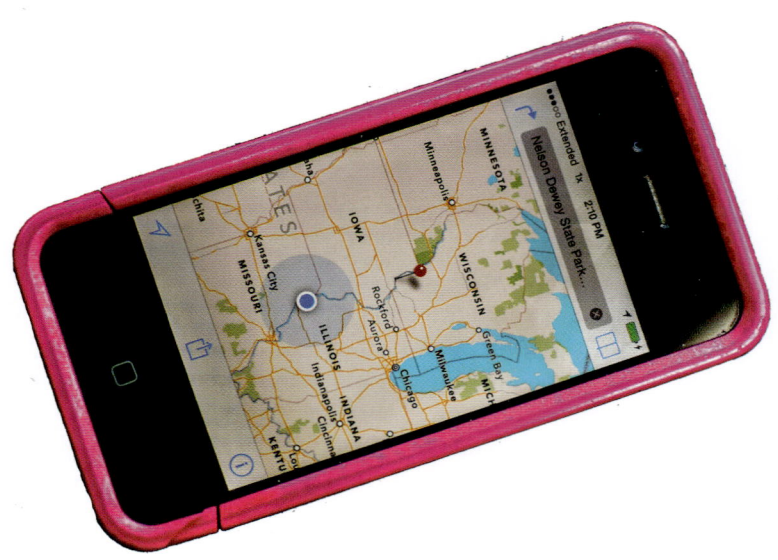

FIGURE 75 Upstream along the Great River Road (Illinois, 2014).

Great River Road (Figure 75) has always stayed with me and has been one of this book's great inspirations. I also thank Brad Johnson, Thorn Chen, Brendan McGillicuddy, Andrea Gyenge, and Richard Leppert. From my time in Toronto I thank Brian Price for his academic support. I thank Christine Lucy Latimer. And I thank, with all my heart, Kathleen Watt for our lovely times, our unforgettable Parkdale pizza nights and our ongoing conversations.

In 2016, I moved back to the Netherlands. From the period since, I thank first of all Rianne Riemens and Nuno Atalaia for our collaborations and conversations. They have sharpened my thinking, about platformization, ideology, the climate crisis, and much more. I thank Anneke Smelik for her belief in the project at an early stage and for guiding me in finding funding for it. I thank Jeroen Boom, for our wonderful collaborations during and after the Covid-19 seasons. I thank Floor Haalboom, for our time together, for our friendship, and for being so enthusiastic about the book long before it was a reality. I thank Jos Winters and Tessa Hendriks for our friendship and for having me over so many times in Amsterdam. I thank Pola Jane O'Mara, for our conversations about Instagram, and for our short, shared life and dreams of a life shared in Munich. I thank

Robert Buzink, for our bike rides and our conversations about tech, even the ones in which we disagree. I thank Markus Haringa for our lasting friendship and also his kind wisdom (we should go on more walks). I thank Salomé Mooij for our encounter and for helping me to think through the book's title (which was, for a long time, *The End of Everyday Life*). I also thank all other people I have befriended, loved, and been inspired by over the years, in particular Adriaan Graas, Hadrian Ferran, Monique Veenswijk, Angelina Kancheva, Patrick Hoop, Tessa de Boer, Rots Brouwer (who opened my eyes to the injustices surrounding cobalt mining), Ismani Nieuweboer (for our conversations about "social" media, "artificial" "intelligence," and Extinction Rebellion), Julie Mèle (for our conversations about anarchism and common freedom), Sophia Parvez (for her comments on the first chapter and for her kindness), and Diana Svihlova (for our conversations about advertising and for reading so much of the book).

Finally, I thank my parents, for everything, and my dad for reading everything in all of its iterations over the years.

Minneapolis-Toronto-Utrecht, 2013-2025

BIBLIOGRAPHY

Access Now, "Meta's Actions 'Adversely Impacted' Palestinians' Rights: Access Now Welcomes BSR Findings" (September 27, 2022, updated January 26, 2023), accessed October 30, 2024, https://www.accessnow.org/press-release/bsr-findings-meta-palestinian-rights.

Ahmed, Sara, "Against Students," *The New Inquiry* (June 29, 2015), accessed October 30, 2024, https://thenewinquiry.com/against-students.

Ahmed, Sara, *Living a Feminist Life* (Durham: Duke University Press, 2017).

Ahmed, Sara, *Queer Phenomenology: Orientations, Objects, Others* (Durham: Duke University Press, 2006).

Ahmed, Sara, "Selfcare as Warfare," *feministkilljoys* (August 25, 2014), accessed October 30, 2024, https://feministkilljoys.com/2014/08/25/selfcare-as-warfare.

Ahmed, Sara, *Strange Encounters: Embodied Others in Postcoloniality* (London: Routledge, 2000).

Ahmed, Sara, *Willful Subjects* (Durham: Duke University Press, 2014).

Alimardani, Mahsa, "How Instagram Is Failing Protesters in Iran," *Slate* (June 2, 2022), accessed October 30, 2024, https://slate.com/technology/2022/06/instagram-meta-iran-protests-exceptions.html.

Althusser, Louis, *"Lenin and Philosophy" and Other Essays*, trans. Ben Brewster (New York: Monthly Review Press, 1971).

Amnesty International, "Democratic Republic of the Congo: Industrial Mining of Cobalt and Copper for Rechargeable Batteries is Leading to Grievous Human Rights Abuses" (September 12, 2023), accessed October 30, 2024, https://www.amnesty.ie/congo-cobalt-copper.

Amnesty International, "Powering Change or Business as Usual: Forced Evictions at Industrial Cobalt and Copper Mines in the Democratic Republic of the Congo" (September 12, 2023), accessed October 30, 2024, https://www.amnesty.org/en/latest/news/2023/09/drc-cobalt-and-copper-mining-for-batteries-leading-to-human-rights-abuses.

Apple, "Apple Will Use 100 Percent Recycled Cobalt in Batteries by 2025" (April 13, 2023), accessed October 30, 2024, https://www.apple.com/newsroom/2023/04/apple-will-use-100-percent-recycled-cobalt-in-batteries-by-2025.

Arikha, Noga, "Up Close and Personal: The Evolution of Personal Ads, from the Newspaper to the Social Network," *Lapham's Quarterly* [no date], accessed October 30, 2024, https://www.laphamsquarterly.org/eros/close-and-personal.

Aster, Hannah, "Digital Sweatshops: The Dark Side of Artificial Intelligence," *Shortform* (October 3, 2023), accessed October 30, 2024, https://www.shortform.com/blog/digital-sweatshop.

Badiou, Alain and Nicolas Truong, *In Praise of Love*, trans. Peter Bush (New York: The New Press, 2012).

Baer, Drake, "Here's What Google Teaches Employees in its 'Search Inside Yourself' Course," *Insider* (August 5, 2014), accessed October 30, 2024, https://www.businessinsider.com/search-inside-yourself-googles-life-changing-mindfulness-course-2014-8.

Bailey, Merridee L., "Hornbooks," *Journal of the History of Childhood & Youth* 6.1 (2013): 5–14.

Bakardjieva, Maria, *Internet Society: The Internet in Everyday Life* (London: Sage, 2005).

Bard, "Meet Bard," accessed 27 April 2023, https://bard.google.com.

Barns, Sarah, *Platform Urbanism: Negotiating Platform Ecosystems in Connected Cities* (Singapore: Palgrave Macmillan, 2020).

Baudelaire, Charles, *The Painter of Modern Life, and Other Essays*, trans./ed. Jonathan Mayne (New York: Phaidon Press, 1967).

BBC, "A Short History of Dating," *Bitesize* [BBC blog] [no year], accessed October 30, 2024, https://www.bbc.co.uk/bitesize/articles/ztrptrd.

Bejarano, Carolina Alonso and Stina Soderling, "Against Grading: Feminist Studies beyond the Neoliberal University," *Feminist Formations* 33.2 (2021): 208–32.

Bengio, Yoshua et al., "Pause Giant AI Experiments: An Open Letter," *Future of Life Institute* (March 22, 2023), accessed October 30, 2024, https://futureoflife.org/open-letter/pause-giant-ai-experiments.

Benjamin, Walter, *Essays and Reflections* (New York: Schocken Books, 2007).

Bergström, Marie, *The New Laws of Love: Online Dating and the Privatization of Intimacy* (Cambridge: Polity Press, 2022).

Berlant, Lauren, *Cruel Optimism* (Durham: Duke University Press, 2011).

Berlant, Lauren, *On the Inconvenience of Other People* (Durham: Duke University Press, 2022).

Bliss, Laura, "Meet the Jane Jacobs of the Smart Cities Age," *Citylab* (December 12, 2018), accessed October 30, 2024, https://www.bloomberg.com/news/articles/2018-12-21/toronto-privacy-advocate-bianca-wylie-v-sidewalk-labs.

Bluemink, Matt, "The Politics of Modulation: Simondon's Influence on Deleuze's 'Societies of Control,'" *Blue Labyrinths* 3 (2021), accessed October 30, 2024, https://bluelabyrinths.com/2021/03/17/the-politics-of-modulation-simondons-influence-on-deleuzes-societies-of-control.

Bonini, Tiziano and Emiliano Treré, *Algorithms of Resistance: The Everyday Fight against Platform Power* (Cambridge, MA: MIT Press, 2024).

Bonnington, Christina, "OkCupid Says People Have to Use their Real Names—and then Changes its Mind," *Daily Dot* (January 3, 2018), accessed October 30, 2024, https://www.dailydot.com/debug/okcupid-real-name-policy-backtrack.

Bostrom, Nick, "A History of Transhumanist Thought," *Journal of Evolution and Technology* 14.1 (2005): 1–30.

Bostrom, Nick, *Superintelligence: Paths, Dangers, Strategies* (Oxford: Oxford University Press, 2014).

Bostrom, Nick, "What Is Transhumanism?" (2001), accessed October 30, 2024, https://nickbostrom.com/old/transhumanism.

Bowles, Nellie, "Where Silicon Valley Is Going to Get in Touch with its Soul," *New York Times* (December 4, 2017), accessed October 30, 2024, https://www.nytimes.com/2017/12/04/technology/silicon-valley-esalen-institute.html.

Braidotti, Rosi, *The Posthuman* (Cambridge: Polity Press, 2013).

Braidotti, Rosi, "A Theoretical Framework for the Critical Posthumanities," *Theory, Culture & Society* 36.6 (2019): 31–61.

Bratton, Benjamin, *The Stack: On Software and Sovereignty* (Cambridge, MA: MIT Press, 2016).

Brevini, Benedetta, *Is AI Good for the Planet?* (Cambridge: Polity Press, 2022).

Broken Chain, "Apple's Uyghur Dilemma Grows," *Tech Transparency Project* (June 8, 2021), accessed October 30, 2024, https://www.techtransparencyproject.org/articles/apples-uyghur-dilemma-grows.

Burgess, Jean, Kath Albury, Anthony McCosker, and Rowan Wilken, *Everyday Data Cultures* (Cambridge: Polity, 2022).

Cameron, Julia. *The Artist's Way: A Spiritual Path to Higher Creativity* (London: Souvenir Press, 2020).

Cardoso, Tom, and Josh O'Kane, "Sidewalk Labs Document Reveals Company's Early Vision for Data Collection, Tax Powers, Criminal Justice," *The Globe and Mail* (October 30, 2019), accessed October 30, 2024, https://www.theglobeandmail.com/business/article-sidewalk-labs-document-reveals-companys-early-plans-for-data.

Cecco, Leyland, "'Surveillance Capitalism': Critic Urges Toronto to Abandon Smart City Project," *The Guardian* (May 7, 2020), accessed October 30, 2024, https://www.theguardian.com/technology/2020/may/07/google-sidewalk-labs-toronto-smart-city-abandoned.

Certeau, Michel de, *The Practice of Everyday Life*, trans. Steven Rendall (Berkeley: University of California Press, 1988).

Certeau, Michel de, *The Practice of Everyday Life, Volume 2: Living & Cooking*, trans. Timothy J. Tomasik (Minneapolis: University of Minnesota Press, 1998).

Cheney-Lippold, John, "A New Algorithmic Identity: Soft Biopolitics and the Modulation of Control," *Theory Culture Society* 28.6 (2011): 164–81.

Cheney-Lippold, John, *We Are Data: Algorithms and the Making of Our Digital Selves* (New York: New York University Press, 2017).

Chokrane, Boutayna Chokrane, "What Is Deinfluencing? Unpacking TikTok's Unlikeliest Shopping Trend," *Vogue* (December 21, 2023), accessed October 30, 2024, https://www.vogue.com/article/what-is-deinfluencing.

Choreographic Translations, *Invisible Dances for Everyday Survivors* (Rotterdam: Choreographic Translations, 2022).

Chun, Wendy, "Big Data as Drama," *ELH* 83.2 (2016): 363–82.

Citton, Yves, *The Ecology of Attention*, trans. Barnaby Norman (Cambridge: Polity Press, 2017).

Cobalt Institute, "Quarterly Cobalt Market Update Overview 2024 Q1" (2024), accessed October 30, 2024, https://www.cobaltinstitute.org/wp-content/uploads/2024/04/Cobalt-Institute-Q1-2024-market-report.pdf.

Cohen, Noam, "Wikipedia is Finally Asking Big Tech to Pay Up," *Wired* (March 16, 2021), accessed October 30, 2024, https://www.wired.com/story/wikipedia-finally-asking-big-tech-to-pay-up.

Conger, Kate, "Google Removes 'Don't Be Evil' Clause from its Code of Conduct," *Gizmodo* (May 18, 2018), accessed October 30, 2024, https://gizmodo.com/google-removes-nearly-all-mentions-of-dont-be-evil-from-1826153393.

Cooke, Richard, "Wikipedia Is the Last Best Place on the Internet," *Wired* (February 17, 2020), accessed October 30, 2024, https://www.wired.com/story/wikipedia-online-encyclopedia-best-place-internet.

Cooper, Kelly, "An Open Letter on Why We're Removing Usernames, Addressed to the Worst Ones We've Seen," *OkCupid Blog* (December 21, 2017), accessed October 30, 2024, https://theblog.okcupid.com/an-open-letter-on-why-were-removing-usernames-addressed-to-the-worst-ones-we-ve-ever-seen-dd017c75d49a.

Couldry, Nick and Ulises A. Mejias, *The Costs of Connection: How Data Is Colonizing Human Life and Appropriating It for Capitalism* (Stanford: Stanford University Press, 2019).

Crary, Jonathan, *24/7: Late Capitalism and the Ends of Sleep* (London: Verso, 2014).

Cross, Tristan, "You Know Modern Life Is Hard When Even Adverts Don't Try to Persuade You Otherwise," *The Guardian* (January 17, 2022), accessed October 30, 2024, https://www.theguardian.com/commentisfree/2022/jan/17/modern-life-hard-adverts-work-uber-eats.

Dam, Rikke Friis and Teo Yu Siang, "Design Thinking: Get a Quick Overview of the History," Interaction Design Foundation (2020), accessed October 30, 2024, https://www.interaction-design.org/literature/article/design-thinking-get-a-quick-overview-of-the-history.

Davie, Michael, "Blood Cobalt," *ABC* (September 5, 2022), accessed October 30, 2024, https://www.abc.net.au/news/2022-02-24/cobalt-mining-in-the-congo-green-energy/100802588.

Davis, Allison P., "New OkCupid Data on Race Is Pretty Depressing," *The Cut* (September 11, 2014), accessed October 30, 2024, https://www.thecut.com/2014/09/new-okcupid-data-on-race-is-pretty-depressing.html.

Deleuze, Gilles, *Negotiations 1972–1990*, trans. Martin Joughin (New York: Columbia University Press, 1990).

Deleuze, Gilles and Félix Guattari, *What Is Philosophy?*, trans. Hugh Tomlinson and Graham Burchell (New York: Columbia University Press, 1994).

Dijck, José van, "The Platform Society," Association of Internet Research conference (2016), accessed October 30, 2024, https://www.youtube.com/watch?v=-ypiiSQTNqo.

Dijck, José van, Thomas Poell, and Martijn de Waal, *The Platform Society: Public Values in a Connective World* (New York: Oxford University Press, 2018).

Dittus, Martin, "The Uneven Geography of Wikipedia," Oxford Internet Institute (October 16, 2018), accessed October 30, 2024, https://geography.oii.ox.ac.uk/the-uneven-geography-of-wikipedia.

Doctoroff, Daniel L., "Reimaging Cities from the Internet Up," *Sidewalk Talk* (November 30, 2016), accessed October 30, 2024, https://medium.com/sidewalk-talk/reimagining-cities-from-the-internet-up-5923d6be63ba.

Doctoroff, Daniel L., "Why We're No Longer Pursuing the Quayside Project—and What's Next for Sidewalk Labs," *Sidewalk Talk* (May 7, 2020), accessed October 30, 2024, https://medium.com/sidewalk-talk/why-were-no-longer-pursuing-the-quayside-project-and-what-s-next-for-sidewalk-labs-9a61de3fee3a.

Doctorow, Cory, "WiFi Isn't Short for 'Wireless Fidelity,'" *Boingboing* (November 8, 2005), accessed October 30, 2024, https://boingboing.net/2005/11/08/wifi-isnt-short-for.html.

Downey, Sarah A., "Your Privacy on OkCupid: The Unromantic Truth," *The Online Privacy Blog* (2012), accessed October 30, 2024, http://www.abine.com/blog/2012/your-privacy-on-okcupid-the-unromantic-truth.

Drake, Leah Bodine, *A Hornbook for Witches: Poems of Fantasy* (Sauk City: Arkham House, 1950).

Dubrofsky, Rachel E. and Megan M. Wood, "Gender, Race, and Authenticity: Celebrity Women Tweeting for the Gaze," in Rachel E. Dubrofsky and Shoshana Amielle Magnet, eds., *Feminist Surveillance Studies* (Durham: Duke University Press, 2015), 93–106.

Dumitrescu, Irina and Caleb Smith, "The Demon of Distraction" in "Posts from the Pandemic," *Critical Inquiry* blog (April 22, 2020), accessed October 30, 2024, https://critinq.wordpress.com/2020/04/22/the-demon-of-distraction.

Eagleton, Terry, *Hope without Optimism* (New Haven: Yale University Press, 2017).

Easton, Dossie and Catherine A. Liszt, *The Ethical Slut: A Guide to Infinite Sexual Possibilities* (San Francisco: Greenery Press, 1997).

Extinction Rebellion, "What Are Regenerative Cultures" [no year], accessed October 30, 2024, https://xr-regenerativecultures.org.

Felski, Rita, *Doing Time: Feminist Theory and Posthuman Culture* (New York: New York University Press, 2000).

Fern, Jessica, *Polysecure: Attachment, Trauma and Consensual Non-Monogamy* (Melbourne: Scribe, 2023).

Forbruker Radet, "Out of Control—How Consumers Are Exploited by the Online Advertising Industry" [report] (January 14, 2020), accessed October 30, 2024, https://www.marketingdirecto.com/wp-content/uploads/2020/01/2020-01-14-out-of-control.pdf.

Foucault, Michel, *Discipline and Punish: The Birth of the Prison*, trans. Alan Sheridan (New York: Vintage Books, 1995).

Foucault, Michel, *Ethics: Subjectivity and Truth*, ed. Paul Rabinow, trans. Robert Hurley (New York: The New Press, 1998).

Foucault, Michel, *Histoire de la sexualité II: L'Usage des Plaisirs* (Paris: Gallimard, 2013).

Franco, James, "Who is 'Her'?" *Vice* (June 2, 2014), accessed October 30, 2024, https://www.vice.com/en/article/7b7b8a/who-is-her.

Franklin-Wallis, Oliver, "Inside X, Google's Top-Secret Moonshot Factory," *Wired* (February 17, 2020), accessed October 30, 2024, https://www.wired.co.uk/article/ten-years-of-google-x.

Freire, Paolo, *Pedagogy of the Oppressed*, trans. Myra Bergman Ramos (New York: Continuum, 2005).

Future of Life Institute, "AI Principles" (August 11, 2017), accessed October 30, 2024, https://futureoflife.org/open-letter/ai-principles.

Gary, Cauleen Suzanne, "Bildung and Gender in 19th Century Bourgeois Germany: A Cultural Studies Analysis of Texts by Women Writers," PhD thesis, University of Maryland, 2008.

Gentile, Ginger, "Is Instagram Censoring Influencers Who Support Iranian Protestors?," *Forbes* (November 10, 2022), accessed October 30, 2024, https://www.forbes.com/sites/gingergentile/2022/11/10/is-instagram-censoring-influencers-who-support-iranian-protestors.

Gilbert, Jeremy and Alex Williams, *Hegemony Now: How Big Tech and Wall Street Won the World (and How We Win it Back)* (London: Verso, 2022).

Gillespie, Tarleton, "The Politics of 'Platforms,'" *New Media & Society* 12:3 (2010): 347–64.

Goldin, Melissa, "Zoom Says It Isn't Training AI on Calls without Consent. But Other Data Is Fair Game," *AP* (August 9, 2023), accessed October 30, 2024, https://apnews.com/article/fact-check-zoom-ai-privacy-terms-of-service-06ff47e47439c2173390a4ca1389f652.

Goodman, Ellen P. and Julia Powles, "Urbanism under Google: Lessons from Sidewalk Toronto," *Fordham Law Review* 88 (2019): 457–98.

Google, "About," accessed October 30, 2024, https://www.google.com/doodles/about.

Google, "Create & Grade Quizzes with Google Forms," accessed October 30, 2024, https://support.google.com/docs/answer/7032287.

Google, "Facts about Google and Competition," https://www.google.com/competition/howgooglesearchworks.html (August 26, 2011), via The Internet Archive, accessed October 30, 2024, https://web.archive.org/web/20111104131332/https://www.google.com/competition/howgooglesearchworks.html.

Google, "Mundaneum Co-Founder Paul Otlet's 147th Birthday" (August 23, 2015), accessed October 30, 2024, https://www.google.com/doodles/mundaneum-co-founder-paul-otlets-147th-birthday.

Google Arts & Culture, "Slogans for the Class of 2030 by Douglas Coupland," accessed October 30, 2024, https://artsandculture.google.com/story/slogans-for-the-class-of-2030-by-douglas-coupland/vQURjwPHHpa5uw.

Google Arts & Culture, "Take a Virtual Field Trip: Where Do You Want to Go Today?" [no date], accessed October 30, 2024, https://artsandculture.google.com/project/expeditions.

Google Cloud, "Google Workspace for Education Data Protection Implementation Guide," accessed 30 October 2024, https://services.google.com/fh/files/misc/google_workspace_edu_data_protection_implementation_guide.pdf.

"Google Expeditions: Bringing the World to your Classroom in Virtual Reality" slide show (no year), accessed October 26, 2024, https://sites.google.com/tcsnc.org/tcs-g-expeditions/google-expeditions-app.

Google for Education, "Elevate Education with Simple, Flexible and Secure Tools with Google Workspace for Education" [no date], accessed October 30, 2024, https://edu.google.com/intl/ALL_uk/workspace-for-education/editions/overview.

Google for Education, *Future of the Classroom: Emerging Trends in K-12 Education (Global Edition)* (2018), accessed October 30, 2024, https://services.google.com/fh/files/misc/future_of_the_classroom_emerging_trends_in_k12_education.pdf.

Google for Education, "Emerging Technologies: A Conversation with Michael Bodaeker" (2018), accessed October 30, 2024, https://edu.google.com/intl/ALL_au/future-of-the-classroom/emerging-technologies.

Google for Education, "Google Workspace for Education" (2023), accessed October 30, 2024, https://edu.google.com/intl/ALL_us/workspace-for-education/classroom.

Google for Education, "Helping Expand Learning for Everyone," accessed October 30, 2024, https://edu.google.com/intl/ALL_uk/why-google/our-commitment.

Google for Education, "Privacy and Security Centre," accessed October 30, 2024, https://edu.google.com/intl/ALL_uk/why-google/privacy-security.

Google for Education, "Products that Power Education," accessed October 30, 2024, https://edu.google.com/intl/ALL_uk.

Google for Education, "The Anywhere School 2021" (2021), accessed October 30, 2024, https://educationonair.withgoogle.com/events/the-anywhere-school-2021.

Google for Education, "Turning Commute Time into Learning Time," accessed October 30, 2024, https://edu.google.com/intl/ALL_uk/why-google/our-commitment/rolling-study-halls.

Gray, Mary L., *Out in the Country: Youth, Media, and Queer Visibility in Rural America* (New York: New York University Press, 2009).

Green, Ben, "The Responsible City," [Chapter 5] in *The Smart Enough City* (Cambridge, MA: MIT Press, 2019), accessed October 30, 2024, https://smartenoughcity.mitpress.mit.edu/pub/yvyv9j2i/release/1.

Günther, Karl-Heinz, "Profiles of Educators: Wilhelm von Humboldt (1767–1835)," *Prospects* 18: 1 (1988): 127–36.

Halberstam, Jack, *Trans** (Oakland: University of California Press, 2018).

Hall, Stuart, "Cultural Studies: Two Paradigms," *Media, Culture and Society* 2 (1980): 57-72.

Han, Byung-Chul, *The Burnout Society*, trans. Erik Butler (Stanford: Stanford Briefs, 2015).

Hanisch, Carol, "Introduction" to "The Personal Is Political: The Women's Liberation Movement Classic with a New Explanatory Introduction" (January 2006), accessed October 30, 2024, http://www.carolhanisch.org/CHwritings/PIP.html.

Haraway, Donna J., *The Companion Species Manifesto: Dogs, People, and Significant Otherness* (Chicago: Prickly Paradigm Press, 2003).

Haraway, Donna J., *A Cyborg Manifesto: Science, Technology, and Socialist-Feminism in the Late Twentieth Century* (Minneapolis: University of Minnesota Press, 2016).

Hardt, Michael, "The Common in Communism," *Rethinking Marxism: A Journal of Economics, Culture & Society* 22.3 (2010): 346–56.

Harris, Malcolm, "Are We Living under 'Technofeudalism'?," *New York Magazine* (October 28, 2022), accessed October 30, 2024, https://nymag.com/intelligencer/2022/10/what-is-technofeudalism.html.

Hayles, Katherine, *How We Became Posthuman* (Chicago: Chicago University Press, 1999).

Hern, Alex, "OkCupid: We Experiment on Users, Everyone Does," *The Guardian* (July 29, 2014), accessed October 30, 2024, https://www.theguardian.com/technology/2014/jul/29/okcupid-experiment-human-beings-dating.

Hester, Lilyn, "Rolling Study Halls: Turning Bus Time into Learning Time," *Google The Keyword* (April 2, 2018), accessed October 30, 2024, https://www.blog.google/outreach-initiatives/grow-with-google/rolling-study-halls-turning-bus-time-learning-time.

Hickel, Jason, *Less Is More: How Degrowth Will Save the World* (London: Penguin Random House UK, 2022).

Hicks, Mar, "Computer Love: Replicating Social Order through Early Computer Dating Systems," *Ada: A Journal of Gender, New Media and Technology* (November 10, 2016), accessed October 30, 2024, https://adanewmedia.org/category/issue-no-10.

Hodgson, Nichi, *The Curious History of Dating: From Jane Austen to Tinder* (London: Robinson, 2022).

Holland, Jennifer, "Expanding Google Arts & Culture with Expeditions," *Google The Keyword* (November 30, 2020), accessed October 30, 2024, https://blog.google/outreach-initiatives/education/expanding-google-arts-and-culture-expeditions.

hooks, bell, *Teaching to Transgress: Education as the Practice of Freedom* (Routledge: Francis & Taylor Group, 1994).

Howard, Ebenezer, *Garden Cities of Tomorrow* (London: Swan Sonnenschein, 2014).

Human Rights Watch, "Israel/Palestine: Facebook Censors Discussion of Rights Issues" (October 8, 2021), accessed October 30, 2024, https://www.hrw.org/news/2021/10/08/israel/palestine-facebook-censors-discussion-rights-issues.

Huxley, Julian, *New Bottles for New Wine* (London: Chatto & Windus, 1957).

Hvas Mortensen, Ditte, "Stage 1 in the Design Thinking Process: Empathise with Your Users," *Interaction Design Foundation* (July 2020), accessed

October 30, 2024, https://www.interaction-design.org/literature/article/stage-1-in-the-design-thinking-process-empathise-with-your-users.

Illich, Ivan, *Deschooling Society* (New York: Harrow Books, 1970), https://archive.org/details/deschoolingsocieOOOOunse.

Illich, Ivan, *Tools for Conviviality* (London: Marion Boyars Publishing, 2021).

Illouz, Eva, *Cold Intimacies: The Making of Emotional Capitalism* (Cambridge: Polity Press, 2007).

Interaction Design Thinking, "What Is Design Thinking," *Interaction Design Foundation*, accessed October 30, 2024, https://www.interaction-design.org/literature/topics/design-thinking.

Jacobs, Jane, *The Death and Life of Great American Cities* (New York: Vintage Books, 1992).

Jaffe, Eric, "Zoning: The Legal and Social Codes of Urban Planning," *Sidewalk Labs* blog (September 21, 2017), accessed October 30, 2024, https://www.sidewalklabs.com/insights/zoning-the-legal-and-social-codes-of-urban-planning.

Jane's Walk, "Revisiting the Jane's Walk Principles in 2021" (2021), accessed November 22, 2021, https://janeswalk.org/new-principles.

Jarrett, Kylie, *Feminism, Labour, and Digital Media: The Digital Housewife* (New York: Routledge, 2016).

Jeffries, Adrianne, "OkCupid: We Didn't Censor Our Match.com Bashing Blog Post," *Observer* (February 2, 2011), accessed October 30, 2024, https://observer.com/2011/02/okcupid-we-didnt-censor-our-matchcombashing-blog-post.

Johnson, Bobbie, "Wikipedia Wins the Google Lottery—but Why?," *The Guardian* (February 18, 2010), accessed October 30, 2024, https://www.theguardian.com/technology/blog/2010/feb/18/wikipedia-google.

Johnston, Malcolm, "Q&A: Dan Doctoroff on Building the Neighbourhood of Tomorrow," *Toronto Life* (April 9, 2018), accessed October 30, 2024, https://torontolife.com/city/qa-dan-doctoroff-building-neighbourhood-tomorrow.

Kastrenakes, Jacob, "Apple Suppliers Linked to Uyghur Forced Labor," *The Verge* (May 10, 2021), accessed October 30, 2024, https://www.theverge.com/2021/5/10/22428899/apple-suppliers-china-uyghur-forced-labor-report.

Kennedy, Maev, "Finding your Valentine—17th Century-Style," *The Guardian* (February 12, 2010), accessed October 30, 2024, https://www.theguardian.com/lifeandstyle/2010/feb/12/valentine-17th-century-lonely-hearts.

Kern, Leslie, *Feminist City* (London: Verso, 2021).

Kerssens, Niels and José van Dijck, "The Platformization of Primary Education in the Netherlands," *Learning, Media and Technology* 46:3 (2021): 250–63.

Khoudary, Hind, "Social Media Giant Meta Carries Out 'Digital Massacre' of Palestinian Posts," *Middle East Eye* (August 11, 2022), accessed October 30, 2024, https://www.middleeasteye.net/news/meta-palestine-posts-social-media-digital-massacre.

Kleinberg, Jon M. "Authoritative Sources in a Hyperlinked Environment," Proc. 9th ACM-SIAM Symposium on Discrete Algorithms (1998), accessed October 30, 2024, https://www.cs.cornell.edu/home/kleinber/auth.pdf.

Koch, Richie, "Using Zoom? Here Are the Privacy Issues You Need to Be Aware of," *Proton Blog* (March 20, 2020, updated January 10, 2023), accessed October 30, 2024, https://proton.me/blog/zoom-privacy-issues.

Kuitenbrouwer, Klaas, "The Stack and the Post-Human User: An Interview with Benjamin Bratton," *Garden of Machines* (February 28, 2015), accessed October 30, 2024, https://tuinvanmachines.hetnieuweinstituut.nl/en/stack-and-posthuman-user-interview-benjamin-bratton.

Kumar, Priya, Jessica Vitak, Marshini Chetty, and Tamara L. Clegg, "The Platformization of the Classroom: Teachers as Surveillance Consumers," *Surveillance & Society* 17.1/2 (2019): 145–52.

Kurzweil, Ray, "AI Will Not Displace Humans, It's Going to Enhance Us," *Futurism* (July 11, 2017), accessed October 30, 2024, https://futurism.com/ray-kurzweil-ai-displace-humans-going-enhance.

Kurzweil, Ray, *The Singularity Is Near: When Humans Transcend Biology* (New York: Viking, 2005).

Landry, Donna and Gerald Maclean, "Introduction: Reading Spivak," in Donna Landry and Gerald Maclean, eds., *The Spivak Reader* (London: Routledge, 1996), 1–14.

Lazare, Melanie, "A Peek at What's Next for Google Classroom," *Google The Keyword* (February 17, 2021), accessed October 30, 2024, https://blog.google/outreach-initiatives/education/classroom-roadmap.

Lazzarato, Maurizio, *Signs and Machines: Capitalism and the Production of Subjectivity*, trans. David Jordan (Los Angeles: Semiotext(e), 2017).

Lefebvre, Henri. *Everyday Life in the Modern World*, trans. Sacha Rabinovitch (New York: Bloomsburg, 2018).

Letzing, John, "Google Hires Famed Futurist Ray Kurzweil," *The Wall Street Journal* (December 14, 2012), accessed October 30, 2024, https://www.wsj.com/articles/BL-DGB-25711.

Lindh, Maria and Jan Nolin, "Information We Collect: Surveillance and Privacy in the Implementation of Google Apps for Education," *European Education Research Journal* 15.6 (2016): 644–63.

Loukaitou-Sideris, Anastasia Ehrenfeucht, and Renia Ehrenfeucht, *Sidewalks: Conflict and Negotiation over Public Space* (Cambridge, MA: MIT Press, 2009).

Lugo, Jorge, "Google Assignments, Your New Grading Companion," *Google The Keyword* (August 14, 2019), accessed October 30, 2024, https://blog.google/outreach-initiatives/education/introducing-assignments.

Madianou, Mirca, "Technocolonialism: Digital Innovation and Data Practices in the Humanitarian Response to Refugee Crises," *Social Media and Society* 5.3 (2019), accessed October 30, 2024, https://doi.org/10.1177/2056305119863146.

Madrigal, Alexis C., "Take the Data out of Dating," *The Atlantic* (December 2010), accessed October 30, 2024, https://www.theatlantic.com/magazine/archive/2010/12/take-the-data-out-of-dating/308299.

Malabou, Catherine, "To Quarantine from Quarantine: Rousseau, Robinson Crusoe, and 'I'," in "Posts from the Pandemic," *Critical Inquiry* blog (March 23, 2020), accessed October 30, 2024, https://critinq.wordpress.

com/2020/03/23/to-quarantine-from-quarantine-rousseau-robinson-crusoe-and-i.

Marantz, Andrew, "Silicon Valley's Crisis of Conscience: Where Big Tech Goes to Ask Deep Questions," *The New Yorker* (August 19, 2019), accessed October 30, 2024, https://www.newyorker.com/magazine/2019/08/26/silicon-valleys-crisis-of-conscience.

Martínez, Antonio García, "Facebook's Not Listening through Your Phone. It Doesn't Have To," *Wired* (November 10, 2017), accessed October 30, 2024, https://www.wired.com/story/facebooks-listening-smartphone-microphone.

Marx, Karl, *Grundrisse: Foundations of the Critique of Political Economy* (Rough Draft), trans. Martin Nicolaus (London: Penguin Books, 1993).

Matias, Yossi, "How We're Using AI to Help Address the Climate Crisis," *Google The Keyword* (November 2, 2022), accessed October 30, 2024, https://blog.google/outreach-initiatives/sustainability/cop27-adaptation-efforts.

Mattern, Shannon, "Post-It Note City," *Places* (February 2020), accessed October 30, 2024, https://placesjournal.org/article/post-it-note-city.

Mazzucato, Mariana, "Preventing Digital Feudalism," *Project Syndicate* (October 2, 2019), accessed October 30, 2024, https://www.project-syndicate.org/commentary/platform-economy-digital-feudalism-by-mariana-mazzucato-2019-10.

Mbembe, Achille, *Critique of Black Reason*, trans. Laurent Dubois (Durham: Duke University Press, 2017).

Mbembe, Achille, "The Universal Right to Breathe," trans. Carolyn Shread, in "Posts from the Pandemic," *Critical Inquiry* blog (April 13, 2020), accessed October 30, 2024, https://critinq.wordpress.com/2020/04/13/the-universal-right-to-breathe.

McKie, Robin, "Deep-Sea Mining for Rare Minerals Will Destroy Ecosystems, Say Scientists," *The Guardian* (March 26, 2023), accessed October 30, 2024, https://www.theguardian.com/environment/2023/mar/26/deep-sea-mining-for-rare-metals-will-destroy-ecosystems-say-scientists.

McLuhan, Marshall, *Understanding Media: The Extensions of Man* (New York: Signet Books, 1964).

Mejias, Ulises A. and Nick Couldry, *Data Grab: The New Colonialism of Big Tech and How to Fight Back* (Chicago: University of Chicago Press, 2024).

Microsoft, "A Digital Geneva Convention to Protect Cyberspace" (2017), accessed October 14, 2019, https://www.microsoft.com/en-us/cybersecurity/content-hub/a-digital-geneva-convention-to-protect-cyberspace.

Microsoft, "AI for Earth," accessed October 30, 2024, https://www.microsoft.com/en-us/ai/ai-for-earth.

Microsoft, "AI for Earth: A Gamechanger for Our Planet," *The Guardian* [no date], accessed October 30, 2024, https://www.theguardian.com/advertiser-content/microsoft-ai-for-earth/microsoft-ai-research.

Microsoft, "Discover the Power of AI with Copilot in Windows," accessed October 30, 2024, https://www.microsoft.com/en-us/windows/copilot-ai-features.

Microsoft, "Microsoft Mesh," accessed October 30, 2024, https://www.microsoft.com/en-us/mesh.

Milner, Marion, *A Life of One's Own* (London: Routledge, 2011),

Mitchell, W. J. T., "Groundhog Day and the Epoché," in "Posts from the Pandemic," *Critical Inquiry* blog (May 11, 2020), accessed October 30, 2024, https://critinq.wordpress.com/2020/05/11/groundhog-day-and-the-epoche.

Morozov, Evgeny, "Critique of Technofeudal Reason," *New Left Review* 133/134 (January/April 2022), accessed October 30, 2024, https://newleftreview.org/issues/ii133/articles/evgeny-morozov-critique-of-techno-feudal-reason.

Morozov, Evgeny, "Google May Have Changed its Name but the Game Remains the Same," *The Guardian* (August 16, 2015), accessed October 30, 2024, https://www.theguardian.com/commentisfree/2015/aug/16/google-alphabet-name-change-same-game-evgeny-morozov.

Morton, Timothy, *Being Ecological* (London: Pelican Books, 2018).

Muldoon, James, *Platform Socialism: How to Reclaim our Digital Future from Big Tech* (London: Pluto Press, 2022).

Mundaneum, "Support the 'Paper Google,'" accessed October 30, 2024, http://expositions.mundaneum.org/en/soutenez-le-google-de-papier.

Myrtl Swchwrm, *Doodly Doodles* [Exhibition text as seen at Grounded festival, June 25, 2022, Utrecht, the Netherlands].

Nelson, Maggie, *On Freedom: Four Songs of Care and Constraint* (London: Jonathan Cape, 2021).

Niarchos, Nicolas, "Dark Side of Congo's Cobalt Rush"; International Rights Advocates, "Cobalt DRC Case," accessed October 30, 2024, https://www.internationalrightsadvocates.org/case/cobalt-drc-case.

Niarchos, Nicolas, "The Dark Side of Congo's Cobalt Rush," *The New Yorker* (May 24, 2021), accessed October 30, 2024, https://www.newyorker.com/magazine/2021/05/31/the-dark-side-of-congos-cobalt-rush.

Niessen, Niels, "Mad Men and Mindfulness," *Discourse* 40.3 (2018), 273–307.

Niessen, Niels, "Shot on iPhone: Apple's World Picture," *Advertising & Society Quarterly* 22.2 (2021), accessed October 30, 2024, https://muse.jhu.edu/article/797069.

Niessen, Niels, "The Task of the Film Critic in Times of Streaming Video," *Film Criticism* 40.1 (2016), accessed October 30, 2024, https://quod.lib.umich.edu/f/fc/13761232.0040.124/–task-of-the-film-critic-in-times-of-streaming-video?rgn=main;view=fulltext.

Noble, Safiya Umoja, *Algorithms of Oppression: How Search Engines Reinforce Racism* (New York: New York University Press, 2018).

O'Neill, Shane, "Microsoft's Home of the Future: A Visual Tour," *Computerworld* (July 2, 2010), accessed May 13, 2022, https://www.computerworld.com/article/2826654/microsoft-s-home-of-the-future–a-visual-tour.html

OkCupid, "The Big Lies People Tell in Online Dating," *OkCupid Blog* (July 7, 2010), accessed October 30, 2024, https://theblog.okcupid.com/the-big-lies-people-tell-in-online-dating-a9e3990d6ae2.

OkCupid, "ChatGPT Is the Matchmaker You Didn't Know You Needed," *OkCupid Blog* (February 13, 2023), accessed October 30, 2024, https://theblog.okcupid.com/chatgpt-is-the-matchmaker-you-didnt-know-you-needed-1c79f57416a4.

OkCupid, "Climate Change Is the #1 Issue to Daters in 2022," *OkCupid Dating Blog* (April 6, 2022), accessed October 30, 2024, https://theblog.okcupid.com/climate-change-is-the-1-issue-to-daters-in-2022-2a54fadc2a10.

OkCupid, "The Global State of Digital Dating," *OkCupid Blog* (November 28, 2022), accessed October 30, 2024, https://theblog.okcupid.com/the-global-state-of-digital-dating-2eac672fcb3e.

OkCupid, "How is Match Percentage Calculated? Discover All Our Matching System Secrets" (July 2022), accessed October 14, 2022, https://help.okcupid.com/hc/en-us/articles/5221215995149-How-is-Match-Percentage-Calculated-Discover-All-Our-Matching-System-Secrets.

OkCupid, "Introducing Brand-New Features to Help You Find Deeper Connections," *OkCupid Blog* (February 14, 2017), accessed October 30, 2024, https://theblog.okcupid.com/okcupid-releases-new-product-features-for-valentines-day-dd08c94a8e6e.

OkCupid, "Where Have You Seen Our DTF Campaign?" (March 22, 2018), *OkCupid Dating Blog*, accessed October 30, 2024, https://theblog.okcupid.com/where-have-you-seen-our-dtf-campaign-376331f629f7.

"Origin of the Name of Toronto," *Toronto.ca*, accessed October 30, 2024, https://archive.ph/GhALr#selection-195.8-195.123.

Orr, Andrew, "iPhones Have 100,000 Times More Processing Power than Apollo 11 Computer," *The Mac Observer* (July 17, 2019), accessed October 30, 2024, https://www.macobserver.com/link/iphones-processing-apollo-11-computer.

Otlet, Paul, *Les Aspects du livre* (Brussels: Musée du livre, 1906).

Page, Larry and Sergey Brin, "2004 Founders' IPO Letter: 'An Owner's Manual' for Google's Shareholders," *Alphabet*, https://abc.xyz.

Park, Jihoon, "Zoom + Meta: The Future of AR Learning," *Zoom Blog* (November 20, 2017), accessed October 30, 2024, https://blog.zoom.us/zoom-meta-future-of-ar-learning.

Perrigo, Billy, "OpenAI Used Kenyan Workers on Less Than $2 per Hour to Make ChatGPT Less Toxic," *Time* (January 18, 2023), accessed October 30, 2024, https://time.com/6247678/openai-chatgpt-kenya-workers.

Perrotta, Carlo, Kalervo N. Gulson, Ben Williamson, and Kevin Witzenberger, "Automation, APIs and the Distributed Labour of Platform Pedagogies in Google Classroom," *Critical Studies in Education* 61.1 (2021): 1–17.

Peters, John Durham, *The Marvelous Clouds: Toward a Philosophy of Elemental Media* (Chicago: University of Chicago Press, 2015).

Phillips, Adam, *Attention Seeking* (London: Penguin Books, 2019).

Pilsch, Andrew, *Transhumanism: Evolutionary Futurism and the Human Technologies of Utopia* (Minneapolis: University of Press, 2017).

Piquard, Alexandre, "Musk's X.AI Start-Up Highlights Paradoxical Relationship with AI," *Le Monde* (May 16, 2023), accessed October 30, 2024, https://www.

lemonde.fr/en/economy/article/2023/04/18/musk-s-x-ai-start-up-highlights-paradoxical-relationship-with-ai-anew_6023306_19.html.

Plantin, Jean-Christophe, Carl Lagoze, Paul N. Edwards, and Christian Sandvig, "Infrastructure Studies Meet Platform Studies in the Age of Google and Facebook," *New Media & Society* 20.1 (2016): 1-26.

Plimpton, George A., "The Hornbook and its Use in America," *Proceedings of the American Antiquarian Society* 26 (1916): 264-72.

Prior, Matthew, *The Poems of Matthew Prior, Volume 2* (Press of C. Whittingham, 1822).

Puiu, Tibi, "Your Smartphone Is Millions of Times More Powerful than the Apollo 11 Guidance Computers," *ZME Science* (October 13, 2015), accessed October 30, 2024, https://www.zmescience.com/feature-post/technology-articles/computer-science/smartphone-power-compared-to-apollo.432.

Rancière, Jacques, *The Ignorant Schoolmaster: Five Lessons in Intellectual Emancipation*, trans. Kristin Ross (Stanford: Stanford University Press, 1991).

Rasch, Miriam, *Frictie: Ethiek in Tijden van Dataïsme* (Amsterdam: De Bezige Bij, 2020).

Raunig, Gerald, *Dividuum: Machinic Capitalism and Molecular Revolution* (South Pasadena: Semiotext(e), 2016).

Remie, Mirjam and Menno Sedee, "Techreuzen Willen de School Hervormen," *NRC Handelsblad* (July 19, 2020).

RFE/RL's Radio Farda, "Instagram Removes Iranian Protest Videos, TV Station Says," *Radio Free Europe Radio Liberty* (September 21, 2022), accessed October 30, 2024, https://www.rferl.org/a/iran-instagram-removes-protest-videos-amini/32044798.html.

Righi, Andrea, *The Other Side of the Digital: The Sacrificial Economy of New Media* (Minneapolis: University of Minnesota Press, 2021).

Rogan, Frances and Shelley Budgeon, "The Personal Is Political: Assessing Feminist Fundamentals in the Digital Age," *Social Sciences* 7.132 (2018): 11-19.

Rooney, Sally, *Conversations with Friends* (New York: Faber & Faber, 2017).

Rudder, Christian, *Dataclysm: Love, Sex, Race, and Identity—What Our Online Lives Tell Us about Our Offline Selves* (New York: Broadway Books, 2014).

Rushkoff, Douglas, *Team Human* (New York: W. W. Norton & Company, 2019).

Russell, Andy, "Share Your Ideas with Chromebook," *Google The Keyword* (July 7, 2022), accessed October 30, 2024, https://blog.google/outreach-initiatives/education/theanywhereschool-chromebook.

Sadowski, Jathan and Roy Bendor, "Selling Smartness: Corporate Narratives and the Smart City as a Sociotechnical Imaginary," *Science, Technology, and Human Values* 44.3 (2019): 540-63.

Salami, Minna, *Sensuous Knowledge: A Black Feminist Approach for Everyone* (London: Bloomsbury Academic, 2020).

Schmelzer, Matthias, Andrea Vetter, and Aaron Vansintjan, *The Future Is Degrowth: A Guide to a World beyond Capitalism* (London: Verso, 2022).

Schmidt, Eric and Jonathan Rosenberg, *How Google Works* (New York: Grand Central Publishing, 2017).

Scott-Heron, Gil, "Home Is Where the Hatred Is" (song), *Pieces of a Man* (1971).

Selwyn, Neil, *Is Technology Good for Education?* (Cambridge: Polity Press, 2016).

Selwyn, Neil, *Should Robots Replace Teachers? AI and the Future of Education* (Cambridge: Polity Press, 2019).

Sennett, Richard, *Building and Dwelling: Ethics for the City* (London: Penguin, 2018).

Shachtman, Noah, "In Silicon Valley, Meditation Is No Fad. It Could Make Your Career," *Wired* (June 18, 2013), accessed October 30, 2024, https://www.wired.com/2013/06/meditation-mindfulness-silicon-valley.

Shakespeare, William, *Love's Labour's Lost* (New York: Penguin, 2015).

Sidewalk Labs, *MIDP* [Master Innovation and Development Plan] *Volume 1: The Plans: Introduction and Chapter 1: Quayside* (*Toronto Tomorrow: A New Approach for Inclusive Growth*) (2019), accessed 1 March 2020, https://www.sidewalklabs.com/Toronto.

Sidewalk Labs, "Presentation to York Quay Neighbourhood Association" (March 13, 2018), accessed 1 March 2020, https://quaysideto.ca/wp-content/uploads/2019/04/York-Quay-Neighbourhood-Association-Presentation-March-13-2018.pdf.

Sidewalk Labs, *Project Vision* (October 17, 2017), https://storage.googleapis.com/sidewalk-toronto-ca/wp-content/uploads/2017/10/13210553/Sidewalk-Labs-Vision-Sections-of-RFP-Submission.pdf, accessed October 30, 2024 https://perma.cc/6ZTMQ6J9.

Sidewalk Labs, *Public Engagement* (brochure) (2019), accessed 1 March 2020, https://sidewalk-toronto-ca.storage.googleapis.com/wp-content/uploads/2019/06/21195824/The-Public-Engagement-Process-for-Sidewalk-Toronto.pdf.

Silberling, Amanda, "Google Workers Protest $1,2B Project Nimbus Contract with Israeli Military," *Techcrunch* (September 1, 2022), accessed October 30, 2024, https://techcrunch.com/2022/09/01/google-workers-protest-1-2b-project-nimbus-contract-with-israeli-military.

Simmel, Georg, *Simmel on Culture*, eds. David Frisby and Mike Featherstone (London: Sage Publications, 1997).

Simondon, Gilbert, *Individuation in Light of Notions of Form and Information*, trans. Taylor Adkins (Minneapolis: University of Minnesota Press, 2020).

Singer, Natasha, "How Google Took over the Classroom," *New York Times* (May 13, 2017), accessed October 30, 2024, https://www.nytimes.com/2017/05/13/technology/google-education-chromebooks-schools.html.

Slater, Dan, "Love in the Technology Era," *Boston Globe* (January 13, 2013), accessed October 30, 2024, https://www.bostonglobe.com/magazine/2013/01/13/love-technology-era/rhd89MA2B0RMzYJm0CUJjN/story.html.

Solnit, Rebecca, *Wanderlust: A History of Walking* (London: Granta Publications, 2001).

Spek, Annelies, *Autismespectrum Stoornissen bij Volwassenen: Een Praktische Gids voor Volwassenen met ASS, Naastbetrokkenen en Hulpverleners* (Amsterdam: Hogrefe, 2013).

Spinoza, Benedict de, *The Chief Works of Spinoza: A Theologico-Political Treatise and A Political Treatise*, trans. R. H. M. Elwes (New York: Dover Publications, 1951).

Srinivasan, Amia, *The Right to Sex* (London: Bloomsbury Publishing, 2021).

Srnicek, Nick, *Platform Capitalism* (Cambridge: Polity Press, 2016).

Stephenson, Neal, *Snowcrash* (Bantam Books, 1993).

Stevens, Kyle, "When Movies Get Sick," in "Posts from the Pandemic," *Critical Inquiry* blog (March 25, 2020), accessed October 30, 2024, https://critinq.wordpress.com/2020/03/25/when-movies-get-sick.

Stewart, Kathleen, *Ordinary Affects* (Durham: Duke University Press, 2007).

Stewart, Matthew, "The Deceptive Platform Utopianism of Google's Sidewalk Labs," *Failed Architecture* (July 25, 2019), accessed October 30, 2024, https://failedarchitecture.com/the-deceptive-platform-utopianism-of-googles-sidewalk-labs.

Sujon, Zoetanya, *The Social Media Age* (London: Sage Publications, 2021).

Trafton, Anne, "Cobalt-Free Batteries Could Power Cars of the Future," *MIT News* (January 18, 2024), accessed October 30, 2024, https://news.mit.edu/2024/cobalt-free-batteries-could-power-future-cars-0118.

Tan, Chade-Meng, *Search Inside Yourself: The Unexpected Path to Achieving Success, Happiness (and World Peace)* (San Francisco: Harper One, 2015).

Tan, Rebecca and Regine Cabato, "Behind the AI Boom, an Army of Overseas Workers in 'Digital Sweatshops,'" *The Washington Post* (August 28, 2023), accessed October 30, 2024, https://www.washingtonpost.com/world/2023/08/28/scale-ai-remotasks-philippines-artificial-intelligence.

Taylor, Carol A., "The Gendered History of *Bildung* as Concept and Practice: A Speculative Feminist Analysis," in Carol A. Taylor, Chantal Amade-Escot, and Andrea Abbas, eds., *Gender in Learning and Teaching: Feminist Dialogues across International Boundaries* (London: Routledge, 2019), 11–23.

Terranova, Tiziana, "Free Labor: Producing Culture for the Digital Economy," *Social Text* 63 (18.2) (2000): 33–58.

Terranova, Tiziana, *After the Internet: Digital Networks between Capital and the Common* (South Pasadena: Semiotext(e), 2022).

Townsend, Anthony M., *Smart Cities: Big Data, Civic Hackers, and the Quest for a New Utopia* (New York: W. W. Norton & Company, 2014).

Tuer, Andrew W., *History of the Hornbook* (London: The Leadenhall Press, 1897).

Turkle, Sherry, *Reclaiming Conversation: The Power of Talk in a Digital Age* (New York: Penguin Press, 2015).

Vaidhyanathan, Siva, *The Googlization of Everything (and Why We Should Worry)* (Berkeley: University of California Press, 2011).

Vamvakitis, John, "Around the World and Back with Google for Education," *Google Blog* (January 22, 2019), accessed October 30, 2024, https://www.blog.google/outreach-initiatives/education/around-the-world-and-back.

Varia, Constant, TTTiPI, Digital Discomfort Workgroup, "Introduction for the Panel: Anti-Colonial Tech through Resistance and Discomforts," [planned for:] Transmediale in Berlin, Germany (February 2, 2024), accessed October 30, 2024, https://pad.riseup.net/p/r.5e8fb6bd54cdce773db487845244e55d.

Varoufakis, Yanis, *Another Now: Dispatches From an Alternative Present* (London: The Bodley Head, 2020).

Varoufakis, Yanis, "Techno-Feudalism Is Taking Over," *Project Syndicate* (June 28, 2021), accessed October 30, 2024, https://www.project-syndicate.org/commentary/techno-feudalism-replacing-market-capitalism-by-yanis-varoufakis-2021-06.

Varoufakis, Yanis, *Technofeudalism: What Killed Capitalism* (London: The Bodley Head, 2023).

Varsava, Nina, "Dating Markets and Love Stories: Freedom and Fairness in the Pursuit of Intimacy and Love," *Cultural Critique* 95 (2017): 162–96.

Verbeken, Pascal, *Brutopia: De Dromen van Brussel* (Amsterdam: De Bezige Bij, 2019).

Wark, McKenzie, *Capital Is Dead: Is This Something Worse* (London: Verso, 2019).

Wark, McKenzie, *Sensoria: Thinkers for the Twenty-First Century* (London: Verso, 2020).

Warner, Michael, "Public/Private," in Catharine R. Simpson and Gilbert Herdt, eds., *Critical Terms for the Study of Gender* (Chicago: University of Chicago Press, 2014).

Webb, Amy, *Data, a Love Story: How I Cracked the Online Dating Code to Meet My Match* (New York: Plume, 2014).

Webb, Lawrence, "When Harry Met Siri: Digital Romcom and the Global City in Spike Jonze' *Her*," in Lawrence Webb and Johan Andersson, *Global Cinematic Cities: New Landscapes of Film and Media* (London: Wallflower Press, 2016), 95–118.

Weeks, Linton, "Speed Dating in the 19th Century," *NPR* (December 15, 2014), accessed October 30, 2024, https://www.npr.org/sections/theprotojournalist/2014/12/15/370323910/speed-dating-in-the-19th-century.

Weldon, Glen, "Why Hasn't Online Dating Made it Onscreen?" *NPR* (June 14, 2017), accessed October 30, 2024, http://www.npr.org/sections/monkeysee/2017/06/14/532752841/why-hasnt-online-dating-made-it-onscreen.

Wikipedia, "Wikipedia," accessed October 30, 2024, https://en.wikipedia.org/wiki/Wikipedia.

Williams, Raymond, *The Long Revolution* (Cardigan: The Old Surgery, 2013).

Williams, Raymond, *Marxism and Literature* (Oxford: Oxford University Press, 1977).

Winterson, Jeanette, *Frankisstein: A Love Story* (London: Vintage, 2019).

Winterson, Jeanette, *12 Bytes: How We Got Here, Where We Might Go Next* (London: Jonathan Cape, 2021).

Woodcock, Ramsey, cited in VPRO television, *Tegenlicht: Rebellen tegen Reclame* (April 26, 2020), accessed October 30, 2024, https://www.vpro.nl/programmas/tegenlicht/kijk/afleveringen/2019-2020/reclame-rebellen.html.

Woods, Heather Suzanne, "Asking More of Siri and Alexa: Feminine Persona in Service of Surveillance Capitalism," *Critical Studies in Media and Communication* 35.4 (2018): 334–9.

World Economic Forum, *Harnessing Artificial Intelligence for the Earth* (January 2018), accessed October 30, 2024, https://www3.weforum.org/docs/Harnessing_Artificial_Intelligence_for_the_Earth_report_2018.pdf.

Woyke, Elizabeth, "A Smarter Smart City," *MIT Technology Review* (February 21, 2018), accessed October 30, 2024, https://www.technologyreview.com/2018/02/21/145310/a-smarter-smart-city.

Wright, Alex, *Cataloging the World: Paul Otlet and the Birth of the Information Age* (New York: Oxford University Press, 2014).

Wylie, Bianca, "Debrief on Sidewalk Toronto Public Meeting 3" (August 20, 2018), accessed October 30, 2024, https://biancawylie.medium.com/debrief-on-sidewalk-toronto-public-meeting-3-a-master-class-in-gaslighting-and-arrogance-c1c5dd918c16.

X, "Moonshot," accessed October 30, 2024, https://x.company/moonshot.

X, *Moonshots: A Game of Radical Thinking* [online game] (2021), accessed October 30, 2024, https://x.company/moonshots-game/intro#step-two.

xAI, "Announcing Grok," *X.AI Blog* (November 3, 2023), accessed October 30, 2024, x.ai/blog.

YouSuckOKC, "An Open Letter on Why We're Removing Usernames, Addressed to the Worst Ones We've Seen," *Medium* (December 22, 2017), accessed October 30, 2024, https://medium.com/@kevan.cummings/seriously-stop-it-842c5ad52129.

Yuan, Eric S., "A Message to Our Users," *Zoom Blog* (April 1, 2020), accessed October 30, 2024, https://blog.zoom.us/a-message-to-our-users.

Zizek, Slavoj, *Like a Thief in Broad Daylight: Power in the Era of Post-Humanity* (New York: Penguin Books, 2018).

Zizek, Slavoj, "Is Barbarism with a Human Face Our Fate?" (March 18, 2020), in "Posts from the Pandemic," *Critical Inquiry* blog, accessed October 30, 2024, https://critinq.wordpress.com/2020/03/18/is-barbarism-with-a-human-face-our-fate.

Zoom, "Zoom Privacy Statement" (February 24, 2023), accessed October 30, 2024, https://explore.zoom.us/en/privacy.

Zuboff, Shoshana, *The Age of Surveillance Capitalism: The Fight for a Human Future at the Frontier of Power* (London: Profile Books, 2019).

Zuckerberg, Mark, "Building Global Community," Facebook.com (February 16, 2017), accessed October 30, 2024, https://www.facebook.com/notes/mark-zuckerberg/building-global-community/10154544292806634.

INDEX

24/7: Late Capitalism and the Ends of Sleep (Crary) 4–5
"307" participatory space, Sidewalk Labs 121, 124–5

L'Abécédaire de Gilles Deleuze 146, 147–8, 156, 171–2
abecedarium 143–4
abuse of market power 150–1
"acedia" 70–2
Ade, George 194
After the Internet: Digital Networks between Capital and the Common (Terranova) 16
"Against Grading" (Bejarano & Soderling) 141
"Against the Stream for Ecological Justice" 25–6
The Age of Spiritual Machines (Kurzwell) 56
The Age of Surveillance Capitalism (Zuboff) 18, 35, 37, 136
Aggarwala, Rit 101
Ahmed, Sara 2, 195, 228, 236, 242–3
   Living a Feminist Life 64
   Queer Phenomenology 37, 118
   Strange Encounters: Embodied Others in Postcoloniality 57, 213
   Willful Subjects 215–16
AI *see* artificial intelligence
AI for Earth program (Google) 237–8
Airbnb 12, 33, 35, 36, 236
Alexa (Amazon) 42–3
Algorithms of Oppression (Noble) 140
Algorithms of Resistance (Bonini & Treré) 19
Allen, Ricj 154

Alphabet 20–1, 86, 131–2, 168–9
Althusser, Louis 9–10, 11–12
Amazon 15, 42–3, 247
American Dream 1, 22, 101–2
Amnesty International 246, 249–50
Anatolia (now Turkey) 85
Android 101–2, 134–5
Another Now: Dispatches from an Alternative Present (Varoufakis) 220
"Anti-Colonial Tech" 247, 251
anti-colonialism 219
   see also decolonization movements
anti-racism 24, 25, 119–20
antisemitism 246–7
Anti-Vietnam protests 65–6
Anybot 227–32
ANYONE concepts 20–1, 131–3, 170
Anywhere School and concepts 33–9, 43, 53–4, 69, 132–3, 158, 170–1
Apple 101–2, 232–6, 248–9
   Siri 42–3, 63
   see also smartphones
apprenticeships 141
AR *see* augmented reality
art and expression, open-city concepts 122
artificial intelligence (AI) 6–7, 51, 183, 210–15
   degrowth 237–8
   EU's AI Act 150–1
   home, consciousness principles 38
   objectification of the teacher 162–3
   Soul (generation AI) 160–2
   see also OpenAI

Arts and Culture (Google) 160, 166
  Wikimedia Commons 166–7
Les Aspects du Livre (Otlet) 150
association(s) 1–2, 4, 50–1, 64, 69, 70–6
AT&T 44
Athena 153
Athenian polis 214
Attention Seeking (Phlips) 72
Atwood, Margaret 106
augmented reality (AR) 46, 48
  see also Mesh
autism 72, 170–1
automatic writing 142

Babu, Anand 102–3
"Bad Company" (Drake) 153
Badiou, Alain 191–3
Baldwin, James 119–20
Ball, Joan 196
ballet, sidewalks 85, 87–8, 113, 117–20
banking models of education 132–3, 148
Bard 54, 141–2
  see also Gemini
Barns, Sarah 112–13
Bastille Day, France 136
Baudelaire, Charles 195
begreifen concepts 222
Being Ecological (Morton) 239–40
Bejarano, Carolina Alonso 141
Belgian Mining Union of Haut-Katanga 247–8
bell hooks 162
Belmont, Arizona 95
Benbow, Sophie 250–1
Bendor, Roy 94
"Beneficial AI" 227–32
Benjamin, Walter 195
Bergström, Marie 200–1
Berlant, Lauren 8–10, 13–14, 112–13, 213–14, 228, 241–2
Besant, Annie 194
bias 68, 167–8
  see also individual forms of discrimination & oppression...

bicycles 194–5, 249–50
"Big Critique" 18–19
"Big Data as Drama" (Chun) 170
Big Tech definitions 1
BigBlueButton 44, 214
Bildung 155–6
binaries *see* dualisms; privacy, privatization, and the private-public binary
Black condition, Black experience 108–10, 113, 119–20, 217, 219, 251–2
  Civil Rights 2, 37, 65–6, 214, 219
  see also racism
BlackLivesMatter 2–3, 219
Bleeding Edge (Pynchon) 208–9
#BlockSidewalk activist group 87
Blood Cobalt: The Congo's Dangerous and Deadly Green Energy Mines (Davies) 248
Bluemink, Matt 112
body-mind dualisms, *see also* Cartesian body-mind dualisms
Bonini, Tiziano 19
Books (Google) 133–4
Borges, Jorge Luis 147–8
Bostrom, Nick 55, 227–32
Braidotti, Rosi 22–3, 115, 212
Brain (X) 169
Bratton, Benjamin 110
Brautigan, Richard 63
Braze analytics company 206
Brevini, Benedetta 238
Brin, Sergey 136, 167
Buddhism 20–1, 131–2, 171–2, 212
Budgeon, Shelley 68
Building and Dwelling: Ethics for the City (Sennet) 117–19, 121–2
Bumble 184
Burgess, Jean 18–19
Burning Man festival 136
burn-out culture 25–6, 38, 69
The Burnout Society (Müdigkeitsgesellschaft) by Byung-Chul Han 58–9

INDEX 279

Callamard, Agnès 249–50
Capital Is Dead: Is this Something Worse? (Wark) 16, 205
capitalism 3, 4–5, 8–10, 14–19, 26, 40–2, 59–61, 108–9, 113, 115, 215, 216, 220, 228–9, 236–9, 247
   24/7: Late Capitalism and the Ends of Sleep by Crary 4–5
   After the Internet: Digital Networks between Capital and the Common by Terranova 16
   degrowth 236, 238–9
   dividuals 108–16
   home, consciousness principles 61
   love, Everyone concepts 183–7
   neoliberalism 8–10, 141, 155–6, 210
   Surveillance Capitalism by Zuboff 35, 37, 136
   technofeudalism 14–18, 25, 59–60, 63, 115, 163–4, 228–30
   see also patriarchy; technocolonialism
capitalism. *Dividuum: Machinic Capitalism and Molecular Evolution* by Raunig 108, 110
Cardboard (Google) 165–6
Cartesian body-mind dualisms 22, 57, 120–1, 235–6
"centers of vibrations" 146–7
The Century of Self (Curtis) 66
ChatGPT 2, 6–7, 16–18, 43, 51, 54, 63, 141–2, 183, 212–13, 214, 232, 243
Cheney-Lippold, John 10, 73–5
Chicago 94–5
child labor *see* enslaved, exploitative labor
Chinese Revolution 65
Choreographic Translations 244
Christianity 143–4, 150
Chromebook 132, 134–5, 137, 158, 160, 170–1
Chun, Wendy 170
Citton, Yves 140

The City (1939) 95
"the city stack" 110
city/sidewalk colonialism 85–130
   dividuals 108–16
   empathy 89–96
   everybody 85–9
   open data 117–22
   smartphones 96–102
   Toronto 122–5
   urban data 102–8
city-as-platform philosophy 87, 101–4, 106–7, 109
city-as-smartphone analogies 96–102
Civil Rights movements 65–6
Classroom (Google) 134–5
climate crisis *see* ecological justice
clouded crowds 109–10, 118–19, 210–15
cobalt/copper mining 246–52
cogito ergo sum 235–6
Cold Intimacies (Illouz) 191
colonialism 63–4
   city/sidewalk colonialism 85–130
   de-Google education 131–81
   post-coloniality 24, 57, 213
   see also decolonization movements; patriarchy; technocolonialism
common integrity 74–5
common and ordinary life 1–32, 205–10, 240–6
common spaces 25–6
communism 25–6
   see also socialism
Community Health Initiative 167–8
"communitywide speed dating" 196
Com-Pat (Computer Dating Services Ltd) 196–7
Congo Dongfang 248
consciousness, consciousness-raising
   city/sidewalk colonialism 110–11, 113
   counter-culture 21–2, 66–7, 233, 235
   decolonizing of Google education 131, 136–7, 143–4, 146, 156–8

and everyday life 2–4, 17, 19–20, 23–6
see also home, consciousness principles
consent 49–50, 215–21
content creators 104, 108, 121
control 109
control, control society 10–11, 40–1, 109, 148–9
con-versare (to converse) 215
conversations (a clouded crowd) 210–15
Conversations with Friends (Rooney) 183, 215
convivial tools 25–6
Copilot (Microsoft) 38, 51, 54–5
Coppock, Nathan 158
Costs of Connection (Couldry & Mejias) 14, 18
The Costs of Connection (Couldry & Mejias) 108
Couldry, Nick 14–15, 17–18, 23–4, 63, 108, 113
counter-culture 21–2, 56–7, 233, 235
Coupland, Douglas 160–2
COVID pandemic 33–5, 38–9, 40, 44–5, 49, 51, 61, 70, 131–2, 135, 137–8, 165–6, 186, 239–40
city/sidewalk colonialism 86–7
Crary, Jonathan 4–5
creuseurs (diggers) of the cobalt mines 248
crisis ordinary 8–9
Critical Inquiry 70
critique, "Big Critique" 18–19
Critique of Black Reason (Mbembe) 13
"Critique of Technofeudal Reason" (Morozov) 18
Cross, Tristan 61
crowds and orientation 195
Cruel Optimism (Berlant) 8–10, 213–14
Cryptpad 214, 251
curation, cura 60, 243

The Curious History of Dating: From Jane Austen to Tinder (Hodgson) 193–5
Curtis, Adam 63, 66

Data*, OkCupid 199–205
Data, A Love Story: How I Cracked the Online Dating Code to Meet My Match (Webb) 207
data colonialism *see* technocolonialism
Data Grab (Mejias & Couldry) 14–15, 23–4
"data" and surveillance 145
*Dataclysm: Who We Really Are** (Rudder) 199, 201–5
data-extraction, extractivism 3–4, 8–9, 14, 36–7, 214, 238
datafication
  city/sidewalk colonialism 122
  ecological justice 229, 245–6
  and everyday life 6–7, 14, 16–19, 22, 24
  home, consciousness principles 58, 63–4
  love via online dating 184, 187, 193, 198, 201, 204–5, 208, 210, 214, 219
dataisms 58, 201–5
dating
  one's self 198–9
  online services 12, 20–2, 183–226
Davies, Michael 248
DayDreams (Google) 165–6
de Certeau, Michel 8, 41
deafness 170–1
The Death and Life of Great American Cities (Jacobs) 85, 87–8, 95
Decimal Classification System 151
decolonization movements 214
  de-Google education 131–81, 243
deep-learning 160–2, 169
DeepMind (Google) 237
de-Google education 131–81, 243
  ANYONE concepts 131–3
  Books 133–4

Classroom 134–5
　　　Doodle 136–7
　　　Educare 137–9
　　　Find 139–40
　　　Grading 140–2
　　　Hornbook 143–4
　　　Information 144–5
　　　Joy 146–7
　　　Knowledge 147–8
　　　Life-long 148–50
　　　Naive 152–3
　　　Owl 153–5
　　　Public 155–6
　　　Query 156–8
　　　"Rolling Study Halls" 158–60
　　　Soul (generation AI) 160–2
　　　Teacher 162–4
　　　Unlearning 164–5
　　　Virtual 165–6
　　　Wikipedia 166–8
　　　X (formerly Twitter) 168–70
　　　You 170–1
　　　Zen 171–2
　degrowth 232–40
　dehumanization 2, 19, 20, 113, 217, 219, 246
　　　Palestinian genocide 246–52
　　　see also posthuman, the; racism
　deindividuation/dividualization
　　　city/sidewalk colonialism 88–9, 108–16, 118–19
　　　decolonizing of Google education 148–50, 171
　　　and everyday life 4, 13, 16–19, 23–4
　　　home, consciousness principles 35, 37–8, 42, 58, 59–61, 73–5
　　　love via online dating 215–16, 219–21
　　　see also posthuman, the
　Deleuze, Gilles 9–13, 40–1, 112, 228
　　　L'Abécédaire de Gilles Deleuze 146–8, 156, 171–2
　　　"Postscript on the Control Society" 10, 109, 148–9
　　　What Is Philosophy? 146–7

Dell 248–9
democracy, democratization 124–5, 139, 153–5, 163, 236–7
Democratic Republic of Congo (DRC) 15, 246–52
Descartes, René 22, 57
Deschooling Society (Illich) 155
design thinking process, empathy 89–96
desire 59–60, 146–7, 157–8, 219–20
detachment 112–13
Diamanti, Jeff 38
"Digital Detox: Unplug and Reimagine your life" 67–8
digital feudalism 15–16
"Digital Geneva Convention" 11
"digital layering" 103–4
Digital Markets Act 150–1
Digital Service Act 150–1
disabilities 72, 170–1
Discipline and Punish (Foucault) 38–9, 141, 228–9
disinformation/misinformation 150–1
disorganized "ordinary" 8–14
disorientation *see* orientation, disorientation
dissociation 50
dividuals *see* deindividuation/dividualization
Dividuum: Machinic Capitalism and Molecular Evolution (Raunig) 108, 110
Doctoroff, Daniel 86, 91, 96–7, 101, 103
domestic life *see* privacy, privatization, and the private-public binary
"Don't be evil" (Google) 152–3
"Don't Mess with Mother" 232–3, 234
Doodle (Google) 136–7
double consciousness 113
DoubleTake systems 206
Drake, Leah Bodine 143, 153
Driving Change with Rolling Study Halls 158

"DTF" (down to fix) advertising 184–6, 190–1, 204
dualisms 111
　see also mind-body dualisms
Dubois, W. E. B. 113
DuckDuckGo 140, 251
Dumitrescu, Irina 70–1
Durand, Cédric 15–16
dwelling 117
dyslexia 170–1
dystopias 46, 49, 63–4, 87, 106

Eagleton, Terry 245
"Earth Shot on iPhone" World Gallery campaign 232–4
Easton, Dossie 211
ecofeminism 236
ecological justice 24–5, 227–56
ecology 64
Educare (Google) 137–9
educational level and dating 209
Eggers, Dave 49, 62
Ehrenfeucht, Renia 85
electric transport 249–50
electronics industry 15
　see also cobalt/copper mining; smartphones
"embodied internet" 46–7
empathy 89–96, 120–1, 242
empowerment 3, 14, 68–9, 74–5, 121–2, 186, 204, 213–15, 216, 221, 231–2, 237
　see also feminism
encounters 57
enlightenment 153–4
　see also democracy, democratization
enslaved, exploitative labor 15, 16, 246–52
Ephron, Nora *see You've Got Mail*
Epic of Gilgamesh 22
"epistemic resistance" 237
epistemic shift 228–9
epistemology 156
Eros Friendship 196

Esalen Institute, California 66–7, 233, 235–6
The Ethical Slut: A Guide to Infinite Sexual Possibilities (Easton & Liszt) 211
etymonline.com 70
European Union (EU) 150–1, 206
The Every (Eggers) 49
Everyday Data Culture (Burgess et al.) 18–19
everyday life, everything concepts 1–8
　see also common and ordinary life
Everyday Life in the Modern World (Lefebvre) 1, 4–5
"Everyone" concepts of love 183–7
Ex Machina (2014) 212
examination 141
Expeditions (Google) 165–6
Extinction Rebellion (XR) 244–5
extraction (value) 14–20
　see also data-extraction, extractivism

Facebook 12, 198
　see also Meta, and the Metaverse
Facemash 198
FaceTime 60
Fairphone 248–9
Fauna & Flora wildlife charity 250–1
feedback loops 10, 206
Felski, Rita 5
feminism 2, 24–5, 119–21
　consent 216–17, 219, 221, 241
　dating 194–5
　degrowth 236
　ecofeminism 236
　homework 64–9
　#MeToo movement 2, 68, 219
　postfeminism 68–9
　radical feminism 3, 65–6, 68, 216–17
　see also individual feminist authors…; patriarchy
Feminism, Labour and Digital Media (Jarrett) 3, 41–2

Feminist City (Kern) 119–20
Feminist Surveillance Studies (Wood) 68
Fern, Jessica 211
Find (Google) 139–40
Fitzgerald, Bill 135
Fleissig, Will 91, 96
Floyd, George 37
folded/intergenerational time 241
fossil fuels 244–5
  see also ecological justice
Foucault, Michel 38–9, 72, 141, 228–9, 240–1
Fourth Industrial Revolution 102–3, 237–8
"Fragment on Machines" (Marx) 110
Frankisstein: A Love Story (Winterson) 231–2
Franklin, Benjamin 153
"free love" movement 194
Free Palestine 246–52
freedom
  city/sidewalk colonialism 108, 119–20, 124–5
  Civil Rights 2, 37, 65–6, 214, 219
  decolonizing of Google education 153, 162
  ecological justice 227–9, 237, 240–6
  and everyday life 2–3, 6–8, 10, 25
  Genocide in Gaza report, University Network of Human Rights 246
  International Rights Advocates 248–9
  love via online dating 195, 214–15, 219–20
  On Freedom: Four Songs of Care and Constraint by Nelson 227–8, 240–1
  to associate 1–2, 64, 69
  United Nations 246, 247
  see also empowerment; privacy, privatization, and the private-public binary

Freire, Paolo 131, 152, 243
  banking models of education 132–3, 148
  problem-posing education 148, 156
friction, flow and
  city/sidewalk colonialism 98, 101–2, 123–4
  ecological justice 236–7
  and everyday life 21–2, 26
  home, consciousness principles 43–4, 46, 55–6, 58–9, 63–4
  love via online dating 208
from-the-internet-up ideology 86, 88–9, 100–1, 102, 104
The Future of the Classroom (Google for Education) 166
The Future is Degrowth (Schmelzer et al.) 236
Future of Life Institute 227–32

Gaither, Kim 158
Garden City movement 94–5
Garland, Alex 212
gated and modulated communities 111–12
Gates, Bill 95
Gaza 246–52
gaze-worthy bodies 68
  see also male domination; patriarchy
Gemini (Google) 6–7, 38, 51, 54, 141–2, 150, 153, 155, 156–7, 212–13
gender bias 68, 167–8
  see also feminism; misogyny; transphobia
gender identity 68, 155–6, 205
General Data Protection Regulation (GDPR) 150–1, 206
Generation X: Tales of an Accelerated Culture (Coupland) 160
genocide 246–52
Genocide in Gaza report (University Network of Human Rights) 246

gentrification 114–15, 119–20, 122, 210
    see also racism
Gilbert, Jeremy 18
Gillespie, Tarleton 103
"Global Community" manifesto 12
"Global State of Online Dating" 199
God 70–1
GoGuardian 135
Goodman, Ellen P. 87, 103–4, 105
Google 15, 17–19, 23–4, 49, 60
    city/sidewalk colonialism 86–7, 91, 102–3, 122–3
    degrowth 237, 238–40
    ecological justuce 247–9
    home, consciousness principles 35, 36, 54
    see also Alphabet; de-Google education; Gemini
Google Drive 251
Google Forms 141
Google Home 42–3, 107–8
Google Maps 113–14, 118–19
Google Search 139, 150, 153, 155, 156–7, 167, 243
Google TechTalks 102–3, 107–8
Googleplex 117–18
The Googlization of Everything (Vaidhyanathan) 157
Gorillas delivery service 61
GPT-4 OpenAI model 231
Grading (Google) 140–2
Gray, Mary 193
Great Fire of London, 1666 85
"Great Rebuilding" of Chicago 94–5
Great Reset 238–9
Greek mythology 153
Green, Ben 122
Greenwich Village neighborhood in Manhattan 87–8, 117–20
Grenoble, France 122
Grindr 184, 217
grocery shopping 61–3, 70–2
"Grow with Google" 158–60
Guattari, Félix 146–7
guild systems 141

H2E devices 169
Halberstam, Jack 205
Han, Byung-Chul 58–9
Hanisch, Carol 65–6, 216–17
harassment 167–8
Haraway, Donna 24–5
Hardt, Michael 25–6, 210
Harnessing Artificial Intelligence for Earth 237–8
Harney, Stefano 241–2
Harris, Malcolm 18
Haut-Katanga (Mining Union) 247–8
Hayles, Katherine 20, 23, 56–7, 115
hegemony 3, 4, 9–11, 23, 25, 64, 69, 133–4, 140, 164, 187, 246–7
    burn-out culture 25–6, 38, 69
    grading 140
    hornbook 143–4
    information 144–5
    see also patriarchy
Hegemony Now: How Big Tech and Wall Street Won the World (Gilbert & Williams) 18
Her (2013) 118–19, 210–15
Hester, Lilyn 158
heuristics 241–2
Hickel, Jason 26, 232, 235–6
Hicks, Mar 197
highways 208–9
Hinge 184, 200–1, 205–6
History of the Horn-Book (Tuer) 143–4
The Hobo's hornbook (Milburn) 143
Hodgson, Nichi 193–5
Holocaust scholars *see* Palestine
holoportation 35, 53, 55–6
    see also Mesh
holoportation platforms 36
    see also Mesh
home, consciousness principles 33–83
    anywhere concepts 33–9
    association (*chez soi*) 70–6
    homework 64–9
    presence 51–8
    resistance 58–64
    Wi-Fi 39–44

homework 64–9
Homo economicus 235–6
Hoover, Herbert 44
hope 245
The Horn Book magazine 143
Hornbook (Google) 143–4
Hornbook on Torts 143
A Hornbook for Witches (Drake) 143, 153
How We Became Posthuman (Hayles) 20, 23, 56–7
Howard, Elbenezer 94–5
Human Potential Movement 66–7, 233, 235
human rights *see* freedom
"human-thing" (Mbembe) 13, 58, 88–9, 110–11, 164–5, 187, 219, 240, 247
Huxley, Julian 22
Hwang, Dennis 136
hybridity 43–4, 56

IDEA districts 86–7, 123
identity 49, 209
    gender identity 68, 155–6, 205
    queer identity 24, 25, 119–20
    see also individuals, individualism, and individualization
ideological bias 167–8
ideological state apparatuses (ISAs) 10
ideology theory 9–10, 11–12
The Ignorant Schoolmaster (*Le Maître ignorant*) by Jacques Rancière 163–4
illegal content 150–1
Illich, Ivan 25–6, 155
Illouz, Eva 191
immanence 212
In Praise of Love (*Eloge de l'amour*) by Alain Badiou 191–3
inclusivity 63–4, 91, 122, 170–1, 243
individuals, individualism, and individualization
    city/sidewalk colonialism 108–13

decolonizing of Google education 162–4
and everyday life 2–5, 8–10, 13–14
home, consciousness principles 41–3, 59–60, 66
individuation, preindividual potential 112–16, 171, 219–20
love via online dating 191–6, 212, 219–21
see also deindividuation/dividualization; freedom; privacy, privatization, and the private-public binary
industrial mining 246–52
Industrial Revolution 102–3, 237–8
Information (Google) 144–5
"Information We Collect: Surveillance and Privacy in the Implementation of Google Apps for Education" (Lindh & Nolin) 145
inner dialogue, consent 220
inner process 73–4
    see also consciousness, consciousness-raising
"Innovative Design and Economic Acceleration" (IDEA) 86–7, 123
Instagram 1–3, 37, 46–7, 57–8, 68, 69, 212–13, 251
integrity *see* individuals, individualism, and individualization
"intelligent lockdown" 33–4
International Court of Justice (ICJ) 247
International Rights Advocates 248–9
intersectionality 24
intimate public places 86, 98–100
Intrinsic (X) 169
"Introducing Sidewalk Toronto" 89–90, 98, 107
invasion of integrity and community 14–15
"The Invention of Everyday Life" (Felski) 5

iOS 101–2
iPhones
   launch of in 2007 23
   see also smartphones
Is Technology Good for Education? (Selwyn) 137
ISAs (ideological state apparatuses) 10

Jacobs, Jane 112–13, 117–22
   The Death and Life of Great American Cities 85, 87–8, 95
   sidewalk ballet 85, 87–9, 113, 117–20
Jaffe, Eric 104
Jarrett, Kylie 2, 3, 41–2
JDate 207
Jitsi 44, 251
Jones, Spike, *see also Her*
Jonze, Spike 118–19
Joy (Google) 146–7
Judeo-Christian mythology 153

Kale, Brewster 139
kedos 70–1
Kennedy, John F. 168–9
Kern, Leslie 119–20
Kerssens, Niels 132–3
The Keyword blog 134–5, 158
Kleenex 40
Kleinberg, Jon 139
Knol, *knol* 167
"Know Thy Selves: Past Lives" (workshop) 66–7
knowledge 243
   see also self-learning; unlearning
Knowledge (Google) 147–8
   see also Information
"Koala mounts" 104
Kolwezi, southern Congo 247–8
Kracauer, Siegfried 1–2
Kumar, Priya 135
Kurzweil, Ray 22, 56, 227–32

Lafontaine, Henri 151
Lake Simcoe, Ontario 124
land acknowledgment (city/sidewalk colonialism) 85–130
Landry, Donna 164
The Law of Population (Besant) 194
Lazzarato, Maurizio 13, 111
learning
   management system 135
   see also de-Google education
Lefebvre, Henri 1, 4–5, 8, 9, 11, 37, 59–60, 63, 72, 228
legal education 143
Leopold (King) 247–8
Less Is More: How Degrowth Will Save the World (Hickel) 26, 232, 235–6
"Let's Talk Consent" 217, 218
LGBTQI+ 24, 25, 37, 118, 119–20, 184, 217
The Library of Babel (Borges) 147
A Life of One's Own (Milner) 72
Life-long (Google) 148–50
Like a Thief in Broad Daylight: Power in the Era of Post-Humanity (Zizek) 25
Lindh, Maria 145
Liszt, Catherine 211
Living a Feminist Life (Ahmed) 64
LMS (learning management system) 135
lockdown era 33–4, 44, 47–50, 63, 70, 72–3
   see also COVID pandemic
London 85, 94–5
Loon networks 169
Lorde, Audre 69
Los Angeles, USA 118–19
Loukaitou-Sideris, Anastasia 85
love *see* dating services
love "at last sight" 195
Love's Labour Lost (Shakespeare) 143
Lower Manhattan Expressway 87–8
Lukács, Georg 1–2
"Lust Horizons: Is the Women's Movement Pro-Sex" (Willis) 216

Maclean, Gerald 164
McLuhan, Marshall 39–40
McNamee, Roger 87
Madianou, Mirca 14
MAGA (Make America Great Again) *see* Trump, Donald
Malabou, Catherine 70–1
male domination 65–6
  see also patriarchy
"The Man of the Crowd" (Poe) 118–19
Manhattan's West Village 95
Marantz, Andrew 67–8
Marcuse, Herbert 66
Married Women's Property Act 194
Martínez, Antonio García 60
Marx, Karl 110
mass customization of education 149
Master Innovation and Development Plan (MIDP) 91, 98
'master' plans and mastery, feminist cities 120–1
"Master's tools" analogy 69
  see also technocolonialism
mastery and the feminist city 120–1
Mastodon 214, 251
Match.com 184, 186–7, 205–6
  see also OkCupid
Mattern, Shannon 121
Mayer, Merrisa 152
Mazzucato, Mariana 15–16
Mbembe, Achille 39, 63, 113, 228
  Critique of Black Reason 13
  "human-thing" 13, 58, 88–9, 110–11, 164–5, 187, 219, 240, 247
meaning-making 163–4
media literacy 165
Meditations on First Philosophy (Descartes) 57
Meetic 191–3
Mejias, Ulises A. 14–15, 17–18, 23–4, 63, 108, 113
Mesh (Microsoft) 33, 36, 38, 52, 53–4

Meta, and the Metaverse 6, 17, 18–19, 24, 38, 46–7, 50–2, 57–8, 60–1
  decolonizing of Google education 166
  ecological justice 242, 247
  home, consciousness principles 33, 35, 53–6
  see also Instagram
Metalife (Metaleven) 49
The Metaverse and How We'll Build It Together 46
#MeToo movement 2, 68, 219
"The Metropolis and Mental Life" (Simmel) 112–13
Microsoft 19, 33, 38, 47–8, 51, 55–6
  degrowth 237–40
  home, consciousness principles 35, 36, 54–6
  see also Teams
MIDP (Master Innovation and Development Plan) 91, 98
Milburn, George 143
Milner, Marion 72
mind-body dualisms 22, 26, 57
mindfulness 14, 99, 244–5
  see also consciousness
Minority Report (2002) 107
misinformation *see* disinformation/misinformation
misogyny 41–2, 48–9, 68, 140, 167–8, 197
  see also feminism; patriarchy
mixed-reality (MR) 48
  see also Mesh
modern forms of oppression 25, 108–10, 113, 167–8
  see also patriarchy
modulation 10, 112
Moonshot Factory (Alphabet) 168–9
Morozov, Evgeny 18
Morozow, Evgeny 133
Morrison, Helen 195–6
Morton, Timothy 239–40
Moten, Fred 241–2
MR *see* mixed-reality

Muldoon, James 25, 214, 236–7
Mundaneum museum, Mons 151, 167–8
Musk, Elon 12–13, 227–32
  see also X (formerly Twitter)
"my-wi" 61, 63
  see also streams

Nair, Sonam 217, 218
Naive(ty), Google 152–3
Nature 115–16
"natureculture" 24–5
negative liberty 214
Nelson, Maggie 227–8, 240–1
neoliberalism 8–10, 141, 153, 155–6, 210
neologisms 167, 232
Netflix 43
New Bottles for New Wine (Huxley) 22
new capitalism, new colonialism 14–16
  see also technocolonialism
The New Laws of Love: Online Dating and the Privatization of Intimacy (Bergström) 200–1
New Year's call, open house and invite in the dating scene 196
New York Radical Women 65
Nextcloud 214, 251
Noble, Safiya Umoja 140
Nolin, Jan 145
non-prescriptive infrastructures, open-city philosophies 118
Norwegian Consumer Council 206
Notes from the Second Year: Women's Liberation (Hanisch) 65
Nupedia 166–7

Occupied Palestinian Territories *see* Palestine
ocean mining 250–1
Office of Healthy Tourism 11
offline map making 116
off-line spaces 20
oikonomia 26, 235–6

OkCupid 12, 20–2, 183–226
  common (and ordinary life) 205–10
  consent 215–21
  conversations (a clouded crowd) 210–15
  Data* 199–205
  dating 193–9
  Everyone concepts 183–7
  Willingness 188–93
Old and New Left movements 65–6
On Freedom: Four Songs of Care and Constraint (Nelson) 227–8, 240–1
On Gender Differences and their Impact on Organic Nature (von Humboldt) 155–6
On the Inconvenience of Other People (Berlant) 241–2
One-Dimensional Man (Marcuse) 66
online dating *see* OkCupid
open house and invite in the dating scene 196
"open space alliance" 104
open/inclusive *living rooms* 63–4
OpenAI 6–7, 12–13, 17–19, 54, 231–2
  see also ChatGPT
open-city philosophies 117–22
"openness" 67–8, 70–1
Operation Match 196–8
Operation Spark 197
optimism 8–10, 213–14, 245
orientation, disorientation 113–14, 118, 195
Oryx and Crake (Atwood) 106
The Other Side of the Digital (Righi) 153
Otherness 164–5, 217, 220
  see also bias; individual forms of discrimination & oppression…
Otlet, Paul 150, 151, 167–8
"Ouentaronk" (poles that cross) 124
"Our Father" prayer 143–4
Owl (Google) 153–5

Page, Larry 86, 136
PageRank 139–40
The Painter of Modern Life (Baudelaire) 195
Palestine 246–52
panopticon 228–9
para- or *post-*state apparatuses 11–12
Parc du Conquantenaire, Brussels 151
Parkdale neighborhood in Toronto 114–15
Parnet, Claire 146
Patel, Amit 152
patriarchy 2–3, 25, 42, 65–6, 68, 75
 city/sidewalk colonialism 108–9, 115–16
 decolonizing of Google education 149, 153, 155–6
 ecological justice 236, 247, 251
 love via online dating 187, 209–10, 213, 216, 219
 see also technocolonialism
pedagogy 131–5, 152–3, 166
Pedagogy of the Oppressed (Freire) 131
"people-first" philosophy 86, 99–104, 120–1
Perrotta, Carlo 135
Peters, John Durham 148, 156–7
Philips, Adam 72
Pieces of Man (Scott-Heron) 37
Pilsch, Andrew 55
"pink coding", zoning 104
pink-washing 184
Pinto, Denise 96
Plantin, Jean-Christope 133–4
platform socialism 25, 214
Platform Socialism: How to Raclaim our Digital Future from Big Tech (Muldoon) 25
The Platform Society (Dijck et al.) 11, 155
Platform Urbanism (Barns) 112–13
"The Platformization of the Classroom" (Kumar et al.) 135
Plenty of Fish 205–6

Plexiglass 40
Poe, Edgar Allen 118–19
"Political Ecologies" 38, 49–50
"The Politics of Platforms" (Gillespie) 103
polyamory 211–12
Polysecure (Fern) 211
Poor Richard's Almanac (Franklin) 153
post-capitalist alternatives 24
post-coloniality 24, 57, 213
 see also decolonization
postfeminism 68–9
The Posthuman (Braidotti) 212
posthuman, the 8, 19, 20–6, 56–8, 69, 73–5
 city/sidewalk colonialism 88–9, 108, 115–22
 consent 219–20
 decolonizing of Google education 148, 152–3, 165
 de-Google education 152–3
 ecological justice 237
 freedom to associate 69
 How We Became Posthuman by Hayles 20, 23, 56–7
 love via online dating 187, 212, 214, 219–20
 open-city philosophies 117–22
 The Posthuman by Braidotti 212
"Posts from the Pandemic" (Stevens) 39, 70
"Postscript on the Control Society" (Deleuze) 10, 109, 148–9
potestas and *potentia/pouvoir* and *puissance* 146–7
Powles, Julia 87, 103–4, 105
The Practice of Everyday Life (de Certeau) 41
Practice Sets 131–2
precarity 112–13
prejudice 217, 219
 see also bias; dehumanization
presence 51–8, 66–7, 115–16, 119–21
priesthood 150
primers 143–4

Print (Google) 133
privacy, privatization, and the private-public binary 1–16, 25–6
   city/sidewalk 86–7, 97–100, 102, 104–8, 111
   decolonizing of Google education 145, 149–51, 156–8, 169
   home, consciousness principles 37–8, 41–4, 49–50, 57, 59, 62–6, 69, 73–5
   love via online dating 184, 190, 193–4, 199–201, 208–14, 216–17, 219
   surveillance 18, 35, 37, 68, 136, 145
problem-posing education 148, 156
Protonmail 214
public and common conversation 121–2
Public (Google) 155–6
public and private space *see* privacy, privatization, and the private-public binary
public-washing 12–13, 96, 98, 124–5
Pynchon, Thomas 208–9

Quayside design 85–130
queer identity 24, 25, 37, 118, 119–20
   see also LGBTQI+
Queer Phenomenology (Ahmed) 37, 118
Query (Google) 156–8

racism 2–3, 42, 48–9, 68, 140
   anti-racism 24–5, 64, 113, 119–20
   ecological justice 251
   love via online dating 210, 213–14, 217, 219
   see also patriarchy
radical feminism 3, 65–6, 68, 216–17
Rancière, Jacques 163–4
Rasch, Miriam 58–9, 73–4
Raunig, Gerald 108, 110
Reclaiming Conversation: The Power of Talk in a Digital Age (Turkle) 213

Regional Planning Association of America 95
"Reimaging the City as a Digital Platform" 102–3
Replika 212–13
repressive state apparatuses (RSAs) 10
resistance, resilience
   "epistemic resistance" 237
   home concepts 58–64
   see also empowerment
"Riding the Blinds" (Nelson) 241
Righi, Andrea 153
The Right to Sex (Srinivasan) 215–17
Robid, Albert 44
Rochelle, Jonathan 135
Rogan, Frances 68
"Rolling Study Halls" (Google) 158–60
Roman Empire 85
Rooney, Sally 183, 215
RSAs (repressive state apparatuses) 10
Rudder, Christian 187, 201–5, 217

sadness and debt 150
Sadwoski, Jathan 94
safe haven 41–2
safe spaces 64, 65–6, 74–5
   see also inclusivity; privacy
St. James Computer Dating Service 196–7
St. Lawrence Centre of the Arts, Toronto 96–7, 121
Salami, Minna 219, 251–2
scattered multiplicity of identifying selves 114–15
Schmelzer, Matthias 236
Schmidt, Eric 91
schools 208–9
Scott-Heron, Gil 37
Screencast 131–2
Search Inside Yourself: The Unexpected Path to Achieving Success, Happiness (and World Peace) by Tan 172

"Search Inside yourself" (SIY) 172
"Select to Speak" tool (Google) 170–1
self-dating 198–9
self-determination 113, 194–5, 214
   see also empowerment
self-driving cars 169
self-learning 6–7, 131, 134, 153, 243
   see also artificial intelligence
self-organization 241–2
"Selling Smartness: Corporate Narratives and the Smart City as a Sociotechnical Imaginary" (Sadowski & Bendor) 94
Selwyn, Neil 137, 149
Sennet, Richard 117–19, 121–2
Sensuous Knowledge: A Black Feminist Approach for Everyone (Salami) 219, 251–2
sexism *see* misogyny
sexual assault/violence, and sexualization 217, 221
   #MeToo movement 2, 68, 219
   see also patriarchy
sexual diversity 68
sexual orientation 24, 25, 37, 118, 119–20, 205
Shakespeare, William 143
"sharing" platforms 123–4
shattered/scattered (disorganized) "ordinary" 8–14
Sidewalk Labs 85–130
Signal 212–14
Signs and Machines (Lazzarato) 13
Simmel, Georg 112–13
singularity 55–6
The Singularity Is Near: When Humans Transcend Biology (Kurzwell) 22, 56
Siri (Apple) 42–3, 63
SIY ("Search Inside yourself") 172
Skaria, Simon 51, 53
slave labor 15, 16, 246–52
Slogans for the Class of 2030 160–2, 170

Smart Cities: Big Data, Civic Hackers, and the Quest for a New Utopia (Townsend) 95
The Smart Enough City (Green) 122
smart homes 42–3
smartphones 23, 63, 96–102, 119–20, 232–3, 234
   city-as-smartphone analogies 96–102
   cobalt/copper mining 246–52
   "Earth Shot on iPhone" World Gallery campaign 232–4
Smith, Caleb 70–1
Snapchat 212–13
Snowcrash (Stephenson) 44
The Social Dilemma (2020) 18
social distancing 70–1
   see also lockdown era
The Social Media Age (Sujon) 207
social organization 208–9
social reproductive labor 41–2
"social safety" discourse 246–7
socialism 25, 214
socioeconomic class 209
Soderling, Stina 141
software for industrial robots 169
Solnit, Rebecca 118
Songdo, South Korea 95
soul concepts 11, 21–2, 51, 53, 57, 63, 98, 160–2, 166, 169, 170, 190, 231
space invasion 14–16
   see also colonialism
spaces of misogyny, racism, surveillance 68
spacetime 40–1
"Speak Pains to Recall Pains" 65
Spielberg, Steven 107
Spinoza, Benedict de 25, 72, 115–16, 146, 235–6
Spivak, Gayatri Chakravorty 164
Spivak Reader 164
splitting 113
Spotify 43
Srinivasan, Amia 215–17
Srnicek, Nick 16–17, 24

"the Stack" 110
steam engine 194–5
Steckley, John 122–3
Stephenson, Neal 44
stereotypes *see* Otherness
Stevens, Kyle 39, 40, 70
Stewart, Matthew 5–6, 100–1
"stoa" space 99–100, 104
strange encounters 242–3
Strange Encounters: Embodied Others in Postcoloniality (Ahmed) 57, 213
streams, streamification 1–2, 24–6, 43–4, 60–1, 63, 69
 city/sidewalk colonialism 110–11
 decolonizing of Google education 148–9, 152–3
 ecological justice 227–56
 unstreaming 26, 242, 245–6
 see also individuals, individualism, and individualization
structures of feeling 59
Sujon, Zoetanya 6, 207
superintelligence 21, 55, 227–32
 see also artificial intelligence
Supernature: Esalen and the Human Potential (2018) 233, 235–6
surveillance 18, 35, 37, 68, 136, 145
Surveillance Capitalism (Zuboff) 18, 35, 37, 136
Swchwrm, Myrtle 136

Talinn, Jaan 227–32
Tan, Chade-Meng 172
Taylor, Carol 156
Teacher (Google) 162–4
Teaching to Transgress (bell hooks) 162
Teams (Microsoft) 1–2, 44, 48, 49, 51, 54, 72
technocolonialism 3, 8–10, 14–20, 22, 40–2, 43–4, 58, 63, 64, 69, 75, 86, 89, 109, 113, 124–5, 156, 164, 172, 183, 187, 209–10, 231, 233–4, 239–40, 242–3, 247, 250

technofeudalism 14–18, 25, 59–60, 63, 115, 163–4, 228–30
Technofeudalism: What Killed Capitalism (Varoufakis) 15–16, 63
"Technofeudalism is Taking Over" (Varoufakis) 14
telegraphs 208–9
telepathy 50
telepresence 53–4
Terranova, Tiziana 16
Tesla 248–9
"therapy" 65
'thick time' 241
TikTok 1–3, 110–11
 home, consciousness principles 57, 69
Tinder 13–14, 43, 184, 194, 205–6, 209, 217, 218, 219
To-Morrow: A Peaceful Path to Real Reform (Howard) 94–5
Toronto, city/sidewalk colonialism 86–7, 89–93, 96, 120–1
"Toronto or is that Taranteau" (Steckley) 122–3
Toronto Tomorrow: A New Approach for Inclusive Growth 85–130
Townsend, Anthony 95
tracing associations 75–6
Trans* (Halberstam) 205
trans exclusionary radical feminism 68
 see also radical feminism
Transcendent Man (2009) 55–6
transhumanism 21–3, 26, 35, 38, 45–6, 50–8, 66–7
 city/sidewalk colonialism 88–90, 94, 107–8, 115, 120–1
 decolonizing of Google education 148, 162
 ecological justice 231–2, 233, 235
 Evolutionary Futurism and the Human Technologies of Utopia by Pilsch 55
 love via online dating 187, 202, 212
Soul (generation AI) 162

Transmediale festival, Berlin 247
transparency 124–5, 204–5
　see also democracy, democratization
transphobia 25, 68, 251
　see also radical feminism
transportation and communications 72–3, 194–5, 206, 208–9
　bicycles 194–5, 249–50
　electric transport 249–50
　self-driving cars 169
　see also bicycles
Treré, Emiliano 19
Truman Show (1998) 101–2
Trump, Donald 12–13, 230
Tuer, Andrew W. 143–4
Tumblr 68
Turkle, Sherry 213–15

Uber 17, 110–11, 112–13, 236
unconscious *see* consciousness, consciousness-raising
The Undercommons (Harney & Moten) 241–2
Understanding Media (McLuhan) 39–40
United Nations (UN) 246, 247
"universal" nature of home 35, 37
universities 208–9
University Network of Human Rights 246
unlearning 164–5, 243
unstreaming 26, 242, 245–6
Urban Data Trust 105
urban data, urbanism 87, 102–8, 112–13
user-machine attachment 13–14
utopianism 55, 94–5, 122
　see also dystopias
Utrecht organic market 70–2

Vaidhyanathan, Siva 157
value extraction 14–20
van Dijck, José 11, 24, 132–3, 137, 139, 155

Varoufakis, Yanis 14, 15–16, 18–19, 63, 220
Varsava, Nina 192–3
vectoralism 15–16
Verbeken, Pascal 151
"vernacular systems" 205
Victorian England and marriage 194
video calling/videotelephony 44–50
　see also Zoom/Zooming
Vietnam War 65–6
Le Vingtième siècle: La vie électrique (Robid) 44
Virtual Reality (VR) 48, 55–6, 165–6
　see also Mesh
virtuality and resistance 58–9
von Humboldt, Wilhelm 155–6
"vulnerability" 67–8

walkability, open-city philosophies 118–19
Walker, Rachel Loewen 241
Walloon region, Belgium 151
Wanderlust (Solnit) 118
Wark, McKenzie 15–16, 18–19, 26, 108, 110, 122, 205
Warner, Michael 3, 5–6, 65–6
water technologies 169
Waterfront Toronto 85–130
Watts, Alan 210, 212
Waymo (X) 169
We Are data: Algorithms and the Making of Our Digital Selves (Cheney-Lippold) 73–5
We Need to Talk: A Film about Consent (Nair) 217–18
Webb, Amy 207
Webb, Lawrence 210
Weller, Catherine 250–1
West Bank 246–52
'wexting' (walking while texting) 112–13
"What Is a Metaverse?" 53–4
What Is Philosophy? (Qu'est-ce que la philosophie?) by Deleuze & Guattari 146–7

WhatsApp 7, 13–14, 16–17, 23, 43, 46–7, 123–4, 212–13
   home, consciousness principles 57, 60
When Harry Met Sally (1989) 192–3
"When Harry Met Siri" (Webb) 210
wholeness 74–5
"Why Hasn't Online Dating Made It Onscreen?" 188
Wi-Fi 39–44, 108–10
   Alliance in Texas 40
Wikimedia Foundation 167–8
Wikipedia 166–8
"Wild Eros in a Fragmented World" workshop 66–7
Willful Subjects (Ahmed) 215–16
Williams, Alex 18
willing/willful subjects 188–93, 219–21
Willis, Ellen 216
Winterson, Jeanette 43–4, 61, 231–2
woke-ness 184
Women's Liberation Movement 25, 65–6
wonder 72
Wood, Megan 68
Woodcock, Ramsi 122
Woods, Heather Suzanne 43

World Economic Forum (WEF) 237–40
Wylie, Bianca 96, 98

X (formerly Twitter) 2, 12–13, 168–70, 219
   home, consciousness principles 37, 57, 68
Xinjiang province, China 15
XR (Extinction Rebellion) 244–5

"yellow book" of Sidewalk Labs 105–7
Yeskel, Zach 135
You (Google) 170–1
YouTube 2, 150
You've Got Mail (1998) 188–90, 210
Yuan, Eric 45–6

Zen Buddhism 20–1, 131–2, 171–2, 212
Zoom/Zooming 17, 40, 43–50, 72
"Zoomtopia" 45–6
Zuboff, Shoshana 18, 35, 37, 136
Zuckerberg, Mark 6, 33, 35, 46–7, 54, 198
   see also Facebook; Meta, and the Metaverse